The Humanitarian Civilian

OXFORD MONOGRAPHS IN INTERNATIONAL HUMANITARIAN AND CRIMINAL LAW

The aim of this series is to publish original and innovative books on fundamental, topical, or cutting-edge issues in international humanitarian law and international criminal justice. The primary purpose of the series is to publish books which, in addition to critically surveying existing law, also suggest new avenues for improving the law.

ALSO PUBLISHED IN THIS SERIES

Detention in Non-International Armed Conflict
Lawrence Hill-Cawthorne

Rules of Engagement and the International Law of Military Operations
J.F.R. Boddens Hosang

To Serve the Enemy
Informers, Collaborators, and the Laws of Armed Conflict
Shane Darcy

The Humanitarian Civilian

How the Idea of Distinction Circulates Within and Beyond International Humanitarian Law

REBECCA SUTTON

OXFORD
UNIVERSITY PRESS

OXFORD
UNIVERSITY PRESS

Great Clarendon Street, Oxford, OX2 6DP,
United Kingdom

Oxford University Press is a department of the University of Oxford.
It furthers the University's objective of excellence in research, scholarship,
and education by publishing worldwide. Oxford is a registered trade mark of
Oxford University Press in the UK and in certain other countries

First Edition published in 2021

Published in the United States of America by Oxford University Press
198 Madison Avenue, New York, NY 10016, United States of America

British Library Cataloguing in Publication Data

Data available

Library of Congress Control Number: 2020945212

ISBN 978–0–19–886381–6

DOI: 10.1093/oso/9780198863816.001.0001

For my parents, Patricia and Randy

Series Editors' Preface

Dr Rebecca Sutton's monograph, *The Humanitarian Civilian: How the Idea of Distinction Circulates Within and Beyond International Humanitarian Law*, tackles a topic of great interest: the position of humanitarian actors under International Humanitarian Law (IHL). She does this with an acute and original perspective which robustly takes into account the realities of IHL. These underlying realities are well known to the author, who has been in the field in her previous 'boots on the ground' (*absit injuria verbis*) career, working in Sudan. Indeed, this experience brings to the study depth and understanding, as well as an innovative element in the methodology and the contents. The book is nourished by an empirical approach that goes beyond the personal experience of the author and relies on surveys, interviews, and focus groups with various relevant actors.

While IHL is basically premised on the assumption that there is an essential divide between civilians and combatants, which sometimes is seen as a tool that could almost *per se* serve as a shelter for civilians, the reality is that parties to conflicts too often ignore the divide. As is well known, against this background, the ordinary reaction of lawyers and activists is to advocate for a stronger implementation of the dividing line and reaffirm how fundamental the principle of distinction is, and the role it plays as a construct that must inform IHL and remain its backbone.

This monograph by Dr Sutton departs from and takes issue with the dominant approach, emphasizing that there is a lot of fluidity in the notion of distinction in actual practice. She builds on strands of scholarship which highlight how the distinction between combatants and non-combatants is dynamic, contested, and not fixed. Further developing these critical assessments, she offers a different perspective towards a 'reconceptualization' of distinction, particularly in so far as humanitarian actors are concerned. In so doing the author presents real-life practices and explains them in an engaging way. She offers interesting thoughts on the special position of humanitarian workers and on the notion of a 'civilian plus status', which she regards with caution.

The book is organized into five chapters, preceded by a very stimulating introduction. This enticing introductory chapter presents the main conceptual and methodological underpinnings of the author's quest for the various shades of distinction through 'three realms' ('Kinetic', 'Pedagogical', and 'Intellectual'). This introductory chapter whets the appetite to go on with the book. And let us not say more, to avoid spoilers! Chapter 2 deals with the notion of distinction and its 'perception' in various groups of relevant actors. Chapter 3 illustrates the process and relevant players in the ascertainment of the status of civilian/non-combatant v. combatant. Chapter 4 discusses definitions and introduces the notion of variants in civilian status, with different ranges of 'civilianness'. Chapter 5 brings to light the notion of 'civilian plus' and delves into its relationships with the broader discussions concerning the distinction principle. The final chapter offers some conclusions on the general aspiration that rules should be actually applicable, and presents nuanced and well-argued thoughts on the measure of caution that could be appropriate in identifying new notions to capture the fluidity of distinction with regard to humanitarian actors.

This book adopts an intellectual approach that, from the outset, goes beyond the debate among lawyers and represents an extremely welcome addition to scholarship in the field of IHL. Dr Sutton's professional trajectory seems also to fit well into Antonio Cassese's vision when the series was created nearly 10 years ago (aimed at including professionals developing their career paths at the crossroads of practice and academia, engaging in cross-cutting, original academic work, keeping a close relationship to practice – as laws are not only made to rest as abstract notions). This book is one that will undoubtedly stimulate further discussion. For all these reasons we are very pleased to publish it as part of the *Oxford Monograph Series in International Criminal and Humanitarian Law.*

The editors

Acknowledgements

Throughout the process of writing and editing this monograph, Merel Alstein and the team at Oxford University Press have been nothing short of fabulous. It has been a great comfort to always know that the book was in good hands. I would also like to thank two anonymous reviewers for OUP, whose incisive feedback was of great value in shaping the book into its current form.

This book began its life in the form of a PhD thesis, and that thesis would not have come to fruition without the guidance and encouragement of many people. I would first like to thank my brilliant supervisors in the Department of Law at the London School of Economics, Gerry Simpson and Devika Hovell. Gerry and Devika supported my vision for this interdisciplinary project and encouraged me to take risks. They provided counsel, wisdom, and humour throughout the PhD journey, and I feel spoiled that this has continued on beyond the doctorate. It was because of the generous engagement of my Viva examiners, Sarah Nouwen and Mark Drumbl, that I was able to step back from the thesis, muster courage, and eventually bring the project to life in its present form. Sarah and Mark invited me to leap out of the realm of the graduate student, and to claim an identity as a scholar in my own right. For their ongoing counsel and support, I am immensely grateful.

I have been fortunate to receive advice and feedback on earlier versions of this work from a number of scholars and practitioners in the fields of international law, socio-legal studies, humanitarianism, and peacekeeping. Heartfelt thanks go to the following individuals for their generosity: Anne Orford, Bruce Oswald, Christine Bell, Christopher Gevers, Dapo Akande, David Keen, David Kennedy, Elizabeth Stubbins Bates, Emily Kidd White, Emily Paddon, Frédéric Mégret, Georgette Gagnon, Heidi Matthews, Hugo Slim, Jennifer Welsh, Karen Engle, Katharine Fortin, Linda Mulcahy, Martin Clark, Meredith Rossner, Naz Modirzadeh, Orly Stern, Rajesh Venugopal, Severine Autessere, Stuart Gordon, Susan Marks, and Tim Allen. Any mistakes that remain in this work are, of course, my own.

Field research in South Sudan and at civil–military training grounds in Sweden, Germany, Italy, and Ghana would not have been possible without the support of funding from the Pierre Elliot Trudeau Foundation and the Social Science and Humanities Research Council of Canada. I am indebted to the hundreds of individuals who shared their time and insights with me during the course of this research. For reasons of confidentiality, I cannot name individual respondents here, but I would like to express particular gratitude to all of the displaced persons in South Sudan who spoke with me. I also thank Paul O'Hagan and Samantha Nutt for their mentorship, and for encouraging me to ground my scholarship in the world of humanitarian practice.

On a personal note, I would like to thank my family and friends, who tirelessly support me and keep my feet on the ground. Last but not least, I would like to thank my husband Duncan Harte, for helping me live a creative life and for inspiring me to write.

Early career academia is not an easy time, and I count myself one of the lucky ones. Much of this book was written in the early morning hours, at night, and on weekends, as the demands of postdoctoral and teaching fellowships consumed my time. I am fortunate to have been able to grab those precious moments to write (and to have had those fellowships); a recent grant from the Leverhulme Trust has been a complete game-changer on this front. I hope that we can build an academic system in which more early career scholars, from more diverse backgrounds, have access to the same opportunities.

Contents

Table of Cases

FRANCE

INTERNATIONAL COURT OF JUSTICE (ICJ)

INTERNATIONAL CRIMINAL TRIBUNAL FOR THE FORMER YUGOSLAVIA (ICTY)

INTERNATIONAL CRIMINAL TRIBUNAL FOR RWANDA (ICTR)

SPECIAL COURT FOR SIERRA LEONE (SCSL)

EXTRAORDINARY CHAMBERS IN THE COURTS OF CAMBODIA (ECCC)

INTERNATIONAL CRIMINAL COURT (ICC)

1
Introduction

Introduction

A common vision of the principle of distinction in international humanitarian law (IHL) positions civilians and combatants as separate entities, divided by a fixed and stable bright line. As soon as one reaches for distinction and its promise of clarity, however, the line dissolves. It dims, moves, or disappears. Even as distinction eludes one's grasp, many people reach for it in many different places and in many different ways. In settings as disparate as Protection of Civilians sites in South Sudan, civil–military training spaces, and Geneva and the Hague, international actors can be found producing distinction. In many instances, the things they are doing with distinction render it unrecognizable as a civilian–combatant binary. A deceptively simple discovery arises here, one that implicates our fundamental assumptions about the practice of IHL: distinction means many things to many people.

Distinction's disorder is routinely downplayed, however, as incentives abound to conceal the chaos it produces. Particularly important here is the desire to live in a world in which civilians are robustly protected and do not come under deliberate attack. This protective impulse leads many international lawyers and protection advocates to suppress the fluidity of distinction and, when confronted by signs of strain, to double down on the bright-line vision. Such accounts lament the erosion of the civilian concept and the blurring of the civilian–combatant boundary, all the while holding the principle of distinction firmly in place as an otherwise stable rule.

Taking a sideways look at distinction, this monograph explores the way in which it circulates within and beyond IHL. A burgeoning critical scholarship shows that the distinction between combatants and non-combatants is not fixed, predictable, or reciprocally understood, but is instead contested and dynamic.[1]

[1] Andrew Barros and Martin Thomas (eds.), *The Civilianization of War: The Changing Civil–military Divide 1914–2014* (Cambridge: Cambridge University Press, 2018) (*Civilianization*); Helen Kinsella, *The Image Before the Weapon: A Critical History of the Distinction between Combatant and Civilian* (Ithaca, NY and London: Cornell University Press, 2011) ('*Image*'); Claire Garbett, *The Concept of the Civilian: Legal Recognition, Adjudication and the Trials of International Criminal Justice* (Oxford: Routledge, 2015) (*The Concept of the Civilian*); Amanda Alexander, 'The Genesis of the Civilian', *Leiden Journal of International Law*, Vol. 20, 2007, pp. 359–376; Emily Crawford, *Identifying the Enemy: Civilian Participation in Armed Conflict* (Oxford: Oxford University Press, 2015) ('*Identifying the Enemy*'); Anicée van Engeland, *Civilian or Combatant? A Challenge for the 21st Century*

The Humanitarian Civilian. Rebecca Sutton, Oxford University Press (2021). © Rebecca Sutton.
DOI: 10.1093/oso/9780198863816.003.0001

Building on these contributions, the present study redirects attention to international humanitarian actors, a set of civilian actors who are caught up in the contradictions of the law in fascinating ways. By virtue of their role delivering assistance to war-affected populations, humanitarian actors bear responsibilities towards these populations, as well as to the parties to the conflict and to IHL. This professional role is imbued with great social value, but also brings attendant dangers that render them vulnerable. Seizing upon signifiers of 'civilianness', humanitarian actors present themselves as harmless, innocent, and outside the fight. They enact a range of everyday distinction practices that set them apart from those actors with whom they do not wish to be associated. Crucially, this includes other civilians, some of whom have qualities of 'combatantness' swirling around them as they appear to be complicit, dangerous, and participating in the conflict. These practices inevitably draw humanitarian actors into clashes with others, and this monograph focuses on tensions that arise with the international peacekeeping and military actors who populate comprehensive missions. As these differently situated actors collide on a routine basis, distinction is made and remade through struggle and contestation.

Drawing on the insights of multi-sited ethnography,[2] this bottom-up study follows the idea of distinction across different global sites, from South Sudan to Geneva. Contests unfold along multiple fault lines, and three figures emerge that are unfamiliar to IHL. The 'civilian plus' represents an especially pure civilian status that humanitarian actors long for, the 'mere civilian' is a default status that humanitarians wish to transcend, and the 'civilian minus' is a tainted status that haunts humanitarian practices. Insofar as the distinctions that are enacted do not map onto a civilian–combatant binary, these dynamics are typically obscured in IHL. This monograph makes these practices legible in all of their complexity, treating them as valid engagements with a legal rule that is already deeply disrupted.

(Oxford: Oxford University Press, 2011) ('*Civilian or Combatant*'); Hugo Slim, *Killing Civilians: Method, Madness, and Morality in War* (Oxford: Oxford University Press, 2010), 210 ('*Killing Civilians*').

[2] George Marcus, 'Ethnography in/of the World System: The Emergence of Multi-Sited Ethnography', *Annual Review of Anthropology*, Vol. 24, 1995, pp. 95–117; Sally Engle Merry, 'Ethnography of the Global', Workshop at the Berkeley Centre for the Study of Law and Society, February 2013; Akhil Gupta and James Ferguson (eds.), *Anthropological Locations: Boundaries and Grounds of a Field Science* (Oakland, CA: University of California Press, 1997). See also Mark-Anthony Falzon, 'Introduction: Multi-Sited Ethnography: Theory, Praxis and Locality in Contemporary Research', in Mark-Anthony Falzon (ed.), *Multi-Sited Ethnography: Theory, Praxis and Locality in Contemporary Research* (Burlington, VT: Ashgate, 2009), pp. 1–24. For an example in international law scholarship see: Sarah Nouwen, *Complementarity in the Line of Fire: The Catalysing Effect of the International Criminal Court in Uganda and Sudan* (Cambridge: Cambridge University Press, 2013), 235, n 45 (*Complementarity*): ('Moving between The Hague, Gulu, Khartoum, Darfur, Kampala, and headquarters of international organizations, the study does not focus, like classic anthropology, on the culture of one community, traditionally a village.')

1.1 Background to the study

The impetus for this study came from my personal experience as an international humanitarian actor. While based in West Darfur, Sudan as Head of Mission for the non-governmental organization (NGO) War Child Canada from 2009 to 2011, I experienced first hand how international actors struggle with distinction. On a day-to-day basis, international humanitarian NGOs in Darfur grappled with whether they should: participate in joint security planning with non-humanitarian actors; accept military offers of in-kind resources; conduct joint projects with the African Union (AU)/UN hybrid mission, UNAMID; travel in armed convoys; and/or engage in long-term development work and human rights advocacy. While the answers to these questions shifted as conflict dynamics fluctuated, what was striking was how these answers were routinely formulated in terms of distinction. Notably, this distinction did not always track along with a civilian–combatant binary. The more relevant divide was sometimes humanitarian–military or humanitarian–civilian, or even humanitarian–humanitarian. Moreover, the idea of distinction was often collapsed together with other priorities and cherished values. Yes, we brandished our organizational logo to safeguard our civilian status, but did so also to demonstrate 'visibility' for donors so that we could secure the necessary funds to continue operating. In the same vein, we did not only avoid an affiliation with UNAMID because of the dangers presented by the mission's military aspects—though this was a live concern. It was also because we doubted the mission's competence and we wanted to protect our good reputation.

When I left Darfur and returned to law school in Canada, I developed a more in-depth knowledge of IHL as lawyers understand it. As I was taught the civilian–combatant distinction in a JD classroom, I struggled to make sense of how this rule governed the intricate practices I had observed and participated in on the ground. My inability to piece this together satisfyingly alerted me to the fact that I had a significant puzzle to solve. This led me back to South Sudan, where I began to search for distinction in unusual spaces and places. The chance opportunity to become a trainer for soldiers and peacekeepers in West Africa led to a serendipitous discovery. That is, training spaces, and especially civil–military training sites, are also sites in which distinction is taught, learned, and brought into question. This uncovering of a middle realm in which people were modelling, simulating, and role-playing distinction challenged my initial expectation that this would be a straightforward story about conflict zone practices versus IHL rules 'in the book'. The assumption that a bright-line binary distinction even exists at the level of text and doctrine was also, eventually, upended. Searching for a stable distinction in the Geneva Conventions and the Additional Protocols, in historical approaches to protection, and in the decisions of international tribunals, I realized that there is no bright line to be found.

1.2 The principle of distinction and the civilian concept in IHL

As a 'second best' to eradicating the use of force globally, IHL's aim is to limit destruction and suffering in armed conflict.[3] While contemporary international lawyers often use IHL, 'laws of war', or 'laws of armed conflict' interchangeably as translations of *jus in bello*,[4] the respective terms have symbolic and political implications that must be acknowledged.[5] Though the present study employs the term IHL, this does not indicate a belief that concerns of humanity eclipse military imperatives in the relevant doctrine.[6] So long as an appreciation of military imperatives is required for securing state buy-in,[7] it can be said that IHL is animated by a 'push and pull' between humanity and military necessity.[8]

The principle of distinction, which functions narrowly to govern targeting in the conduct of hostilities, reflects this balancing act. This rule allows parties to the conflict to attack military objectives and kill those deemed legitimate targets, while offering protection to civilians and civilian objects.[9] Article 48 of AP I provides:[10]

[3] Gabriella Blum, 'The Laws of War and the "Lesser Evil"', *Yale Journal of International Law*, Vol. 35, No. 1, 2010, pp. 1–69, 7 ('Lesser Evil').

[4] As in Theodor Meron, 'The Humanization of Humanitarian Law', *American Journal of International Law*, Vol. 94, No. 2, 2000, pp. 239–278. For a critique of this practice, see Amanda Alexander, 'A Short History of International Humanitarian Law', *European Journal of International Law*, Vol. 26, No. 1, 2015, pp. 109–138, 112–113 ('Short History').

[5] David Kennedy, *Of War and Law* (Princeton, NJ: Princeton University Press, 2006), 83 (*War*); Blum, supra, 8 ('Lesser Evil').

[6] Alexander, supra, 135 ('Short History'). On the concept of unnecessary suffering, see Chris Jochnick and Roger Normand, 'The Legitimation of Violence: A Critical History of the Laws of War', *Harvard International Law Journal*, Vol. 35, No. 1, Winter 1994, pp. 49–95, 66 ('Critical History').

[7] Frédéric Mégret, 'Thinking about what International Humanitarian Lawyers "Do": An Examination of the Laws of War as a Field of Professional Practice', in Wouter Werner, Marieke de Hoon, and Alexis Galán (eds.), *The Law of International Lawyers: Reading Martti Koskenniemi* (Cambridge: Cambridge University Press, 2017), pp. 265–296, 271 ('IHL Lawyers').

[8] In the present study, military necessity relates to achieving a legitimate military purpose or meeting an identified military objective. On debates about the status of humanity as an IHL principle, compare Meron, supra (arguing that humanity is at the centre of IHL), with, e.g.: Michael Schmitt, 'Discriminate Warfare: The Military Necessity–Humanity Dialectic of International Humanitarian Law', in David Lovell and Igor Primoratz (eds.), *Protecting Civilians During Violent Conflict: Theoretical and Practical Issues for the 21st Century* (Abingdon and New York: Ashgate, 2012), Chapter 6, 87–88 ('Discriminate Warfare'). The 'push and pull' dynamic is discussed in Sandesh Sivakumaran, 'Making and Shaping the Law of Armed Conflict', *Current Legal Problems*, Vol. 71, No. 1, 2018, pp. 119–160, 156 ('Making and Shaping'); Michael Schmitt, 'Military Necessity and Humanity in International Humanitarian Law: Preserving the Delicate Balance', *Virginia Journal of International Law*, Vol. 50, No. 4, 2010, pp. 796–839. But see Adil Haque, 'Indeterminacy in the Law of Armed Conflict', *International Law Studies*, Vol. 95, No. 118, 2019, pp. 118–160 ('Indeterminacy') (challenging claims that IHL involves a balance of humanity against military necessity).

[9] While there is some mention of civilian objects and IHL's 'protected persons' in this study, the focus is on individual civilians and civilian populations.

[10] Article 48 of the Protocol Additional to the Geneva Conventions of 12 August 1949, and Relating to the Protection of Victims of International Armed Conflicts, 8 June 1977, 1125 UNTS 3, Can TS 1991 No. 1 ('AP I'). See also Article 13 of the Protocol Additional to the Geneva Conventions of 12 August 1949, and Relating to the Protection of Victims of Non-International Armed Conflicts, 8 June 1977, 1125 UNTS 609, Can TS 1991 No. 2 ('AP II').

> In order to ensure respect for and protection of the civilian population and civilian objects, the Parties to the conflict shall at all times distinguish between the civilian population and combatants and between civilian objects and military objectives and accordingly shall direct their operations only against military objectives.

In the same instrument, the civilian is formally defined in international law for the first time.[11] AP I defines the civilian in a negative or residual manner, essentially referring to anyone who is not a combatant.[12] Article 50(1) stipulates:

> A civilian is any person who does not belong to one of the categories of persons referred to in Article 4 A (1), (2), (3) and (6) of the Third Convention and in Article 43 of this Protocol. In case of doubt whether a person is a civilian, that person shall be considered to be a civilian.

It has been suggested that the AP I definition treats the civilian as something of an afterthought. Crawford says the civilian is given 'short shrift' in AP I,[13] Dinstein writes that IHL doesn't 'tell us who or what the protected persons and objects are',[14] and Garbett notes the lack of identifiable features and visual signifiers associated with the civilian.[15] The ICRC Commentary to the APs explain that the drafters of AP I purposely selected a negative definition, however.[16] The aim was to expand the breadth of coverage to all those who are not combatants, rendering the civilian category more—not less—precise. A further stated benefit of the binary is that it does away with the problem of having an 'undistributed middle' between the civilian and combatant categories.[17] The formulation is ostensibly alternative and exhaustive: every individual must fall into one of these two categories, and those who belong to one do not belong to the other.[18]

[11] As per Alexander, supra, 359–360 ('Genesis'). See below in this section.

[12] Discussed in Cecilie Hellestveit, 'The Geneva Conventions and the Dichotomy between International and Non-International Armed Conflict: Curse or Blessing for the "Principle of Humanity"', in Kjetil Mujezinovic Larsen, Camilla Guldahl Cooper, and Gro Nystuen (eds.), *Searching for a 'Principle of Humanity' in International Humanitarian Law* (Cambridge: Cambridge University Press, 2013), pp. 86–123, 102; Avril McDonald, 'The Challenges to International Humanitarian Law and the Principles of Distinction and Protection from the Increased Participation of Civilians in Hostilities', *Spotlight on Issues of Contemporary Concern in International Humanitarian Law and International Criminal Law*, Working Paper, University of Tehran Round Table, April 2004.

[13] Crawford, supra, 233 (*Identifying the Enemy*).

[14] Yoram Dinstein, *The Conduct of Hostilities under the Law of International Armed Conflict* (Cambridge: Cambridge University Press, 2004), 114 (*CoH*).

[15] Garbett, supra, 100 (*The Concept of the Civilian*).

[16] Claude Pilloud, Yves Sandoz, Christophe Swinarski, et al. (eds.), *ICRC Commentary on Additional Protocols of 8 June 1977 to the Geneva Conventions of 12 August 1949* (Geneva: ICRC, 1987), 609–611 (*AP Commentary*). Discussed also in Kinsella, supra, 142 (*Image*).

[17] Dinstein, supra, 142 (*CoH*).

[18] Andrew Alexandra, 'Private Military and Security Companies and the "Civilianization" of War', in David Lovell and Igor Primoratz (eds.), *Protecting Civilians During Violent Conflict: Theoretical*

This approach espouses the benefits of inclusiveness, comprehensiveness, and clarity.[19]

The promise of clarity quickly fades as soon as one contemplates the contemporary basis of civilian protection in armed conflict. According to the same ICRC Commentary, the protection of civilians under IHL is connected to 'the inoffensive character of the persons to be spared and the situation in which they find themselves'.[20] The implication is that protection under the APs of 1977 is not solely based on an individual's status as either civilian or combatant, but instead hinges on an individual's conduct.[21] While the armed/unarmed marker may thus serve as an indicator of civilian status, protection depends upon the nuances of actual participation.[22] The concept of direct participation in hostilities (DPH) was introduced into IHL for this reason.[23] Along with other targeting rules, it unsettles the notion of a fixed and stable line. As Kinsella remarks, the introduction of a temporal element into the distinction, through the DPH concept, upends the notion that the civilian and the combatant are only 'conceived in opposition to each other'.[24]

Kindersley and Rolandsen identify a 'self-imposed blind spot', whereby practitioners knowingly disregard the complexities of civilian identity in the operating environment.[25] I would go further and suggest that, in addition to issues of on-the-ground practice, there is a discernible reluctance to confront distinction's fragility as a legal idea.[26] To understand why a bright-line binary framework remains in circulation as the reference point, it is important to note how high the stakes are from an IHL perspective. Not only is the principle of distinction positioned as a central IHL rule, but also it is framed as the apotheosis of historical advancements in legal protections for those outside the fight.

and Practical Issues for the 21st Century (Abingdon and New York: Ashgate, 2012), pp. 183–189, 187 ('Private Military Companies').

19 Pilloud et al. (eds.), supra, 610–611 (*AP Commentary*).

20 Ibid., 610 (*AP Commentary*).

21 GC IV of 1949 implies that the primary basis for protecting civilians from harm is their lack of combatant status.

22 Slim, supra, 210 (*Killing Civilians*). See also *Prosecutor v. Blagoje Simić et al.*, Case No. IT-95-9-T, Trial Judgment, ICTY, 17 October 2003, para. 659 (mere possession of a weapon does not create 'reasonable doubt' of civilian status); *Prosecutor v. Pavle Strugar*, Case No. IT-01-42-A, Appeal Judgment, ICTY, 17 July 2008, paras. 167, 178 (emphasizing actual harm caused by the civilian who directly participates in hostilities).

23 DPH is addressed in Chapter 2 and Section 5.3.1. Civilian objects, in contrast, lose protection when they make an effective contribution to military action. See Article 52(2) of AP I.

24 Kinsella, supra, 144 (*Image*).

25 Nicki Kindersley and Øystein H. Rolandsen, 'Who are the Civilians in the Wars of South Sudan?', *Security Dialogue*, Vol. 50, No. 5, 2019, pp. 383–397, 393 ('Who are the Civilians?').

26 On distinction as a fragile idea see Karma Nabulsi, *Traditions of War: Occupation, Resistance, and the Law* (Oxford: Oxford University Press, 1999), 1 (*Traditions of War*); Kinsella, supra, 3 (*Image*).

First, distinction has been described as 'the basis for the law of armed conflict',[27] 'the foundation of the whole system' of IHL,[28] a 'fundamental' component,[29] and a 'cornerstone'[30] of IHL. While IHL instruments do not provide a civilian–combatant distinction in non-international armed conflicts (NIACs),[31] Sassoli et al. propose that a distinction must exist in NIACs if IHL is to be respected.[32] The logic is simple: if distinction fails, the wider body of law might fall apart. Berman critiques this tendency to tie the principle of distinction to IHL's functioning. Assessing the ICRC's strict approach to distinction, he contends: 'The destabilization of *jus in bello* by means of its own categories ... cannot be held back through avowedly counter-realistic fiats about the rigorous difference between combatants and civilians.'[33] He holds that such decrees, in fact, facilitate the very destabilization that the ICRC is trying to avert.[34]

Second, the temptation to conceal distinction's disorder is heightened when the AP I rule is treated as the culmination of age-old efforts to protect civilians. Some cite GC 1864 as the first legal moment at which victims of war became the focal point,[35] though this instrument focuses on wounded combatants. Others highlight protections advanced in the Hague Regulations of 1899 and 1907,[36] though protections in these instruments are primarily assigned to prisoners and inhabitants of occupied territories. What is more, the Hague Regulations do not prohibit the bombing or starvation of those outside the fight, nor do they prohibit reprisals.[37] It is not until GC IV of 1949 that protections are advanced for the civilian as a legal entity,[38] but

[27] Pilloud et al. (eds.), supra, 438 (*AP Commentary*).

[28] Alejandro Lorite Escorihuela, 'Humanitarian Law and Human Rights Law: The Politics of Distinction', *Michigan State Journal of International Law*, Vol. 19, No. 2, 2013, pp. 300–407, 319.

[29] *Legality of the Threat or Use of Nuclear Weapons*, Advisory Opinion, ICJ Reports 1996, International Court of Justice, 8 July 1996, para. 257.

[30] Crawford, supra, 1 (*Identifying the Enemy*).

[31] Ibid., 15, 73. On the under-regulation of NIACs, in general, see: Sandesh Sivakumaran, 'Re-Envisaging the International Law of Internal Armed Conflict', *European Journal of International Law*, Vol. 22, No. 1, 2011, pp. 219–264, 219 ('Re-Envisaging'); Dino Kritsiotis, 'Humanitarian Warfare: Towards an African Appreciation', in Jeremy I. Levitt (ed.), *Africa: Mapping New Boundaries in International Law* (Oxford: Hart, 2008), pp. 149–180, 152 ('Humanitarian Warfare').

[32] Marco Sassoli, Antoine Bouvier, and Anne Quintin (eds.), *How Does Law Protect in War?* (Geneva: ICRC, 2011), Chapter 5, 1 ('civilians can and will only be respected if government soldiers and rebel fighters can expect those looking like civilians not to attack them') (*How Does Law Protect?*). The principle of distinction in NIACs is sourced in customary international law. See Jean-Marie Henckaerts and Louise Doswald-Beck, *Customary International Humanitarian Law* (Geneva: ICRC, 2005) (*ICRC Customary IHL Study*).

[33] Nathaniel Berman, 'Privileging Combat? Contemporary Conflict and the Legal Construction of War', *Columbia Journal of Transnational Law*, Vol. 43, No. 1, 2004, pp. 1–71, 54 ('Privileging Combat?') (discussing the 'part-time combatant').

[34] Ibid. See also Nicholette Boehland, *The People's Perspectives: Civilian Involvement in Armed Conflict* (Oxford: Oxford University Press, 2010).

[35] Daniel Thurer, 'Dunant's Pyramid: Thoughts on the "Humanitarian Space"', *International Review of the Red Cross*, Vol. 89, No. 865, 2007, pp. 47–61, 50 ('Dunant's Pyramid').

[36] Crawford, supra, 14, 50 (*Identifying the Enemy*), citing the example of Pilloud et al. (eds.), supra, 598 (*AP Commentary*); Judith Gardam, *Non-Combatant Immunity as a Norm of International Humanitarian Law* (Dordrecht: Martinus Nijhoff Publishers, 1993) ('*Non-Combatant Immunity*'). See also Richard Shelley Hartigan, *The Forgotten Victim: A History of the Civilian* (Chicago, IL: Precedent Publishing, 1982).

[37] Jochnick and Normand, supra, 76 ('Critical History'); Alexandra, supra, 116 ('Short History').

[38] See e.g. Article 33 of GC IV; Article 49 of GC IV.

even then the civilian is not defined and the relevant protections are circumscribed in numerous ways.[39] And yet, as Alexander shows, delegates at the AP conferences in the 1970s behaved as though strong protections for civilians were already in place, and indeed at the core of IHL.[40] She argues that the seemingly broad protections ultimately introduced in the APs were in fact open to competing interpretations, containing a range of 'cautious disclaimers and imprecise provisions'.[41] On this account the AP I definition of the civilian does not remedy,[42] but instead introduces an ambiguous civilian status. Like many other rules of international law,[43] it can be said that the principle of distinction is plagued by indeterminacy and ambiguity—some of which might be intentional and, indeed, considered advantageous.[44]

This monograph takes the view that when it comes to the civilian concept, the problem is not so much that IHL sets up the civilian as a black box—though the negative definition presents some difficulties. It is rather that the principle of distinction rests on ambiguity, uncertainty, and contingency. Dominant narratives of IHL somehow manage to convey precisely nothing about the civilian, while at the same time establishing a nebulous and even contradictory civilian figure. This haziness continues in the treatment of the international humanitarian actor in IHL doctrine, and again with respect to the relationship between the international humanitarian actor and the civilian category. The fuzzy treatment of both the humanitarian actor and the civilian concept in IHL makes it possible to set up (some) humanitarian actors as the subjects of special protection and privilege—without framing this as a carve-out from IHL's civilian category.

1.3 The actors of interest

This study explores the way in which distinction circulates globally, focusing on the practices of international actors in comprehensive missions governed by IHL. The international humanitarian actor is positioned as the central actor of interest, and the same qualities that make the humanitarian actor an intriguing figure to study

[39] Nabulsi, supra, 11 (*Traditions of War*); Crawford, supra, 233 (*Identifying the Enemy*).

[40] Amanda Alexander, 'International Humanitarian Law: Postcolonialism and the 1977 Geneva Protocol I', *Melbourne Journal of International Law*, Vol. 17, No. 1, 2016, pp. 1–36, 21–22 ('Postcolonialism').

[41] Ibid.

[42] This argument is advanced in Garbett, supra, 100 (*Concept of the Civilian*).

[43] On indeterminacy in international legal rules see Martti Koskenniemi, *From Apology to Utopia: The Structure of International Legal Argument* (Cambridge: Cambridge University Press, 2009). On indeterminacy in IHL see Haque, supra ('Indeterminacy').

[44] Kinsella, supra (*Image*), 189. Citing Abram Chayes and Antonia Chayes, 'On Compliance', *International Organization*, Vol. 47, No. 2, 1993, pp. 175–205, 189 (on indeterminacy); Theodor Meron, *War Crimes Law Comes of Age* (Oxford: Oxford University Press, 1998), 159 (on deliberate ambiguity). See also Chapter 2.

also pose definitional hurdles. Even before the term 'humanitarian' is brought into contact with IHL, it suffers from indeterminacy.[45] It is too simplistic to declare, for example, that a humanitarian actor is someone who provides humanitarian assistance.[46] This is potentially a useful point of departure, but it gathers inside the category peacekeeping and military actors who deliver (so-called) humanitarian assistance. A further challenge is that no category of 'humanitarian actor' exists as such in IHL doctrine.[47] I argue in this monograph that IHL positions the Red Cross figure as the paradigmatic humanitarian actor, but this only tells us so much because the bulk of international actors who actively deliver humanitarian assistance in contemporary armed conflicts do not resemble this entity. While some available typologies of humanitarian actors usefully grapple with the diversity of the role,[48] none explicitly engage with IHL. Nor, for that matter, do they account for the presence of non-humanitarian actors in the operational space. The concept of 'humanitarian space', which generally refers to the room humanitarian actors have to carry out their tasks unimpeded, is also limited in this respect.[49]

This monograph situates humanitarian actors alongside other international actors engaged in political, military, and peacekeeping responses to armed conflict. The imperative to incorporate other international actors into the narrative flows from the fact that humanitarian actors do not simply 'distinguish themselves' in isolation. Instead, distinction is something that must be worked out and navigated in relationship with others. The relevant 'field' is defined here as the relational social space in which differently situated actors come into contact and struggle

[45] Monika Krause, *The Good Project: Humanitarian Relief NGOs and the Fragmentation of Reason* (Chicago, IL and London: University of Chicago Press, 2014), 109 (*Good Project*); Samir Elhawary and Sara Pantuliano, 'UN Integration and Humanitarian Space', Panel at University of Ottawa Centre for International Policy Studies, 31 January 2012. Available at: https://www.youtube.com/watch?v=3SfTYAVvHyU.

[46] Humanitarian assistance is defined here as the provision of humanitarian relief—namely humanitarian and protection assistance involving food, water, sanitation, shelter, and health services, as well as humanitarian coordination. This excludes post-conflict development activities, while recognizing that many actors who identify as humanitarian also engage in work across the relief–development continuum. For a similar definition, see: Kubo Macak, 'Principles of Neutrality and Impartiality of Humanitarian Action in the Aftermath of the 2011 Libyan Conflict', in Andrew J. Zwitter et al. (eds.), *Humanitarian Action: Global, Regional and Domestic Legal Responses* (Cambridge: Cambridge University Press, 2014), pp. 447–474, 447 ('Principles').

[47] See Section 2.3.1.

[48] Discussed in Abby Stoddard, 'Humanitarian NGOs: Challenges and Trends', *Humanitarian Policy Group*, Briefing paper, No. 1, July 2003, 3; Krause, supra, 110 (*Good Project*).

[49] For debates on the humanitarian space see Sarah Collinson and Samir Elhawary, *Humanitarian Space: A Review of Trends and Issues* (London: Overseas Development Institute, 2012) (*Humanitarian Space*); Marcos Ferreiro, 'Blurring of Lines in Complex Emergencies: Consequences for the Humanitarian Community', *Journal of Humanitarian Assistance*, December 2012, available at http://sites.tufts.edu/jha/archives/1625 ('Blurring'). For accounts of humanitarian space that engage with IHL see Johanna Grombach Wagner, 'An IHL/ICRC Perspective on "Humanitarian Space"', *Humanitarian Exchange Magazine*, No. 32, 2005 ('IHL/ICRC Perspective'); Thurer, supra ('Dunant's Pyramid'); Sylvain Beauchamp, 'Humanitarian Space in Search of a New Home', in Benjamin Perrin (ed.), *Modern Warfare: Armed Groups, Private Militaries, Humanitarian Organizations, and the Law* (Vancouver: UBC Press, 2012), pp. 199–234 ('Humanitarian Space').

over distinction.[50] Ultimately, I have organized the relevant actors into three broad categories:[51]

1. International humanitarian actors:
   a. '*ICRC actor*': humanitarian actors working for the International Committee of the Red Cross (ICRC) and Red Cross family;
   b. '*humanitarian NGO actor*': humanitarian actors working for NGOs such as MSF, Oxfam, Mercy Corps;
   c. '*UN humanitarian actor*': humanitarian actors working for UN humanitarian agencies such as UNHCR, UNICEF, and OCHA.
2. International peacekeeping actors:
   a. '*peacekeeping actor/peacekeeper*': forces who populate peacekeeping battalions of missions such as UNMISS, MONUSCO, EUPROFOR, UNAMID;
   b. '*civilian/civilian staff*': civilians working in civil affairs, human rights monitors, political and diplomatic actors working for the same missions.
3. International military actors:
   a. '*military actor*': soldiers, civil–military liaison officers, and other military actors deployed in multinational military missions and coalitions led by NATO, the US, and others (e.g. ISAF in Afghanistan).

Having outlined the relevant categories in this way, I want to emphasize that, more than the actors themselves, it is the boundaries between them that are of interest in this investigation.[52] What is being tracked across global sites is thus not any particular individual or bounded group, but rather the idea of distinction and, especially, the civilian concept. In keeping with the bottom-up approach of the study and its emphasis on practice, I am tentatively reserving conclusions about the way in which these groupings interact with IHL's civilian–combatant distinction. That is a central puzzle of this monograph, and it will be pieced together gradually over the course of the discussion. From a doctrinal IHL perspective, however, the reader will note that many of the international actors belonging to these three groups are

[50] Drawing on Lohne and Sandvick's definition of the field in their legal sociology of humanitarianism, adding an IHL focus and a more explicit role for non-humanitarian actors. Kjersti Lohne and Kristin Bergtora Sandvik, 'Bringing Law into the Political Sociology of Humanitarianism', *Oslo Law Review*, Vol. 4, No. 1, 2017, pp. 4–27, 10–11, 15 ('Political Sociology'). For a general discussion of the field see Pierre Bourdieu, *The Field of Cultural Production* (Cambridge: Cambridge University Press, 1993) ('*The Field*').

[51] At the training sites, actors will additionally have the designation of 'trainer' or 'trainee'. The listed organizations comprise a non-exhaustive set of examples of the relevant actors. Police and private international actors, such as those engaged in business activities or employed by private military and security companies, are not considered in detail.

[52] Following the insights of relational ethnography. See e.g. Matthew Desmond, 'Relational Ethnography', *Theory and Society*, Vol. 43, No. 5, 2014, pp. 547–579 ('Relational Ethnography').

entitled to civilian protection in international law. Already, then, we see hints that the idea of distinction is circulating in civilian–civilian relations.

1.4 Central claims of the monograph

This monograph advances three main claims. The first is about the everyday life of international (humanitarian) law, the second is about distinction's perpetually disrupted nature, and the third is about the existence of a 'civilian plus' figure in international practice.

1.4.1 The everyday life of IHL

This claim concerns the wide range of unconventional actors who are shaping the idea of distinction and the civilian concept through their everyday practices and interactions.

This study connects the socio-legal study of law in everyday life to the study of everyday humanitarianism.[53] The latter occupies a corner of the broader literature on humanitarianism, situated in what some refer to as the field of humanitarian studies.[54] Relatively speaking, scholars of international law have been slow to embark on a comprehensively interdisciplinary engagement with humanitarianism.[55] As a consequence, the rich insights of the humanitarianism literature have not yet

[53] On everyday humanitarianism see: Lisa Ann Richey, 'Conceptualizing "Everyday Humanitarianism": Ethics, Affects, and Practices of Contemporary Global Helping', *New Political Science*, Vol. 40, No. 4, 2018, pp. 625–639 ('Everyday Humanitarianism'); Udan Fernando and Dorothea Hilhorst, 'Everyday Practices of Humanitarian Aid: Tsunami Response in Sri Lanka', *Development in Practice*, Vol. 16, No. 3/4, 2006, pp. 292–302 ('Everyday Practices'); Anais Aresseguier, 'The Moral Sense of Humanitarian Actors: An Empirical Exploration', *Disasters*, Vol. 42, No. 1, 2018, pp. 62–80 ('Moral Sense').

[54] Contributions to the broader literature on humanitarianism have been generated by academics in a wide range of individual disciplines, including anthropology, sociology, political science, and international relations. See, e.g.: Liisa H. Malkki, *The Need to Help: The Domestic Arts of International Humanitarianism* (North Carolina: Duke University Press, 2015) (*Need to Help*); David Mosse (ed.), *Adventures in Aidland: The Anthropology of Professionals in International Development* (New York: Berghahn, 2013) (*Aidland*); Silke Roth, *Passionate Professionals: The Paradoxes of Aid Work* (Abingdon and New York: Routledge, 2015) (*Paradoxes of Aid*); Didier Fassin and Mariella Pandolfini (eds.), *Contemporary States of Emergency: The Politics of Military and Humanitarian Interventions* (New York: Zone Books, 2010) (*States of Emergency*); Didier Fassin, *Humanitarian Reason: A Moral History of the Present* (University of California Press, 2011) (*Humanitarian Reason*); Krause, supra (*Good Project*); Antonio Donini (ed.), *The Golden Fleece: Manipulation and Independence in Humanitarian Action* (Virginia: Kumarian Press, 2012) (*Golden Fleece*); Zoe Marriage, *Not Breaking the Rules, Not Playing the Game: International Assistance to Countries at War* (London: Hurst, 2006) (*Not Breaking the Rules*). The present study also benefits from insights from the literature on everyday peacekeeping, especially: Severine Autessere, *Peaceland: Conflict Resolution and the Everyday Politics of International Intervention* (Cambridge: Cambridge University Press, 2014) (*Peaceland*).

[55] Lohne and Sandvik, supra, 5 ('Political Sociology').

meaningfully infused what Drumbl terms the 'international legal imagination'.[56] Where IHL scholars have taken up the issue of humanitarianism, a doctrinal and normative approach to law has predominated. This can be explained, in part, by the need to clarify IHL's application to issues such as state consent for humanitarian activities, humanitarian access to beneficiaries, and the deliberate targeting of humanitarian actors by violent actors.[57] Without denying the pressing nature of such concerns, much could also be learned from a more critical, socio-legal approach to the theory and practice of humanitarianism.[58] An important methodological contribution of the present study is to demonstrate the form that such an inquiry might take.

In socio-legal studies, law is viewed as a historical and culturally specific mode of social organization, taking different forms both within and across social strata.[59] With this bottom-up approach to the study of law, it is a legitimate task to study how rules work in practice.[60] One might ask, for example, how a given actor perceives, understands, experiences, uses, or avoids law.[61] This has the potential to reveal how individual actors engage with law in unexpected ways.[62] Scrutiny of practice is also instructive because, as noted above, IHL rules are open to alternative—and potentially contradictory—meanings. Focusing on practice can thus illuminate subtle dynamics that might otherwise be unaccounted for, such as the fact that that IHL's civilian–combatant distinction is not the only fault line along which the relationships of international actors are organized.

The international actors examined in this study avoid, ignore, adopt, apply, develop, and promulgate IHL norms and rules. However, their engagement with IHL is not simply instrumental. These actors also self-conceptualize according to IHL's civilian and combatant categories, such that law plays a constitutive role. The

[56] Mark Drumbl, *Re-imagining Child Soldiers in International Law and Policy* (Oxford: Oxford University Press, 2012), 9 (*Child Soldiers*) (referring to a 'normative, aspirational, and operational mix of international law, policy, and practice—constituted as it is directly and indirectly by a broad constellation of actors').

[57] See, e.g.: Claudie Barrat, *Status of NGOs in International Humanitarian Law* (Leiden: Brill Nijhoff, 2014) (*Status of NGOs*); Wagner, supra ('IHL/ICRC Perspective'); Dapo Akande and Emanuela-Chiara Gillard, 'Arbitrary Withholding of Consent to Humanitarian Relief Operations in Armed Conflict', *International Law Studies*, Vol. 92, 2016, pp. 483–511 ('Consent').

[58] On the need for a legal sociology of humanitarianism, see Lohne and Sandvik, supra ('Political Sociology').

[59] As articulated by the Centre for Socio-Legal Studies at the University of Oxford.

[60] On law from the 'bottom up' and from outside legal institutions, see: Susan Silbey and Ayn Cavicchi, 'The Common Place of Law: Transforming Matters of Concern into the Objects of Everyday Life', in Bruno Latour and Peter Weibel (eds.), *Making Things Public: Atmospheres of Democracy* (Cambridge, MA: MIT Press, 2005), pp. 556–565 ('Common Place of Law'); David Cowan, Linda Mulcahy, and Sally Wheeler, 'Introduction', in David Cowan, Linda Mulcahy, and Sally Wheeler (eds.), *Major Works in Socio-Legal Studies* (London: Routledge, 2013), 5 ('Introduction').

[61] Paraphrasing Cowan, Mulcahy, and Wheeler, supra, 5 ('Introduction').

[62] Susan Silbey and Austin Sarat, 'Critical Traditions in Law and Research', *Law and Society Review*, Vol. 21, 1987, pp. 165–174, 173; Austin Sarat and Thomas R. Kearns, 'Beyond the Great Divide: Forms of Legal Scholarship and Everyday Life', in Austin Sarat and Thomas R. Kearns (eds.), *Law in Everyday Life* (University of Michigan Press, 1993), pp. 21–62, 60 ('Beyond the Great Divide').

socio-legal study of law in everyday life engages with law's instrumental and constitutive aspects;[63] this recognizes that law is shaped by the way in which actors use it, but also that its constitutive power delimits the way in which actors are able to employ it.[64] This introduces an important caveat to the approach delineated above—namely that actors cannot *avoid* or *ignore* law, entirely. Even if international humanitarian actors in South Sudan were to fail to cite IHL on a daily basis, their civilian identity would continue to shape their self-perception and the organization of their affairs.

This monograph also makes a deeper point about legal pluralism, about who might shape IHL's meaning beyond the usual suspects and outside the usual venues.[65] Settings as dissimilar as Geneva and South Sudan are treated here as sites where the meaning of IHL is articulated, disseminated, and shaped.[66] The fact that distinction takes on myriad forms and surfaces in a variety of contexts for different reasons, is in itself noteworthy. Moreover, distinction is being constituted and reconstituted on a daily basis by those we might not tend to think of as legal actors. Traditionally, states have been positioned as the main actors engaged in making international law,[67] including IHL.[68] Yet the development of IHL has been demonstrably pluralistic, with non-state actors playing a significant role.[69] This study understands IHL as a body of law and a practice with room for the contributions of non-traditional actors. Moving away from a focus on collective entities, the study contributes to the burgeoning legal literature on individual actors—particularly

[63] Sarat and Kearns, supra, 29, 32 ('Beyond the Great Divide').

[64] Ibid., 55; Barbara Yngvesson, 'Inventing Law in Local Settings: Rethinking Popular Legal Culture', *Yale Law Journal*, Vol. 98, No. 8, 1989, pp. 1689–1709.

[65] See Sally Engle Merry, 'International Law and Sociolegal Scholarship: Towards a Spatial Global Legal Pluralism', in Austin Sarat (ed.), *Special Issue: Law and Society Reconsidered (Studies in Law, Politics and Society)*, Vol. 21, 2007, pp. 149–168 (linking socio-legal studies and legal pluralism). See also Lianne M. Boer, 'The Greater Part of Juriconsults: On Consensus Claims and their Footnotes in Legal Scholarship', *Leiden Journal of International Law*, Vol. 29, 2016, pp. 1021–1042, 1041–1042 (study of practice shows that 'the law is "made" by those working with it, and there are very many people doing so, in many different capacities').

[66] On the need to study unorthodox locales, see David M. Trubeck and John Esser, 'Critical Empiricism in American Legal Studies: Paradox, Program, or Pandora's Box?', *Law and Social Inquiry*, Vol. 14, 1989, pp. 1–52, 45.

[67] Jean d'Aspremont, 'International Law-Making by Non-State Actors: Changing the Model or Putting the Phenomenon into Perspective?', in Math Noortmann and Cedric Ryngaert (eds.), *Non-State Actor Dynamics in International Law: From Law-Takers to Law Makers* (London: Routledge, 2010).

[68] Michael Schmitt and Sean Watts, 'State *Opinio Juris* and International Humanitarian Law Pluralism', *International Law Studies*, Vol. 91, 2015, pp. 171–215 ('IHL Pluralism'); Sivakumaran, supra ('Making and Shaping').

[69] Leslie Green, *The Contemporary Law of Armed Conflict*, 3rd edition (Manchester: Manchester University Press, 2008), pp. 26–64; Martha Finnemore, *National Interests in International Society* (Ithaca, New York: Cornell University Press, 1996), Chapter 1; Schmitt and Watts, supra, 172 ('IHL Pluralism'). On the desirability of a role for non-state actors, compare Schmitt and Watts, supra, 174 ('IHL Pluralism') (calling for a narrower state-based approach) with Sivakumaran, supra ('Making and Shaping') (IHL is made by the 'community of international humanitarian lawyers', which includes states, 'state-empowered' actors and non-state actors).

those occupying lower-level and frontline roles.[70] The monograph does not assert that these unconventional actors are enacting positive law in the sense of contributing to treaties and legal conventions (though some might). The claim, rather, is that they are producing the meaning of international legal rules through their everyday practices and interactions.[71] We might thus think of them as 'lawmakers', in the broadest sense of the word.[72]

As a point of clarification, not everything needs to be considered law to be of interest in this interdisciplinary inquiry. A socio-legal examination of the everyday invites a closer look at practices that might, on the surface, seem to have very little to do with law.[73] As Sarat and Kearns point out, 'motives, needs, emotions, anxieties, aspirations that are not entirely fixed by legal meanings or by legal forces operate throughout without totally losing their identity to law'.[74] The empirical material gathered for this study demonstrates that turf battles, power struggles, status anxiety, feelings of affinity or resentment, jealousy, and petty gripes all play a role in the everyday life of distinction.

1.4.2 Distinction as a perpetually disrupted idea

The second claim is about the idea of distinction being disrupted apart from, and prior to, anything that is going on in the everyday practices of international actors.

It should be emphasized at the outset that this is not a study of IHL compliance. The question animating this investigation is thus not whether a given actor follows the law of distinction, but how international actors make and remake distinction as a matter of grounded practice. There are two reasons for which a compliance focus would be limiting here. First, a compliance focus potentially obscures significant aspects of actual practice.[75] It assumes, for example, that the civilian–combatant distinction is in fact the distinction of greatest significance—an assumption belied

[70] Jutta Brunée and Stephen Toope, *Legitimacy and Legality in International Law* (Cambridge: Cambridge University Press, 2010); Kate Parlett, *The Individual in the International Legal System: Continuity and Change in International Law* (Cambridge: Cambridge University Press, 2011), Chapter 3; Michael P. Scharf, 'International Law in Crisis: A Qualitative Empirical Contribution to the Compliance Debate', *Cardozo Law Review*, Vol. 31, 2009, pp. 45–97; Lassa Oppenheim, *International Law: A Treatise* (London and New York: Longmans, Green, 1905).

[71] This brings an IHL focus to the growing literature on the everyday life of international law. See, e.g. Luis Eslava, *Local Space, Global Life: The Everyday Operation of International Law and Development* (Cambridge: Cambridge University Press, 2015).

[72] For a similarly broad approach to law-making, see Itamar Mann, *Humanity at Sea: Maritime Migration and the Foundations of International Law* (Cambridge: Cambridge University Press, 2016); Sivakumaran, supra, n 5 ('Making and Shaping').

[73] Sarat and Kearns, supra, 55 ('Beyond the Great Divide').

[74] Ibid.

[75] On the limits of a compliance focus see Martti Koskenniemi, *The Gentle Civilizer of Nations: The Rise and Fall of International Law 1870–1960* (Cambridge: Cambridge University Press, 2001), 485 (a compliance focus 'silently assumes that the political question—what the objectives are—has already been solved'). See also Kinsella, supra, 4 (*Image*).

by the civilian–civilian tensions that this study brings to light. Second, in a compliance study those practices that depart from a civilian–combatant binary would be regarded as violations of the law, or perhaps as extra-legal and therefore irrelevant. Such accounts treat the IHL rule as both stable and valuable, obfuscating distinction's more troubling aspects.

Adopting a different tack, the study does not simplistically juxtapose the practices of international actors with an inert legal doctrine. Nor does it frame the practices in question as interfering with a rule that is otherwise orderly. Instead, the study uncovers the messiness of distinction at every level: from the AP I codification of the principle of distinction, to other IHL targeting rules that dim or move the line, to the co-location of humanitarian actors with armed UN forces in South Sudan. The crucial point being conveyed here is that it is not simply the case that international humanitarian actors are disrupting distinction through their practices—though that may well be true. The claim, instead, is that distinction is a deeply disrupted idea that is plagued by pre-existing disorder.

1.4.3 The existence of the 'civilian plus'

The third claim is about the existence in international practice of a special civilian figure and its corollaries.

As the empirical findings show, the routine interactions that take place between international humanitarian actors and others in the operational space are shaped by contests over distinction. In the vision of distinction that animates these practices, the notion of static civilian and combatant entities is supplanted by more fluid qualities of 'civilianness' and 'combatantness'. It is as though these qualities float in the air, potentially affixing to any individual at any given moment—depending upon one's self-presentation and behaviour, and the surrounding context. This is a world in which civilianness is more a matter of degree than category, and we thus find international actors jostling with one another for positioning on a civilianness continuum. The relationship of 'humanitarianness' to civilianness (and combatantness) is also a live question, one that is pursued across the multi-sited study.

To capture the way in which the civilian concept is diffracted through the lenses of various international actors, I introduce three new figures: the 'civilian plus', 'mere civilian', and 'civilian minus'. This triptych relies upon a concept of civilianness that is relative, contingent, and aligned with an already-fragmented civilian category in IHL. While all three civilian figures attract the same target immunity IHL accords to civilians in armed conflict, they are situated differently in other respects. The 'civilian plus' is a special status that provides an extra layer of inviolability to individuals who express particularly pure iterations of civilian characteristics. The 'mere civilian' denotes a default status given to those who are 'only' ordinary civilians, and who have done nothing to attract a 'plus' or 'minus' designation. The 'civilian minus' is a tainted status accompanied by swirling qualities of combatantness, assigned to otherwise-civilian individuals who creep too close to the fight. The engagement with these three civilian figures in the monograph is both descriptive and analytical, but judgement on whether IHL should accommodate a special civilian status is reserved until the concluding chapter. This deferral of the normative question is intended as a corrective, so that we might first understand these grounded practices before making pronouncements on their destabilizing potential.

Coming now to the normative question, I am sympathetic to the desire for a special status but, in the end, I propose that the 'civilian plus' is a dangerous proposition. While a special status for international humanitarian actors responds to their genuine security anxieties and incentivizes the crucial tasks they perform in war, it also (further) splinters IHL's civilian category and sets some civilians apart from others. My main concern is that the 'civilian plus' entrenches humanitarian exceptionalism, giving legal imprimatur to the differential treatment of the lives of humanitarian actors as compared to those of other civilians—including the war-affected populations whose suffering provides humanitarians with their *raison d'etre*.[76] This conundrum highlights the paradoxical nature of the 'civilian plus'. The power of a special civilian figure derives from the notion that lesser civilians exist, and this serves to weaken the general norm of civilian protection. The more beleaguered or undermined the civilian ideal becomes, however, the more desirable the prospect of a special civilian status appears.

1.5 A note on methodology

While it might seem perverse to introduce a special civilian figure only to conclude that it is a dangerous idea, this outcome flows naturally from deliberate methodological choices and the epistemology that underpins the study.

To begin with, the empirical component[77] of this monograph was developed through a grounded theory approach.[78] This approach involves an iterative process that is primarily inductive, but has deductive aspects as well.[79] Although the

[76] Building on Didier Fassin, 'Inequality of Lives, Hierarchies of Humanity: Moral Commitments and Ethical Dilemmas of Humanitarianism', in Ilana Feldman and Miriam Ticktin (eds.), *In the Name of Humanity* (Durham, NC: Duke University Press, 2010), pp. 239–255 ('Inequality of Lives').

[77] On empirical approaches in international legal scholarship, see: Elena Baylis, 'The Transformative Potential of Rigorous Empirical Research', *American Society of International Law Annual Meeting*, Vol. 104, March 2010 ('Empirical Research'); Gregory Shafer and Tom Ginsburg, 'The Empirical Turn in International Legal Scholarship', *American Journal of International Law*, Vol. 106, No. 1, 2012, pp. 1–48 ('Empirical Turn').

[78] See Kathy Charmaz, *Constructing Grounded Theory: A Practical Guide Through Qualitative Analysis* (London: SAGE, 2006) (*Grounded Theory*).

[79] Ibid., 4, 188.

research was guided by a foreshadowed problem (i.e. how the idea of distinction circulates in international practices), it did not begin with a specific hypothesis.[80] Rather, it left open the possibility of adjusting the research plan in response to surprising discoveries.[81] Riles describes the task of sorting out the relationships between various discoveries as a process of 'unwinding'; in this process, the scholar faces an intellectual risk, as she must follow where the material leads her.[82]

The empirical material this study draws on was generated by interviews, surveys, focus group discussions, and participant observation I conducted in South Sudan and at civil–military training grounds. Informed by ethnographic approaches developed in the discipline of anthropology, these empirical methods aim to see through the eyes of international actors, describing and explaining their motivations, actions, interpretations, values, and patterns of meaning.[83] I conducted research in South Sudan in 2015, in the states of Central Equatoria, Jonglei, and Unity.[84] Across the fieldwork sites, I completed 100 hours of participant observation and conducted 113 interviews; 55 of these interviews were with key informants and the rest took the form of focus group discussions. I carried out fieldwork on civil–military training sites in 2016 in Italy (NATO CIMIC), Germany (Zif), and Sweden (SWEDINT) (see Section 1.6.2). At the training grounds, I logged over 200 hours of participant observation; I conducted 38 interviews with trainers and trainees, mostly in the form of small focus group discussions, and also administered 17 supplementary perception surveys.[85]

The gathering, synthesizing, and coding of empirical material for this study led to the discovery of the 'civilian plus' figure, as described. While traces of this figure's dark side lingered around the edges of my attempts to describe the grounded practices, I deferred the question of whether a special civilian is something we should want. This move is also linked to the epistemological framework I am working within. This study falls closer to the interpretive end of the positivist–interpretivist

[80] Bronislaw Malinowski, *Argonauts of the Western Pacific: An Account of Native Enterprise and Adventure in the Archipelagoes of Melanesian New Guinea* (London: Routledge, 1922/1984), 9.

[81] Alan Bryman, 'The Debate about Quantitative and Qualitative Research: A Question of Method or Epistemology', *The British Journal of Sociology*, Vol. 35, No. 1, 1984, pp. 75–92, 78 ('The Debate'); David Silverman (ed.), *Doing Qualitative Research: A Practical Handbook*, 3rd edition (London: SAGE, 2010), 274 ('*Doing Qualitative Research*').

[82] Annelise Riles, 'Afterword: A Method More than a Subject', in David Cowan and Daniel Wincott (eds.), *Exploring the 'Legal' in Socio-Legal Studies* (London: Palgrave, 2016), pp. 257–264, 260; Annelise Riles, 'Anthropology, Human Rights and Legal Knowledge: Culture in the Iron Cage', *American Anthropologist*, Vol. 108, 2008, pp. 52–65.

[83] Bryman, supra, 77–88 ('The Debate'). On methodological borrowing in socio-legal studies, see David Cowan and Daniel Wincott, 'Exploring the "Legal"', in David Cowan and Daniel Wincott (eds.), *Exploring the 'Legal' in Socio-Legal Studies* (London: Palgrave, 2016), pp. 1–32, 5, 14. For a socio-legal study of international law employing anthropological methods, see Nouwen, supra (*Complementarity*).

[84] The research is also informed by earlier visits I made to South Sudan in 2010, 2011, and 2014 as an aid practitioner.

[85] A more extensive account of methodology, research ethics, and positionality is provided in Rebecca Sutton, *The Humanitarian Actor as 'Civilian Plus': The Circulation of the Idea of Distinction in International Law* (Unpublished PhD Thesis, 2018).

spectrum, aiming not to explain so much as to engender understanding.[86] For this reason, it focuses on descriptive inference, which permits high levels of authenticity, richness, and trustworthiness in the findings.[87] In order to enhance the reliability of the research, a well-defined and vigorous coding frame involving precise coding rules was developed.[88] To strengthen the validity of the research, both data triangulation (i.e. drawing on different sources of data) and method triangulation (i.e. drawing on mixed methods) were employed.[89] In terms of the falsifiability of the research, it should be pointed out that this study does not concentrate on causal relationships. However, the intention is not to ignore potential causal relationships, but to keep the causal aspect open-ended.[90] Finally, as for the generalizability of the research,[91] the study's multi-sited approach permits a certain level of typicality and transferability. In particular, the inclusion of the civil–military training sites helps to situate the findings from South Sudan in a wider global context.

1.6 Introduction to the three realms: distinction from the bottom up

This multi-sited study interrogates the idea of distinction across three domains: the Kinetic, where distinction is in motion in the operational context (South Sudan); the Pedagogical, where distinction is taught to practitioners in a classroom setting (civil–military training grounds in Italy, Germany, and Sweden); and the Intellectual, where distinction is adjudicated, theorized, and made into policy (Geneva and the Hague). Eschewing the assumption that the most important divide is a civilian–combatant one, this study investigates a wide range of line-drawing practices and captures numerous distinctions at play. As the bottom-up discussion within each chapter progresses across the three realms, the findings become increasingly normative and abstract—and more obviously relevant for international law. Yet a point the monograph conveys is that all of these sites are spaces in which the idea of distinction is produced. The civilian concept is to be found not only in the Geneva Conventions or the verdict of an international criminal tribunal, but also in the 'no weapons allowed' sign erected outside an NGO office in

[86] John Macionis and Linda Gerber, *Sociology*, 7th edition (Toronto: Pearson, 2011), 33.

[87] On the value of a descriptive approach in the study of law, see Anne Orford, 'In Praise of Description', *Leiden Journal of International Law*, Vol. 25, No. 3, 2012, pp. 609–625, 616; Drumbl, supra, Preface and Acknowledgments (*Child Soldiers*).

[88] As per Lee Epstein and Gary King, 'The Rules of Inference', *University of Chicago Law Review*, Vol. 69, No. 1, 2002, 85.

[89] Uwe Flick, *An Introduction to Qualitative Research* (London: SAGE, 2009), 136, 443–453.

[90] Anna MacDonald, 'Local Understandings and Experiences of Transitional Justice: A Review of the Evidence', *London School of Economics Justice and Security Research Program*, Paper No. 6, July 2013, 7.

[91] On ethnographic methods and generalizability, see John Gerring, 'Mere Description', *British Journal of Political Science*, Vol. 42, No. 4, 2012, pp. 721–746, 726. See also Desmond, supra ('Relational Ethnography') 573 (the most important part about generalizability is being right).

Juba and the virtual reality game that teaches Swedish soldiers how to interact with NGOs on the battlefield.

To make these dynamics legible as part of the everyday life of distinction, this study employs the concept of *everyday distinction practices*. These refer to the day-to-day competent performances[92] that international humanitarian actors engage in to operationalize their distinction project. These performances are profoundly relational; even as humanitarian actors strive to distance themselves and maintain separation, they are often still intertwined and bound together with other actors.[93] These distinction practices materialize mainly in the Kinetic and Pedagogical realms, assuming different forms to reflect the demands of each respective context. Distinction circulates in the Intellectual realm in something less of a quotidian manner, befitting the more normative qualities of this domain. Each realm is now outlined in turn.

1.6.1 The Kinetic realm

Of all three realms, Kinetic practices tend to be the most practical—and potentially reactive. As the Kinetic realm is where one finds distinction in motion, it sheds light on the way in which distinction is enacted as a day-to-day matter on the ground. Here, official policies and normative debates are brought into contact with the mundaneness of daily decision-making, revealing the nuances of what international actors actually do. It is also in the Kinetic realm that the most intense relationships between international actors are formed, as these actors routinely come into physical contact.[94]

This attention to grounded practice builds on the insights of scholars such as de Waal, Marriage, and Koddenbrock, whose respective works illuminate the way in which the commitments of humanitarian actors are (not) implemented. De Waal entreats us to consider 'actually existing humanitarianism',[95] and Marriage likewise instructs us to look beyond official discourse: humanitarian actors may invoke rules or principles at the same time as they ignore or breach them, in practice.[96]

[92] The reference to 'competent performances' comes from Emanuel Adler and Vincent Pouliot (eds.), *International Practices* (Cambridge: Cambridge University Press, 2011), 6, 15. Drawing more generally on Pierre Bourdieu, *Outline of a Theory of Practice* (Cambridge: Cambridge University Press, 1977), 78–86 (*Outline*).

[93] See George Marcus, *Ethnography through Thick and Thin* (Princeton, NJ: Princeton University Press, 1998), 90; Desmond, supra, 554 ('Relational Ethnography'). For relational accounts of humanitarian practice see Larissa Fast, *Aid in Danger: The Perils and Promise of Humanitarianism* (Philadelphia, PA: University of Pennsylvania Press, 2014), 8; Roth, supra, 91 (*Paradoxes of Aid*).

[94] Slim makes a similar point regarding civil–military policies; see Hugo Slim, 'The Stretcher and the Drum: Civil–Military Relations in Peace Support Operations', *International Peacekeeping*, Vol. 3, No. 2, 1996, pp. 123–140, 129, 131 ('Stretcher').

[95] Alex de Waal, *Famine Crimes: Politics and the Disaster Relief Industry in Africa* (Melton, Suffolk: James Currey, 1997), 66(*Famine Crimes*).

[96] Marriage, supra, 10 (*Not Breaking the Rules*).

Koddenbrock further argues that a disregard for operational practice sustains the visible and public face of international intervention.[97] Normative debates about the traditional humanitarian principles, for example, tend to treat the principles as untethered by what goes on 'on the ground'.[98] Taking these findings about humanitarian practice in a new direction, this monograph centres the idea of distinction.

South Sudan has been selected as the operational site that serves as the focal point of the Kinetic realm discussions. There is a long history of intentionally targeting civilians in the region's conflicts, and those claiming to be outside the fight are typically regarded with suspicion in South Sudan. Focusing on the period since 2013, South Sudan has been the site of an armed conflict in which international humanitarian actors struggle to secure sustained access to populations in need, while facing threats to their own safety. From 2013 to 2018, at least 100 aid workers were reportedly killed in the country.[99] South Sudan was ranked the most dangerous place in the world for humanitarian actors to operate in 2017,[100] with a record number of aid workers being killed by gunfire.[101] In a study from 2018, South Sudan had the highest number of both major global attacks on humanitarian actors (55 incidents) and of victims (111).[102] South Sudan is also a context in which diverse intervening actors converge. International humanitarian actors share the operational space with other civilian and military actors, including members of a UN integrated mission with a robust 'Protection of Civilians' mandate, UNMISS. The presence of a UN integrated mission that is empowered to use force poses numerous challenges for humanitarian actors, some of whom live with peacekeepers in close quarters and rely upon UN military assets.

In South Sudan, IHL rules are not a habitual topic of conversation for international actors. Nonetheless, distinction influences these actors' self-conceptualization and their encounters with each other. Distinction is activated when humanitarian actors eject armed actors from a site where they deliver services, or when a humanitarian actor travels on a UNMISS helicopter and everyone gossips about it. A crucial element of Kinetic practices is thus the relevance of optics: distinction has a more explicit visual life in the operational context, and the

[97] Kai Koddenbrock, *The Practice of Humanitarian Intervention: Aid Workers, Agencies, and Institutions in the Democratic Republic of the Congo* (New York: Routledge, 2016), 59, 62 (*Humanitarian Intervention*).

[98] Ibid., 68.

[99] African Press Organization, 'South Sudan: Aid Workers Freed, Humanitarian Deaths Reach 100 since 2013', Press Release, Distributed by APO Group on Behalf of OCHA, 1 May 2018. Available at: https://www.africa-newsroom.com/press/south-sudan-aid-workers-freed-humanitarian-deaths-reach-100-since-december-2013.

[100] Humanitarian Outcomes, *Aid Worker Security Report: 2018*, August 2018. Available at: https://reliefweb.int/report/world/aid-worker-security-report-figures-glance-2018.

[101] Adele Harmer, 'Aid Worker Deaths: The Numbers Tell the Story', *OCHA News*, 16 August 2018. Available at: https://www.unocha.org/story/aid-worker-deaths-numbers-tell-story.

[102] Humanitarian Outcomes, *Aid Worker Security Report: 2019*, August 2019. The main types of attacks in 2018 in South Sudan were shooting (76), bodily assault (50), and kidnapping (15). Available at: https://www.humanitarianoutcomes.org/sites/default/files/publications/awsr_figures2019.pdf.

deployment of signs and symbols reveals much about whose perceptions are being managed, and why. A final noteworthy aspect of the Kinetic realm is the way in which it exposes conflicts that are otherwise concealed. This study draws attention, in particular, to a tension that arises in daily practice between the traditional humanitarian principle of humanity and the idea of distinction.

1.6.2 The Pedagogical realm

While South Sudan is perhaps more obviously a site of everyday life—albeit a conflict-affected one—professional training spaces are also venues where everyday life unfolds.[103] The Pedagogical realm is a middle zone that lies in between the conflict zone and the legal text; it is a space between theory and practice. Whereas Kinetic practices are more reactive and responsive to grounded realities, Pedagogical practices have a very strong normative component. This is where the idea of distinction is taught and critiqued. In treating the Pedagogical realm as its own domain, this study makes the case that training reveals something new that cannot be gleaned from the doctrine, scholarship, and practice of the Intellectual realm, nor from the day-to-day operations of the Kinetic realm. Three benefits of studying training sites will now be outlined.

First, civil–military training grounds are venues where overt attempts are made to disseminate international rules and norms and to shape the behavioural ideals of international actors. Given that civil–military training programmes are explicitly designed to address the contact point between civilian and military actors, they inevitably implicate IHL's principle of distinction. Unlike in South Sudan, international actors in the training spaces have explicit and sustained conversations about the civilian–combatant distinction and other rules governing the conduct of hostilities.

Second, the exploration of training spaces complements the investigation of civil–military interaction in operational contexts. Almost all of the actors in the civil–military training programmes are returning from frontline work in the field, on a break between stints, or preparing for a new mission. At their most useful, the programmes establish a temporary space where these international actors can take stock and make sense of their time in the field. Trainees bring their knowledge and experiences with them from the operational context, and their unique individual experiences also shape their engagement with the lessons. Trainees' first-hand accounts of their experiences in deployment zones offer granular, thick descriptions of how contests over distinction materialize in the operational

[103] Bureaucratic conferences and meetings are treated as a site of everyday life in Sarat and Kearns, supra ('The Great Divide').

context.[104] To varying degrees, these training grounds also bring civilian and military actors together in face-to-face interaction. It is because of these differently situated actors' varied outlooks that the training grounds are also sites of struggle, and it is through these struggles that distinction is constituted and reconstituted.

Third, rather than measuring how well the training programmes mimic the 'real' world, this monograph looks at the artificial aspects of the trainings, showcasing facets of distinction that are often hidden from view. Simulation exercises, for example, afford an opportunity to observe complex patterns of interaction as if in slow motion. Trainees can literally pause the action as a simulation exercise unfolds, and they might even be granted a chance at a 'do-over'. This kind of iterative process is rarely witnessed in other contexts. It is also through these types of exercises that tensions between competing ideals start to emerge. Commitments that seem possible to uphold simultaneously in the relevant texts, or in the classroom, suddenly rub up against each other and trainees must negotiate this friction. This more practical aspect of training thus begins to edge closer to the operational context.

Three civil–military training programmes were selected for scrutiny in this study. The programmes are led, respectively, by: NATO's Multi-National Civil–Military Cooperation Group (CIMIC) in Motto di Livenza, Italy; the Swedish Armed Forces (SWEDINT) training centre outside Stockholm; and the German Centre for Peace Operations (Zif) outside Berlin. These trainings deal with one variant of civil–military relations, which is the interaction of external or international civilian and military actors who are involved in international missions in armed conflicts.[105] While the selected training programmes are all delivered in Europe, they have a global dimension, as they prepare a diverse set of international actors to deploy to a variety of conflict contexts. Of particular importance is that the trainings share the aim of preparing international actors to participate in comprehensive-type missions. Since the end of the Cold War, international institutions such as the EU, the UN, and NATO have steadily moved towards comprehensive, integrated, and multidimensional international missions.[106] These missions are imbued with values such as 'working together' and are accompanied by imagery of walls coming down between different kinds of international actors.[107] The

[104] Some stories told at trainings that relate to South Sudan have thus been included in the Kinetic part of the study.

[105] Michael Pugh, 'The Challenge of Civil–Military Relations in International Peace Operations', *Disasters*, Vol. 25, No. 4, 2001, pp. 345–357, 346 ('Civil–Military Relations').

[106] Joanna Macrae and Nicholas Leader, 'Shifting Sands: The Search for "Coherence" Between Political and Humanitarian Responses to Complex Emergencies', *Humanitarian Policy Group Report*, No. 8, August 2000, 9 ('Shifting Sands').

[107] Jonathan Goodhand, 'Contested Boundaries: NGOs and Civil–Military Relations in Afghanistan', *Central Asian Survey*, Vol. 32, No. 3, 2013, pp. 287–305, 287 ('Contested Boundaries'); Victoria Metcalfe et al., 'UN Integration and Humanitarian Space: An Independent Study Commissioned by the UN Integration Steering Group', *Stimson Center and Overseas Development Institute*, 2011 ('Stimson Report').

selected training spaces thus showcase the way in which the idea of distinction circulates in settings in which civilian and military actors are encouraged to traverse the boundaries that separate them.

1.6.3 The Intellectual realm

The Intellectual realm encompasses a collection of sites more traditionally associated with law-making. It focuses on the legal rules encoded in the Geneva Conventions, historical approaches to legal protection in war, and decision-making at the International Criminal Tribunal for the Former Yugoslavia (ICTY). This is a realm in which lawyers, legal officials, judges, and (legal) academics, formally trained in international law, codify, adjudicate, and theorize distinction. It is also a domain in which policymakers and practitioners devise soft law guidelines and rules for civilian–military interaction. While one might expect that here, finally, we will find a bright-line civilian–combatant distinction intact, this quickly unravels as distinction is disrupted historically, doctrinally, and in practice. As the notion of a unified civilian category crumbles, the civilian figure that emerges is beset by contradiction. The civilian is at once a cherished ideal, imbued with extraordinarily high expectations and aspirations, and a fragile entity, routinely questioned, beleaguered, and undermined. These findings shed light on why international humanitarian actors would seek to transcend the civilian's vulnerability by asserting a special status.

1.7 Structure of the monograph

Pursuing the motif of a bright line, the main substantive chapters (Chapters 2–5) examine the circulation of the idea of distinction across the three realms. The narrative in each chapter begins in South Sudan, then progresses to the civil–military trainings, and finally on to Geneva and the Hague. In the Kinetic and Pedagogical realms, the discussion is organized around a series of encounters, inspired by Goffman's understanding of an encounter as 'the natural unit of social organization in which focused interaction occurs'.[108] These opening passages distil the relevant empirical findings into composite interactions that are representative and easily digestible, presaging the themes that will be developed in the discussion to follow.

[108] Erving Goffman, *Encounters: Two Studies in the Sociology of Interaction* (Eastford, CT: Martino Fine Books, 2013/1961), 8 (*Encounters*).

1.7.1 Chapter 2: What is the distinction?

Chapter 2 introduces, but does not resolve, the conundrum of what the idea of distinction *is* that is circulating in international practices, and how it relates to the IHL targeting rule. The main point conveyed is that distinction in the conduct of hostilities sense is in play, but that it is being deployed in ways we might not expect. Actors routinely move the line to assert intra-civilian distinctions, for example. They also collapse IHL's principle of distinction together with other values, ideas and principles to compose what we might think of as the 'distinction vernacular'.[109] The muddling of distinction is easier to observe in the training spaces than in South Sudan, as conversations about IHL are more explicit in the former. Trainees can be found struggling to locate a civilian–combatant binary in the conduct of hostilities sense, and they extend this fuzzy treatment to their categorization of humanitarian actors. The chapter also outlines the comprehensive ethos that guides contemporary international missions, explaining how the 'working together' mentality shapes intervention in South Sudan and the goings on at the three civil–military training sites. From the perspective of international humanitarian actors, international military and peacekeeping actors are encroaching upon them and blurring the lines—though what lines, exactly, is an issue not easily settled. Finally, the discussion of the Intellectual realm examines the status of these differently situated international actors in IHL, canvasses civil–military guidance documents, and considers high-level pronouncements about distinction. Attention is drawn to slippage between a civilian–combatant distinction and other fault lines, as distinction's haziness prevails at the level of doctrine, soft law, and policy.

1.7.2 Chapter 3: Who draws the line?

In a world in which international actors are intermingled and different spheres of activity coalesce, international humanitarian actors take it upon themselves to assert distinction. Crucially, this is not only about being distinct from other types of actors, but also about being *seen* to be distinct. It emerges in South Sudan that safeguarding distinction is in many respects a project of managing perceptions. The perceptions in question, I argue, belong to an amorphous onlooker: the 'phantom local'. This imagined local audience—which folds together the varied perspectives of armed actors, authorities, and beneficiaries—ultimately decides

[109] The concept of vernacularization is developed in Peggy Levitt and Sally Merry, 'Vernacularization on the Ground: Local Uses of Global Women's Rights in Peru, China, India and the United States', *Global Networks*, Vol. 9, No. 4, 2009, pp. 441–461 ('Vernacularization'). The authors define vernacularization as a 'process of appropriation and local adoption of globally generated ideas and strategies'.

who is who amongst international actors and whether appropriate lines are being drawn. A concern for perceptions is also palpable in the Pedagogical realm, though here humanitarian actors additionally ground their vision of distinction in law. In both South Sudan and in the training spaces, other international actors contest the vision of distinction that humanitarians promulgate. A power struggle ensues as these other actors remonstrate, push back, and adjust the lines humanitarian actors draw. Notably, international military trainees are explicitly encouraged to foster proximity with humanitarian actors (and other civilians) in operational settings. The exploration of the Intellectual realm focuses squarely on the figure of the humanitarian actor in IHL, examining the historical evolution of this figure and its treatment in AP I. I propose that IHL projects a Red Cross fantasy, such that protections for humanitarian actors are grounded in a very particular vision of humanitarianness. This leaves other humanitarians with status anxiety, yet their efforts to emulate this vision serve to further entrench the Red Cross actor's paradigmatic status.

1.7.3 Chapter 4: How is the line drawn?

Building on observations made previously about the importance of perceptions, Chapter 4 presents distinction as a performance. Jettisoning the notion that there is a line, as such, being drawn, the discussion conveys the dynamism of everyday distinction practices. Distinction takes on an explicit visual life in the Kinetic realm: humanitarian actors deploy signs and symbols, and carry themselves in deliberate ways, so as to ensure that their civilianness is unimpeachable. It is not a question of being civilian or not-civilian, but rather being more or less civilian; everything is a matter of degree and subtle gradation. Other international actors emerge here as potential sources of contamination, and these include (armed) actors who would be entitled to civilian protection in IHL. Humanitarian actors embark on dogged attempts to assert distinction from these other actors, but they do so in a wider context in which distinction is always already compromised. While the possible futility of their distinction project leads some humanitarian actors to rally behind distinction even more strongly, other humanitarians balance distinction with other pressing priorities. In the Pedagogical realm, international military and peacekeeping actors voice incredulity about the logic of humanitarian distinction practices. From the perspective of these other actors, humanitarians are behaving erratically and prevaricating. The Intellectual realm zeroes in on the civilian concept, locating a continuum of civilianness in international law. The discussion examines qualities that have historically been associated with civilianness—such as harmlessness, innocence, and non-participation in fighting—and highlights the shifting relevance of an armed/unarmed marker. Engaging with the adjudication of crimes against humanity cases at the ICTY,[110] it is shown even in international tribunals that civilianness might be a matter of degree. The chapter closes by introducing three unfamiliar figures: the 'civilian plus', 'mere civilian', and 'civilian minus'.

1.7.4 Chapter 5: Where is the line drawn?

This chapter pursues the 'civilian plus' and its corollaries across the three realms, exploring where the line is being drawn within the civilian category. Adopting parallel structures, the discussions in the Kinetic and Pedagogical realms first consider the humanitarian actor as a 'civilian plus' figure, and then examine arguments that humanitarian actors instead merit 'civilian minus' status. It is shown that in everyday practice, humanitarian actors strive to escape the vulnerability of the 'mere civilian' and to disperse any qualities of combatantness that might swirl around them. They root their claims to the 'civilian plus' in their important professional role and in the risk of harm it exposes them to; they also emphasize the expertise required to carry out humanitarian work. Other international actors detect a humanitarian superiority complex at play, sensing that humanitarian actors look down on them from a virtuous perch. Intriguingly, it is the very same professional role that could legitimate a claim to a special status that also impugns the civilianness of humanitarian actors—as when they are accused of 'feeding the enemy'. The discussion in the Intellectual realm conveys that these intra-civilian distinctions are not disturbing an otherwise stable binary framework. Attention is drawn to IHL targeting rules, such as DPH, that trouble a bright-line distinction. It is further shown that before the civilian was defined in AP I, the category was disaggregated for purposes of protection and access to services. Finally, returning to the notion of a Red Cross fantasy, it is proposed that IHL sets some humanitarian actors apart from the general civilian population.

1.7.5 Chapter 6: Conclusion

The final chapter opens with one last encounter from South Sudan, highlighting the importance of the temporal element to everyday distinction practices. As is shown, struggles over distinction unfold at the most micro of levels: within a single individual. Having deferred normative questions, the discussion now confronts the conundrum of whether a special status for humanitarian actors is desirable.

[110] *Prosecutor v. Milan Martić*, Case No. IT-95-II-A, Appeal Judgment, ICTY, 8 October 2008 ('*Martić* Appeal Judgment'); *Prosecutor v. Dragomir Milošević*, Case No. IT-98-29/1-T, Trial Judgment, ICTY, 12 December 2007 ('*Milošević* Trial Judgment').

A debate is presented between two composite perspectives: the 'help the helpers' view (in favour of a special status for humanitarian actors) and the 'against humanitarian exceptionalism' view (wary of a special status). Ultimately siding with the latter outlook, I argue that caution is merited in the face of proposals to give humanitarian actors something more than civilian status. Emphasizing the relational nature of distinction, I query whether further fragmentation of IHL's civilian category might adversely impact all those civilians not singled out for special treatment. This is a live issue that extends beyond the realm of humanitarian actors: advocates are increasingly calling for more *lex specialis* for different types of civilians, such as children and journalists. After contemplating the implications of this wider investigation for a range of issues, such as humanitarian practice and the civilian concept, the discussion gestures towards potential avenues for further inquiry.

Conclusion

As this monograph pursues line-drawing practices across the three realms, the civilian–combatant distinction is broken up and other, unfamiliar distinctions are also introduced and broken up—such as that between 'civilian plus' and 'mere civilian'. We find that so many people are reaching for distinction, in so many different ways, even as a bright-line binary distinction eludes their grasp. To lay the foundation for the broader inquiry, the next chapter embarks on an exploration of what the idea of distinction is that is circulating in the practices of international actors.

2
What is the distinction?

Introduction

This monograph is concerned with the way in which the idea of distinction circulates across different global sites, specifically in the context of integrated or comprehensive missions that are governed by IHL. This chapter contemplates the comprehensive ethos that guides these types of international missions, setting the scene for the examination of distinction practices to follow. A question that lies at the heart of this discussion, that will be of interest to international lawyers, is the following: what is this idea of distinction and how does it relate to the IHL targeting rule? This chapter does not set out to answer this question definitively so much as to introduce possibilities that are explored throughout the rest of the inquiry.

The discussion begins in the Kinetic realm. After providing an overview of the recent history of conflict and intervention in South Sudan, the discussion exposes anxieties amongst humanitarian actors that lines are being blurred between themselves and the integrated UN peacekeeping mission in South Sudan, UNMISS. This sets up a tense relationship between international humanitarian actors and all components of the peacekeeping mission, as the former seek to distance themselves and dissociate from the latter.

Next, in the Pedagogical realm, military and peacekeeping trainees learn about the comprehensive ethos of 'working together', which chafes against lessons on the importance of distinction. After outlining the three civil–military training spaces, it is shown that military trainees struggle to locate a distinction in the conduct of hostilities sense. This murky perception of the civilian and combatant categories spills over into their articulation of how the distinction applies to humanitarian actors. When humanitarian actors enter the training space and convey the need for separation, trainees intuit that such boundaries will only impede mission success.

The third part follows the idea of distinction to the Intellectual realm, examining the principle's application to international actors who operate in and around comprehensive missions. The discussion considers the formulation of distinction in AP I, in civil–military guidance documents, and in the communications of international actors. It is noted that many of the actors from whom humanitarian actors strive to assert a distinction are, like humanitarian actors themselves, generally entitled to the protections IHL affords to civilians. Considerable slippage is also detected in public communications and soft law guidance between different distinctions—such as civilian–combatant, civilian–military, and

The Humanitarian Civilian. Rebecca Sutton, Oxford University Press (2021). © Rebecca Sutton.
DOI: 10.1093/oso/9780198863816.003.0002

civilian–humanitarian. The implication is that distinction does not break down in operational practice, so much as grounded practice carries on the pre-existing fuzziness that is embedded in guidance and discourse from above.

It was explained in the introductory chapter that this is not a compliance study, meaning that the overall intention in the monograph is not to assess whether international actors are following the IHL rule. The present chapter is exceptional in this respect, as it considers whether the distinction being enacted matches with the IHL targeting rule. The objective here is simply to establish that IHL's civilian–combatant distinction is in play in the daily practices of international actors, while foreshadowing the rich array of practices that take distinction far beyond this narrow meaning.

2.1 Distinction in integrated missions: the Kinetic realm

This section opens with an examination of conflict dynamics and international intervention in South Sudan, and then considers humanitarian entanglements with the integrated UN mission, UNMISS. As is shown, humanitarian actors believe that UNMISS peacekeepers are encroaching on the humanitarian sphere and endangering commitments to distinction.[1] Although international actors in South Sudan overtly engage with IHL rules only rarely, law is in play as individuals invoke the 'rule book' and self-conceptualize as civilians or combatants. South Sudan is thus a site where the everyday life of distinction unfolds.

2.1.1 Conflict and intervention in South Sudan

This part of the discussion gives a broad overview of the contemporary conflict context and then focuses on intervention—and specifically the UN integrated mission—in South Sudan.

Conflict history

The place that is now South Sudan has been shaped by multiple colonial interventions, and law has historically been twinned with violence to sustain the rule of governing elites. Sudan was administered by Ottoman–Egyptian colonial forces from the 1820s to the 1880s, after which 'the Mahdi', religious leader Muhammad bin Abdalla, asserted his influence.[2] By the late nineteenth century Sudan was under British control, and this continued up until 1955—with an Anglo-Egyptian

[1] Chapter 4 discusses how humanitarian actors themselves may blur the lines.

[2] Girma Kebedde, 'Sudan: The North-South Conflict in Historical Perspective', *Contributions in Black Studies*, Vol. 15, 1997, pp. 15–45 ('Sudan').

Condominium in place from 1899 to 1923.[3] As a result of these successive regimes, the legal systems in Sudan and South Sudan are not only rooted in local customary law but also have been inflected with Islamic Law, British common law, and Egyptian civil law—not to mention the frequent and prolonged use of emergency law regimes.[4] South Sudan is thus host to a complex, plural, and contested legal landscape; Ibreck aptly describes law in South Sudan as a 'morass of plural institutions, norms and practices'.[5]

In the mid twentieth century, the growing desire for Sudanese autonomy pushed the British to grant self-governance in 1953, and independence followed three years later. For the population of Southern Sudan, which was (and remains today) largely Christian and animist, this meant being governed by mostly Muslim rulers from the remote northern administrative capital of Khartoum. A Southern push for autonomy from the North was the impetus for the 1955–1972 civil war,[6] which pitted Southern military officials against Khartoum. At the end of this conflict, the secular leader Colonel Nimeiri guaranteed more autonomy to Southern Sudan. This promise faded by the 1980s, however, as oil deposits were discovered in the South in the late 1970s[7] and regional support grew for an Islamic state under Arab-Muslim control.

By 1985, a North–South conflict was raging as the newly formed Sudan People's Liberation Movement/Army (SPLM/A) in the South fought the Sudanese government in the North.[8] The civilian population bore the brunt of the conflict for two decades: civilians were directly targeted with violence, forcibly recruited to fight, starved, and deprived of their livelihoods. The violence became particularly brutal in Southern Sudan following a split in the SPLA between leader John Garang, and Lam Akol and Riek Machar, over eminence and competing visions of the South's future.[9] The official end to North–South fighting was marked by the signing of the Comprehensive Peace Agreement (CPA) in 2005.[10] Within the next decade, however, conflict erupted again in the South (see below in this section).

The CPA called for a future referendum on Southern Sudanese independence,[11] and 2011 ushered in a newly independent Republic of South Sudan after

[3] Rachel Ibreck, *South Sudan's Injustice System: Law and Activism on the Front Line* (London: Zed, 2019), 33 ('*Injustice System*').

[4] Ibid., 7, 38.

[5] Ibid, 7.

[6] On the role of identity in the conflict see Francis M. Deng, *War of Visions: Conflict of Identities in the Sudan* (Washington, DC: The Brookings Institution, 1995) (*War of Visions*).

[7] Kebedde, supra, 7 ('Sudan').

[8] The roots of this conflict are discussed in Deng, supra, (*War of Visions*); Francis Deng and Daniel Deng, *Bound by Conflict: Dilemmas of the Two Sudans* (New York: Fordham University Press, 2015).

[9] Ibreck, supra, 38 (*Injustice System*).

[10] For a chronological analysis of the peace process that led to the CPA see: Øystein H. Rolandsen, 'A Quick Fix? A Retrospective Analysis of the Sudan Comprehensive Peace Agreement', *African Political Economy*, Vo. 38, No. 130, 2011, pp. 551–564 ('CPA').

[11] *The Comprehensive Peace Agreement: Between the Government of the Republic of the Sudan and the Sudan People's Liberation Movement/Sudan People's Liberation Army*, signed at Naivasha, Kenya,

an overwhelming majority voted in favour.[12] The advent of independence brought with it various rule of law efforts, along with high hopes for renewal, strong leadership, economic progress, and meaningful development in the South. Advancement in all of these areas was soon thwarted, however, as violence broke out in the new country's capital, Juba, in December 2013. The legacy of the earlier SPLA fragmentation, mentioned above, was evident here: a struggle for political and military power between Riek Machar—who was now the Vice President of the SPLA—and incumbent President Salva Kiir ignited the initial violence.[13] Early fighting was mainly between different SPLA factions, and the conflict took on an ethnic dimension as the two leaders' respective supporters roughly cut along Nuer–Dinka ethnic lines.[14] Violence quickly swept Juba, and government security forces began to seek out and attack men of Nuer ethnicity—often inside their homes.[15] It was alleged that those targeted were not civilians at all, but were instead rebels.[16] Fighting soon spread to outside the capital, and within a few months attacks on civilians were routine and widespread across the country.[17]

That civilians would bear the brunt of the violence is not a new phenomenon in South Sudan. It fits both a wider regional pattern of treating civilians as legitimate targets in armed conflicts, especially where they are deemed loyal to the opposition,[18] and also historical patterns of sexual and gender-based violence.[19] More

26 May, 2005, Part A, I.3. Available at: https://peacemaker.un.org/sites/peacemaker.un.org/files/SD_060000_The%20Comprehensive%20Peace%20Agreement.pdf.

[12] In the final count, 98.87 per cent of those who voted were in favour of independence, with 97.58 per cent of registered voters casting a ballot. The Carter Center, 'Observing the 2011 Referendum on the Self-Determination of Southern Sudan: Final Report', 2012, 5. Eligibility requirements for voting are laid out in Article 25 of the *Southern Sudan Referendum Act*, 2009.

[13] Lauren Ploch Blanchard, *Conflict in South Sudan and the Challenges Ahead* (Washington, DC: Congressional Research Service, 2016).

[14] African Affairs, 'Making Sense of South Sudan, Virtual Issue', 2016. Available at: https://academic.oup.com/afraf/pages/south_sudan_virtual_issue.

[15] The Sentry, 'War Crimes Shouldn't Pay: Stopping the Looting and Destruction in South Sudan', September 2016. Available at: https://thesentry.org/reports/warcrimesshouldntpay/.

[16] Nicki Kindersley and Øystein H. Rolandsen, 'Who are the Civilians in the Wars of South Sudan?', *Security Dialogue*, Vol. 50, No. 5, 2019, pp. 383–397, 393 ('Who are the Civilians'); Øystein H. Rolandsen et al., 'A Year of South Sudan's Third Civil War', *International Area Studies Review*, Vol. 18, No. 1, 2015, pp. 87–104, 90 ('A Year').

[17] Nicki Kindersley and Øystein H. Rolandsen, 'Civil War on a Shoestring: Rebellion in South Sudan's Equatoria Region', *Civil Wars*, Vol. 19, No. 3, 2017, pp. 308–324 ('Shoestring').

[18] Michael Arensen, *If We Leave We Are Killed: Lessons Learned from South Sudan Protection of Civilians Sites* (Geneva: International Organization for Migration, 2016), 15 (*If We Leave*); Jana Krause, 'Stabilization and Local Conflicts: Communal and Civil War in South Sudan', *Ethnopolitics*, Vol. 18, No. 5, 2019, pp. 478–493, 487 ('Stabilization') (support for government or opposition forces turned entire communities in Jonglei state, South Sudan, into targets).

[19] On the root causes of sexual and gender-based violence in South Sudan see Alicia Luedke and Hannah Logan, 'That Thing of Human Rights: Discourse, Emergency Assistance, and Sexual Violence in South Sudan's Current Civil War', *Disasters*, Vol. 42, No. S1, 2017, pp. S99–S118 ('That Thing') (critiquing the narrow focus on sexual violence as a 'weapon of war'). See also Marjoke A. Oosterom, 'It May Approach as Quickly as Bushfire: Gendered Violence and Insecurity in South Sudan', *IDS Research Report*, 2014 ('Bushfire').

broadly, civilians have long been seen in South Sudan, and Sudan, as important conflict resources to capture and control.[20] Going back at least to the Anglo-Egyptian Condominium period, practices such as mass displacement, collective punishment, and population control have been the norm rather than the exception.[21] The treatment of the civilian population in South Sudan will be revisited in Chapter 3.

In terms of conflict status, it is generally agreed that South Sudan has been in a non-international armed conflict from December 2013.[22] As of early 2019 the death toll of the conflict had reached 400,000, with just under half of this number killed directly in fighting.[23] Up to 4.5 million people, that is approximately one in three citizens, have been displaced and forced to leave their homes.[24] The main parties to the conflict, and many of their allies and supporters, stand accused of committing atrocities and employing tactics in the conflict—including sexual and gender-based violence—that violate international human rights law and IHL.[25] While this study does not focus on issues of criminal justice and human rights, it will be shown that humanitarian actors distance themselves from civilian actors who advocate on accountability issues.

Peace agreements signed in 2015[26] and 2018[27] failed to endure, and a further agreement was signed later in 2018 to 'revitalize' and revise the earlier transitional agreement for South Sudan.[28] There was some hope that peace might take a

[20] Kindersley and Rolandsen, supra ('Who are the Civilians?').

[21] Ibid., 387.

[22] See, e.g., Geneva Academy, *Rule of Law in Armed Conflicts (RULAC)* project, 'Non-International Armed Conflict in South Sudan'. Available at: http://www.rulac.org/browse/conflicts/non-international-armed-conflict-in-south-sudan#collapse4accord.

[23] Francesco Checchi et al., *Estimates of Crisis-Attributable Mortality in South Sudan: December 2013–April 2018* (London: London School of Hygiene and Tropical Medicine, 2018).

[24] Ibid.; 'South Sudan: The Humanitarian Toll of a Decade of War', *The New Humanitarian,* 21 March 2019. Available at: https://www.thenewhumanitarian.org/in-depth/south-sudan-humanitarian-toll-half-decade-war.

[25] See the reports of the Commission on Human Rights in South Sudan, established by the UN Human Rights Council in March 2016. See e.g. *Report of the Commission on Human Rights in South Sudan*, A/HRC/40/69, 12 March 2019. See also Laila Matar, 'UN Human Rights Body Should Renew South Sudan Investigation', *Human Rights Watch*, 20 February 2019. Available at: https://www.hrw.org/news/2019/02/20/un-human-rights-body-should-renew-south-sudan-investigation.

[26] *Agreement on the Resolution of the Conflict in the Republic of South Sudan*, 17 August 2015. Available at: https://unmiss.unmissions.org/sites/default/files/final_proposed_compromise_agreement_for_south_sudan_conflict.pdf.

[27] *Agreement on Outstanding Issues on Governance and Security Arrangements*, 5 August 2018. Available at: https://www.peaceagreements.org/masterdocument/2111.

[28] *The Revitalized Agreement on the Resolution of the Conflict in South Sudan (R-ARCISS)*, 12 September 2018. Available at: https://www.peaceagreements.org/wview/2112/Revitalised%20Agreement%20on%20the%20Resolution%20of%20the%20Conflict%20in%20the%20Republic%20of%20South%20Sudan%20(R-ARCSS). Francesca Mold, 'Bitter Foes Reunite to Sign Revitalized Peace Agreement to End Civil War in South Sudan,' *UNMISS*, 13 September 2018. Available at: https://unmiss.unmissions.org/bitter-foes-reunite-sign-revitalized-peace-agreement-end-civil-war-south-sudan. A permanent ceasefire had been agreed earlier in the *Khartoum Declaration of Agreement Between Parties of the Conflict in South Sudan*, 27 June 2018. Available at: https://igad.int/attachments/article/1874/Khartoum%20Declaration.pdf.

sustainable hold at this point, and humanitarian conditions in the country had also begun to improve.[29] The empirical material from South Sudan that is discussed in this book focuses on the 2013–2015 period, when violence was still relatively acute and civilians rarely ventured outside of the Protection of Civilians (PoC) sites. The next section brings contemporary intervention actors into the conversation, outlining recent international efforts to address the conflict and its effects in South Sudan.

Intervention in South Sudan

This examination of contemporary intervention in South Sudan will consider the international humanitarian presence, the integrated UN mission, and integration policies as they apply in South Sudan and similar contexts.[30] The UN's Protection of Civilians (PoC) agenda, which is addressed in Chapter 3, can be understood as separate from the coherence or integration agendas—though they are not mutually exclusive and PoC mandates often give rise to similar issues.[31]

The North–South conflict that engulfed Sudan and Southern Sudan from the 1980s to 2005 galvanized one of the largest international humanitarian responses of that era, Operation Lifeline Sudan (OLS). OLS was ground-breaking in scope and scale: international humanitarian agencies secured the consent of the parties to hold 'humanitarian ceasefires' and open 'corridors of tranquility' so they could access affected populations.[32] The initiative also struggled with diversion of aid by fighting parties and perception problems regarding the neutrality of the intervention.[33] Further critiques were made of OLS, namely that it: actually prolonged the conflict; negatively influenced local attitudes to aid; tore at the social fabric of aid recipient communities; and empowered problematic non-state actors.[34]

[29] Samuel Okiror, 'Briefing: All You Need to Know about South Sudan's New Power Sharing Accord', *The New Humanitarian*, 14 August 2018. A 2019 report finds that the post-2018 agreement violence is mostly communal. See International Peace Institute, 'Prioritization and Sequencing of Security Council Mandates: The case of UNMISS' (International Peace Institute, The Stimson Center and Security Council Report, 2019).

[30] Regional interveners are not covered in detail here. On the role of oil actors, Uganda, and other regional players see International Crisis Group, 'South Sudan: A Civil War by Any Other Name', *Africa Report*, No. 217, 2014, pp. 18–26. Available at: https://www.crisisgroup.org/africa/horn-africa/south-sudan/south-sudan-civil-war-any-other-name.

[31] For a historical perspective on the overlap and cyclical recurrence of stabilization and integrated intervention modes, see Sultan Barakat, Sean Deely, and Steven Zyck, '"A Tradition of Forgetting": Stabilization and Humanitarian Action in Historical Perspective', *Disasters*, Vol. 34, No. S2, 2010, pp. 297–319 ('Forgetting').

[32] Larry Minear (ed.), *Humanitarianism Under Siege: A Critical Review of Operation Lifeline Sudan* (New Jersey: Red Sea Press, 1991).

[33] Holly Philpot, 'Operation Lifeline Sudan: Challenges During Conflict and Lessons Learned', *University of Denver Case-Specific Briefing Paper*, 2011. Available at: https://www.du.edu/korbel/crric/media/documents/hollyphilpot.pdf.

[34] Lydia Tanner and Leben Moro, 'Missed Out: The Role of Local Actors in the Humanitarian Response in the South Sudan Conflict', *Consortium Report for CAFOD UK, Christian Aid, Oxfam and Tearfund*, 2016 ('Missed Out'). https://www.alnap.org/help-library/missed-out-the-role-of-local-actors-in-the-humanitarian-response-in-the-south-sudan.

A large international humanitarian presence remained in the area after the signing of the CPA in 2005, mostly focused on recovery and post-conflict development.[35] These actors were not sufficiently resourced or prepared to scale up and refocus their interventions in the wake of the humanitarian emergency that accompanied the December 2013 violence. Local churches and national organizations stepped in and played a pivotal role as first responders, but many felt sidelined by the international presence.[36] As the experience of OLS shows, concerns about a lack of local ownership of, and control over, aid initiatives are perennial in South Sudan.[37]

With respect to the humanitarian presence following independence, more than 9.5 Billion USD was allocated for humanitarian aid in South Sudan from 2011 to 2018; much of this was funnelled through the South Sudan Humanitarian Response Plan.[38] As of 2018, OCHA reports that 192 humanitarian organizations are operating in South Sudan.[39] The main organizations delivering humanitarian assistance are national NGOs (95), International NGOs (79), UN agencies (7), government (4), and faith-based organizations (4).[40] Collectively, these organizations are trying to assist roughly half of South Sudan's population, that is 7 million people, who are deemed to be in need of aid.[41] As many as 5.3 million people in South Sudan are considered 'food insecure'.[42] Along with food security and livelihoods, the main humanitarian 'clusters'[43] operating in South Sudan are protection, nutrition, and education.[44]

Moving on, the international peacekeeping presence in South Sudan will now be considered. When the CPA was signed in 2005, the multi-dimensional integrated UN Mission in the Sudan (UNMIS) was installed with headquarters in Khartoum.[45] Following South Sudan's independence in 2011, this mission was officially replaced by the UN Mission in South Sudan (UNMISS).[46] Authorized under

[35] Ibid., 10.

[36] Ibid.

[37] Ibid.; Mark Bradbury, 'Normalising the Crisis in Africa', *Disasters*, Vol. 22, No. 4, 2002, pp. 328–338.

[38] UN OCHA, 'Republic of South Sudan 2018 (Humanitarian Response Plan),' *Financial Tracking Service*, 2018. Available at: https://fts.unocha.org/appeals/646/summary.

[39] UN OCHA, 'South Sudan: Operational Presence (3W: Who, What, Where),' June 2018. Available at: https://reliefweb.int/report/south-sudan/south-sudan-county-level-operational-presence-3w-who-what-where-june-2018 ('Operational Presence').

[40] Ibid.

[41] Erol Yayboke, 'Accessing South Sudan: Humanitarian Aid in a Time of Crisis', *Centre for Strategic and International Studies Brief*, May 2018. Available at: https://www.csis.org/analysis/accessing-south-sudan-humanitarian-aid-time-crisis.

[42] Ibid.

[43] Clusters are groups of humanitarian organizations that operate in the same sector. For an overview see UN OCHA, 'Clusters'. Available at: https://www.humanitarianresponse.info/en/coordination/clusters.

[44] UN OCHA, supra ('Operational Presence').

[45] As per UNSC, *Security Council Resolution* 1590 (2005), 24 March 2005, S/RES/1590 ('UNSC Resolution 1590').

[46] UNSC, *Security Council Resolution* 1996 (2011), 8 July 2011, S/RES/1996 ('UNSC Resolution 1996').

Chapter VII of the UN Charter, the mission's mandate was to 'consolidate peace and security and to help establish conditions for development' in South Sudan.[47] As stated in the Status of Forces Agreement (SoFA) signed by UNMISS and the Government of South Sudan (GoSS), UNMISS committed to following the international legal rules regarding the conduct of military personnel, including the 1949 GCs and the APs.[48] In response to the December 2013 violence, UN Security Council Resolution 2155 of May 2014 reinforced UNMISS and 'reprioritized' its robust PoC mandate, as well as its human rights monitoring activities, support for the delivery of humanitarian assistance, and oversight of the implementation of the Cessation of Hostilities (COH) agreement.[49]

Focusing now on UN integration policies, integration is often conceptualized as a specific variant of the comprehensive approach.[50] Integration policies envision particular postures and mindsets, and they are a site of contestation in which differently situated actors work out their preferred relationships. The landmark Brahimi Report in 2000 garnered a shift in the UN towards more robust peace support operations, greater emphasis on PoC mandates, and the introduction of Integrated Mission Task Forces.[51] Integration, as a general concept, gained momentum in subsequent years.[52] An explicit linkage of development and security was asserted by the mid 2000s,[53] along with the conceptualization of a relief–development continuum.[54] The integrated approach was to apply to all contexts where the UN had a country team and multidimensional peacekeeping operation or political mission. For UN actors, the integrated presence entailed: a shared vision of strategic objectives; closely aligned or integrated planning; a set of agreed results, timelines, and

[47] Ibid. Chapter VII entitles UN forces to engage in robust use of force, and to use 'all necessary means' to protect civilians and humanitarian actors, and for self-protection. See Kai Koddenbrock, *The Practice of Humanitarian Intervention: Aid Workers, Agencies, and Institutions in the Democratic Republic of the Congo* (London and New York: Routledge, 2016), 79 (Humanitarian Intervention).

[48] See Section Four of the *Status of Forces Agreement between the United Nations and the Government of the Republic of South Sudan Concerning the United Nations Mission in South Sudan*, 2011. South Sudan acceded to the 1949 Geneva Conventions and their Additional Protocols in 2013.

[49] UNSC, *Security Council Resolution* 2155 (2014), 27 May 2014, S/RES/2155 ('UNSC Resolution 2155').

[50] The comprehensive approach is explored further in Section 2.2. below. Note that many participants in civil–military training programmes deploy as part of an integrated mission, similar to the one in South Sudan.

[51] United Nations, *UN Report of the Panel on United Nations Peace Operations*, UN Report A/55/305–S/2000/809, 21 August 2000, 34–37 ('Brahimi Report').

[52] On UN Integration policies generally see Victoria Metcalfe et al., 'UN Integration and Humanitarian Space: An Independent Study Commissioned by the UN Integration Steering Group', *Stimson Center and Overseas Development Institute*, 2011 ('Stimson Report').

[53] United Nations, *UN High-Level Panel on Threats, Challenges, and Change. A More Secure World: Our Shared Responsibility*, UN Report A/59/565, 2 December 2004 ('Our Shared Responsibility').

[54] United Nations, *Delivering as One: UN Report of the Secretary General's High-Level Panel* (New York, NY: United Nations, 2006) (*Delivering as One*). Available at: https://www.undp.org/content/undp/en/home/librarypage/capacity-building/delivering-as-one-report-of-the-secretary-generals-high-level-panel.html

responsibility for delivering tasks relating to the consolidation of peace; and agreed mechanisms for monitoring and evaluation.[55]

The conversation about UN integration focused on structural issues up until 2008 or so,[56] at which time it shifted towards strategic planning and issues of implementation. A question that continues to trouble practitioners is where humanitarian actors—especially NGOs—should fit in in relation to the civilian and military components of these missions. Through integration and the coordination mechanisms that accompany it, the overall trend has been to draw humanitarian assistance into the fold of political and peacekeeping missions.[57] Humanitarian actors can be pulled into the orbit of an integrated mission where they participate in the humanitarian cluster system and rely upon the UN for logistical support. Equally, humanitarians must contend with the presence of armed actors in their operational space, as well as UN efforts to represent their interests in humanitarian access negotiations. Different agencies and types of humanitarian organizations might navigate these dynamics in dissimilar ways: UN humanitarian agencies, for example, sometimes colocate offices with the mission.[58]

Those who value greater proximity between the humanitarian sphere and UN missions emphasize the overall aim of attaining peace and the importance of coordination and unified action.[59] The integrated mission ethos thus echoes the 'working together' mantra of the comprehensive approach.[60] Opponents of the push towards integration counter that it blurs the lines between different spheres of activity, undermines the ability of humanitarian actors to access and earn beneficiary trust, increases threats to aid worker security, subordinates humanitarian action to political agendas, and dilutes humanitarian leadership.[61] Concerns about distinction are implicit in these latter accounts, and they are also sometimes voiced more overtly. In a 2015 survey, humanitarian actors report a perceived 'lack of

[55] Metcalfe et al., supra, 1 ('Stimson Report').

[56] For a discussion of the 'triple hat' approach to UN leadership and colocation under UN integration, see UN OCHA, 'Policy Instruction: OCHA's Structural Relationships within an Integrated UN Presence', 1 May 2009 ('Policy Instruction'). Available at: https://www.humanitarianresponse.info/sites/www.humanitarianresponse.info/files/documents/files/OCHA%E2%80%99s%20Structural%20Relationships%20Within%20An%20Integrated%20UN%20Presence.pdf.

[57] Claudie Barrat, *Status of NGOs in International Humanitarian Law* (Leiden: Brill Nijhoff, 2014), 345 (*Status of NGOs*).

[58] UN OCHA, supra ('Policy Instruction').

[59] Discussed in Daniel Philpott and Gerard Powers (eds.), *Strategies of Peace: Transforming Conflict in a Violent World* (Oxford: Oxford University Press, 2010), 280 (*Strategies*).

[60] See Section 2.2.

[61] Metcalfe et al., supra ('Stimson Report'); Lisa Schirch, 'Research Gaps on Civil–Military Policy Trends', *Humanitarian Practice Network*, May 2014. Available at: https://odihpn.org/magazine/research-gaps-on-civil-military-policy-trends/ ('Gaps'); Marit Glad, *A Partnership at Risk? The UN–NGO Relationship in Light of Integration* (Norwegian Refugee Council, 2011), 5 (*Partnership at Risk*); Steering Committee for Humanitarian Response, 'Some NGO Views on the Humanitarian Implications of Implementing the Brahimi Report', 2000; Antonio Donini, 'Between a Rock and a Hard Place: Integration or Independence of Humanitarian Action', *International Review of the Red Cross*, Vol. 92, No. 880, 2010, pp. 141–157, ('Integration'); Cecilia Hull, *Integrated Missions: A Liberia Case Study* (Division of Defence Analysis, Swedish Defence Research Agency, 2008 (*Liberia*).

distinction' between themselves and integrated peacekeeping operations (or special political missions) in six countries, including South Sudan.[62] An ambition of this study is to interrogate the idea of distinction circulating in such claims.

Humanitarian actors often claim that integration, as a general proposition, threatens to undermine the traditional humanitarian principles. A brief overview of these principles is in order.[63] First, *humanity* denotes that human suffering must be addressed wherever it is found.[64] This is sometimes also referred to as the 'humanitarian imperative'. In Pictet's original formulation of the principles, humanity is positioned as the core principle at the top of a hierarchy.[65] Today, the more common practice is to place the principles on equal footing. Second, the principle of *neutrality* requires that a humanitarian actor 'may not take sides in hostilities or engage at any time in controversies of a political, racial, religious or ideological nature'.[66] In Pictet's words: 'Like the swimmer, who advances in the water but who drowns if he swallows it, the ICRC must reckon with politics without becoming a part of it.'[67] Third, the principle of *impartiality* denotes a commitment to focusing on the needs of individuals and the urgency of their distress, rather than discriminating on the basis of nationality, race, religious belief, class, or political opinion.[68] It is the needs-based nature of humanitarian assistance that distinguishes it from other, politically oriented, activities. Finally, the principle of *independence* holds that it is not permissible for an outside power to influence or cause a humanitarian actor to deviate from his or her ideals.[69] Although the principle of independence

[62] The six countries listed are Afghanistan, South Sudan, Somalia, Democratic Republic of the Congo, Sudan, and the Central African Republic. See Inter-Agency Standing Committee (IASC), *Review of the Impact of UN Integration on Humanitarian Action*, 2015, 36–37 ('IASC Review'). Available at: https://interagencystandingcommittee.org/system/files/150908_un_integration_review_-_iasc_pha_tt_2015.pdf.

[63] For a more in-depth treatment see Jean Pictet, *The Fundamental Principles of the Red Cross, Commentary* (Geneva: Henry Dunant Institute, 1979) (*Principles*); Denise Plattner, 'ICRC Neutrality and Neutrality in Humanitarian Assistance', *International Review of the Red Cross*, No. 311, 1996; Francois Bugnion, *The International Committee of the Red Cross and the Protection of War Victims* (Geneva: Macmillan, 2003). Note that many humanitarian actors do not claim to be neutral in contemporary conflicts. See Hugo Slim, *Humanitarian Ethics: A Guide to the Morality of Aid in War and Disaster* (Oxford: Oxford University Press, 2015), 70 (*Humanitarian Ethics*).

[64] IASC, *Civil–Military Relationship in Complex Emergency: A Reference Paper*, 2004 ('IASC Reference Paper'). Available at: http://www.refworld.org/pdfid/4289ea8c4.pdf.

[65] Pictet, supra ('Principles') (listing the seven fundamental principles hierarchically as humanity, impartiality, neutrality, independence, voluntary service, unity, and universality).

[66] International Federation of the Red Cross (IFRC), 'The Seven Fundamental Principles: Neutrality'. Available at: http://www.ifrc.org/en/who-we-are/vision-and-mission/the-seven-fundamental-principles/neutrality/.

[67] Quoted in Slim, supra, 67 FN 7 (*Humanitarian Ethics*).

[68] See IFRC, 'The Seven Fundamental Principles: Impartiality'. Available at: http://www.ifrc.org/en/who-we-are/vision-and-mission/the-seven-fundamental-principles/impartiality/. See also: Article 70(1) of the Protocol Additional to the Geneva Conventions of 12 August 1949, and Relating to the Protection of Victims of International Armed Conflicts, 8 June 1977, 1125 UNTS 3, Can TS 1991 No 1 ('AP I'); Article 18(2) of the Protocol Additional to the Geneva Conventions of 12 August 1949, and Relating to the Protection of Victims of Non-International Armed Conflicts, 8 June 1977, 1125 UNTS 609, Can TS 1991 No 2 ('AP II').

[69] Pictet, supra, 61–62 (*Principles*).

emphasizes autonomy, the delivery of humanitarian assistance inevitably forces humanitarian actors to make contact with—or rely upon—warring parties, beneficiaries, donors, and others.[70]

On a final note, while humanitarian anxieties about peacekeeper encroachment are starkly present in the integration era, it should be acknowledged that tensions amongst these international actors are longstanding.[71] The next section delves into everyday humanitarian–UNMISS interactions, examining how concerns about distinction are articulated vis à vis the UN integrated mission.

2.1.2 Distinction in the Kinetic realm: humanitarian–UNMISS interactions

This empirical discussion introduces some of the tensions that arise as international humanitarian actors strive to safeguard distinction, while other international actors—and the structures within which they are all working—encourage interaction. In this context, UNMISS actors tend to view the calls humanitarian actors make for separation as an obstacle that needs to be surmounted.

'Everything is blurred'

Many struggles over distinction in South Sudan are traced back to the presence of an integrated UN mission. As one humanitarian NGO actor sums up: 'A huge problem right now is humanitarian distinction in the context of the UN integrated mission.' Other humanitarian actors say, of integration's impact: 'We've created a problem', and 'everything is blurred'. A consistent refrain amongst humanitarian NGO actors is that there needs to be a humanitarian 'carve out'—a clear separation between themselves and international actors who participate in integration structures and policies. International actors who belong to the integrated UN mission in South Sudan articulate varied responses to these calls for separation. One UNMISS peacekeeper appreciates that humanitarian actors need to draw the distinction line as they see fit. He accepts that they should take the lead, and simply offers: 'If they need help we're happy to support.' Other members of the UN forces, however, wish to exert an influence on how and where the line is drawn; they actively strive to close the distance that humanitarian actors introduce between them. A Military Liaison Officer (MLO) who works for UNMISS

[70] Slim, supra, 73 (*Humanitarian Ethics*).

[71] For an overview of humanitarian–peacekeeper relationships until the late 1990s see Larry Minear, 'Humanitarian Action and Peacekeeping Operations', *Background paper for UNITAR/IPS/NIRA Singapore Conference*, 1997. Available at: https://sites.tufts.edu/jha/archives/110. See also Kirsten Young, 'UNHCR and ICRC in the Former Yugoslavia: Bosnia-Herzegovina', *International Review of the Red Cross,* Vol. 83, No. 843, 2001, pp. 781–805 (humanitarian actors tried to dissociate from peacekeepers working for UNPROFOR, as they thought any affiliation would endanger them).

proposes that the trick is to not act too much like a soldier. 'You really have to adapt yourself and think of people's interests and speak to who they are. When I'm talking to humanitarians, maybe I'll say [here he switches to a much softer and high-pitched voice, adopting a mischievous look] "Is everything ok? Do you need help?" Like, sympathetic.' A UN peacekeeper goes further: 'In our training, we get the impression that the humanitarians will not talk to us because we are military, but there are ways to make it happen. For example, I will wear civilian clothes to go visit MSF in the north. I won't carry a gun to go to Pibor.'

Integration policy and the push to interact

While much of this monograph focuses on the interactions of individual actors, it is important to elucidate the structures and wider forces that shape daily struggles over distinction. In many instances, the behaviour of individual UNMISS actors that humanitarian actors impugn is a straightforward implementation of the mission's goals, values, and priorities—as opposed to a deviation from the same. From the point of view of humanitarian actors in South Sudan, serious sticking points in this respect include: the militarized aspects of the mission and the combatant-like features of UN peacekeepers; the political nature of the mission and its lack of neutrality in the conflict; and differing visions as to how the protection of civilian populations is secured. The integration ethos presents an overarching concern here, raising the spectre of blurring and merger.

Contemplating these structural issues from an IHL perspective, the combatant-like appearance of UN forces jumps out as potentially bearing upon targeting concerns. The other issues mentioned could potentially implicate the civilian–combatant distinction, but not necessarily. For example, the political nature of the mission does not, in and of itself, make the mission a party to the conflict and thus a legitimate target in IHL.[72] As a matter of practice, however, a lack of neutrality on the part of the mission may lead fighting parties to view UNMISS, and those who are associated with the mission, as part of the conflict. But politicization also clearly has implications that go beyond targeting concerns, such as the undermining of the traditional humanitarian principles.

There is also the issue of disappointed expectations on both sides, which transcends concerns of IHL. Humanitarian actors and UNMISS actors fault each other for concentrating resources within the PoC sites, for example. One humanitarian actor traces the tensions between international actors in South Sudan—which she describes as 'palpable'—to such unmet expectations. 'UNMISS wanted humanitarians to do certain things. Humanitarians thought UNMISS should do things as [part of] its PoC mandate.' In her view, it is imperative that UNMISS actors come to grips with the limitations of humanitarian NGOs—for example, in terms of

[72] The legal status of peacekeeping actors is examined in Section 3.3.1.

capacity. A UNMISS civilian actor counters that it is not capacity so much as a lack of will to deliver services outside the PoC sites: humanitarian actors want to stay inside the sites, where life is easier. Humanitarian actors are also seen as slow to accept that UNMISS actors must make decisions on the basis of mission priorities, including the safety of UN staff, reputation, and UN 'stay and deliver' policies.[73] One UNMISS civilian actor sees humanitarian actors as having wildly unrealistic expectations of the UN mission, treating it as 'a redeemer or Jesus Christ'.[74] In contrast to concerns that humanitarian actors look down on others—which surface repeatedly in South Sudan and at the civil–military trainings—the claim here is that humanitarian actors expect too much.

Focusing on humanitarian NGOs, one such actor in Juba asserts that 'NGOs need to find ways to maintain their independence from all parts of the mission' but concedes that simple necessity often drives engagement with UNMISS. Another humanitarian NGO actor proposes that UN integration policy is not necessarily problematic in and of itself, but its practical implementation discourages respect for distinction. Concerns about implementation extend upwards to the highest levels of public communication, demonstrating the natural overlap between the three realms addressed in this monograph—in this case the Kinetic and the Intellectual. UNMISS leadership has, at times, depicted a close association between the mission and humanitarian actors in South Sudan. When Hilde Johnson was the head of UNMISS in 2014, for example, she stated that UNMISS had successfully built an important partnership with humanitarian actors who had remained in South Sudan when the violence spiked.[75] This implied alignment undermined humanitarian actors' vision of distinction.[76] As an aside, this study's empirical findings belie the mission-level narrative of 'a' partnership or a singular relationship between UNMISS and humanitarian actors in South Sudan.

UNMISS actors' separation anxiety

Coming back to the opening vignette (see above), a UN peacekeeper says he is happy to help when humanitarian actors need support. He also observes that not all humanitarian actors enact distinction in the same way, suggesting that distinction practices vary by organization: 'Some want to keep it, others are more flexible.' This UNMISS actor's rather accommodating approach to humanitarian distinction practices does not extend across the mission. Many of his colleagues are quick

[73] See, more generally, Jan Egeland, Adele Harmer, and Abby Stoddard, *To Stay and Deliver: Good Practice for Humanitarians in Complex Security Environments* (Geneva and New York: OCHA, 2011) (*Stay and Deliver*).

[74] This interview took place at the SWEDINT training.

[75] International Peace Institute, 'UN Special Representative to the Secretary General Hilde Johnson: South Sudan Crisis Changed UNMISS Mindset', July 2014. Available at: https://www.ipinst.org/2014/07/srsg-johnson-south-sudan-crisis-changed-unmiss-mindset.

[76] Civil–military guidelines for South Sudan also call for the promotion of distinction in both public communication and conduct. See Section 2.3.2.

to question what this notion of being 'distinct' encompasses, and they are intent on pushing for as much cooperation and interaction with humanitarian actors as possible. This generates a power struggle over who draws the line, which is explored in Chapter 3.

One UNMISS peacekeeper states that he understands the need for separation between different kinds of actors. That being said, he still expects humanitarian actors to share information with UN forces. He would be satisfied if humanitarian actors were to 'give us info about bad guys doing A, B, C, D' and then say 'you guys go'. This would allow UN forces to do their job, while recognizing that humanitarian actors must prioritize access to people in need. He believes such information exchanges leave the civilian identity of humanitarian actors intact.

A UNMISS civilian actor is puzzled by the way that humanitarian actors treat UN forces in South Sudan,[77] alleging that they take the implementation of distinction too far. Humanitarian actors have requested, for example, that her uniformed UNMISS colleagues refrain from participating in local patrols in certain parts of South Sudan. She relays that UN peacekeepers are incredulous about such requests for physical separation: 'We can't be here because of a uniform?!' Particularly in the early days of the mission, she explains, 'because we were not used to working so closely with humanitarians, our uniformed colleagues were unhappy and could not understand why [humanitarians] would not want them, but then would call whenever they heard a shooting'.

There are two issues to highlight here. First, some UNMISS actors evidently feel that humanitarian actors are implementing distinction in a muddled, and even hostile manner. As will be shown in Chapter 4, the one thing that seems to frustrate international military and peacekeeping actors more than humanitarians strictly enforcing distinction is when humanitarian actors send mixed signals. The second issue is the way in which UNMISS actors depict themselves, in terms of which side they fall on in the civilian–combatant divide. It will be shown throughout this study that many UNMISS peacekeepers refer to themselves as military actors and translate this to combatant status, despite the fact that they will generally be protected as civilians under IHL. Confusion also reigns in the training spaces regarding the legal status of international military actors, and some peacekeeping trainees are taught to think of themselves as combatants.

Whatever their self-conceptualization, UNMISS peacekeepers are divided on whether it would undermine the civilian status of humanitarian actors to be seen with them. While some UN forces insist that such proximity will not make humanitarian actors a target, others are alive to this possibility or, at least, aware that it presents an anxiety for humanitarian actors. Those in the latter camp seek to downplay their own combatant-like characteristics when interacting with humanitarians.

[77] The interviews in this paragraph took place at the SWEDINT training ground.

This is the case with the UN peacekeeper in the opening vignette (see above) who wears civilian clothing and leaves his weapon behind when visiting MSF.

Further interpersonal dynamics merit attention, including professional jealousy and inklings that humanitarian actors deem themselves superior. Donini has critiqued the treatment of humanitarian actors as saviours, proposing that it potentially sets up false expectations of what humanitarian actors can deliver and encourages 'delusions of grandeur'.[78] However problematic a saviour mentality may be, Slim observes that the humanitarian attachment to an 'all-powerful, self-sufficient and heroic rescuer' has been difficult to shake.[79] Noting that UN military actors tend to rotate in and out of South Sudan fairly frequently, one UNMISS actor has the impression that humanitarian actors see the questions asked by UNMISS actors as 'very basic'. He is convinced that 'We bore them. It's more about humanitarians being busy and not having time [for] us'. A UNMISS peacekeeper confesses his envy of humanitarian actors: 'Sometimes I am a bit jealous of how much [humanitarian actors] know. They seem quite effective in what they do. For us, our mission, it is a huge beast. It has to be that way. Maybe they envy us for our access to resources.' The first UNMISS speaker further remarks: 'If there is no conflict we have nothing to offer, because we just do security.'

This last claim rubs up against the general sentiment that, in times of conflict, humanitarian actors must be especially careful to maintain separation from military actors. It is noteworthy that the very instances in which UNMISS peacekeepers expect that humanitarian actors would allow proximity—that is, when violence spikes—are the moments in which peacekeepers take on combatant-like features that drive humanitarian actors away. One UNMISS peacekeeping actor cannot fathom why inter-reliance does not lead to respect. 'They might not like us, but they fucking need us. We feel dismissed as arrogant.' Evidently, non-humanitarian actors take these everyday distinction practices personally.

Elsewhere in South Sudan, one UNMISS peacekeeping actor appears to be catching more flies with honey. The UN MLO who is cited in the opening vignette adapts his behaviour for humanitarian actors. He changes the pitch of his voice and works hard to endear himself to them. He understands this shapeshifting to be an integral part of his liaison role.[80] Notably, his efforts to 'make people feel special' are not reserved solely for humanitarian actors. He does the same thing when visiting other international civilian actors, such as UN Civil Affairs and UN Human Rights officers. When he approaches these civilians, he will say: 'I really need your

[78] Antonio Donini et al., *Humanitarian Agenda 2015: Final Report: The State of the Humanitarian Enterprise* (Boston: Feinstein International Famine Centre, 2008), 4 (*Agenda 2015*).

[79] Slim, supra, 73 (*Humanitarian Ethics*). But see Liisa H. Malkki, *The Need to Help: The Domestic Arts of International Humanitarianism* (Durham, NC: Duke University Press, 2015), 29 (*Need to Help*) (finding annoyance amongst humanitarian aid workers that heroism would be attributed to them).

[80] The MLO mainly serves as a conduit between the civilian and military components of the UN mission.

help on this patrol. I have this specific task for you, it's so valuable.' This is perhaps the smoothest example of the 'rush to the intimate',[81] which will be elaborated upon in Chapter 3.

The techniques employed by the UNMISS MLO attest to the importance of individual personalities in shaping relationships at the institutional level in South Sudan. A UNMISS civilian actor observes: 'Things are so personality based; what you get at HQ is not what you will see in implementation.' A humanitarian NGO actor confirms this. He contrasts his 'very poor' relationship with a particular UNMISS coordinator in one location with his generally 'good' relationship with UNMISS elsewhere, highlighting the trust he has for particular individuals in specific locations. Moreover, his feelings towards individual UNMISS actors have concrete implications for whether or not he lets them come close. He will bring along with him to places and share information with a UNMISS actor he gets along with and trusts. In contrast, a humanitarian NGO actor in the Bor PoC site explains: 'We don't tell the UN everything, and when we accompany people to a given place we will not say to the UN "Come with us".' The latter approach appears to be the norm in South Sudan. While it is not simply the case that everything can be neatly traced to feelings of affinity between individuals,[82] interpersonal relationships and trust clearly exert influence on dynamics at the institutional level.

Leaving the Kinetic realm behind, the next section follows the idea of distinction to training spaces, where trainees from integrated and comprehensive missions imbibe the 'working together' ethos.

2.2 Distinction in integrated missions: the Pedagogical realm

This section delves into the comprehensive approach as it is taught at civil–military training sites, highlighting the tension between upholding distinction and 'working together'. Training participants explicitly engage with IHL and the civilian–combatant distinction, affording an opportunity to assess how distinction circulates in the conduct of hostilities sense.[83] The empirical findings show that international military and peacekeeping actors struggle to locate a bright line but nonetheless set about forging the distinction in practice. They formulate the

[81] The phrase comes from Ann Laura Stoler and David Bond, 'Refractions Off Empire: Untimely Comparisons in Harsh Times', *Radical History Review*, Vol. 95, 2006, pp. 93–107 ('Refractions'). Discussed also in Derek Gregory, 'The Rush to the Intimate: Counterinsurgency and the Cultural Turn', *Radical Philosophy*, Vol. 150, 2008, pp. 8–23 ('Rush to the Intimate').

[82] While not discussed in this monograph, findings from this study about humanitarian actors' perspectives on UN Police show that humanitarian actors sometimes enforce distinction with other actors they feel great affinity for. This suggests that there is not necessarily a straightforward correlation, in practice, between distinction practices and feelings of affinity. See also Section 5.1.1.

[83] As these kinds of explicit discussions about the principle of distinction are less common in the Kinetic realm, this part of the chapter is structured differently.

civilian–combatant distinction in a fragmented way at the outset, and then incorporate humanitarian actors into this messy vision. Introducing a theme that will be developed throughout this study, these international actors are keen to foster proximity and to erase the lines that humanitarian actors draw.

2.2.1 Overview of the training spaces

Civil–military training spaces serve as sites where struggles over distinction naturally arise, whether they materialize face to face, virtually, or in the form of stories shared from the operational context. The three training programmes investigated in this study are designed to help military and peacekeeping actors navigate their relationships with civilians in general, and humanitarian actors in particular. While the civilian–combatant distinction circulates at the trainings, this is not to say that the goal of the programmes is to engender respect for the distinction between different actors. On the contrary, the CIMIC, CAMPO, and SWEDINT programmes transmit the message that it is appropriate—and indeed desirable—to merge different spheres of activity. Their cherished mantra is not 'safeguarding distinction', so much as 'working together'. Shaped by the comprehensive push and its attendant emphasis on demolishing boundaries,[84] these training programmes showcase the external forces that push back against humanitarian distinction practices. The comprehensive push is entangled with a number of more specific policies and practices that also potentially implicate distinction, which arise to varying degrees at each of the training spaces. Particularly important here are Protection of Civilians mandates, mentioned earlier; CIMIC approaches; counterinsurgency (COIN) doctrine; and stabilization efforts.[85] The three training programmes are now outlined in turn.

NATO CIMIC training

In terms of contemporary global trends, international governments are tying humanitarian assistance ever more closely to political and security goals while, at the same time, military forces are receiving mandates and funding to work closely with humanitarian actors.[86] More and more, military forces are interacting with the same local populations that humanitarian actors typically engage with to deliver

[84] Jonathan Goodhand, 'Contested Boundaries: NGOs and Civil–Military Relations in Afghanistan', *Central Asian Survey*, Vol. 32, No. 3, 2013, pp. 287–305, 297 ('Contested Boundaries').

[85] The controversial 'Human Terrain System', whereby civilian anthropologists and social scientists have been deployed to conflict zones to advise military missions, is not addressed in this monograph. See Montgomery McFate and Janice Laurence, *Social Science Goes to War: The Human Terrain System in Iraq and Afghanistan* (Oxford: Oxford University Press, 2015) (*Human Terrain*); Maximilian Forte, 'The Human Terrain System and Anthropology: A Review of Ongoing Public Debates', *American Anthropologist*, Vol. 113, No. 1, 2011, pp. 149–153 ('Human Terrain').

[86] Schirch, supra, ('Gaps').

assistance.[87] The NATO CIMIC training programme examined here responds to all of these trends and prepares actors to adapt to this state of affairs.

The one-week Functional Specialist CIMIC course is run by the NATO Multi-National Civil–Military Cooperation Group (MNCG) and takes place in Motta di Livenza, Italy. It has the stated goal of providing trainees with a basic understanding of NATO CIMIC policies, principles, and tasks.[88] The training is specifically geared towards 'functional specialists'—soldiers with a civilian area of expertise, such as medicine or psychology. Serving as 'CIMIC personnel' in NATO missions, these individuals bridge the gap between military institutions and civilian organizations. CIMIC, or civil–military cooperation, is the main rubric under which NATO soldiers engage with civilian actors. CIMIC is a specific variant of civil–military relations, one that presupposes cooperation between the relevant actors. This terminology, and that of 'civil–military dialogue',[89] is also employed by military actors to govern interactions with (civilian) humanitarian actors.

NATO's approach to civil–military relationships is organized around the achievement of military objectives. Military actors learn about, and work closely with, civilian actors in order to fulfil the military mission.[90] The civilian activities that CIMIC units engage in are considered part of a range of non-combat tools a commander may employ 'to dominate whatever landscape is being faced'.[91] A landscape might refer to the media, the civilian population, intelligence, or broader nation-building objectives.[92] When military actors deliver services to the local population as part of CIMIC, they do not do so to provide assistance to those in need, per se, but to ensure force protection and to win 'hearts and minds'.[93] The aim is to 'create civil–military conditions that will offer the Commander the greatest possible moral, material and tactical advantages'.[94]

CIMIC approaches overlap somewhat with COIN, which institutions such as NATO, and the US and UK militaries, have developed. COIN marshals civilian

[87] Ibid.

[88] NATO Multi-National CIMIC Group, *Functional Specialist Course.* Available at: https://www.cimicgroup.org/c_id/119.

[89] Simone Haysom and Ashley Jackson, '"You Don't Need to Love Us": Civil–Military Relations in Afghanistan, 2002–2013', *Stability*, Vol. 2, No. 2, 2013, pp. 1–16 ('Love Us').

[90] Michael Pugh, 'Civil-Military Relations in Peace Support Operations: Hegemony or Emancipation?', *Overseas Development Institute Seminar on Aid and Politics*, February 2001 ('ODI Seminar'). Available at: https://www.odi.org/sites/odi.org.uk/files/odi-assets/events-documents/3774.pdf. Citing Western European Union, WEU 1999—WEU (1999), *WEU Draft Concept on Civil–Military Cooperation (CIMIC)*, WEU Brussels, WEU—DMS 99246, 17 February 1999 ('WEU Draft Concept on CIMIC').

[91] Raj Rana, 'Contemporary Challenges in the Civil–Military Relationship: Complementarity or Incompatibility?', *International Review of the Red Cross*, Vol. 86, No. 855, 2004, pp. 565–591, 573–574 ('Challenges').

[92] Ibid., 574.

[93] Georg Frerks, 'Who Are They? Encountering International and Local Civilians in Civil–Military Interaction', in Gerard Lucius and Sebastiaan Rietjens (eds.), *Effective Civil–Military Interaction in Peace Operations: Theory and Practice* (New York: Springer, 2016), pp. 29–44, 31 ('Who Are They?').

[94] WEU Draft Concept on CIMIC, supra.

and military players to address the root causes of insurgencies, in the hope of appeasing, marginalizing, or defeating insurgents.[95] While COIN doctrine also espouses the aims of protecting and promoting the rights of local populations, it is explicitly a form of warfare that—like CIMIC activities—seeks to win 'hearts and minds' for strategic aims.[96] Humanitarian and development projects are often enlisted to this end.[97]

Civil–military relations at SWEDINT

The Swedish Armed Forces offer a two-week training programme on Civil–Military Relations (CMR) at the Swedish Armed Forces International Centre (SWEDINT), located on a military base an hour outside of Stockholm. The course prepares international civilian, military, and police actors to cooperate and coordinate with each other in international peace-support operations under the aegis of the UN, the EU, or NATO. The relations of interest in this training programme are those between soldiers or peacekeepers working for an international mission, on one hand, and the wide array of local and international civilian actors in the conflict context, on the other. The training also responds to the fact that international military forces play an increasingly prominent role in crisis-response and peace-support operations. In an effort to help trainees learn the requisite skills, the training makes use of innovative 'mixed reality'[98] simulation exercises which employ virtual reality technology.

The CMR training is not a course run by, or devoted to the practices of, the UN Office for the Coordination of Humanitarian Affairs (OCHA). However, many of the trainees are preparing to serve as peacekeepers in UN missions. The SWEDINT training thus provides some coverage of the OCHA approach to civil–military relations, which is very different from the NATO CIMIC approach outlined previously. OCHA is tasked with overseeing the relationships between various international (UN) actors, and it plays a particularly active role in settings with an integrated UN mission such as South Sudan.[99] OCHA is also the UN agency responsible for humanitarian coordination, and it guides what the UN terms 'humanitarian civil–military' relations. This terminology fuses the humanitarian sphere with

[95] See, generally, Austin Long, 'Counter Insurgency', in Alexandra Gheciu and William Wohlforth (eds.), *The Oxford Handbook of International Security* (Oxford: Oxford University Press, 2018) ('Counter Insurgency').

[96] For a critique of COIN that engages with the civilian–combatant distinction see Heidi Matthews, 'The Other Side of COIN: The Civilian-Combatant Distinction, Terrorism, and the Laws of War', SSRN, 2013. Available at: https://ssrn.com/abstract=2316758.

[97] Paul Fishtein and Andrew Wilder, 'Winning Hearts and Minds? Examining the Relationship between Aid and Security in Afghanistan', *Feinstein International Centre Report*, January 2012 ('Hearts and Minds').

[98] 'Mixed Reality' brings together virtual reality exercises with other forms of simulation, such as live role play.

[99] UN OCHA, 'Humanitarian Civil–Military Coordination (UN-CMCoord)'. Available at: https://www.unocha.org/themes/humanitarian-civil-military-coordination.

the traditional civil–military relations paradigm. In contrast to NATO's CIMIC approach, OCHA uses the framework of civil–military coordination, or CM-Coord. While CIMIC presupposes cooperation—which can include joint planning and shared assets—OCHA keeps the level of interaction open. Typically, OCHA aims for a more modest arrangement of coordination, or simple co-existence. Co-existence involves, at most, information sharing about the needs of the local population and the movements of humanitarian actors.[100] UN CM-Coord also emphasizes civilian leadership and does not orient civilian–military dialogue towards winning a military mission.

The goal of winning 'hearts and minds' also arises at the SWEDINT and CAMPO trainings, in connection with the stabilization mandates that UN peacekeeping missions are increasingly being given.[101] While there is no coherent global definition of stabilization, UN stabilization activities typically include supporting state authority, building the capacity of state forces, using (robust) force to protect civilians and members of the mission, and re-establishing rule of law.[102] At all three trainings, 'hearts and minds' initiatives are the subject of controversy.

Comprehensive approaches at Zif

The final training programme analysed here is the Comprehensive Approach in Multi-Dimensional Peace Operations (CAMPO). This week-long programme is run by the German Centre for International Peace Operations (Zif),[103] and it takes place at the Akademie Schmöckwitz outside of Berlin. It is facilitated by training staff from Zif and the Command and Staff College of the German Armed Forces in Hamburg, and it involves guest lectures by high-level actors such as UN diplomats. The stated aim of the CAMPO training programme is to prepare trainees to follow a comprehensive approach when deploying as members of multidimensional peacekeeping operations. Participants include a mixture of civilian and military actors, most of whom are engaged in EU or UN missions. Because of the dominant presence of UN peacekeeping actors at the CAMPO programme, trainees also engage quite heavily with the UN OCHA CM-Coord approach.

[100] Victoria Wheeler and Adele Harmer (eds.), 'Resetting the Rules of Engagement: Trends and Issues in Military–Humanitarian Relations', *Humanitarian Policy Group Report*, March 2006, 13 ('Rules of Engagement').

[101] Cedric de Coning, 'Is Stabilization the New Normal? Implications of Stabilization Mandates for the Use of Force in UN Peace Operations', in Peter Nadin (ed.), *The Use of Force in UN Peacekeeping* (Oxford and New York: Routledge, 2018), pp. 85–99 ('Stabilization').

[102] Alexander Gilder, 'The Effect of "Stabilization" in the Mandates and Practice of UN Peace Operations', *Netherlands International Law Review*, Vol. 66, No. 1, 2019, pp. 47–73, 51 ('Effect of Stabilization'). On the evolution of the concept see Roger MacGinty, 'Against Stabilization', *Stability*, Vol. 1, No. 1, pp. 20–30 ('Against Stabilization').

[103] In German: *Zentrum fur Internationale Friedenseinsatz* (Zif). English description of the course: Zif, 'Comprehensive Approach to Multi-Dimensional Peacekeeping Operations'. Available at: http://www.zif-berlin.org/en/training/zif-training-courses/specialization-courses/campo.html.

At all three of the training grounds, civilian and military trainers deliver the classroom sessions.[104] Both NATO and SWEDINT invite international humanitarian actors who are active practitioners to supplement the lessons delivered by non-humanitarian trainers.[105] This presents a fascinating opportunity to examine the way in which humanitarian actors explain concepts to trainees, as compared with routine humanitarian practice in the Kinetic realm. The boundaries between the different types of trainers are not always rigid. Some of the (non-humanitarian) civilian trainers have either previously worked as humanitarian actors or have engaged extensively with them. It is the invited humanitarian trainers who exert themselves most vigorously to impart a vision of distinction to the trainees. These humanitarians seek to deepen the military's appreciation for humanitarian principles and to enrich the military's understanding of the diversity of international civilian actors.[106] While some of the trainers are of a more academic bent, few have extensive formal legal training. This reflects the fact that these civil–military training programmes are designed to practically prepare international actors to engage in comprehensive missions.

Trainer and trainee attitudes towards the comprehensive approach and the idea of distinction will now be explored across the Pedagogical realm.

2.2.2 Distinction in the Pedagogical realm: the conduct of hostilities

The discussion begins at the CAMPO training, where military and peacekeeping trainees try to discern the boundaries of the civilian category in a role-play exercise. IHL's principle of distinction is explicitly engaged here, presenting an opportunity to investigate how various international actors understand this legal rule. When international actors reach for a bright-line civilian–combatant distinction—and they do reach for it, repeatedly—what they tend to find in its place is a confused, fuzzy, and fragmented idea. This complicated engagement with distinction, as it relates to the conduct of hostilities, serves as the shaky foundation upon which the status of international humanitarian actors is overlaid.

[104] I served as a trainer myself in some of the civil–military trainings, and this raises issues for reflexivity that I discuss in Rebecca Sutton, *The Humanitarian Actor as 'Civilian Plus': The Circulation of the Idea of Distinction in International Law* (Unpublished PhD Thesis, 2018).

[105] The organizational identities of these humanitarian actors have been withheld to preserve confidentiality.

[106] This is reminiscent of humanitarian actors who engage in joint doctrine development exercises with military actors. See Victoria Metcalfe and Michelle Berg, 'Country-Specific Civil–Military Coordination Guidelines', *Humanitarian Policy Group Working Paper*, August 2012 ('Civil–Military Guidelines').

'It's very rough to say "civilians"'

In the elaborate fictional land of the Batari people, an armed conflict is being fought between state armed forces and the Batari Liberation Army fighters. Members of the Batari civilian population are caught in between, and they are in urgent need of life-saving humanitarian services as well as protection from the ongoing violence. It is into this context that the CAMPO trainees are plunged, tasked with designing and implementing an international response to the unfolding crisis. Initially, the trainees are arranged into 'mixed' groups of international actors; each group contains a police officer, a peacekeeper, a human rights officer, and so on. The groups are tasked with identifying who is a civilian in the land of Batari. Remarks on the haziness of the civilian category fly around the room, as trainees struggle in earnest to come to a consensus. In an earlier training session, the CAMPO trainees have learned that 'It's very rough to say "civilians"', and that the civilian is 'not that easy to describe'. Now, they wonder: Is it only the members of the local Batari population who are truly civilians under international law? What about individuals belonging to the non-Batari population who also reside in the area? Might some of the Batari Liberation Army fighters who do not carry weapons be civilians? To cope with this complexity, one group establishes different compartments in the civilian category. They differentiate unarmed liberation fighters from members of the local population, labelling them as different kinds of civilians. The other groups mostly arrive at indeterminate answers to this question. At the outset of the next exercise, the CAMPO trainer instructs trainees to leave their 'mixed' groups behind and gather in what he jokingly refers to as their 'single ethnicities'. He tells them to sort themselves into four groups representing four possible categories of international actor: group 1: humanitarian and development; group 2: civilian; group 3: military; and group 4: police. The civilian group, the CAMPO trainer explains, includes international civilian actors who are 'political and diplomatic and everything'. Everything, evidently, except for humanitarian (or development) actors.[107] After group 1, comprised of humanitarian actors, concludes their presentation, the military trainer invites group 2, comprised of civilians, to the front of the room with the following prompt: 'OK, now it's the civilians, since we are already in that sector.'

This set of encounters will serve as a jumping-off point for exploring the conceptualization of distinction across the three training spaces.

A confusion of categories at CAMPO

In the scholarly literature on civil–military relations, civilian actors are generally treated as a bounded group, juxtaposed with military actors as their 'other'.

[107] Two further issues that are not examined here include the pairing of humanitarian actors with actors carrying out long-term development work, and the treatment of police actors as civilians or combatants.

This is not to say that there is a complete lack of nuance: some scholars and practitioners of civil–military relations nod to plurality within the civilian and military categories.[108] In the vignette from the CAMPO training programme, above, trainees grapple with IHL's civilian category in different ways. When the trainees are immersed in the fictional land of the Batari, they strain to fit every actor on the ground into the civilian–combatant binary. While most groups find themselves at a loss, one group forges ahead by delineating sub-categories of civilians. This does not contravene the formal lessons of the CAMPO training, but instead amplifies a trainer's earlier observation that the category of the civilian is something of an approximation.

As the focus shifts to international actors, the fuzziness around the civilian category is carried forward. A number of unstated assumptions about the international civilian are discernible in the second exercise. First, the move to establish group 1 (the humanitarian and development group) as a separate category from group 2 (the civilian group) notionally splits the humanitarian actor from the civilian. When the trainer jokingly invites trainees to leave their 'mixed' groups behind and return to their 'single ethnicities', this insinuates that humanitarian actors might even belong to a different ethnicity from other international civilians.[109] But then, when the humanitarian group finishes delivering their presentation, the trainer treats them as part of the civilian sector. This latter framing suggests that the humanitarian actor is not in a category of its own so much as it is a subset of the wider civilian category. This endorses the suggestion of another CAMPO trainer, who transmitted in an earlier session: 'Within the civilians, we have humanitarians.' This comment was made during a CAMPO lesson on the different 'categories' of international civilians that the CAMPO trainees needed to be familiar with. Waving a hand at the multitude of actors falling within the broader civilian category, the trainer advises vaguely that trainees 'have to understand and distinguish the different things'. There is a nod to diversity within the humanitarian category, as well, as the trainer states that there is no such thing as a monolithic humanitarian community.

The main point being stressed here is that CAMPO participants treat IHL's civilian–combatant distinction merely as a point of departure that is both unsatisfactory and malleable. A further observation—that will soon be investigated more thoroughly—is that many of these international actors reject the notion that humanitarian actors would be treated as special civilians. And yet, as a perceptual

[108] See, e.g.: Hugo Slim, 'The Stretcher and the Drum: Civil–Military Relations in Peace Support Operations', *International Peacekeeping*, Vol. 3, No. 2, 1996, pp. 123–140, 126, 128 ('Stretcher'); Pugh, supra, 2 ('ODI Seminar').

[109] Garbett finds that some civilian witnesses at the ICTY subdivide the civilian population into different ethnic groupings and other affiliations. Claire Garbett, *The Concept of the Civilian: Legal Recognition, Adjudication and the Trials of International Criminal Justice* (Oxford: Routledge, 2015), 130 (*The Concept of the Civilian*).

matter, their shaky interpretation of the civilian category makes room for this possibility. The trainees openly contemplate intra-civilian distinctions, and they often tacitly treat humanitarian actors differently from other civilians.

On a further note, in another CAMPO exercise international actors are divided not into civilians and combatants, but into state and non-state actors. A trainer suggests that various non-state actors can be differentiated according to a metric of 'niceness': 'On the nice side, we have NGOs. On the not-too-nice side, we have armed actors and privatization of violence.' While humanitarian NGOs are given a high 'niceness' ranking in this formulation, their positioning in a category with armed actors is also treated as unproblematic. Notably, no mention is made of the civilian–combatant distinction in connection with this framework.

In search of a bright line at SWEDINT

During a training session at SWEDINT, a military trainer asks trainees what they would do in situations of hybrid warfare where they cannot discern between civilians and combatants. A UN civilian trainee responds that, following the UN Department of Peacekeeping Operations (DPKO) policy for UN missions, 'when in doubt, assume someone is civilian'. When the same question arises with respect to international actors, a military trainee proposes dividing international actors into armed versus unarmed categories. He points out that this fits with the framework of civil–military relations and 'it's the best term we have'. He goes on to note the difficulty of drawing this line when civilian security actors are armed, or when politicians and donors take on the appearance of military actors. Still, he believes that the preferred approach is to situate all international civilians together in one unified category; he includes humanitarian actors in this category, as well.

Later, during a chat in the hallway outside the classroom, a civilian trainer at SWEDINT reflects on these exchanges. He proposes that, in theory, anyone should be able to look at international actors and say 'You're either a combatant or you're not'. However, he laments that there are blurred lines in practice, especially where military forces engage in humanitarian activities or humanitarian actors use military assets and start to resemble a military force. He describes a photograph he once took of a military officer wearing civilian clothes, recalling: 'It was a conflict area and he wanted to melt into the population. I know that is illegal, but you also have humanitarians dressing up in field gear . . . and you start asking, who is who?' He identifies a grey zone of relationships between international humanitarian actors and other civilian actors. He proposes that this is not a legal issue to be resolved by IHL, but a matter of 'what our respective organization means'.

Several SWEDINT trainees also weigh in on the civilian–combatant distinction. One military trainee pronounces: 'Not all civilians are civilians. There are different kinds.' Another military trainee vociferously opposes this splitting, and his comments reflect an important strand of pushback against a special status for humanitarian actors. He alleges that the humanitarian actors he encounters in conflict zones seek special treatment. In his words: 'They don't want to associate with the military ... but again they want an extra distinction.' He offers the example of the MSF hospital bombing in Kunduz, Afghanistan by US forces.[110] 'They want to say the hospital in Kunduz is MSF, to be seen as special. But all I know: they are civilians.' He ventures: 'Next thing you will have special groups, like "MSF civilian".' His colleague backs him up, stating resolutely that all non-military actors are just 'civvies'. For both of these SWEDINT trainees, there is no room for different kinds of civilians in a bright-line civilian–combatant binary framework.

Competing visions of distinction at NATO

At the NATO CIMIC training, trainees also learn about what NATO terms the 'civil dimension' of the operational context. They are taught that it encompasses a plethora of actors, including NGOs, governmental organizations, donors, international organizations, media, internally displaced persons (IDPs), refugees, civilian populations, and local authorities. With a faint echo of the CAMPO trainer's 'niceness' metric described earlier, one NATO military trainer sorts actors into good and bad—leaving room for a disorderly in-between. In conflict zones, he proposes, 'We have good guys and bad guys. Everything in the middle is a mess, including NGOs'. Contemplating who is civilian amongst international actors, one NATO trainer reaches for a bright-line binary that positions civilians who directly participate in hostilities (DPH) on the combatant side. He asserts: 'It is very simple. You're civilian if you are not carrying a weapon and you're not participating in hostilities.'[111] When I ask him in a subsequent interview how this perspective translates in comprehensive international missions, he ponders, 'Now that is interesting .... This is so hard, this is the nub edge of it. It's about perceptions'. It is noteworthy that international military and peacekeeping actors have the sense that onlookers observe and make judgements about international actors in the operational context. This suggests potential receptivity to the importance of local perceptions, a concern that animates humanitarian distinction practices.

At another point in the NATO training, international civilian actors are configured similarly to Russian nesting dolls. First there are international humanitarian actors, who are nestled within international civilian actors, who are nestled within the larger civilian landscape. In this conceptualization, humanitarian actors are depicted as a subcategory of civilian actors, much as in the conceptualization at CAMPO described previously. Intriguingly, one of the military trainers at NATO also refers to humanitarian actors as '*civilian* civilians'. Expanding on this, she says that when military actors use the word 'civilian' in the context of a UN peacekeeping mission, they typically use it as shorthand for UN police; they do not

[110] The Kunduz incident is discussed in Section 3.2.1.

[111] Civilians who directly participate in hostilities do not forfeit their civilian status in IHL, but they are treated differently from civilians who do not directly participate. See Section 5.2.1.

digest it as a reference to humanitarian actors. Another military trainer at NATO counters that the term 'civilian' is meant to capture all international civilian actors. Here, again, is potential pushback against the notion of a special civilian status for humanitarian actors. First, he emphasizes that, under international law, 'humanitarians are just civilians. There is no other kind of civilian'. Following this, he suggests that if humanitarian actors were to say otherwise, 'this must be something special the humanitarians have created for themselves, because that's not the law'.

As with the SWEDINT trainee mentioned earlier who scoffs at the notion of the 'MSF civilian', this NATO trainer depicts humanitarian actors as clamouring to claim a special status for themselves. The possibility that international law allocates such a status to humanitarian actors is precluded, as is the prospect that other (non-humanitarian) international actors might actively disseminate a carve-out for humanitarian actors. Meanwhile, some international military actors who participate in the civil–military training do exactly that. Several examples of this have been offered here, such as the reference at the CAMPO training to the separate ethnicity of humanitarian actors. In addition, the NATO military trainer who uses the phrase '*civilian* civilians' casually refers to 'our civilian and humanitarian colleagues' during a coffee break. When asked to expand on this remark, she attributes it to unconscious impulse. She simply thinks of them as two separate groups.

2.2.3 Distinction in the Pedagogical realm: humanitarian–military interactions

Now, the discussion brings humanitarian actors more fully into the room, showing how they assert distinction in the training spaces and reject the comprehensive mission embrace. This section offers the most direct comparison of the earlier discussion of distinction in the Kinetic realm.

'Are you not here? You *are* here!'

At the NATO CIMIC training, an experienced humanitarian trainer finds himself standing at the front of the classroom, facing a group of uniformed trainees whom he must convince about the importance of distinction. Broaching the issue of comprehensive missions, he breaks the bad news:

> It's beautiful, fantastic, but we are not part of it. We are not part of the end state; our job is not to have peace and security. This is your job, and [the job] of politicians and governments. Our job is to take care of victims of armed conflict. We're in the picture, but not contributing.

Plunging forward, he notes that when humanitarian actors make such pronouncements to their military counterparts in war zones, they are typically met with denial. Soldiers will say: 'Great to have you on board. Are you not here? You *are* here! So great to have you as part of the comprehensive approach.' He softens

> his tone now, perhaps recognizing the looming prospect of trainee alienation. He allows: 'They have the right to have this perception.' Concessions made, he returns firmly to his original course. Perceptions are invoked again, but this time it is those of an undefined omnipresent observer. 'But in the end the issue is this perceived neutrality: we are not going to plan, analyse, deploy together.' Intimating that the trainees sitting before him will get it right, he concludes 'As far as this is understood, life is beautiful and everything is happy'.

As discussed previously, attendees of civil–military training programmes are taught the importance of simultaneously 'working together' and 'upholding distinction'. The overall impression is one of humanitarian actors scrambling to draw and safeguard lines faster than other international actors can move or erase them. Chapter 3 will grapple with the way in which humanitarian actors take the lead in forging distinction, but for now the focus is on the challenges that comprehensive missions pose for distinction.

The inevitability of the comprehensive approach

A uniting theme of the three civil–military training programmes is the inevitability of the comprehensive approach. At the outset of the NATO CIMIC training, a military trainer asserts that resistance is an exercise in futility. 'We don't have a choice. We operate in the same environment ... we have to interact with each other. We have a dialogue, it must take place at all levels, so it's better for us to prepare for this and get ready for it.' At the CAMPO training site, a trainer likewise notes that, in any global contemporary intervention, international military and civilian actors find themselves together, and international humanitarian actors must simply 'swallow the pill' that peacekeeping, military, and police actors are all involved. Ultimately, the trainer explains, the comprehensive approach requires every participant to know the whole picture. A high-level UN guest speaker at the CAMPO training also encourages trainees not to let their individual roles take on undue importance. 'It's not really about being a police officer, a political affairs officer ... it's about being part of a political process.'

Once the vision for the wider mission is intact, a CAMPO trainer explains, room can be made for different perspectives, clear definitions of the scope of work for all parties, and the delineation of boundaries. The trainer imposes the following temporal sequence: work together first, enact distinction second. Another CAMPO trainer proposes that upholding the civilian–combatant distinction should not constrain attempts to collaborate with humanitarian actors. On the contrary, military actors should actively pursue joint planning and coordination. Cast in this light, any refusal on the part of humanitarian actors to interact with international military actors is both disagreeable and surmountable. These teachings do not consider the possibility that such contact might taint humanitarian actors by giving them the appearance of being entangled with military actors. With ominous implications for the distinction humanitarian actors forge, this trainer advises 'Don't think about boundaries, "this I cannot cross"'. A CAMPO peacekeeping trainee deduces from these training sessions that when international actors adopt competing mindsets it entrenches divisions and generates friction in the mission. The trainee surmises that international actors must find better ways to relate to humanitarian actors, for the simple reason that they need each other. Although humanitarian actors insist that they are not part of the comprehensive approach, another trainee adds that they still need to 'know its results'.

As Dorussen and de Vooght show in a 2018 Report, international humanitarian NGO actors grasp the inevitability of comprehensive approaches.[112] They are well aware that both 'black UN' (UN forces and their affiliates) and 'blue UN' (UN humanitarian and development actors) will be present in any conflict zone in which they operate; they know that they will need to find ways of navigating relationships with these persons.[113] This is not to imply, however, that humanitarians entertain the same visions as other international actors regarding the kinds of relationships that are desirable. The next section demonstrates that 'blue UN' actors like UN OCHA sometimes join NGOs in expressing concerns about the comprehensive push.[114]

Humanitarian actors' wariness of the comprehensive approach

When a humanitarian trainer leads a training session at NATO, she articulates the perspective of UN humanitarian actors regarding comprehensive approaches.[115] Echoing comments that a different humanitarian trainer made during his session (see opening vignette, above), she states: 'We say to NATO, do not include us under your umbrella because we are nearby and maybe working in the same environment or doing the same things. We are not part of this comprehensive approach.' She explains that humanitarian actors handle civil–military relations in a different way, guided not by CIMIC but instead by Civil–Military Coordination (CM-Coord). The latter approach, the trainer explains, is not about succeeding in a military mission. Instead, it aims to 'protect and promote the humanitarian principles, avoid competition, minimize inconsistency and, when appropriate, pursue common goals'.

One humanitarian trainer quizzes the NATO trainees on whether a military commander can sit with a humanitarian actor at a table in a conflict zone and give orders: 'You do a hospital here, change that convoy time.' When the NATO trainees tentatively answer this question in the negative, the trainer responds emphatically

112 Han Dorussen and Marian de Vooght, 'Putting Civilians First: NGO Perceptions and Expectations of UN Peacebuilding', *Folke Bernadotte Academy*, Brief 01, 2018 ('FBA Report').

113 Ibid., 3.

114 But see Section 5.1.2 for a discussion of NGO distinction practices that push UN humanitarian actors to the other side of the line.

115 This session is delivered via Skype, rather than in person.

that her organization 'will never sit at [a] table with military partners'. It becomes clear later in her training session that she does not intend this literally, because her organization does, in practice, engage with military actors discreetly behind the scenes. Her point is that the advent of comprehensive missions does not make organizations like hers a 'partner' of military actors in any sense of the word.

The SWEDINT training also includes a series of sessions facilitated by invited representatives of humanitarian organizations, all of whom extol the importance of distinction. Reflecting on these sessions, one SWEDINT military trainee shares that she was very surprised when humanitarian trainers came in on day one of training and said 'No contact': 'Why not?' On further reflection, she says that she could 'sort of understand' where the humanitarian actors were coming from. Her military colleague offers: 'I found it a bit provocative. It's like you have your goal, and we have our goal and we can't cooperate. But we *do* have the same goal, we're all here for the country to get better.' In this trainee's view, the humanitarian trainer who calls for separation between actors is 'making it too easy for himself to distinguish himself. It should be an integrated mission—see how flexible the military are'. When he deploys to conflict zones, he shares: 'We do CIMIC hugs in my team.'

A final observation from the trainings is that peacekeeping trainees at CAMPO and SWEDINT also struggle to locate themselves on the civilian–combatant divide. Unlike the military trainees at NATO, who will fall into IHL's combatant category when they intervene as soldiers, peacekeeping actors will often be categorized as civilians in IHL.[116] When this issue arises at the CAMPO training, the formal training sessions teach that (UN) peacekeepers should be categorized as combatants. As one trainer explains, peacekeeping actors are increasingly being given Chapter VII mandates under the UN Charter and Rules of Engagement. This renders them military contingents, and the peace operations they engage in are, in essence, combat operations—even if softer-sounding terms are employed. The implication is that the peacekeeping trainees are to think of themselves as combatants from whom humanitarian actors seek to distinguish themselves. Another CAMPO trainer adds that it is not only the robust mandate and the use of force that create tensions between humanitarian actors and peacekeeping actors, but also a (perceived) lack of impartiality on the part of peacekeepers.[117]

The application of the AP I rule to international actors will be examined in the next section, along with global guidelines and public communications on the relationships of international actors.

[116] Members of peacekeeping operations benefit from the protection afforded to civilians by IHL, with some exceptions. See Section 2.3.1.

[117] On impartiality in peacekeeping more generally, see Emily Paddon Rhoads, *Taking Sides in Peacekeeping: Impartiality and the Future of the United Nations* (Oxford: Oxford University Press, 2016).

2.3 Distinction in integrated missions: the Intellectual realm

This section considers the way in which the idea of distinction circulates with respect to international actors who engage in interventions governed by IHL. The discussion visits three sites of the Intellectual realm: the categorization of international actors in IHL doctrine; civil–military guidelines that delineate norms to guide international actors' interactions; and the high-level pronouncements of humanitarian actors regarding IHL's principle of distinction. Attention is drawn to intra-civilian distinctions, and to slippage between a civilian–combatant binary and other formulations.

2.3.1 The status of international actors in IHL

This section considers how the civilian–combatant distinction applies to international peacekeeping, military, and humanitarian actors respectively. The two key points distilled are that peacekeeping actors will often be entitled to civilian protection in IHL, and that IHL treats different humanitarian actors differently—an observation that underpins the argument about IHL's Red Cross fantasy.[118]

International peacekeeping actors

Focusing here on the case of UNMISS, international peacekeeping forces and civilian staff of peacekeeping missions will be considered in turn. Starting with UN peacekeeping forces—that is, the 'blue helmets' who populate peacekeeping battalions—these actors generally benefit from the protection afforded to civilians in IHL. This is with the exception of scenarios where the operation as a whole becomes a party to the conflict.[119] This danger is especially present with robust peace-enforcement missions, as opposed to traditional peacekeeping. Civilian immunity may also be forfeited if the individual member of the operation engages in DPH.[120] The military aspects of the mission,[121] along with the uniforms that peacekeepers

[118] Drawing on Mégret's description of IHL's treatment of warfare as a 'fantasy of sameness', wherein two opposing armies face each other on the battlefield, each in uniform and bearing arms. See Frédéric Mégret, 'From "Savages" to "Unlawful Combatants": A Postcolonial Look at International Humanitarian Law's "Other"', in Anne Orford (ed.), *International Law and its Others* (Cambridge: Cambridge University Press, 2006), pp. 265–317, 307 ('IHL's Other').

[119] A contemporary scenario that tests these limits is the mandate of the Force Intervention Brigade affiliated with MONUSCO in the Democratic Republic of the Congo. See UNSC, *Security Council Resolution* 2098 (2013), 28 March 2013, S/RES/2098 ('UNSC Resolution 2098'); Scott Sheeran and Stephanie Case, 'The Intervention Brigade: Legal Issues for the UN in the Democratic Republic of the Congo' (International Peace Institute, 2014) ('Intervention Brigade'). See also Katarina Grenfell, 'Perspective on the Applicability and Application of International Humanitarian Law: the UN Context', *International Review of the Red Cross*, Vol. 95, No. 891/2, 2013, pp. 645–652 ('UN Context').

[120] See International Group of Experts, *Leuven Manual on the International Law Applicable to Peace Operations* (Cambridge: Cambridge University Press, 2017), 97–99 (*Leuven Manual*).

[121] See above note 48 on UNMISS-GoSS SoFA; UNSC Resolution 2155, supra.

wear and the weapons some carry, do not in and of themselves amount to combatant status under IHL.

As for civilian peacekeeping staff, such as those engaging in political and human rights activities for UNMISS, these staff members will generally be categorized as civilians in IHL. Unlike their colleagues in UN forces battalions, these individuals will continue to benefit from the protection IHL affords civilians, even if the operation becomes a party to the conflict.[122] Civilian immunity is maintained, as long as an individual's conduct does not meet the threshold for DPH.[123]

We have already seen that the treatment of these two sets of peacekeeping actors in the operational context and training spaces diverges from IHL doctrine. First, peacekeepers routinely self-conceptualize as combatant-like or combatants outright, and humanitarians also think of them this way. The armed/unarmed marker evidently serves as a basis for distinction in practice, even though IHL provides that civilians might carry arms in certain circumstances. This muddling is not helped by civil–military guidance that swaps 'military' and 'combatant' terms, nor by the fact that some trainees will deploy to peace-enforcement missions—such as MONUSCO in the DRC—that have become parties to the conflict.[124] Second, it will be shown that humanitarian actors assert a distinction from UNMISS civilian staff as a way of affirming their own civilian identity. Humanitarian actors thus have the impression that UNMISS peacekeeping forces are *not civilians*, and that UNMISS civilian staff are *the wrong kind of civilians*. This claim will be expanded upon in later chapters.

International military actors

Those trainees from the civil–military training spaces who participate as peacekeeping forces in international missions will be afforded the same treatment in IHL as UNMISS peacekeepers. They are generally protected as civilians, but this can change in accordance with the nature of the mission and the conduct of individual members of the forces. Aside from these peacekeeping actors, many trainees participate as soldiers in military missions—such as the NATO-led International Security Assistance Force (ISAF) mission in Afghanistan. While medical and religious personnel of armed forces have a particular legal status,[125] most soldiers

[122] *Leuven Manual*, supra, 97–99.

[123] Ibid.

[124] Sheeran and Case, supra ('Intervention Brigade').

[125] On military medical personnel see: Article 24 and 25 of GC I; Article 36 and 37 of GC II; Article 15 and 16 of AP I; Rules 25–30 of the ICRC Customary Law Study. Rule 25 of the ICRC Study provides that 'Medical personnel exclusively assigned to medical duties must be respected and protected in all circumstances. They lose their protection if they commit, outside their humanitarian function, acts harmful to the enemy'. Jean-Marie Henckaerts and Louise Doswald-Beck, *Customary International Humanitarian Law* (Geneva: ICRC, 2005) ('ICRC Customary IHL Study'). Religious personnel are generally afforded the same treatment as medical personnel in IHL. Rule 27 of the ICRC Customary Law Study assigns similar protections to religious personnel. Discussed in Barrat, supra, 303 (*Status of NGOs*); Julia Brooks, 'Protecting Humanitarian Action: Key Challenges and Lessons From the Field', *A*

who participate in military missions will be categorized as combatants under IHL. These soldiers are given a mandate to use force, they are authorized to engage in offensive operations, and they are entitled to the various privileges that come with belligerency. Other members of these military missions addressed in this monograph, such as Civil Affairs officers who engage in civil–military interaction, will also generally be categorized as combatants in IHL.[126]

International humanitarian actors

Finally, international humanitarian actors are the group at the centre of this investigation. This brief discussion broadly outlines their treatment under AP I.

As noted in Chapter 1, there is no category of 'humanitarian actor', as such, in IHL. The GCs of 1949 do not contain any special provisions relating to personnel participating in relief actions,[127] and the draft version of AP I initially contained no separate provision for such personnel.[128] In their ultimate formulation, the APs introduce explicit protections for certain humanitarian actors—typically referring to them as 'relief personnel'. As a matter of customary IHL, civilian humanitarian relief personnel are protected from attack in accordance with the principle of distinction.[129] Article 71(2) of AP I requires parties to the conflict to 'respect and protect' humanitarian actors,[130] and Article 71(3) stipulates that relief personnel shall be assisted by each party to the conflict to the fullest extent practicable.[131] The movements and activities of relief personnel are only to be limited in cases of imperative military necessity.[132] Humanitarian actors are also entitled to humane treatment.[133] The protection IHL affords to humanitarian actors is premised on their ability to deliver assistance in a manner that is humanitarian, impartial, and without adverse distinction.[134] This emphasis on conduct and modalities of assistance helps to explain the slipperiness of the humanitarian actor category, a theme which re-emerges throughout this study.

Report for Harvard Humanitarian Initiative and ATHA, October 2016, 10 ('Protecting Humanitarian Action').

126 This is in contrast to their Civil Affairs counterparts in UN peacekeeping missions who, as noted, will generally be entitled to civilian protection in IHL.

127 Claude Pilloud, Yves Sandoz, Christophe Swinarski, et al. (eds.), *ICRC Commentary on Additional Protocols of 8 June 1977 to the Geneva Conventions of 12 August 1949* (Geneva: ICRC, 1987), 831 (*AP Commentary*).

128 Ibid.

129 Rule 31 of the ICRC Customary IHL Study. Henckaerts and Doswald-Beck, supra ('ICRC Customary IHL Study') ('Humanitarian relief personnel must be respected and protected').

130 Article 71(2) of AP I.

131 Article 71(3) of AP I.

132 Ibid.

133 Article 75 of AP I; Article 4 of AP II.

134 Dapo Akande and Emanuela-Chiara Gillard, *Oxford Guidance on the Law Relating to Humanitarian Relief Operations in Situations of Armed Conflict* (UN OCHA, 2016), 14 (*Oxford Guidance*).

IHL also prescribes limits to the conduct of humanitarian actors. Relief personnel must not exceed the terms of their mission,[135] for example, and they must adhere to the security requirements of the party in whose territory they carry out their duties.[136] If they violate these rules humanitarian actors may be denied permission to operate, but they will not automatically become legitimate targets in IHL. Likewise, carrying out humanitarian activities without state consent will not cause humanitarian actors to forfeit civilian status.[137] Like other civilians, however, humanitarian actors may lose civilian immunity where they directly participate in hostilities. Direct participation in a robust peace-enforcement mission could also compromise their civilian status,[138] though other types of UN affiliation could equally afford protective benefits (see below in this section).

The differential treatment of Red Cross, NGO, and UN humanitarian actors in IHL merits attention. It will be shown here that Red Cross actors are the humanitarian actors most clearly protected in IHL. While UN humanitarians also have recourse to some special protections in international law, the protected status of humanitarian NGOs is much less certain.

Focusing first on Red Cross actors, the ICRC, the International Federation of the Red Cross and Red Crescent Societies (IFRC) and national Red Cross societies[139] have a special position in IHL treaties.[140] They are also mentioned by name in AP I. In the Geneva conferences of 1863–1864, the Red Cross emblem was the only humanitarian symbol accorded legal protection. At the time, it was deemed universal and easy to recognize, with its key stated role being to protect medical personnel and medical facilities in armed conflict.[141] The GCs of 1949 also recognized the legitimacy of three further humanitarian emblems: the red crescent, the red lion and the red sun; a red crystal followed in 2003 in the Third Additional Protocol to the GCs.[142] Use of these emblems was restricted to members of the Red Cross family, as well as to medics and some military actors.[143]

[135] Article 71(4) of AP I.

[136] Ibid. For a discussion of the wider regulatory environment, see also Harvard Program on Humanitarian Policy and Conflict Research, 'Humanitarian Action under Scrutiny: Criminalizing Humanitarian Engagement', *Harvard Program on Humanitarian Policy and Conflict Research Working Paper*, February 2011 ('Humanitarian Action').

[137] Akande and Gillard, supra, 51 (*Oxford Guidance*).

[138] A. P. V. Rogers, *Law on the Battlefield* (Manchester: Manchester University Press, 2012), 319 (*Law on the Battlefield*).

[139] In this study, the term 'Red Cross' refers to these actors, collectively.

[140] Barrat, supra, 4 (*Status of NGOs*). For an account of the ICRC as an organization see Steven Ratner, 'Law Promotion Beyond Law Talk: The Red Cross, Persuasion, and the Laws of War', *European Journal of International Law*, Vol. 22, No. 2, 2011, pp. 459–506 ('Law Talk').

[141] International Federation of the Red Cross (IFRC), 'The Emblem Debate'. Available at: http://www.ifrc.org/en/who-we-are/the-movement/emblems/the-emblem-debate/.

[142] Protocol Additional to the Geneva Conventions of 12 August 1949, and Relating to the Adoption of an Additional Distinctive Emblem, 8 December 2005 ('AP III').

[143] Baptiste Rolle and Edith Lafontaine, 'The Emblem that Cried Wolf: ICRC Study on the Use of Emblems', *International Review of the Red Cross*, Vol. 91, No. 876, 2009, pp. 759–778 ('Emblem').

The second group, humanitarian NGOs, is the most precariously situated in terms of a legal status in IHL. Humanitarian NGOs do not (yet) have a crystallized international legal personality,[144] and their logos and emblems are not protected under IHL in the same manner as those of the Red Cross.[145] Aside from the category of Red Cross actors, Barrat catalogues 13 categories under which humanitarian actors could claim protection in international armed conflicts.[146] The NGO MSF, for example, might be categorized as: medical personnel; substitute protecting power; impartial humanitarian body; relief society; social organization; and organization assisting protected persons.[147] It is less clear how other humanitarian organizations will fare, such as those multi-mandate NGOs who engage in human rights, state-building, and peace-building activities.[148] Barrat's conclusion that humanitarian NGOs as a larger group are 'comprehensively covered' by IHL thus comes with serious caveats.[149] Some humanitarian NGOs may be afforded extra protection through relationships with other international actors; they might have an affiliation with the Red Cross,[150] for example, or serve as UN 'associated personnel' who subcontract or implement activities for the UN.[151] The latter scenario, which implies operating under UN control, may be untenable for independent (and neutral) humanitarian organizations.[152]

[144] Emily E. Kuijt, 'A Humanitarian Crisis: Reframing the Legal Framework on Humanitarian Assistance', in Andrew J. Zwitter et al. (eds.), *Humanitarian Action: Global, Regional and Domestic Legal Responses* (Cambridge: Cambridge University Press, 2014), pp. 54–80, 66–67 ('Humanitarian Crisis').

[145] Koenrad Van Brabant, 'Operational Security Management in Violent Environments', *Humanitarian Policy Network Good Practice Review*, June 2000, 336 ('Security Management'); Bruno Demeyere, 'Turning the Stranger into a Partner: The Role and Responsibilities of Civil Society in International Humanitarian Law Formulation and Application', *Harvard Program on Humanitarian Policy and Conflict Research Thematic Brief*, 2016, 11 ('Stranger').

[146] Barrat, supra, (*Status of NGOs*) 338, Table 1. The listed categories are as follows: voluntary aid society, civil defence organization, medical personnel, religious personnel, substitute protecting power, impartial humanitarian body, organization assisting POWs, relief society, international religious organization, organization approved by parties, social organization, organization engaged in family reunion, and organization assisting protected persons. The listed organizations in NIACs include: the ICRC, the IFRC, the national Red Cross Society, medical personnel, religious personnel, impartial humanitarian bodies, and relief societies.

[147] Ibid., 340, Table 2.

[148] Ibid., 344.

[149] Ibid., 343.

[150] Erin Weir, 'Conflict and Compromise: UN Integrated Missions and the Humanitarian Imperative', *Kofi Annan International Peacekeeping Training Centre Monograph*, 2006, 44 ('Conflict and Compromise').

[151] As provided in the UN Convention on the Safety of United Nations and Associated Personnel, 9 December 1994, 2051 UNTS 363 ('1994 Convention') and its Optional Protocol, adopted on 8 December 2005 ('Optional Protocol to the 1994 Convention'). The Optional Protocol expands the range of situations in which the 1994 Convention applies, but it retains the same concept of 'associated personnel'. Discussed in Kate Mackintosh, 'Beyond the Red Cross: The Protection of Independent Humanitarian Organizations and their Staff in International Humanitarian Law', *International Review of the Red Cross*, Vol. 89, No. 865, 2007, pp. 113–130, 114, 122–123 ('Beyond the Red Cross'); Erin Weir, supra, 44 ('Conflict and Compromise'); Christiane Bourloyannis-Vrailas, 'The Convention on the Safety of United Nations and Associated Personnel', *International and Comparative Law Quarterly*, Vol. 44, 1995, pp. 560–590, 564–566 ('The Convention').

[152] Mackintosh, supra ('Beyond the Red Cross'), 122–123 (noting a further limitation on the Convention's applicability, which is that it does not apply once UN forces are engaged in combat). For

As for UN humanitarian agencies, they are in a different legal position from humanitarian NGOs,[153] and also from Red Cross actors. Aside from whatever protections UN humanitarian actors might claim under IHL,[154] the blue laurel wreath of the UN and its logo are explicitly protected under international law.[155] Additionally, individual actors working for UN humanitarian agencies are covered by international legal instruments such as the 1994 Convention on the Safety of United Nations and Associated Personnel and its Optional Protocol, and the 1946 Convention on the Privileges and Immunities of the United Nations.[156] Although UN humanitarian actors are better protected in law than humanitarian NGOs, this study's empirical findings show that, in practice, the 'UN' designator fuels perceptions that UN humanitarians are not neutral actors. In other words, their fate is more likely to be tied to that of members of the UN political or peacekeeping mission.

2.3.2 Distinction in civil–military guidelines

A number of civil–military guidance documents invoke the principle of distinction, forming part of an authoritative 'rule book' that practitioners might draw upon to organize their relationships. Relevant global guidelines will be considered first, before turning to South Sudan-specific guidance. The main points to take away from the guidance perused here are as follows. First, the guidelines are informed by, and infused with, IHL rules. Second, the distinction being promulgated is only sometimes a civilian–combatant binary aligned with a bright-line vision of distinction. Third, even at this normative level, the emphasis on perceptions is marked: how things appear, and what onlookers witness, is given concerted

debates about the application of the 1994 Convention and its relationship to IHL, see Tristan Ferraro, 'The Applicability of International Humanitarian Law to Multinational Forces', *International Review of the Red Cross*, Vol. 95, No. 891/2, 2013, pp. 561–612 ('Applicability').

[153] This positioning can be attributed to the state-centric nature of international law and the fact that the wider status of the UN is that of an institution composed of member states. Discussed in Larissa Fast, *Aid in Danger: The Perils and Promise of Humanitarianism* (Philadelphia, PA: University of Pennsylvania Press, 2014), 204 (*Aid in Danger*).

[154] Laurie R. Blank, 'The Limits of Inviolability: The Parameters for Protection of United Nations Facilities During Armed Conflict', *International Law Studies*, Vol. 93, 2017, pp. 45–101, 62 ('Inviolability') (on IHL as the *lex specialis* governing protection in armed conflict).

[155] On the treatment of the UN flag and logo in the Rome Statute, see Article 8(2)(b)(vii) of UN General Assembly, Rome Statute of the International Criminal Court (last amended 2010), 17 July 1998 ('Rome Statute').

[156] '1994 Convention', supra; 'Optional Protocol to the 1994 Convention', supra; UN Convention on the Privileges and Immunities of the United Nations, 13 February 1946, 21 UST 1418, TIAS No. 6900, 1 UNTS 15 ('1946 Convention'). Discussed in Bourloyannis-Vrailas, supra ('The Convention'); Blank, supra, 50 ('Inviolability'); Ferraro, supra ('Applicability').

attention. The audience for distinction remains fuzzy, however, and this grounds a claim about the 'phantom local' that will be advanced in Chapter 3.

Global civil–military guidelines

The most widely cited guidelines in the civil–military training spaces are: the 'Oslo Guidelines' on the use of Foreign Military and Civil Defence Assets in Disaster Relief;[157] the 'MCDA Guidelines' on the use of Military and Civil Defence Assets to Support United Nations Humanitarian Activities in Complex Emergencies;[158] the Inter-Agency Standing Committee (IASC) Reference Paper on Civil–Military Relationship in Complex Emergencies;[159] and the IASC Non-Binding Guidelines on the Use of Military or Armed Escorts for Humanitarian Convoys.[160] These guidelines contain operational guidance drawn from IHL and other bodies of law, and the guidelines themselves are typically regarded as a form of non-binding or 'soft' law.[161] This monograph is primarily concerned with the attitudes of international actors to breaches of the rules, rather than the (lack of) formal penalties that flow from alleged breaches.

The global civil–military guidelines highlight the importance of distinction, often citing the need for separation between military and civilian (including humanitarian) spheres.[162] The guidelines stipulate that distinction is achieved by: avoiding the colocation of humanitarian and military actors; ensuring that military actors wear a uniform at all times; clearly identifying vehicles as civilian or military; and promoting distinction in public communication and conduct.[163] The guidelines: limit direct military engagement in humanitarian assistance to exceptional circumstances;[164] enumerate 'last resort' rules pertaining to the use of military assets by humanitarians; discuss the 'red lines'[165] of humanitarian actors; and outline forms of 'area security' by military actors.

[157] UN OCHA, *Guidelines on the Use of Foreign Military and Civil Defence Assets in Disaster Relief*, November 2007 ('Oslo Guidelines'). Available at: https://www.unocha.org/sites/unocha/files/OSLO%20Guidelines%20Rev%201.1%20-%20Nov%2007.pdf

[158] UN OCHA, *Guidelines on the use of Military and Civil Defence Assets to Support United Nations Humanitarian Activities in Complex Emergencies*, March 2003 ('MCDA Guidelines'). Available at: https://www.unocha.org/publication/guidelines-use-military-and-civil-defence-assets-support-united-nations-humanitarian.

[159] IASC Reference Paper, supra.

[160] IASC, *Non-Binding Guidelines on the Use of Armed Escorts for Humanitarian Convoys*, February 2013 ('IASC Guidelines'). Available at: http://www.refworld.org/pdfid/523189ab4.pdf.

[161] See e.g. Gabriella Venturini, 'International Disaster Response Law in Relation to Other Branches of International Law', in Andrea de Guttry, Marco Gestri and Gabriella Venturini (eds.), *International Disaster Response Law* (The Hague, Netherlands: Asser Press, 2012), pp. 45–64, 53 ('Disaster Response Law') (treating the IASC guidance as soft law).

[162] Voluntary Organizations in Cooperation in Emergencies (VOICE), 'VOICE Position on Civil–Military Relations in Humanitarian Action: Recommendations to the European Union', 2009 ('Civil–Military Relations').

[163] Metcalfe and Berg, supra, 1 ('Civil–Military Guidelines').

[164] Ibid., 2.

[165] This typically refers to an upper limit of violence against (or restrictions on) humanitarian personnel, facilities, or activities that humanitarian actors are not willing to tolerate.

While the guidelines engage concretely with distinction, they also emphasize the interdependency of diverse international actors operating in armed conflict.[166] It is assumed that different kinds of actors can take what they need from each other whilst also remaining safely ensconced in their respective spheres, but the findings from the Kinetic realm seriously strain this notion. There is also discernible slippage in these documents between different iterations of distinction, and a humanitarian–military distinction features prominently. While this study is primarily focused on the civilian side of the line—specifically, on the usage of the 'civilian' and 'humanitarian' terms—it merits mention that the terms 'military' and 'combatant' are also not interchangeable in IHL. Members of armed forces who serve as medical and religious personnel, for example, will not be legally categorized as combatants.[167] Recalling the discussion of IHL doctrine in the previous section, such muddling might mislead about the legal status of civilian members of international missions, as well as peacekeeping forces belonging to a UN mission that is not a party to the conflict.

While global civil–military guidelines have traditionally been developed for military interventions, context-specific guidance is increasingly generated for UN peacekeeping missions, as in the case of South Sudan.[168]

Civil–military guidelines for South Sudan

This part of the discussion considers two documents: the South Sudan guidelines for the humanitarian–UNMISS relationship, and the South Sudan humanitarian civil–military coordination guidance document. The idea of distinction circulates within these two documents, sometimes in the form of a civilian–combatant distinction but also as a civilian–military, humanitarian–military, and humanitarian–UNMISS distinction. There is a discernible carve-out for humanitarian actors from the wider civilian category, with no explanation of what the relationship between the civilian and the humanitarian is. The humanitarian–UNMISS distinction is also significant for the way in which it lumps UNMISS civilian staff together with UN peacekeeping forces, tying their fates when they might be entitled to different protections under IHL.[169]

The first document, the South Sudan guidelines for the humanitarian–UNMISS relationship,[170] outlines rules for the use of UNMISS assets and UNMISS armed escorts by humanitarian actors. Weapons, military equipment, or uniformed

[166] VOICE, supra ('Civil–Military Relations').

[167] Also, there is no combatant status, as such, in NIACs. See Rule 3 of Henckaerts and Doswald-Beck, supra ('ICRC Customary IHL Study').

[168] Metcalfe and Berg, supra, 1 ('Civil–Military Guidelines').

[169] See Section 3.3.1.

[170] South Sudan Civil–Military Advisory Group, *Guidelines for the Coordination between Humanitarian Actors and the United Nations Mission in South Sudan (UNMISS)*, endorsed 6 December 2013 ('Humanitarian–UNMISS Guidelines').

personnel are not to be transported on humanitarian assets, unless uniformed personnel are afforded 'IHL protected status'—for example, when conflict casualties are evacuated by air.[171] UNMISS civilian staff are permitted to travel on UN Humanitarian Air Service (UNHAS) flights with UNMISS approval, but the chartering of UNHAS-branded aircraft by UNMISS for the peacekeeping mission is prohibited.[172]

This guidance document also follows global guidelines on 'last resort' use of military assets, promoting a humanitarian–military distinction. Humanitarian actors are only to use military assets as a last resort in exceptional circumstances. Relevant 'last resort' criteria include: the mission maintains humanitarian and civilian character; there is urgent humanitarian need; there is no comparable humanitarian alternative; the use of the asset/escort is limited in time and scale; and it does not affect long-term operations of humanitarians.[173] In Chapter 4, humanitarian actors take an unsanctioned helicopter trip in South Sudan and international actors dispute whether the 'last resort' criteria were satisfied.[174]

The guidance mentions the threat of a 'blurring of lines between the humanitarian community and UNMISS', entreats humanitarian actors and UNMISS to 'ensure distinction of each other's activities', and calls for a 'clear distinction of the identities, functions and roles' of both sets of actors. Specific measures include: UNMISS actors should not carry arms in humanitarian premises; staff, relief supplies, premises, and transport etc. should 'promote distinction of respective identifies'; the purpose and mandate of each actor should be clear in public communications. The guidance also highlights the importance of optics, stipulating: 'Any perception that humanitarian organizations may have become affiliated with the military could impact negatively on the security of their staff and on humanitarian access.'[175] As required by the global UN DPKO Civil–Military Coordination policy,[176] UNMISS is supposed to create a secure environment to facilitate the delivery of humanitarian assistance, and only to deliver relief directly as a last resort. UNMISS is not to deliver assistance with the aim of winning 'hearts and minds'.

The second document is the South Sudan humanitarian civil–military coordination guidelines.[177] This guidance says the following of the civilian–military

[171] This is referred to as CASEVAC. See ibid.

[172] Ibid.

[173] Ibid.

[174] See Section 4.1.2.

[175] UN OCHA, 'Frequently Asked Questions: UN Humanitarian Civil–Military Coordination, Military Civil Defense Assets and the Use of Military Escorts in South Sudan' ('Humanitarian Civil–Military Guidelines').

[176] UN Department of Peacekeeping Operations, *Civil–Military Coordination Policy*, September 2002. Available at: http://www.refworld.org/pdfid/451ba7624.pdf.

[177] 'Humanitarian Civil–Military Guidelines', supra. See Chapter 4 for a discussion of how the humanitarian sphere is grafted onto the civil–military paradigm.

distinction: 'At all times, a clear distinction must be maintained between combatants and civilians, who are granted immunity from attack by IHL. Military personnel must refrain from presenting themselves as civilian/humanitarian workers, and vice versa.' While this framing tracks more closely with the civilian–combatant distinction than the humanitarian–UNMISS guidelines (see above), it singles out the humanitarian actor as an object and a subject of simulation. The guidance notes that the use of military assets is greatly constrained in a context like South Sudan, and provides that 'the importance of distinction becomes paramount as outlined in [IHL]'.[178] As the empirical findings from the Kinetic realm demonstrate, however, distinction does not always serve as a trump in the operational context.

The importance of perceptions is again flagged in this guidance document, as decision-making is to consider implications for the 'perception of humanitarian assistance, access and acceptance, as well as security of affected people . . .'.[179] Further to the issue of optics, the guidance calls for physical separation of humanitarian actors and UNMISS. Rather than rely directly on military assets, for example, humanitarian actors are to request that UNMISS provides 'area security'. This involves clearing and patrolling important road networks, for example, and brings less of a risk of humanitarian actors being visibly connected with UNMISS. While the guidelines acknowledge that direct use of military assets and armed escorts may help facilitate humanitarian work, humanitarian actors are urged to consider the negative impact on the 'neutral perception' of humanitarians. The guidelines caution that the long-term negative effects of such reliance might outweigh the immediate positive benefits.[180] It will be shown later that the temporal horizon is significant in practice: humanitarian actors who adopt short-term versus long-term thinking arrive at different conclusions about using UNMISS assets.

When humanitarian actors resort to the use of UNMISS assets without following the proper 'last resort' guidance for South Sudan, they contravene these civil–military guidelines. Apart from such breaches, however, humanitarian actors who enact intra-civilian distinctions are often *following* the rules. It is also significant that the concern for perceptions is not confined to on-the-ground practice. Rather, the presence of an undefined local observer permeates the guidelines as well as the high-level pronouncements of humanitarian actors. Turning now to the latter, it will be shown that the fuzzy treatment of distinction in civil–military guidance documents continues in humanitarian actors' communications.

[178] Here the guidance directs readers to the 'MCDA Guidelines', supra.

[179] This guidance document does not use the language 'no comparable humanitarian alternative' when discussing resort to military assets. Instead, it refers to a lack of appropriate civilian assets. See 'Humanitarian Civil–Military Guidelines', supra.

[180] 'Humanitarian Civil–Military Guidelines', supra.

2.3.3 High-level pronouncements about distinction in integrated missions

In their routine public communications, policy, and strategy documents, international humanitarian organizations—ranging from the ICRC to NGOs to UN humanitarian actors—appeal to distinction. Different variations of distinction circulate in these public communications, and a carve-out is often made for the humanitarian actor from the wider civilian category.

The ICRC is the humanitarian organization that most consistently cites IHL and explicitly ties the protection of humanitarian actors to IHL's principle of distinction. This makes sense, given the ICRC's positioning as the custodian of IHL.[181] An emblematic ICRC statement is the following: 'The fundamental principle of [IHL] according to which a distinction must always be made between combatants and non-combatants is the cornerstone of the protection afforded to the personnel of humanitarian organizations.'[182] The preamble to the Red Cross Code of Conduct also states that, in the event of armed conflict, the Code will be interpreted in accordance with IHL.[183]

Amongst UN actors, UN OCHA makes the clearest pronouncements on distinction. It also frequently swaps a civilian–combatant distinction for a humanitarian–military one. OCHA's CM-Coord Handbook refers to a humanitarian–military distinction, stipulating that: 'Humanitarian organizations are civilian organizations and unarmed. They rely on the protection provided by IHL and the acceptance of their humanitarian mandate by all parties.'[184] OCHA also cites the Geneva Conventions as the source of the principle of distinction 'between combatants and non-combatants', equating the latter with those no longer participating in hostilities. OCHA states that the civilian–military distinction used in CM-Coord is derived from IHL's principle of distinction, and notes that it 'specifically refers to the distinction between military and humanitarian actors'. Finally, CM-Coord guidance stipulates that the humanitarian–military distinction will be difficult to maintain if the two sets of actors engage in similar activities—even if they are not directly cooperating.[185]

As for humanitarian NGOs, the Humanitarian Charter associated with the *Sphere Handbook*[186] refers to IHL's principle of distinction in the conduct of

181 See Section 3.3.2.

182 ICRC, 'Respect for and Protection of the Personnel of Humanitarian Organizations', *ICRC Report*, September 1998.

183 ICRC, *Red Cross Code of Conduct for the International Red Cross and Red Crescent Movement and Non-Governmental Organizations (NGOs) in Disaster Relief* (ICRC, 1996), Preamble.

184 UN OCHA, *Civil-Military Coordination Handbook* (OCHA, 2015) ('OCHA CM-Coord Handbook').

185 Ibid.

186 Sphere, *The Sphere Project: Humanitarian Charter and Minimum Standards in Humanitarian Response*, 2011 edition (Rugby, UK: Practical Action Publishing, 2011) (*Sphere Handbook*).

hostilities sense, framing it as a civilian–combatant distinction. The same Charter also affirms the primacy of the humanitarian imperative, stating that humanitarian actors should abide by the overriding principle of alleviating human suffering.[187] The Charter is silent on whether or how this implicates the idea of distinction, but the present study uncovers serious tensions between these commitments in the Kinetic realm (see Chapter 4). Various humanitarian NGOs also draw on the principle of distinction in their public communications, often referring to a humanitarian–military divide.[188] No mention is made of whether the military actors in question would be categorized as civilians or combatants under IHL. Humanitarian and development think-tank organizations also promulgate—and muddle—the distinction. A report by the Overseas Development Institute, for example, discusses how integrated missions and 'hearts and minds' initiatives could challenge the humanitarian–military distinction in IHL.[189] This same report refers to the distinction between 'military, civilian, and humanitarian functions', as well as 'the distinction between humanitarian and politico-military responses'.[190]

In the statements canvassed above, humanitarian organizations routinely draw on IHL for authority when appealing to different iterations of distinction. It is intimated that different kinds of civilians might be found in IHL, opening up the possibility of a special civilian status for humanitarian actors.

Some concluding remarks will now be offered on the discoveries that have been made as the idea of distinction was tracked across the Kinetic, Pedagogical, and Intellectual realms.

Conclusion

A central goal of this monograph is to understand the everyday life of the humanitarian civilian, and to discern how this figure is formed within and against the cast of international actors who populate international interventions. To set the scene for this exploration, Chapter 2 introduced the structures, principles, and mindsets that inform the comprehensive or integrated mission ethos. The story being told here, from the perspective of humanitarian actors, is one of encroachment and blurring of lines by outside (non-humanitarian) actors. The distinction humanitarian actors are safeguarding is not always clear, however, and we will soon see that they, too, blur the lines in the operational context. For now, the main point is that humanitarian actors generally retreat from the comprehensive approach, and this generates tensions with international military and peacekeeping actors.

187 Ibid., 20.

188 CARE International, *Policy Framework for CARE International's Relations with Military Forces*, 2009. Available at: https://www.careemergencytoolkit.org/wp-content/uploads/2017/03/39_1.pdf.

189 Wheeler and Harmer (eds.), supra ('Rules of Engagement'), 2.

190 Ibid., 14, 46.

As the idea of distinction was followed from South Sudan to the three civil–military training spaces and on to the Intellectual realm, it was shown that international actors are shaping and reshaping distinction through their practices. Sometimes, the distinction in play directly implicates questions of targeting in the conduct of hostilities: actors struggle to assert a protected civilian status that will shield them, legally if not materially, from attack. In other instances, distinction is invoked in a manner that tracks less discernibly along with a civilian–combatant framework. International actors might move the line inside the civilian category, for example, or collapse the IHL rule together with other important values, needs, and interests—producing the distinction vernacular. As these differing conceptualizations of distinction are gathered under the rubric of everyday distinction practices, we begin to understand how the idea of distinction is circulating within IHL and also beyond it.

The next chapter builds on this attempt to parse out the way in which the idea of distinction circulates across global sites, illuminating the power struggles that arise when humanitarian actors enact their vision of distinction.

3

Who draws the line?

Introduction

International humanitarian law puts the main onus of upholding the civilian–combatant separation on the parties to the conflict: combatants are required to (visually) distinguish themselves, and a warring state must distinguish its armed forces from its civilian population.[1] While IHL imposes clear reciprocal duties on those engaged in fighting to uphold distinction, the responsibilities of civilians in this respect are only implied. It can be gleaned from the AP I definition that civilians will generally not wear a uniform, carry a weapon, or participate in hostilities. However, the notion that civilians might otherwise be obliged to take active steps to distinguish themselves—such as by maintaining physical distance or by modifying their conduct—is not something that IHL attends to.[2] The notion that civilians might assert distinction from other civilians, especially, is unfathomable in this paradigm.

In the civil–military guidelines outlined in Chapter 2, none of the sources canvassed impose the main burden of implementing distinction on humanitarian actors or other civilians. Certainly, there are expectations that humanitarians will minimize reliance upon, and association with, military actors, and that civilian actors will not behave in such a manner as to relinquish their civilian immunity. Aside from this, much distinction-related guidance places specific demands on military actors and those with combatant status. The latter are to wear uniforms, identify their vehicles, communicate their combatant status, and restrict direct

[1] Article 4(a)(4) of Geneva Convention Relative to the Treatment of Prisoners of War, 12 August 1949, 75 UNTS 135, Can TS 1965 No. 20 ('GC III'); Article 51(7) of AP I; Article 58(b) of AP I. Discussed in Michael Bothe et al. (eds.), *New Rules for Victims of Armed Conflicts: Commentary on the Two 1977 Protocols Additional to the Geneva Conventions of 1949*, 2nd edition (The Hague, Netherlands: Brill: 2013/1982), 281–283 (states must ensure their armed forces are easily distinguishable from members of enemy armed forces and civilians); William Ferrell, 'No Shirt, No Shoes, No Status: Uniforms, Distinction, and Special Operations in International Armed Conflict', *Military Law Review*, Vol. 78, 2003, pp. 94–140, 105–106 ('No Shirt') (to qualify for the privilege of combatant immunity, combatants must distinguish themselves from the civilian population).

[2] The closest body of scholarship is the political science and international relations literature on civilian self-protection. See, e.g. Erin Baines and Emily Paddon, '"This is How We Survived": Civilian Agency and Humanitarian Protection', *Security Dialogue*, Vol. 43, No. 3, 2012, pp. 231–247; Betcy Jose and Peace A. Medie, 'Understanding Why and How Civilians Resort to Self-Protection in Armed Conflict', *International Studies Review*, Vol. 17, No. 4, 2015, pp. 515–535; Frédéric Mégret, 'Beyond the "Salvation" Paradigm: Responsibility to Protect (Others) vs. the Power of Protecting Oneself', *Security Dialogue*, Vol. 40, No. 6, 2009, pp. 575–579.

The Humanitarian Civilian. Rebecca Sutton, Oxford University Press (2021). © Rebecca Sutton.
DOI: 10.1093/oso/9780198863816.003.0003

involvement in humanitarian assistance. Regardless of how this burden is distributed on paper, this study's empirical findings establish that humanitarian actors routinely take it upon themselves to assert and safeguard distinction. This chapter embarks on a granular exploration of the vision of distinction humanitarian actors promulgate, highlighting the power struggles that ensue with others in the operational space.

Taking a bottom-up approach once again, Section 3.1 illuminates humanitarian distinction practices in South Sudan. As is shown, humanitarian actors in the Kinetic realm try to distinguish themselves, and they perform their distinct status for an audience: the 'phantom local'. A conflict is also highlighted between humanitarian and UNMISS actors, over how civilians in South Sudan are best protected. Moving on to the training spaces, Section 3.2 demonstrates that once again humanitarian actors take the initiative to draw lines. IHL is more squarely in the picture here, and local perceptions are also deemed crucial. International military and peacekeeping actors contest the appeals humanitarian actors make to distinction, and the former are keen to erase the lines humanitarians draw. Section 3.3 engages with the figure of the international humanitarian actor, charting its historical evolution and scrutinizing the form in which it is enshrined in IHL. I argue that IHL projects a Red Cross fantasy, and that non-Red Cross actors keep this fantasy in circulation through their attempts to simulate the Red Cross. Humanitarian principles, signs, and symbols are also discussed, engaging with critiques of their functions and of the underlying motivations of humanitarian actors who rely upon them.

3.1 The Kinetic realm

This discussion illuminates the dance of distinction that humanitarians engage in with others, focusing on UNMISS actors in South Sudan. The figure of the 'phantom local' also enters the scene, serving as the ultimate audience for the performance of distinction.

3.1.1 Humanitarian actors draw the line

International humanitarian actors find themselves enmeshed with international peacekeeping actors in South Sudan. This is by virtue of sheer physical proximity, inter-reliance, policies and structures designed to foster contact, and the overt efforts peacekeepers make to close the distance. As they navigate entanglement with others in the operational space, international humanitarian actors can be found drawing lines and burnishing their civilian credentials. Focusing on humanitarian actors' perspectives for the moment, it is shown that some humanitarian actors join other, non-humanitarian actors, in questioning these distinction practices.

> **'We constantly negotiate, renegotiate, define, redefine our position'**
> For the head of one international humanitarian NGO in Juba, the effort to safeguard distinction whilst operating alongside an integrated mission is akin to a delicate dance—one, he suggests, that is underappreciated by other international actors. 'Fred Astaire, he got all the fame, but Ginger Rogers danced backwards, in high heels.' The challenge, as he sees it, is to hold the line in the midst of evolving circumstances. 'We constantly negotiate, renegotiate, define, redefine our position. Goalposts are constantly moving and changing, we are changing.' When it comes to implementing IHL's civilian–combatant distinction in South Sudan, one UN humanitarian actor proposes that humanitarian actors in the field play the most significant role. These individuals negotiate distinction on a daily basis, and the decisions they make are of more consequence than what international donors, staff based at HQ or the written rules say. This individual states: 'To be frank, I believe that those in the field are at the coalface and will work out appropriate arrangements regardless of overarching guidelines ... so long as humanity remains the guiding light.' A humanitarian NGO actor contemplates the relationship between the rules in the books and operations on the ground. He suggests that, even where staff can cite the relevant guidelines on military asset use chapter and verse, they tacitly understand that if they follow the proper process they will never accomplish their goals. A UN humanitarian actor corroborates this: 'What is written is good, the policy is really good. But when you're out, on the ground, if you follow every single word, you won't be able to do anything.' This individual suggests: 'In particular situations ... [you] want to react. You just have to bend the rules. I do what I believe is right, whether it's within or against the rules; I just follow my guts.'

The following section considers how humanitarian actors exert themselves to draw lines, with the subsequent section addressing competing views on the protection of civilians in South Sudan.

Humanitarian actors forge the distinction

The struggles over distinction that materialize between humanitarian actors and peacekeepers take the form of a dance, with humanitarian actors drawing lines that others bend, move, and erase. At times, humanitarian actors appear to relinquish agency, or at least they are very constrained; one has the sense that the dance is orchestrated by others and set to music not of humanitarian actors' choosing. A humanitarian actor in the opening vignette thus describes himself as holding the line, and casts himself in the Ginger Rogers role. This is a fraught and sometimes lonely task, as his own humanitarian colleagues might opt not to join him.

In interviews, one humanitarian NGO actor proposes that it is for the head of each humanitarian organization in Juba to translate the rules from HQ to the field. While there might be formal agreement at the HQ level regarding civil–military interactions, 'what it boils down to is practical application. It's really [for the Heads of Mission] to make sure global best practices get filtered down to staff.' Another NGO actor assesses that humanitarian actors based at HQ fall short in this respect. Residing far away from South Sudan, they 'commit a sin of not briefing staff before they go out'; they fail to train staff in IHL and often do not require staff to sign codes of conduct. It is further suggested that HQ staff might not appreciate the importance of safeguarding distinction. One humanitarian actor believes that some HQ staff endorse a short-term vision that aligns with brief project cycles. This leads them to lose sight of the need to maintain humanitarian space[3]—which he equates with enacting distinction—in the years to come. Donor contracts often perpetuate short-term thinking by restricting funding to short periods, though they could conceivably create incentives for upholding distinction—such as by forbidding the use of military assets.

These empirical findings are supported by other scholarly accounts. According to one global study, the implementation of civil–military guidelines by humanitarian actors is uneven and the guidelines are sometimes honoured in the breach.[4] As Metcalfe and Berg find, even those who actively participate in writing the guidelines might not explicitly draw on the rules in their advocacy, training, decision-making, or practice on the ground.[5] Goodhand observes, with respect to NGOs in Afghanistan, that rules dissemination on engagement with military actors is adversely impacted by issues such as staff turnover in the field and the tendency to send low-level staff to coordination meetings.[6] Assessing the implementation of security practices within humanitarian organizations, Beerli highlights fierce power struggles between headquarters staff and senior-level field managers—observing also that the very concepts of 'field' and 'headquarters' are contested.[7]

For some humanitarian actors interviewed for this study, gaps in rules dissemination at field level are not serious cause for concern. One individual in South Sudan asserts that those at the coalface figure out how to conduct themselves 'regardless of overarching guidelines' (see opening vignette, above). He views this as unproblematic, 'so long as humanity remains the guiding light.' Here we come

[3] On humanitarian space see Sarah Collinson and Samir Elhawary, *Humanitarian Space: A Review of Trends and Issues* (London: Overseas Development Institute, 2012) (*Humanitarian Space*). See also Section 1.3.

[4] Victoria Metcalfe and Michelle Berg, 'Country-Specific Civil–Military Coordination Guidelines,' *Humanitarian Policy Group Working Paper*, August 2012, 5–6 ('Civil–Military Guidelines').

[5] Ibid.

[6] Jonathan Goodhand, 'Contested Boundaries: NGOs and Civil–Military Relations in Afghanistan,' *Central Asian Survey*, Vol. 32, No. 3, 2013, pp. 287–305, 297 ('Contested Boundaries').

[7] Monique J. Beerli, 'Saving the Saviors: Security Practices and Professional Struggles in the Humanitarian Space,' *International Political Sociology*, Vol. 12, No. 1, 2018, pp. 70–87 ('Saving the Saviors').

upon a classic example of the important role that ambiguity plays in humanitarian distinction practices, specifically with respect to engagement with the traditional humanitarian principles.[8] This humanitarian actor asserts that humanitarian practice should rightfully be guided by the principle of humanity—that is, the imperative to assist population in need—leaving opaque the implications for distinction. As we will see in subsequent chapters, humanity and distinction routinely chafe against each other in the Kinetic realm.

However delicate and high-stakes the distinction dance is for some humanitarian actors, there are other such actors who view distinction as a constraint or an impediment. There is, unsurprisingly, no such thing as a homogeneous humanitarian vision of distinction. The notion that a humanitarian actor might simply 'follow his guts' in the field—as one individual asserts in the opening vignette—has ominous implications for the observance of international law in conflict zones. The same can be said of his colleagues' assertions that following the 'rule book' means not getting anything done. Some humanitarian actors who dismiss the 'rule book' in this way are perhaps poorly trained or inadequately briefed, but there is more to this story. Crucially, there are humanitarian actors who question distinction's importance and extol, in the same breath, other values that form part of the humanitarian code. These individuals might be reasonably well-acquainted with international legal rules, but simply reject the premise that distinction is a trump.

The dissonant visions of distinction that various humanitarian actors espouse will be elaborated upon throughout the remaining chapters. For now, it is important to note that there are differences horizontally across organizations, and also vertically as individual field workers respond to (different) instructions from their organizational HQs in varied ways.

Zooming out slightly, UNMISS actors are now brought into the picture. Challenges arise in connection with UNMISS's robust PoC mandate, as humanitarian and peacekeeping actors espouse differing approaches to protecting war-affected populations.

Differing visions of protection

Since the 2005 signing of the CPA, the protection of civilians has formed an explicit part of UN missions in Sudan[9] and South Sudan. As noted in Chapter 2, UNMISS has a robust PoC mandate and it is authorized to use force to protect the civilian population. When civil war initially broke out in 2013, tens, and eventually hundreds, of thousands of IDPs sought refuge at UNMISS bases. They did so, in part, because they believed that the mission was essentially a military or governmental authority that could control UN land.[10] At several sites, UNMISS staff opened the

[8] The traditional humanitarian principles are discussed in Sections 2.1.1 and 3.3.3.

[9] For example, the joint AU–UN mission in Darfur, UNAMID.

[10] Nicki Kindersley and Øystein H. Rolandsen, 'Who Are the Civilians in the Wars of South Sudan?', *Security Dialogue*, Vol. 50, No. 5, 2019, pp. 383–397, 393 ('Who Are the Civilians?').

gates and allowed in those seeking physical protection from the armed violence.[11] These settings came to be referred to as 'Protection of Civilians', or PoC, sites. By not referring to them as IDP camps, international actors hoped to emphasize their temporary status.[12]

Understood in historical perspective, South Sudan's PoC sites are only the most recent iteration of encampment and of attempts to manage populations in the region's conflicts.[13] The PoC sites are somewhat unusual in the sense that armed UN forces are tasked with guarding their perimeter—and are also protecting populations, in part, from the state.[14] The problems enumerated here are not unique to South Sudan, however; they have arisen globally in the context of many other displacement settings.[15] Scholars have questioned the very idea that anyone can guarantee the safety of a space and the protection of the people inside it.[16] This point is especially apposite when one recognizes that targeting civilians is often an explicit fighting strategy rather than a side-effect of conflict,[17] that civilians often support those engaged in fighting or participate in the conflict in other ways,[18] and that globally displacement settings routinely serve as sites for fighters to recoup, recruit, and train.[19]

Discerning who merits protection inside South Sudan's PoC sites and delivering this protection is no easy feat. As Kindersley and Rolandsen find in South Sudan (and Sudan), 'People use their own distinctions between fighters and non-combatants, and there are many home-grown norms guiding conduct towards these groups and perceptions of legitimate targets for military action'.[20] As the

[11] Caelin Briggs, *Protection of Civilians Sites: Lessons from South Sudan for Future Operations* (Norwegian Refugee Council, 2017), 12 (*PoC Sites*).

[12] Michael Arensen, *If We Leave We Are Killed: Lessons Learned from South Sudan Protection of Civilians Sites* (International Organization for Migration, 2016), 12 (*If We Leave*); Damian Lilly, 'Protection of Civilians Sites: A New Type of Displacement Settlement?', *Humanitarian Exchange Magazine*, No. 62, September 2014 ('PoC Sites'). Available at: http://odihpn.org/magazine/protection-of-civilians-sites-a-new-type-of-displacement-settlement/.

[13] Kindersley and Rolandsen, supra, 386, 392 ('Who Are the Civilians?'). The authors address the historical use of 'peace villages' in Sudan, including recent Sudanese government-controlled sites in Blue Nile and South Kordofan.

[14] Ibid., 385.

[15] Sarah Kenyon Lischer, *Dangerous Sanctuaries: Refugee Camps, Civil War, and the Dilemmas of Humanitarian Aid* (Ithaca, NY and London: Cornell University Press, 2005) (*Dangerous Sanctuaries*).

[16] Jennifer Hyndman, 'Preventive, Palliative, or Punitive? Safe spaces in Bosnia-Herzegovina, Somalia, and Sri Lanka', *Journal of Refugee Studies*, Vol. 16, No. 2, 2003, pp. 167–185 ('Safe Spaces'); Phil Orchard, 'Revisiting Humanitarian Safe Areas for Civilian Protection', *Global Governance*, Vol. 20, No. 1, 2014, pp. 55–75 ('Safe Areas').

[17] Andrew Barros and Martin Thomas, 'Introduction', in Andrew Barros and Martin Thomas (eds.), *The Civilianization of War: The Changing Civil–military Divide 1914-2014* (Cambridge: Cambridge University Press, 2018), pp. 1–21 ('Introduction'); Benjamin A. Valentino, 'Why We Kill: The Political Science of Political Violence Against Civilians', *Annual Review of Political Science*, Vol. 17, No. 1, 2014, pp. 89–103 ('Why We Kill'); Hugo Slim, *Killing Civilians: Method, Madness, and Morality in War* (Oxford: Oxford University Press, 2010) (*Killing Civilians*).

[18] See discussion on targeting in South Sudan, Section 2.1.1.

[19] See generally David Keen, *The Benefits of Famine: A Political Economy of Famine and Relief in Southwestern Sudan, 1983–1989* (Princeton, NJ: Princeton University Press, 1994) (*Famine*).

[20] Kindersley and Rolandsen, supra, 386 ('Who Are the Civilians?').

authors also observe, South Sudan's PoC sites—along with all those who provide services in them—are viewed by local actors as appealing assets to commandeer and control.[21] While the international community treats the IDPs residing in South Sudan's PoC sites as civilians, the Government of South Sudan and various non-state armed actors routinely question the civilian status of these IDPs. The government has accused UNMISS of protecting rebels inside the sites, especially as most of the sites' residents come from opposition-held areas.[22] There are credible allegations of (ex-) combatants passing through the UN-guarded gates,[23] and of weapons being smuggled inside in charcoal and firewood.[24] One respondent for the present study points out that UNMISS lacks the capacity to search a place like the Bentiu PoC site, which had 130,000 IDPs living inside it at the time of field research.

The performance of humanitarian actors' own civilian identity takes on great importance in this setting. With these murky civilian–combatant dynamics as the baseline in and around the PoC sites, international humanitarian actors are anxious that local armed actors will think there are no real civilians. Matters are not helped by the fact that humanitarian actors and UN forces often engage with the same local populations, albeit to different ends. As one humanitarian NGO actor explains: 'Protection for us relates to the community; for the UN, it is all about force.' She believes it is the responsibility of her organization to implement distinction and hold the line, because otherwise UN forces will not observe it. 'We do not allow them to enter our work areas ... they cannot come in here with their weapons. The [UNMISS] patrol can drive up to the gates or pass by, but no weapons can enter. They know this'. Another humanitarian actor contributes:

> For us humanitarians, protection is all activities that involve individuals receiving assistance with safety and dignity and their rights are respected, as with child protection. But for [UNMISS], they only look at the 'safety' aspect of the people, but not the 'dignity'. So I, as an IDP, am safe—but I'm not dignified.

A humanitarian actor explains how conceptualizations of 'access' also differ:

> We as humanitarians need access free from the military, in order to get to civilians. But for UNMISS they need access for their military patrols. So we need to clarify that 'access' doesn't mean the same thing for us .... If UNMISS has good talks with SPLA or government, they are pleased. They think they are acting on our behalf to get access. But we say 'No, please don't'.

21 Ibid., 393.

22 Ibid. See also: 'South Sudan Army Claims UN Peacekeepers Harbouring Rebels in Juba', *Sudan Tribune*, 19 September 2016. Available at: http://www.sudantribune.com/spip.php?article60283.

23 Briggs, supra, 64–66 (*PoC Sites*) (emphasizing the need to maintain the civilian character of the PoC sites).

24 Arensen, supra, 58 (*If We Leave*) (referring to the Bentiu PoC site in Unity State).

While this perspective on access captures the mainstream view amongst humanitarian actors in South Sudan, some of these actors propose that a certain amount of inter-reliance with UNMISS is inevitable. A humanitarian actor in Unity State explains: 'For the UN to protect the people here, they need humanitarian agencies to come and provide the assistance and all the services. For humanitarians to be more secure and safe, they need UNMISS to provide protection.' This individual does not call for the direct use of UNMISS assets, but instead advocates for a form of area security that the civil–military guidelines in South Sudan permit.[25] This could involve mine-clearing, securing assurances from armed actors that vehicles are allowed to move, or repairing airstrips outside the sites.

The capacity of UNMISS actors to use force, and especially the carrying of weapons, galvanizes a strong impulse in humanitarian actors to assert distinction. And yet, many humanitarian actors sincerely want UN peacekeepers to use force more routinely and more robustly to protect local populations. UNMISS peacekeepers have acquired a reputation for being risk averse, reluctant to leave their bases and use force to protect civilians.[26] Not only have multiple PoC sites suffered serious perimeter breaches under UNMISS's watch,[27] but also protection resources have been concentrated inside of the sites to the neglect of vulnerable populations outside. One UN humanitarian actor describes the sites as the 'visible eyesore of the conflict', and another adds: 'there's 201,000 in PoCs, but four point something million outside PoCs, and the latter are not being served'. Tellingly, in interviews conducted for this study, UN mission actors consistently interpreted questions about their PoC mandate as referring solely to the PoC sites.

Turning the tables, UNMISS actors accuse humanitarian actors of getting too comfortable in the PoC sites and ignoring needs outside.[28] Still, many UNMISS actors voice frustration with the mission's wobbly enforcement of its Chapter VII mandate in South Sudan. One UNMISS actor complains that the implementation of the Rules of Engagement (RoE) is 'not constant or linear, you sensitize the mission on it, and then you start again'. A UNMISS peacekeeping actor emphasizes the instability wrought by changes in command: 'A battalion commander might be around for a year; you need to explain to them that they need to push RoE to the limit, so they feel they can act also outside the PoC site.' The way in which UN forces respond to threats of violence against IDPs is attributed to individual personalities and, many suggest, the national origin of particular battalions. While certain nationalities are perceived as 'going the mile', other nationalities are rumoured to

[25] Area security is discussed in Section 2.3.2.

[26] Arensen, supra, 33 (*If We Leave*). United Nations, *Evaluation of the Implementation and Results of Protection of Civilians Mandates in United Nations Peacekeeping Operations: Report of the Office of Internal Oversight Services*, A/68/787, 7 March 2014, 7–8 (finding UNMISS peacekeepers used force less than 10 per cent of the time when civilians were attacked).

[27] Ibid, 33.

[28] See Chapter 4.

have a 'no body bag policy'. The latter are deemed to lack the will to respond robustly to threats against civilians.[29]

This state of affairs presents a somewhat confounding dynamic. Even as the combatant-like appearance of UN peacekeepers drives humanitarian actors away, humanitarians earnestly wish UNMISS actors would use force when civilian protection demands it. While UNMISS actors are important players in the everyday distinction practices of humanitarian actors, it will now be argued these peacekeeping actors are not the ultimate audience.

3.1.2 The ultimate audience for distinction: the 'phantom local'

As can be discerned from the discussion above, explicit appeals to IHL and international legal norms are infrequent in the Kinetic realm. One detects, more often, that behaviour is guided by tacit expectations or assumptions about local[30] perceptions. Humanitarian actors are clearly hoping to influence the other international actors in their midst, but the most important audience for distinction is an omnipresent onlooker they routinely summon. The humanitarian distinction project thus has a crucial optics component, with signs, symbols, and conduct all deployed to influence this imagined observer.[31] When humanitarian actors imagine how they are perceived by local actors, I find that they collapse a plurality of potential local audiences into a composite observer—termed here the 'phantom local'.[32] This spectral figure embodies (at least) three sets of observers: armed actors, local authorities, and war-affected populations.[33] These actors are real enough, with their

[29] See also 'Sudan Accuses UN Peacekeepers of Killing Seven Civilians in Darfur', *Reuters*, 27 April 2015. Available at: https://uk.reuters.com/article/us-sudan-darfur-unamid/sudan-accuses-u-n-peacekeepers-of-killing-seven-civilians-in-darfur-idUSKBN0NI1SC20150427.

[30] The term 'local' is employed very loosely, referring to someone other than a fellow international actor who intervenes in or responds to a conflict. It can refer to national, regional, or foreign actors. A version of the 'phantom local' argument is articulated in Rebecca Sutton, 'The "Phantom Local" and the Everyday Distinction Practices of Humanitarian Actors in War: A Socio-Legal Perspective', *New Political Science*, Vol. 40, No. 4, 2018, pp. 640–657 ('Phantom Local').

[31] Humanitarian signs and symbols are discussed in Section 3.3.3.

[32] Inspired by Walter Lippman, *The Phantom Public* (Piscataway, New Jersey: Transaction, 2006/1926) ('Phantom Public') (referring to a monolithic public with mythical and fictional qualities); Meredith Rossner et al., *The Process and Dynamics of Restorative Justice: Research on Forum Sentencing* (Sydney: University of Western Sydney, 2013), 43 (*Restorative Justice*) (referring to the phantom magistrate); David Kennedy, *The Dark Sides of Virtue: Reassessing International Humanitarianism* (Princeton, NJ: Princeton University Press, 2005), 29 (*Dark Sides*) (referring to the imaginary bystander of human rights initiatives).

[33] Other important audiences that are not discussed here include donors and the media. See, e.g.: Alexander Cooley and James Ron, 'The NGO Scramble: Organizational Insecurity and the Political Economy of Transnational Action', *International Security*, Vol. 27, 2002, pp. 5–39 ('NGO Scramble'); Monika Krause, *The Good Project: Humanitarian Relief NGOs and the Fragmentation of Reason* (Chicago, IL and London: University of Chicago Press, 2014), 48 (*Good Project*); Kai Koddenbrock, *The Practice of Humanitarian Intervention: Aid Workers, Agencies, and Institutions in the Democratic Republic of the Congo* (London and New York: Routledge, 2016), 56–57 (*Humanitarian Intervention*).

own desires, interests, and motivations, but the distinction project positions them as members of an audience that watches—and judges—the routine practices of humanitarian actors. These local actors are thereby recast, respectively, as attacker-perceivers, authority-perceivers, and beneficiary-perceivers.[34] Humanitarian actors need, and perhaps fear, something different from each type of audience. The attacker-perceiver might wish to harm humanitarian actors or to commandeer humanitarian resources such as money, transportation, facilities, and aid. The authority-perceiver has the power to grant or withhold various types of permission, such as visas to enter the country and authorization to move about or access particular populations. The beneficiary-perceiver might trust and accept humanitarian actors, or not, potentially thwarting the latter's attempts to provide succour to populations in need.[35]

From an IHL perspective, the analytical power of the 'phantom local' lies in its capacity to illuminate whether a particular invocation of distinction implicates targeting in the conduct of hostilities. Of the constellation of figures that make up the phantom local, the attacker-perceiver stands out as most obviously relevant to the issue of violent attack. If humanitarian actors ground a given appeal to distinction in the need to satisfy this figure, then we might thus expect that the IHL targeting rule is in play. When humanitarian actors invoke other audiences, however, this could alert us to the possibility that the distinction in question functions to uphold different interests and values. A particular performance of distinction might be directed to the beneficiary-perceiver, for example, so as to convey the appropriateness and quality of an agency's programming. This could link, or circle back, to concerns about violent attack by armed actors—as when humanitarian actors assert that their mission is genuinely humanitarian to establish their civilian bona fides—but it might not.

Where the connection between reassuring beneficiaries and thwarting violence (against humanitarian actors) is weak, this should not obscure the paramount importance of the former set of actors. It is, after all, populations in need of assistance that create the impetus for the humanitarian presence in the first place. This points to a perverse implication of the 'phantom local', aside from the way in which it potentially flattens real actors out into audiences. That is, the sense that an amorphous local spectator is watching may lead humanitarian actors to conflate recipients of their services with those who would harm humanitarian actors. These dynamics must be contextualized as part of a wider conversation about fear in humanitarian practice. Scholars such as Duffield, Roth, and Hilhorst have shown that humanitarian actors might fear and mistrust even the individuals they seek

[34] In practice, only some parts of the larger war-affected population will in fact benefit from humanitarian services. On those who are not served, see Krause, supra (*Good Project*) 43–44.

[35] For the sake of simplicity, I focus here on civilian recipients of humanitarian assistance, excluding the help provided to wounded and sick soldiers.

to help.[36] More generally, Fast posits that the security practices of humanitarian actors 'help to create a situation in which fear threatens to eclipse the humanitarian imagination'.[37]

It is important to acknowledge that, individually and collectively, humanitarian actors are intellectually aware that there is no such thing as a monolithic observer witnessing their every move. There is a cognitive dissonance at play, though, as the daily effort to implement distinction has the effect of suppressing one's appreciation for multiplicity.[38] Part of the problem here may be that tracking actual perceptions of distinction, an exercise which observers and practitioners in the humanitarian field have sought to do,[39] is notoriously difficult.[40] It is instructive to compare the competing conclusions drawn by two scholars of peacekeeping, Pouligny and Autessere, whose respective works focus on the DRC. Pouligny deduces that local populations do make distinctions: 'On the whole local people are not fooled either by the deceptive appearances of unity given by the UN acronym or by excessive reference to the "international community", even if local discourses often play on appearances.'[41] In contrast, Autessere finds that locals tend to lump all internationals together: '[I]n most conflict zones, despite coordinated efforts by humanitarian agencies to differentiate themselves from military interveners, there is still a major conflation of foreign military and civilian groups .... [H]ost populations rarely distinguish between different types of foreign interveners'.[42]

[36] Mark Duffield, 'Risk-Management and the Fortified Aid Compound: Everyday Life in Post-Interventionary Society', *Journal of Intervention and Statebuilding*, Vol. 4, No. 4, 2010, pp. 453–474, 471 ('Compound'); Silke Roth, *Passionate Professionals: The Paradoxes of Aid Work* (London and New York: Routledge, 2015), 183 (*Paradoxes of Aid*); Dorothea Hilhorst, 'Dead Letter or Living Document? Ten Years of the Code of Conduct for Disaster Relief', *Disasters*, Vol. 29, No. 4, 2005, pp. 351–369, 361 ('Dead Letter').

[37] Larissa Fast, *Aid in Danger: The Perils and Promise of Humanitarianism* (Philadelphia, PA: University of Pennsylvania Press, 2014), 3 (*Aid in Danger*).

[38] For an application of theories of cognitive dissonance to the field of humanitarian assistance see Zoe Marriage, *Not Breaking the Rules, Not Playing the Game: International Assistance to Countries at War* (London: Hurst, 2006) (*Not Breaking the Rules*).

[39] See: Caroline Abu-Sada (ed.), *In the Eyes of Others: How People in Crises Perceive Humanitarian Aid* (MSF and NYU Centre on International Cooperation, 2012) (*Eyes of Others*); Caroline Abu-Sada (ed.), *Dilemmas, Challenges, and Ethics of Humanitarian Action: Reflections on Médecins Sans Frontières Perception Project* (Montreal and Kingston: McGill-Queens University Press, 2012) (*Dilemmas*), especially Francois Cooren and Frederik Matte, 'At the Limits of Perception: Humanitarian Principles in Action', pp. 29–47 ('Limits of Perception'); Antonio Donini et al., 'Mapping the Security Environment: Understanding the Perceptions of Local Communities, Peace Support Operations, and Assistance Agencies', *Feinstein International Famine Centre Report*, June 2005 ('Security').

[40] Caroline Abu-Sada, 'Introduction', in Abu-Sada (ed.), supra, pp. 3–8, 5 (*Dilemmas*). Hugo Slim, 'How We Look: Perceptions of Humanitarian Action', *Centre for Humanitarian Dialogue*, Presentation, April 2004 ('How We Look'). Available at: https://reliefweb.int/sites/reliefweb.int/files/resources/CFBFB047170078CFC1257222004D3AFD-HDC-Apr2004.pdf.

[41] Beatrice Pouligny, *Peace Operations Seen from Below: UN Missions and Local People* (London: C. Hurst and Company, 2006), 128, and 131–141 (*Peace Operations*).

[42] Severine Autessere, *Peaceland: Conflict Resolution and the Everyday Politics of International Intervention* (Cambridge: Cambridge University Press, 2014), 271 (*Peaceland*).

The present study does not purport to settle that debate, but instead focuses on the mirror that humanitarian actors hold up to see how they are reflected in others' eyes. Cooley designates this attempt to discern how one is perceived by others as the 'looking-glass self'.[43] The goal in this inquiry is to shed light on the ascribed perceptions of local actors—to offer a thick sociological description of what are, in essence, perceptions of perceptions.[44] There are further layers to this excavation, as this study uncovers the hidden and ambiguous elements of humanitarian distinction practices. In her study of the Mende in Sierra Leone, Ferme describes how a mirror 'mimetically doubles that which is in front without giving away that which is behind the reflection'.[45] Understanding what is concealed, Ferme observes, is crucial to making sense of the visible.[46] The views espoused by international military and peacekeeping actors who share the operational space with humanitarian actors are instrumental to this investigation. Although these other actors' impressions are equally subjective they provide clues and offer points of departure that help to uncover the actual functions of distinction as enacted by humanitarian actors.

3.2 The Pedagogical realm

This section explores the question of who, amongst international actors, is responsible for forging IHL's civilian–combatant distinction in the Pedagogical realm. As in the Kinetic realm, the empirical findings establish that international humanitarian actors take the lead on this, entreating other international actors to accede to their vision. Not only do other international actors often push back, but they also actively work to erase the lines humanitarian actors are drawing. Reflecting the nature of the empirical material gathered in the training spaces, the present discussion is organized differently to its counterpart in the Kinetic realm. The discussion proceeds in two sections. The first establishes that humanitarian actors take charge with distinction and presents the reactions of other actors. The second introduces a 'rush to the intimate' that military actors engage in to foster proximity to humanitarians.

[43] Charles Horton Cooley, *Human Nature and the Social Order* (New York: Scribner, 1902).

[44] This outlook is grounded in subjectivist ontology, following W. I. Thomas's 'Thomas theorem' that if we believe something to be real, its consequences are real enough because we behave as though it does exist. See W. I. Thomas, 'The Relation of Research to the Social Process', in Morris Janowitz, (ed.), *W.I. Thomas on Social Organization and Social Personality* (Chicago, IL: University of Chicago Press, 1966/1931), pp. 289–305. See also Mark J. Smith, *Social Science in Question* (London: Open University Press/SAGE, 1998).

[45] Mariane Ferme, *The Underneath of Things: Violence, History and the Everyday in Sierra Leone* (Berkeley, CA: University of California Press, 2001), 7 (*The Underneath of Things*).

[46] Ibid., 2.

3.2.1 Humanitarian actors draw the line

In comparison with the frontline actors who operate in South Sudan, humanitarian guest trainers who teach in the civil–military training programmes espouse a clearer and unequivocal vision of distinction.[47] Perceptions again form a crucial piece of the puzzle, but in this more normative realm IHL is also squarely part of the conversation.

> **'This is really IHL'**
>
> It is early spring in Motto di Livenza, Italy, and a group of front-line functional specialists is gathered at the NATO CIMIC training to hear from humanitarian actors. At the beginning of her session, the humanitarian trainer grabs the edge of her shirt between her thumb and forefinger. 'Normally I speak to the Italian military with my uniform on; today is my first time without my uniform. I have my T-shirt, that is my uniform. It's the thing that protects us. For us it is a white T-shirt with a logo.' This mention of a uniform elicits appreciative nods around the classroom. The trainer takes pains to elaborate on why humanitarian actors must position themselves neutrally in the conflict. She states: 'It is a matter of perception: the military is part of the conflict and NGOs will be in danger if seen in this way.' She elaborates on how her organization's strict approach to distinction has also ensured its continued access to populations in need. It has enabled the organization to safely operate in insurgent-controlled parts of Afghanistan, for example, 'where even NATO wasn't able to go'. Later in the training session, the trainer broaches the delicate issue of attacks on humanitarian actors, highlighting the then-recent bombing of the MSF hospital in Kunduz, Afghanistan, by US coalition forces. She implores the trainees—some of whom are US soldiers—to explain to her how this happened. Staving off charges that she is letting her emotions get the best of her, she reiterates that her concerns about the bombing are legally grounded. As she phrases it: 'This is really IHL. We approach this all from IHL.' Reflecting on the session, a trainee who is a military doctor voices approval; he refers solemnly to MSF as 'my brother in uniform'. Another trainee grasps why humanitarian actors would be upset about the Kunduz bombing, but he also senses that MSF is seeking special treatment. 'What makes that an MSF hospital, as opposed to other hospitals they don't call an MSF hospital? It would still be civilian....' Contemplating the emphasis of humanitarian actors on neutrality, one of the military trainers states 'Yes! We get it, totally. But just MSF or ICRC'.

[47] Note that the international humanitarian actors studied in South Sudan represent a much larger range of organizations than the humanitarian trainers who lead sessions at the civil–military training programmes discussed in Part II. This also helps to explain the diversity of views in South Sudan.

The discussion begins with an examination of the way in which humanitarian actors communicate the need for distinction at civil–military training venues. When international military and peacekeeping actors challenge the vision of distinction humanitarian actors propound, power struggles ensue.

Humanitarian actors forge the distinction

At some point in their respective training sessions, all of the humanitarian trainers identify international law as the source of the civilian–combatant distinction. They mention international law in general terms or refer, more specifically, to IHL and the Geneva Conventions. The appeal to law's authority rarely stands on its own, however. Consistently, any use of legal discourse is accompanied by a reference to the importance of perceptions. Here, the 'phantom local' can be found hard at work. In some instances, this imagined observer is summoned as a monolithic entity, as when one refers generically to the prospect of 'being seen'. At other times, a more specific manifestation of the 'phantom local' is called upon to make a particular point. When a humanitarian actor intimates that the 'bad guys' monitor the interactions of international actors, for example, she invokes the attacker-perceiver to ground anxieties about personal safety.

Turning now to the lessons delivered by humanitarian actors at the NATO CIMIC training, in the discussion of the Kunduz bombing (see opening passage, above), the humanitarian trainer is emphatic: 'This is really IHL. We approach this all from IHL.' A few moments before she utters this, however, she also conveys: 'It is a matter of perception.' Although she does not specify whose perceptions pose a concern, the mention of danger suggests that it is the attacker-perceiver who is watching. She draws on the traditional humanitarian principles[48] to clarify the logic of her argument, tacitly putting distinction on the same plane as these principles. She explains that humanitarian actors uphold the humanitarian principles as both a legal obligation and a 'moral and operational necessity', and states that adhering to the principles enables humanitarian actors to access war-affected populations and to keep themselves safe.

Elsewhere in her session, the same humanitarian trainer imparts: 'Distinction is hard; we are all in white cars. This is why the bad guys sometimes target us.' Here, she suggests that local observers cannot discern between a car with a humanitarian NGO flag and a car with a UN logo, nor between the black and blue UN. Humanitarian NGOs, as a larger group, express concern about the adverse impact on local perceptions when black UN actors accompany blue UN actors, or when black UN actors use equipment that is branded blue UN.[49] A humanitarian trainer explains that because of these anxieties about confusion, MSF painted their cars

[48] See Sections 2.1.1 and 3.3.3.

[49] Han Dorussen and Marian de Vooght, 'Putting Civilians First: NGO Perceptions and Expectations of UN Peacebuilding', *Folke Bernadotte Academy*, Brief 01, 2018, 3 ('FBA Report').

pink in the DRC. 'Pink to make the difference. Pink! OK?!' In the edited collection *In the Eyes of Others*, Abu-Sada documents this move by MSF-Switzerland to paint its cars fuchsia in Bunia, Ituri Province, in the DRC in 2005: [50]

> As UN forces were using white all-terrain vehicles similar to those of MSF, the population conflated the two organizations. To add to the confusion, MONUC posted soldiers to 'protect' the space where the MSF teams were based. It became difficult for the organization to explain its neutrality to the local people. MSF-Switzerland decided to repaint its vehicles fuchsia, as that color was not associated with any political or military force present in the region.

At the NATO CIMIC training, another humanitarian explains that, according to IHL, 'if you are in the convoy you are the military objective'. For this reason, this trainer's organization will usually 'bluntly refuse military escorts, because we do not want to be integrated into the military'. Having invoked IHL, the trainer hastily adds, 'And then there is the issue of image—how you are seen on the other side. It's all based on acceptability; we have to walk the talk, live it on a daily basis, so there is no misrepresentation.' He also explains that the intentional targeting of humanitarian staff 'is where we cross the red line. It's not collateral damage, by chance the shell has landed next to our office'. The attacker-perceiver is activated in this account and the trainer conveys the importance of maintaining a purely humanitarian image, without which the organization cannot ensure 'acceptance'. This mention of 'acceptance' refers to a specific risk-management approach that humanitarian actors employ. In contrast to 'deterrence' or 'protection' approaches, acceptance strategies focus on fostering goodwill and ensuring positive perceptions of humanitarian actors so as to reduce others' motivations to harm them.[51]

During a subsequent session at the NATO CIMIC training, another trainer extols the importance of maintaining distinction in the operational context. She states: 'This distinction comes from IHL, between combatant and non-combatant, between the military and the non-military humanitarian aid worker.' Immediately before she cites IHL, she says: 'For the humanitarian community it is not possible to be seen closely interacting with military actors or armed actors that may be seen as parties to the conflict or [as committing] violence against the local population.' This reference to parties to the conflict summons the authority-perceiver and the attacker-perceiver. It is also insinuated that the beneficiary-perceiver will harshly

[50] Caroline Abu-Sada, 'Part I: Studying How MSF is Perceived', in Abu-Sada (ed.), supra, pp. 10–96, 10–11 (*Eyes of Others*).

[51] The concept of 'acceptance' also arises in the civil–military guidelines discussed in Section 2.3.2. On acceptance and humanitarian security practices, see e.g.: Jan Egeland, Adele Harmer, and Abby Stoddard, *To Stay and Deliver: Good Practice for Humanitarians in Complex Security Environments* (Geneva and New York: OCHA, 2011) (*Stay and Deliver*); Ruben Andersson and Florian Weigand, 'Intervention at Risk: The Vicious Cycle of Distance and Danger in Mali and Afghanistan', *Journal of Intervention and Statebuilding*, Vol. 9, 2015, pp. 519–541 ('Intervention at Risk').

judge any humanitarian actor who fails to stay away from armed actors who harm civilian populations.

Turning now to the perspectives of other international actors participating in the training programmes, the proceeding section shows that some are persuaded by the appeal to international law while others are sympathetic to the need to appease the 'phantom local' and still others reject both rationales. Focusing on international military actors, a power struggle is uncovered as humanitarian distinction practices threaten the traditional balance of power between humanitarian and military actors.

Other international actors push back

Generally speaking, military actors hold the position of power in the humanitarian–military relationship.[52] When humanitarian actors erect boundaries in the name of distinction, they may be seen to disturb this arrangement. Although some humanitarians would cast international military and peacekeeping actors in the role of Fred Astaire,[53] the distinction practices of humanitarian actors often lead other actors to feel as if *they* are the ones on the back foot.

During a classroom session at the NATO CIMIC training programme, a military trainer primes trainees for learning about distinction. When teaching them why they need to understand humanitarian actors as a group, he explains: 'Maybe you are working together, maybe it's people you cannot target; your targeting officer needs to know. You can't target their buildings and if you are bombing nearby, you might need to use a special type of bomb.' He elaborates: 'We want to avoid collateral damage, targeting of humanitarian facilities or personnel, or civilians in need, and this is very much in line with IHL.' Other military trainers at NATO link appeals to distinction by humanitarian actors to a commitment to the traditional humanitarian principles. One military trainer says of humanitarian actors, 'especially in theatre, they don't want to link . . . they want to remain impartial'. Touching on the principles as well as optics, another trainer states 'NGOs, international organizations, sometimes they won't meet up. If they share a room and coffee with us, they can be seen as taking sides by people outside. We need to respect their neutrality, independence'. Receptivity to the need for distinction might be impacted by the identity of the humanitarian organization in question. The final comment from the opening vignette ('But just MSF or ICRC') exemplifies the tendency of international military actors to treat the ICRC—and often MSF, as well—differently from other humanitarian actors.

[52] Michael Pugh, 'Civil–Military Relations in Peace Support Operations: Hegemony or Emancipation?', *Overseas Development Institute Seminar on Aid and Politics*, February 2001, 5 ('ODI Seminar'). Available at: https://www.odi.org/sites/odi.org.uk/files/odi-assets/events-documents/3774.pdf; Michael Pugh, 'The Challenge of Civil–Military Relations in International Peace Operations', *Disasters*, Vol. 25, No. 4, 2001, pp. 345–357, 349 ('Civil–Military Relations').

[53] See Section 3.1.1.

At the SWEDINT training venue, one trainer points to perceptions as the reason why it makes sense to let humanitarian actors forge the distinction. This trainer advises military actors to think carefully about why humanitarian actors would assert a separation between actors. He explains that if military actors are themselves targets and meet with humanitarian actors, they put humanitarians 'in harm's way'. He urges military actors to be careful about meeting with humanitarian actors because 'everyone knows'. At the CAMPO training, a trainee reflects on similar lessons about distinction. This trainee is baffled by the notion that humanitarian actors need to keep their distance from military actors. He speculates: 'Shouldn't humanitarians be right there with the military so that their own personnel can be safe, and they can get access to people in need?' A civilian UN trainee responds that humanitarian actors do not see it in this way: 'No, they refuse to be close to [military actors]; they are just separate.' If a particular humanitarian actor uses a military escort, this trainee explains, other 'humanitarians say you are endangering the lives of the relief workers'. In these exchanges, trainees debate whether the distinction humanitarian actors enact satisfies the 'phantom local', who mostly appears in the form of the attacker-perceiver. The first CAMPO speaker believes that the physical protection military actors offer eclipses whatever perception problems might arise through close proximity. While these actors disagree about what, exactly, is perceived and the implications of such perceptions, there is evidently some level of receptivity amongst non-humanitarian actors to the notion that perceptions matter.

One point of contention at the training sessions is whether the blurring of lines between different international actors actually endangers humanitarian actors. Hammond articulates a lucid critique on this front, underscoring what she terms the 'trope of confusion'.[54] She contends that the focus on blurring suggests that humanitarian actors are targeted by mistake or through misunderstanding.[55] Instead, she argues that the intentional violence against humanitarian actors is performative—designed to elicit media attention and to send a message about security levels and a disregard for humanitarian principles.[56] This leads Hammond to suggest that it is aid agencies, themselves, who lack clarity on their own role in armed conflict and who are unable to extricate themselves from conflict dynamics.[57]

[54] Laura Hammond, 'The Power of Holding Humanitarianism Hostage and the Myth of the Protective Principles', in Michael Barnett and Thomas Weiss (eds.), *Humanitarianism in Question: Politics, Power, and Ethics* (Ithaca, NY: Cornell University Press, 2008), pp. 172–195, 176 ('Holding Humanitarianism Hostage').

[55] Ibid. On the intentional targeting of humanitarian actors see also: Silke Roth, 'Aid Work as Edgework: Voluntary Risk-Taking and Security in Humanitarian Assistance, Development and Human Rights Work', *Journal of Risk Research*, Vol. 18, No. 2, 2015, pp. 139–155, 141 ('Edgework'); Roth, supra, 32 (*Paradoxes of Aid*).

[56] Hammond, supra, 177 ('Holding Humanitarianism Hostage').

[57] Ibid.

During a focus group discussion at NATO, a military trainer argues that complaints about blurring are misguided. She contends: 'What we're trying to figure out is where the line *is*. It's not a blurring, it's the *location*.' Although her search for a line seems to conjure a bright-line binary framework, her insistence that the line is not static also constitutes a departure from a stable distinction. From this trainer's vantage point, the question should always be about what arrangement works best in a given setting. She cannot fathom why humanitarian actors would have a monopoly on deciding the location of this line. Listening in, another military trainer gently pushes back: 'You have to respect the distinction between military and civilians. We have to create the environment for military and civilians to do their work.' While he agrees that the line is not static, he is sympathetic to the argument that humanitarian actors should be in control. Invoking the 'phantom local', he says if there is a 'mix up' in the eyes of local actors, it is international civilian actors and humanitarian NGOs who are put at risk. What is remarkable in these exchanges is how the military trainers (do not) engage with IHL. Neither of these NATO trainers believes that one can find the civilian–combatant line 'in the books' of law. Rather, they believe this line is forged anew by international actors in response to the demands of a particular operational context.

Returning to the SWEDINT training, conversation turns to the ascribed views of the beneficiary-perceiver. One military trainee suggests that the main audience for distinction is, in fact, the 'customers' of humanitarian projects.[58] He says of humanitarian actors:

> It is like if they associate with military they will get less customers. If you are in a village and you see NGOs talking to tanks and helicopters, you might be a bit scared of them—even doctors or people who bring you food … so maybe you won't be pushed towards these people.

In this trainee's view, beneficiary populations can tell the different actors apart and they adapt their behaviour accordingly. At the CAMPO training, a military trainer also connects distinction to beneficiary trust. He suggests that when humanitarian actors struggle with other international actors over drawing the line, it is because humanitarian actors 'don't want to lose their privileged position with vulnerable groups'. In contrast to the SWEDINT trainee, however, he doubts that local populations can discern the identity of a given international actor. 'For them, it's all the same.' In this depiction, the 'phantom local' looks on at the blur of international actors and finds its counterpart: the 'phantom foreigner'. Carle and Chkam's account of international actors in Iraq following the 2003 intervention alludes to this nebulous foreign figure, finding that there was 'almost no possibility of distinction'

[58] Krause also treats donors as the customers of humanitarian projects. See Krause, supra (*Good Project*).

amongst international actors in this context.[59] This amorphous foreign intervener makes another appearance in the comments of a police trainee at SWEDINT. The trainee believes that local populations generally cannot tell who is who amongst international actors, though he is confident that international actors can make an impression if they try. When deployed as an EU police officer in Afghanistan, he often conversed casually with local actors about how they saw the passing vehicles of international actors. He relays: 'Some thought they were military, ISAF, NATO, UN … only the few who were interested in the different actors in Afghanistan knew who was who.' [60] From this he concludes: 'If we didn't have time to introduce ourselves and speak to them, they might not know.' A military trainee chimes in: 'Whoever goes near to the people, is the one who will be known.' These perspectives on identification do not dispose of the problem of perceived affiliations between different types of actors, an issue that the next section explores.

3.2.2 International military actors erase the line

In addition to pushback against humanitarian actors' attempts to draw the line, international military actors imperil the humanitarian distinction project in other ways. First, military actors, themselves, sometimes engage in humanitarian-type tasks and assert a humanitarian identity.[61] Second, military actors strive to get close to humanitarian actors, erasing lines faster than humanitarians can draw them.

'What you bring to the fight'

During one of the NATO CIMIC training sessions, a military trainer advises that when trainees arrive in a new area of operation, they should take immediate steps to show 'what you bring to the fight'. It is evident that the battle in question does not take place on the conventional battlefield, and the training sessions on 'CIMIC projects' illuminate the true arena. CIMIC projects are focused and time-bound projects that are designed to have an immediate and tangible impact, thereby increasing acceptance of foreign troops, ensuring force protection and—in some cases—supporting intelligence gathering. Practitioners sometimes refer to them as quick impact projects, or QIPs. To prepare trainees

[59] Alexandre Carle and Hakim Chkam, 'Humanitarian Action in the New Security Environment: Policy and Operational Implications in Iraq', *Humanitarian Policy Group Background Paper*, September 2006, 7 ('Humanitarian Action').

[60] Local perceptions in Afghanistan are also addressed in Larry Minear and Antonio Donini, 'International Troops, Aid Workers, and Local Communities: Mapping the Perceptions Gap', *Humanitarian Exchange Magazine*, No. 32, December 2005, pp. 26–29, 27 ('Perceptions') ('In Afghanistan, people made fewer distinctions among NGOs, perhaps reflecting comments by a senior government official that all NGOs were corrupt, and a growing disenchantment with the aid effort').

[61] Note that under IHL, military actors are not precluded from engaging in the delivery of humanitarian assistance; nowhere in IHL instruments it is specified that only civilian actors can deliver humanitarian assistance.

> to implement such projects, a military trainer shares his experiences working with fishing cooperatives in the Horn of Africa. Testing the trainees, he inquires: 'Why would I work with fishing cooperatives?' Going for laughs, one trainee ventures facetiously: 'Because you like fish?' After allowing a brief moment of levity, the trainer provides the real answer. The end game is to empower the capacity of the fishermen so they won't join the pirates. 'I made some QIPs for them, courses in mending fishing nets, materials, teaching skills . . . .' Another benefit of the contact this fostered, he says, is that fishermen shared information about weapons smuggling in the area. When he asks trainees why certain kinds of CIMIC projects are executed in particular locations, it prompts a chorus of: 'CIMIC is in support of the military mission'. During another training session, a military trainer depicts the daily duties he carried out on a recent afternoon in the conflict zone where he was deployed. He checked on the refurbished water pumps in the IDP camps and approved the release of funds for the water pumping station. Next: 'There were soccer uniforms to be dropped off for a community team, heated disputes to resolve, an influential Mullah to visit.' He concludes: 'It is surely my fight in my area of operation.'

CIMIC activities and quick impact projects (QIPs), which take military actors outside of the scope of their traditional combat role, are the subject of controversy at the trainings. This discussion considers such activities first, before addressing attempts to foster proximity with humanitarian actors.

Military humanitarianism

Discussions about the militarization of humanitarian assistance flow in one of two directions: they either refer to direct engagement by military forces in the delivery of humanitarian assistance or they refer to the use of military logistical, security, and other assets by humanitarian actors.[62] The present discussion is concerned with the former variant, and it focuses on findings collected at NATO and CAMPO (as the issue did not arise at SWEDINT in a significant way).[63] In contrast to the fairly widespread acceptance of the comprehensive approach by military actors, participants in these civil–military training programmes are divided on whether military actors should exceed their traditional combat role. While the discussion here focuses on the need for distinction between humanitarian and military actors, it should be noted that IHL does not preclude military actors from playing a role in the delivery of humanitarian assistance. There is no stipulation in IHL instruments that only civilian actors can deliver humanitarian assistance—though the

[62] Peter Hoffman and Thomas Weiss, *Sword and Salve: Confronting New Wars and Humanitarian Crises* (Lanham, MD: Rowman and Littlefield Publishers, 2006), 20 (*Sword and Salve*). See Pugh, supra, 352 ('Civil–Military Relations').

[63] The issue of military asset use by humanitarian actors is examined in Chapter 4.

requirements that relief be 'exclusively humanitarian' and 'impartial' impose serious limitations on military actors directly engaging in relief activities.[64]

On one hand, trainees are taught that humanitarian actors are not the only ones who can help local populations caught up in war. They learn how to execute CIMIC projects (NATO) and QIPs (CAMPO). It is suggested during a CAMPO training session that the military's job in contemporary conflict should be interpreted broadly. Trainees learn that international military forces are increasingly engaged in stabilization and counter-insurgency tasks that involve humanitarian-like activities. One CAMPO trainer emphasizes that, however humanitarian these tasks might look, they remain combat operations. At the NATO training, participants are also reminded that, even if they 'do a lot of the same things' as humanitarian actors, this does not make them humanitarian actors. Citing the example of military forces building schools, a NATO military trainer tests the trainees: 'Do we have a military NGO?' The trainees respond with an unambiguous collective 'No'. The difference, all agree, is that everything NATO does is designed to achieve its military mission. The trainers convey that humanitarian NGOs primarily seek to support the civilian population and that, unlike NATO, they do not have a military 'second mission'. A military trainee later explains what this means to him: 'In the end we're all soldiers first .... If I'm doing humanitarian relief in a war zone, my hand will be on my weapon. That's a big mental thing. I'm here to help you, but don't try anything, I will kill you.' Still, it bothers him that humanitarian actors might see him as itching to pick up a gun. Having emphasized the centrality of his combatant identity, he insists that 'No one hates war more than a soldier'.

While military actors are frequently reminded that they are not humanitarian actors, many depict themselves as being in a helping role or sharing a concern for 'common humanity'. Contemplating the sessions led by humanitarian trainers on this topic (see later in this section), several NATO trainees are irritated by the concern for the motivations of military actors. One military trainee insists: 'We really can provide a service. Don't worry about what our motives may be, in the end we're helping somebody.' His fellow trainee chimes in: 'I can help you help these people, but you're not letting me help them by providing whatever I can provide.' A NATO trainer validates such reactions: 'Our underlying thing is humane: we *stop* the conflict. Most missions, the most bullets are shot on the [firing] range.' Likewise, another trainer submits: 'The military is not just killing people, or hurting civilians. We are even looking after civilians.' A trainer adds: 'We have in common the humanity ... we do it with kinetic force, they do it by helping.' Here, combatant and

[64] Johanna Grombach Wagner, 'An IHL/ICRC Perspective on "Humanitarian Space"', *Humanitarian Exchange Magazine*, No. 32, 2005 ('IHL/ICRC Perspective') ('The phrase "relief action of an exclusively humanitarian and impartial nature", however, means that the military must not disguise itself as a civilian humanitarian actor in order to deceive the population and collect intelligence for future military action').

humanitarian identity are folded together as though the commonalities outweigh the differences.

As highlighted previously, one CAMPO trainer emphasizes that humanitarian-like activities are combat tasks when performed by military actors—including peacekeeping actors. Undermining this message, another CAMPO trainer asserts that humanitarian actors are not the only ones here 'to save the world'. The armed actors who engage in multidimensional peacekeeping operations, this trainer contends, want the very same thing. Over lunch, the trainer recalls a civil–military training programme for EU actors that he had attended. He reports: 'They reassured each other why they cannot work together, while people drown. No one answered the question "What can I contribute?"' He thinks this is preposterous. 'You're arguing over the colour of the life belt, while people are drowning.'[65] Similar dynamics unfold in South Sudan, where there is discernible friction between humanitarian actors and UNMISS actors regarding technical expertise.[66]

Cutting in the other direction, there is a detectable—albeit marginal—thread at the trainings arguing for military actors to avoid non-combat roles. Coincidentally, at both CAMPO and NATO, this runs through discussions on the construction of schools. At the CAMPO training programme, one trainer makes a disparaging reference to international military forces building schools in the Balkans in the 1990s. The trainer elaborates: 'We now understand this is not our role . . . so we first ask: Is this our job?' Similarly, at NATO, a military trainer describes a scenario in West Africa wherein NATO accidentally damaged a local school. NATO arranged for local civilian contractors to repair the school while NATO forces took care to stay 'out of sight'. In this trainer's view, it would not have been appropriate for soldiers to fix the school themselves. 'That should be the distinction: so you shouldn't see military working on civilian [things].' While the above CAMPO trainer focuses on what properly falls within the military sphere, the NATO trainer asserts that a distinction problem was averted because NATO forces remained out of sight. This emphasis on optics can generate perverse results, as we will see shortly.

The sessions run by humanitarian actors firmly take up this appeal for a narrower military mandate. Humanitarian actors have long recognized military capability and expertise,[67] yet voiced doubts that people engaged in war fighting or peace enforcement can deliver aid appropriately.[68] The underlying aims of CIMIC projects and QIPs—especially the goal of 'winning hearts and minds'—chafe against the imperative to deliver needs-based aid in a neutral and impartial

[65] The reference to the colour of a life belt alludes to the issue of humanitarian signs and symbols, addressed in Section 3.3.3.

[66] See Chapter 5.

[67] Sphere, *The Sphere Project: Humanitarian Charter and Minimum Standards in Humanitarian Response*, 2011 edition (Rugby, UK: Practical Action Publishing, 2011), 60 (*Sphere Handbook*).

[68] Pugh, supra, 352 ('Civil–Military Relations'). These dynamics might be different in situations such as natural disasters and public health emergencies, as opposed to the armed conflict contexts examined here.

manner.[69] During a training session at NATO, a humanitarian trainer notes that humanitarian actors are troubled by 'the association, mobilization, and utilization of humanitarian assistance to achieve other objectives'. When military actors engage directly in so-called humanitarian activities or present their tasks as complementary to that of humanitarian actors, this generates confusion. 'The goal is different. Is the population understanding that? Do you think I will still have access to the Taliban side?' The risk of misunderstanding, she explains, is heightened by a priori local ideas that all foreigners are the same. Both humanitarian and military actors are foreign, have means, operate in times of crisis, and say they are 'here to help'. At the end, she reiterates: 'What's important for us is distinction.' Notably, this humanitarian trainer does not draw on IHL to persuade military actors. It is instead perceptions—and, in particular, the spectre of a 'phantom foreigner'—doing the heavy lifting.

An even starker clash materializes when military actors actively try to close the distance between themselves and humanitarian actors.

A rush to the intimate

Aside from engaging in activities that take them into the civilian sphere, international military actors may also overtly strive to foster proximity with civilians. In the civil–military training spaces, military actors voice an earnest desire to increase contact with international humanitarian actors. The efforts military actors make to learn about, get to know, and approach humanitarian actors are reminiscent of what Stoler and Bond term a 'rush to the intimate' in counter-insurgency operations.[70] Intriguingly, military actors who engage in such conduct tend not to think that it undermines distinction.

Depicting the humanitarian sphere as part of a crowded landscape of international civilian actors, a military trainer at NATO proposes: 'We need to fight complexity with knowledge.' One trainee offers: 'The goal is to have positive feelings between military and NGOs.' A NATO trainer highlights the importance of building friendships and advises trainees to 'show them who you really are, as military and humans'. Another NATO trainer recommends that trainees draw attention to commonalities between humanitarian and military actors, such as a mission-first focus, courage, and an emphasis on getting things done. Ultimately, trainees learn, the onus to foster interactions with humanitarian actors is on

[69] Erin Weir, 'Conflict and Compromise: UN Integrated Missions and the Humanitarian Imperative', *Kofi Annan International Peacekeeping Training Centre Monograph*, 2006, 41 ('Conflict and Compromise'). See also Dorussen and de Vooght, supra ('FBA Report').

[70] Ann Laura Stoler and David Bond, 'Refractions Off Empire: Untimely Comparisons in Harsh Times', *Radical History Review*, Vol. 95, 2006, pp. 93–107 ('Refractions'). Discussed in Derek Gregory, 'The Rush to the Intimate: Counterinsurgency and the Cultural Turn', *Radical Philosophy*, Vol. 150, 2008, pp. 8–23 ('Rush to the Intimate').

military actors. As one NATO trainer puts it: 'We have the gun and uniform, so it's for us to open the door.'

During another training session at NATO, a military trainer explains that smaller and less organized humanitarian actors lack the 'absorptive capacity' to engage with military actors. Another military trainer urges trainees to differentiate between individuals and institutions when fostering relationships in conflict zones. Individuals, it is intimated, offer leverage points for entry. By way of example, the trainer tells the story of a humanitarian organization that initially refused to speak with international military forces in a conflict zone.[71] Eventually, 'one employee said he would talk to me in his brother's shop if [we] didn't tell his boss, so that worked'. The lesson imparted is that what cannot be accomplished at the organizational level can be achieved through one-on-one interaction. This resonates with the techniques that UN civilian trainees at CAMPO say they have developed for improving relations with humanitarian actors.[72] One reservist trainee at NATO, who splits his time between military service and civilian life, says it is easy for him to gain the trust of humanitarian actors because he can 'speak civilian'. He refrains from using acronyms, makes an effort to be less 'aggressive', and strives to put every message in a 'way they want to hear it'. He is adamant that, even when a military actor behaves in this way to get humanitarian actors on side, still, 'you are a soldier'.

Participants in the SWEDINT training also discuss the value of fostering relationships at the individual level. One trainee looks for international humanitarian actors of his own nationality in a conflict zone, so 'we can talk'. Another trainee submits: 'It's all personality. If you connect with someone, it's easy to exchange information.'[73] His fellow trainee adds: 'It's one thing to communicate with the organization as a whole, but easier one on one.' A SWEDINT trainee also proposes that established international humanitarian organizations are easier to work with than new, smaller NGOs because the former are more professional. This comment squares with findings, which will explored in Chapter 5, that smaller and lesser-known NGOs are seen to lack professionalism. At the same time, it is at odds with the NATO trainer's story just mentioned of how a humanitarian actor hid his interaction with the trainer from his boss. It was not professionalism that made the contact possible, but the willingness of the individual humanitarian actor to bend his organization's rules. Moving on, a SWEDINT military trainee who deploys as a UN peacekeeper adds that UN humanitarian actors are 'easier for military' to deal with than NGOs, because the former are part of the UN family. Another military trainee is heartened by potential disconnects between the official pronouncements of humanitarian actors and what they are, in practice, willing to do behind closed doors.

[71] Location withheld to protect confidentiality.

[72] See Section 5.2.1.

[73] Dorussen and de Vooght also find that direct experience with individuals influences humanitarian actors' views of particular organizations or actors. Dorussen and de Vooght, supra, 4 ('FBA Report').

He explains that humanitarian actors sometimes speak with him in private, and that when they face security problems, 'they even stay in our camp'.

It is important to pay close attention to military trainees' interpretation of the emphasis on optics. If concerns about distinction stem from the prospect being seen together, then some military actors believe that their 'rush to the intimate' may continue as long as it takes place outside of the public eye. NATO trainees thus swap stories of how they make headway with humanitarian actors 'behind the scenes'. At the SWEDINT training, one trainee advocates downplaying the differences between military and humanitarian actors. The uniforms that military actors wear, he proposes, are really just 'a piece of cloth'. At the NATO training, it is proposed that military actors should remove their uniforms altogether. Recalling the reservist trainee at NATO who says he is able to 'speak civilian', the suggestion is also floated in that training programme that military actors might make progress by *looking* civilian—that is, by donning civilian clothing. In one of the training sessions, a trainer shows a photo of himself participating in a running race organized by a UN humanitarian agency in the Horn of Africa, in which he wore running kit. Referring to the green military uniform of a NATO soldier, he notes that humanitarian NGOs are usually opposed to 'interacting with people dressed like a vegetable'. He advises, however, that trainees can 'easily take down the wall' by removing their 'vegetable or salad dress'.

In essence, this trainer is advocating that military actors should renounce the combatant-like aspects of their identity to foster interaction with humanitarian actors. Here he sounds very much like the UNMISS peacekeepers cited in Chapter 2, who talk about downplaying features that make them appear more like combatants (and less like civilians) when engaging with humanitarian actors.[74] While military actors might expect that meeting in secret or shedding uniforms will dispel humanitarian actors' anxieties about distinction, this only addresses the optics part of the equation. It does not deal with other concerns that arise with respect to association, such as humanitarian actors actually being influenced by those who are participating in the conflict. Such practices could, in some cases, also violate IHL.[75] In subsequent conversation, several NATO trainees voice discomfort with the notion of removing their uniforms—though not for legal reasons. One trainee likens this to cheating, 'especially in civilian perceptions'.

Not all military trainees think that engendering proximity to humanitarian actors is the right move overall; some recognize that it could bring harm to humanitarian actors. One NATO trainee allows: 'We have a different mission than the humanitarians, and we approach the local population differently.' When another

[74] See Section 2.1.2, especially the peacekeeper who says he will wear civilian clothes and not bring his weapon to visit MSF.

[75] In addition to undermining the principle of distinction, the failure to wear a uniform or distinctive sign could fall foul of IHL rules such as the prohibition on perfidy—most obviously if the military actors are engaged in offensive operations. See Article 37 of AP I; Ferrel, supra ('No Shirt').

trainee, befuddled, inquires, 'Why can't we work together?' his colleague proffers: 'Because humanitarians think we endanger them. We are military and we are political; we are not there for the same reason as humanitarians.' Another trainee contributes: 'When I hear them say they need to stay impartial, it's a challenge for me. But if that's what keeps them safe, I guess they have to use that.' Thus, separation from humanitarian actors is simply something 'we'll have to respect'. These pronouncements regarding the need to reinforce—or at least not interfere with—the lines drawn by humanitarian actors represent the minority view at the training grounds.

The first two parts of this Chapter have shown that humanitarian actors take the lead on enacting their vision of distinction, and they do so in relationship with international military and peacekeeping actors. The question of what it means to protect local populations emerges as a point of contention in South Sudan, and at the civil–military training grounds military actors do more than push back on humanitarian distinction practices: they actively enter the humanitarian sphere. As humanitarian actors draw lines, other international actors can thus be found dimming, moving, and erasing them. Conversations about what the 'phantom local' sees—whether in monolithic form or taking shape as a more specific audience—provide hints about who these performances of distinction are designed to appease and what the stakes are. A further layer of complexity will be introduced in Chapter 4, where it is shown that humanitarian actors sometimes actively blur the lines themselves.

Moving on to the highly normative Intellectual realm, the next section addresses the conceptualization of the humanitarian figure in international law and examines the way in which humanitarian principles, signs, and symbols serve the distinction project. Attention is drawn to the way in which the Red Cross actor is set up as the touchstone of humanitarian assistance.

3.3 The Intellectual realm

In the course of their routine work, a range of international humanitarian actors—including Red Cross actors, UN agencies, and NGOs—implement everyday distinction practices. We saw earlier in the empirical discussion that international military and peacekeeping actors are sometimes more receptive to appeals to distinction when they are uttered by particular humanitarian actors.[76] The Red Cross (and sometimes MSF) is routinely singled out as possessing the requisite authority to invoke distinction. Focusing here on the Red Cross, I advance the claim that the special treatment of this humanitarian actor continues in IHL, where the Red

[76] As indicated by the comments of the military trainer who 'gets' distinction, with the caveat 'but just MSF or ICRC'. See Section 3.2.1.

Cross actor is afforded special status and protections. I call this IHL's Red Cross fantasy. UN humanitarian actors and NGOs too are longing for a special status, and as we will see, their attempts to simulate the Red Cross figure keep the fantasy in circulation.

This three-part discussion charts the emergence of the humanitarian figure in IHL, introduces IHL's Red Cross fantasy, and engages with (critiques of) the traditional humanitarian principles, signs, and symbols.

3.3.1 The historical evolution of the humanitarian figure in law

To understand the significance of humanitarian actors' line-drawing practices, it is important to examine the historical emergence of the humanitarian actor in international law. A discussion of the relationship between this figure and IHL's civilian category will follow in Chapter 5.

While the provision of succour to certain individuals in war formed part of the first GC in 1864, it was not until the 1970s that IHL explicitly attended to the civilian actors delivering what would today be called humanitarian assistance.[77] This study identifies AP I as the moment at which the humanitarian actor enters the legal scene, and I will propose here that the category of the humanitarian actor was effectively split apart before it was explicitly contemplated in AP I. The Red Cross figure, or someone bearing a likeness to this figure, was positioned as the paradigmatic humanitarian actor, while the status of other self-identifying humanitarian actors was left opaque. This points to another parallel in IHL's treatment of the humanitarian actor and the civilian category: before the civilian was defined in AP I, the civilian category was also splintered in GC IV of 1949.[78]

Henri Dunant's mythical experience at the Battle of Solferino is typically cited as the birthplace of contemporary humanitarian assistance, but humanitarianism as a broader practice has much earlier antecedents.[79] A social commitment to caring and providing for society's most vulnerable can historically be identified in diverse societies and a plethora of world religions.[80] In Europe, going back to the Black Death pandemic of the Middle Ages, the introduction of public health boards to care for those who were ill and to dispose of bodies may be considered a prototype

[77] Some elements of this discussion appear in Rebecca Sutton, 'Enacting the "Civilian Plus": Humanitarian Actors and the Conceptualization of Distinction', *Leiden Journal of International Law*, Vol. 33, No. 2, 2020, pp. 429–449 ('Civilian Plus').

[78] See Section 5.3.2.

[79] Michael Barnett, *Empire of Humanity: A History of Humanitarianism* (Ithaca, NY: Cornell University Press, 2011), 5–6 (*Empire*).

[80] Elizabeth Ferris, 'Faith and Humanitarianism: It's Complicated', *Journal of Refugee Studies*, Vol. 24, No. 3, 2011, pp. 606–623, 608 ('Faith'). Again, the focus here is on the Western world.

of contemporary disaster medicine.[81] The Western tradition of Christian charity is also considered to have played a central role, with the movement to abolish slavery in the mid 1800s deemed an early iteration of contemporary humanitarianism.[82] As the burgeoning historical scholarship on humanitarianism and empire also demonstrates, however, the motivations of self-proclaimed humanitarians have not always been altogether altruistic.[83] What is most relevant for our purposes here is that humanitarians who came before Dunant did not limit their activities to emergency relief; rather, they took an expansive view of suffering and made no claims to be outside of politics.[84]

Dunant's vision of humanitarianism, which informed early IHL instruments, was a very specific one. In calling for an international convention that would create European societies dedicated to the care of wounded soldiers, Dunant is credited for having launched 'the idea of a permanent, voluntary, and international organization that would care for victims of war'.[85] Significantly, Dunant's vision revolved primarily around military actors providing medical assistance to sick and wounded soldiers.[86] States were the central actors providing relief at this time, and there was little consideration of private actors engaged in relief activities.[87] Dunant's vision infused the GCs of 1864, and the protection of religious and medical personnel belonging to the military was codified in positive law before any mention was made of civilian actors providing help.[88] This emphasis on military actors as the providers and recipients of assistance continued in several IHL instruments that followed, with some exceptions.[89] Article 15 of the Hague Conventions of 1899 mentioned

[81] Eleanor Davey, with John Borton and Mathew Foley, 'A History of the Humanitarian System: Western Origins and Foundations', *Humanitarian Policy Group Working Paper*, June 2013, 6 ('History').

[82] John Ashworth, 'The Relationship between Capitalism and Humanitarianism', *The American Historical Review*, Vol. 92, No. 4, 1987, pp. 813–828 ('Capitalism').

[83] See especially Emily Baughan et al., 'Empire and Humanitarianism: Special Edition', *Journal of Imperial and Commonwealth History*, Vol. 40, No. 5, 2012, pp. 727–896.

[84] Barnett, supra, 5–6 (*Empire*).

[85] Antonio Cassese, 'Current Challenges to International Humanitarian Law', in Andrew Clapham and Paola Gaeta (ads.), *Oxford Handbook of International Law in Armed Conflict* (Oxford: Oxford University Press, 2014), pp. 3–19, 4 ('Challenges').

[86] Henry Dunant, *A Memory of Solferino* (Geneva: International Committee of the Red Cross, 1986) (*Solferino*). Discussed in Christopher Greenwood, 'Historical Development and Legal Basis', in Dieter Fleck (ed.), *Handbook on International Humanitarian Law*, 2nd edition (Oxford: Oxford University Press, 2008), pp. 1–43, 22 (*Historical Development*) ('What shocked Dunant after the Battle of Solferino was the lack of any systematic effort by the armies concerned to care for the wounded'). On the national societies of the Red Cross as an auxiliary of state armies, see Marc-Antoine Perouse de Montclos, 'The (de)Militarization of Humanitarian Aid: A Historical Perspective', *Humanities*, Vol. 3, 2014, pp. 232–243, 241 ('Militarization').

[87] Nicholas Stockton, 'The Accountable Humanitarian', *Humanitarian Accountability Partnership*, 2005 ('Accountable') Available at: http://hapinternational.org/pool/files/the-accountable-humanitarian-2-12-05.pdf (it was the Great Powers that wanted humanitarian 'neutrality' due to fears that one-sided relief would be advantageous for opponents).

[88] Claudie Barrat, *Status of NGOs in International Humanitarian Law* (Leiden: Brill Nijhoff, 2014), 303 (*Status of NGOs*).

[89] Prior to the Second World War, diaspora populations played a prominent role in assisting civilian populations. See Barnett, supra, 82 (*Empire*).

the 'delegates of relief societies for prisoners of war',[90] and the Hague Convention of 1907 again referred to 'relief societies for prisoners of war'.[91] The GCs of 1929 also referred to 'relief workers', though the actors delivering relief were not addressed in further detail. Prior to the Second World War, Leclerc-Gagné observes, there was no conception that all of the delegates delivering relief in war belonged to a common category.[92] The individuals who delivered assistance were typically connected to the relief societies they worked for, such as the ICRC (see Section 3.3.2) or the Young Men's Christian Association.[93]

During the First and—especially—the Second World War, a marked shift occurred with respect to practice on the ground (see next section). Civilian actors became more engaged in the provision of assistance, and civilians—particularly interned civilians and those in occupied territories—increasingly became the recipients of assistance.[94] This changing landscape was partially captured in GC IV of 1949, wherein IHL referred to the notion of civilian humanitarian actors providing assistance to civilian populations at risk.[95] Crucially, the GCs of 1949 introduced a right of humanitarian initiative.[96] No express mention had yet been made of a humanitarian actor category,[97] though actors providing assistance were said to be protected as 'persons taking no part in hostilities' under Common Article 3 to the GCs.[98] In the GCs of 1949, the relevant provisions on protection and relief were explicitly concerned with the recipient populations, rather than the actors delivering assistance.[99] The protection accorded to relief actors under these legal instruments may be viewed as akin to that provided to the general civilian population in armed conflict.[100]

As of 1949, neither the civilian nor the humanitarian actor had been defined in IHL. A second thread will now be woven into the account in order to introduce some complexity. Before the humanitarian actor was introduced as a category

[90] Article 15 of Final Act of the International Peace Conference, the Hague, 1899, Laws of Armed Conflicts (1899 Hague Convention).

[91] Article 15 of Final Act of the Second International Peace Conference, The Hague, 1907, Laws of Armed Conflicts (1907 Hague Convention).

[92] Elise Leclerc-Gagné, *The Construction of the Humanitarian Worker as Inviolate Actor* (unpublished PhD thesis, 2014), 52 (*Inviolate Actor*).

[93] Ibid.

[94] Ibid., 65.

[95] See, e.g., Article 142 of GC IV (obligations on the detaining power to assist relief societies in performing their tasks).

[96] Article 9 of GC I; Article 9 of GC II; Article 9 of GC III; Article 10 of GC IV. On the role of human rights law in this respect, see Ruth Stoffels, 'Legal Regulation of Humanitarian Assistance in Armed Conflict: Achievements and Gaps', *International Review of the Red Cross*, Vol. 86, No. 855, September 2004, pp. 515–546 ('Legal Regulation'). See also Article 30 of GC IV (the right of all protected persons to have access to 'any organization that might assist them') and Article 142 of GC IV.

[97] Helen Durham and Phoebe Wynn-Pope, 'Protecting the "Helpers": Humanitarians and Health Care Workers During Times of Armed Conflict', *Yearbook of International Humanitarian Law*, Vol. 14, December 2011, pp. 327–346, 334 ('Protecting the Helpers').

[98] Common Article 3 of GC I–IV.

[99] Durham and Wynn-Pope, supra, 336 ('Protecting the Helpers').

[100] Ibid., 334.

(such as it is) in AP I, IHL positioned one type of humanitarian actor as the object of special treatment and privilege.

3.3.2 IHL's Red Cross fantasy

I argue here that IHL's vision of humanitarianness was shaped by its fantasy of the Red Cross[101] figure as the paradigmatic humanitarian actor. This notion of an IHL fantasy draws on Mégret's description of IHL's treatment of warfare as a 'fantasy of sameness', wherein two opposing armies face each other on the battlefield, each in uniform and bearing arms.[102]

Today, the ICRC enjoys international legal personality, and a range of privileges and immunities are ascribed to it under international and domestic law.[103] The ICRC has been described as a hybrid between a classic international—or intergovernmental—organization and an NGO.[104] Returning briefly to Dunant's experience at Solferino, Dunant imagined a Red Cross movement that would promote and safeguard humanitarian ideals.[105] The Red Cross actor materialized in early IHL instruments as a twinkle in Dunant's eye, informing the 1864 Geneva Convention and securing the Red Cross figure as the touchstone of humanitarian assistance.[106] As noted earlier, the Red Cross emblem was the only humanitarian symbol accorded legal protection at the Geneva Conferences of 1863–64. The symbols of other humanitarian actors are examined in Section 3.3.3, below.

Focusing on the GCs of 1949 for a moment, the Red Cross figure is treated as the benchmark for humanitarian relief in a number of ways. Common Article 3 of the GCs refers to an impartial humanitarian body 'such as' the ICRC.[107] Article 63 of

[101] This refers to the ICRC, the International Federation of the Red Cross (IFRC), and the Red Cross national societies.

[102] Frédéric Mégret, 'From "Savages" to "Unlawful Combatants": A Postcolonial Look at International Humanitarian Law's "Other"', in Anne Orford (ed.), *International Law and its Others* (Cambridge: Cambridge University Press, 2006), pp. 265–317, 307 ('IHL's Other').

[103] On the ICRC's international legal personality, see Knut Dormann and Louis Maresca, 'The ICRC and its Contribution to the Development of IHL in Specialized Instruments', *Chicago Journal of International Law*, Vol. 5, No. 1, 2004–5, pp. 217–232, 217 ('The ICRC'). See also: Article 4 of AP I (ICRC serves as a substitute for the Protecting Power, where appropriate); UNGA, General Assembly Resolution 45/6 (1990), A/RES/45/6 (confirming ICRC observer status at the UN General Assembly); Els Debuf, 'Tools to Do the Job: The ICRC's Legal Status, Privileges and Immunities', *International Review of the Red Cross*, Vol. 97, No. 897/8, 2016, pp. 319–344, 324 ('Tools'); Bruno Demeyere, 'Turning the Stranger into a Partner: The Role and Responsibilities of Civil Society in International Humanitarian Law Formulation and Application', *Harvard Program on Humanitarian Policy and Conflict Research Thematic Brief*, 2016, 8–9 ('Stranger') (special privileges and immunities are granted to ICRC and related personnel by states on a case-by-case basis).

[104] Debuf, supra, 324 ('Tools'). While its mandate comes from states, the ICRC was founded in 1863 as a private organization named the International Committee for the Relief of Military Wounded. Since 1994, the ICRC has had international organization status in Switzerland.

[105] See e.g. Greenwood, supra, 22 (*Historical Development*).

[106] Debuf, supra, 320–321 ('Tools').

[107] Common Article 3 of GC I–IV.

GC IV stipulates that, in the context of occupied territories, the occupying power may not require any changes in the personnel or structure of relief societies such as the ICRC that could prejudice relief activities.[108] A common provision of the GCs also stipulates that, with the consent of the parties to the conflict, the ICRC 'or any other impartial humanitarian organization' may undertake humanitarian activities to protect and provide relief to civilian persons.[109] While these IHL provisions make space for non-Red Cross actors,[110] it is also the case that the humanitarian actors envisioned are Red Cross actors or (independent) organizations that resemble the Red Cross. Article 63(c) of GC IV opens out a bit further, according a right of humanitarian initiative to 'special organizations of a non-military character' that work to improve the living conditions of the civilian population.[111]

While this expansion of the category was accelerated with AP I (see below), the positioning of the Red Cross as the relief provider par excellence has been an unchanging feature of IHL. It is not altogether surprising that this was the case in 1949, given the state of practice on the ground at the time. What is striking is how IHL's fixation with the Red Cross continued in AP I, even though the practice of humanitarian assistance had begun to significantly transform. Of particular note, humanitarian NGO actors had started to emerge as key players in humanitarian responses prior to the codification of the APs. The role of humanitarian NGOs and UN humanitarian agencies—the two sets of non-Red Cross humanitarian actors addressed in this monograph—will now be considered.

The first recognizable humanitarian NGO, the Save the Children Fund, was formed in 1919 out of the experience of the First World War.[112] An exponential increase in the number of humanitarian NGOs followed the Second World War, with approximately 200 organizations forming between 1945 and 1949.[113] It was not until the Nigeria–Biafra conflict of the late 1960s, however, that humanitarian NGOs came to truly dominate the international response.[114] De Waal describes the experience in Biafra as both totem and taboo for humanitarian NGOs.[115] It was a ground-breaking logistical effort that demanded considerable courage, but humanitarian actors also found themselves mired in ethical issues relating to the

[108] Art 63(a)(b) of GC IV.

[109] Article 9 of GC I–II/Article 10 of GC IV.

[110] As pointed out in Kate Mackintosh, 'Beyond the Red Cross: The Protection of Independent Humanitarian Organizations and their Staff in International Humanitarian Law', *International Review of the Red Cross*, Vol. 89, No. 865, 2007, pp. 113–130, 115–116 ('Beyond the Red Cross').

[111] Article 63(c) of GC IV.

[112] See Peter Walker and Daniel Maxwell, *Shaping the Humanitarian World* (London: Routledge, 2009), 25 (*Shaping*).

[113] Barnett, supra, 112 (*Empire*).

[114] Alex de Waal, *Famine Crimes: Politics and the Disaster Relief Industry in Africa* (Oxford: James Currey, 1997), 73 (*Famine Crimes*). The UN's involvement in Biafra was marginal, in large part because the conflict was initially categorized as an internal conflict. See Mie Vestergaard, 'Biafra, 1967–1970: Ethical Dilemmas of Humanitarian Relief', *Online Atlas on the History of Humanitarianism and Human Rights* ('Biafra'). Available at: http://hhr-atlas.ieg-mainz.de/articles/vestergaard-biafra.

[115] de Waal, supra, 72–73 (*Famine Crimes*).

diversion of aid and the prolonging of the war.[116] The Biafra conflict was widely publicized and captured the attention of the international community. Media coverage not only highlighted the impact of the famine and the conflict, but it also showcased the role of non-state actors in the humanitarian response.[117] Although the ICRC had, by this time, long been active in its work as IHL guardian and in delivering material relief to wounded soldiers and prisoners of war, Biafra marked its first large-scale relief operation.[118] Perceived shortcomings in the ICRC's handling of this response—particularly the way in which it had interpreted its commitment to neutrality—also galvanized the formation of MSF in 1971.[119] Despite this surge of engagement in the delivery of assistance by humanitarian NGOs, no direct mention of them was made in the APs of 1977.

Many of the UN humanitarian agencies that make routine appearances in this monograph have their antecedents in the (post-) Second World War era. The UN Relief and Rehabilitation Administration (UNRRA), whose activities peaked in the mid 1940s, was subsequently split into separate agencies, including UNICEF and what eventually became UNHCR.[120] WFP emerged in the 1960s as a multilateral experiment in providing food aid; the UN's coordinating body for humanitarian relief, the Office of the UN Disaster Relief Coordinator (UNDRO), was established in 1971. Partly in response to coordination failures in Biafra, UNDRO was given a mandate to mobilize, direct, and co-ordinate international relief efforts and assist with disaster-management planning, with a focus on peacetime operations.[121] Its contemporary iteration, the (non-operational) coordinating agency UN OCHA, works in natural disasters and armed conflicts under the rubric of 'complex emergencies'.

The emergence of these various UN humanitarian players has, overall, met with a different reception in international law than has the emergence of NGOs. Some agencies, like OCHA, come into being through UN General Assembly Resolutions. As noted previously, dedicated international legal conventions also address the protection of UN personnel and the inviolability of premises.[122] Nonetheless, these UN humanitarian agencies share something with humanitarian NGOs: their

[116] Ibid.

[117] Kevin O'Sullivan, 'Humanitarian Encounters: Biafra, NGOs and Imaginings of the Third World in Britain and Ireland, 1967–70', *Journal of Genocide Research*, Vol. 16, No. 2–3, 2014, pp. 299–355, 299 ('Humanitarian Encounters: Biafra').

[118] de Waal, supra (*Famine Crimes*), 67–68 (*Famine Crimes*).

[119] Ibid., 76. See also Eleanor Davey, 'Famine, Aid and Ideology: The Political Activism of Médecins Sans Frontières in the 1980s', *French Historical Studies*, Vol. 34, No. 3, 2011, pp. 529–558 ('Famine').

[120] Davey, supra, 9 ('History').

[121] Mark E. Allen, Zakaria Sibahi, and Earl D. Sohm, *Evaluation of the Office of the United Nations Disaster Relief Coordinator*, JIU/REP/80/11, 1980 ('Evaluation'). Available at: https://www.unjiu.org/sites/www.unjiu.org/files/jiu_document_files/products/en/reports-notes/JIU%20Products/JIU_REP_1980_11_English.pdf.

[122] See Section 2.3.1.

legibility as humanitarians depends on their successful approximation of the Red Cross figure.

In proposing that IHL projects a Red Cross fantasy, I do not mean to suggest that restricting the boundaries of the humanitarian actor category is inherently problematic. There might be very good reasons for ruling out the participation of certain kinds of players, as well as particular modalities of assistance. The claim being advanced is simply that many non-Red Cross actors—who, collectively, carry out the bulk of humanitarian assistance today[123]—are not legible as humanitarians in IHL. In the next section, I suggest that when non-Red Cross actors exert themselves to demonstrate their likeness to Red Cross actors, they keep the Red Cross fantasy in circulation.

3.3.3 Humanitarian principles, signs, and symbols

Much as anxiety about civilian status motivates everyday distinction practices, it is evident that humanitarian line-drawing is also concerned with embodying and safeguarding qualities of humanitarianness. This section of the discussion contemplates what makes someone humanitarian, attending to humanitarian principles, signs, and symbols. Here, once again, the influence of the Red Cross ideal is palpable.

The traditional humanitarian principles

In addition to grounding their distinct civilian status in international law, humanitarian actors draw upon the traditional humanitarian principles of humanity, impartiality, independence, and (sometimes) neutrality to guide their work and assert their identity.[124] The ICRC commits to following the humanitarian principles in all of its humanitarian work, and these principles are enshrined in its Code of Conduct.[125] Hundreds of other humanitarian agencies espouse the same general

[123] The ICRC remains one of the largest operational international humanitarian organizations today, but most humanitarian assistance is delivered by non-Red Cross actors. See Jacob Kellenberger, 'The Role of the International Committee of the Red Cross', in Andrew Clapham and Paola Gaeta (eds.), *Oxford Handbook of International Law in Armed Conflict* (Oxford: Oxford University Press, 2014), pp. 20–36, 20. In 2007, approximately 58 per cent of humanitarian assistance was delivered by NGOs: Peter Walker and Kevin Pepper, *Follow the Money: A Review and Analysis of the State of Humanitarian Funding* (Boston, MA: Feinstein International Center, 2007). In 2015 and 2016, funding to NGOs as a proportion of total international humanitarian assistance (from private, governmental, and EU donors) was 38 and 35 per cent, respectively. This reflects only direct funds and does not account for all of the resources sub-granted to NGOs by other aid recipients, such as UN agencies. See Chapter 4 of Development Initiatives, *Global Humanitarian Assistance Report 2018*. Available at: http://devinit.org/wp-content/uploads/2018/06/GHA-Report-2018.pdf.

[124] The humanitarian principles are introduced in Section 2.1.1.

[125] Peter Walker, 'Cracking the Code: The Genesis, Use and Future of the Code of Conduct', *Disasters*, Vol. 29, No. 4, 2005, pp. 323–336 ('Code'); Hilhorst, supra, 353, 361 ('Dead Letter') (discussing the difference between the traditional humanitarian principles and the code of conduct).

commitment, having signed up to the Code of Conduct and subscribed to a Red Cross meta-narrative.[126] While this buy-in may bring humanitarian actors closer to an approximation of the Red Cross figure, it also sustains the Red Cross fantasy by holding this figure up as the model of humanitarianness.

This is not to say that non-Red Cross actors necessarily do a good job of simulating the Red Cross figure, nor that they all laud the Red Cross approach. There is considerable variation across the humanitarian community with respect to commitment to the traditional humanitarian principles.[127] As Koddenbrock observes, this is the case at the most abstract and rhetorical level, even before one attends to the complexities of on-the-ground implementation.[128] In contemporary practice, for example, many humanitarian actors do not claim to be neutral.[129] A commitment to humanity, impartiality, and independence is shared by a wide array of humanitarian actors, but it is evident that these terms mean different things to different organizations and the individuals within them. An MSF global perceptions study exposes the potential lack of ownership of international rules by local staff working for MSF,[130] and the present investigation uncovers a similar dynamic across other humanitarian organizations.[131]

This variation poses a challenge when attempting to discern precisely how the traditional humanitarian principles connect to IHL's principle of distinction and, more specifically, to everyday distinction practices. In the highly normative Intellectual realm, it might appear that these things are all in harmony—that the traditional humanitarian principles, together with the principle of distinction, set the humanitarian actor apart as a particular kind of entity. In theory, the traditional humanitarian principles are not designed for non-humanitarian actors.[132] Fernando and Hilhorst describe the principles as part of a distancing discourse that

[126] Katherine Davies, *Continuity, Change and Contest: Meanings of 'Humanitarian' from the 'Religion of Humanity' to the Kosovo War* (London: Humanitarian Policy Group, 2012); Urvashi Aneja-Bod, *Contesting the Humanitarian Regime in Political Emergencies: International NGO Policies and Practices in Sri Lanka and Afghanistan, 1990– 2010* (unpublished DPhil thesis, 2013), 7 (*Contesting*); de Waal, supra, 135 (*Famine Crimes*).

[127] On the Dunantist/Wilsonian typology, see Abby Stoddard, 'Humanitarian NGOs: Challenges and Trends', *Humanitarian Policy Group*, Briefing paper, No. 1, July 2003.

[128] Koddenbrock, supra, 57, 63 (*Humanitarian Intervention*).

[129] On neutrality, see Hugo Slim, *Humanitarian Ethics: A Guide to the Morality of Aid in War and Disaster* (Oxford: Oxford University Press, 2015), 70 (*Humanitarian Ethics*); de Waal, supra, 76–77 (*Famine Crimes*).

[130] Abu-Sada, supra (*Eyes of Others*).

[131] Field interviews with local humanitarian actors in South Sudan revealed that national staff of international NGOs also questioned the application of international legal rules to their work.

[132] Joost Herman, 'International Law and the Humanitarian Space in the Twenty-First Century: Challenged Relationships', in Andrew J. Zwitter et al. (eds.), *Humanitarian Action: Global, Regional and Domestic Legal Responses* (Cambridge: Cambridge University Press, 2014), pp. 11–32, 31 ('Humanitarian Space'); Kubo Macak, 'Principles of Neutrality and Impartiality of Humanitarian Action in the Aftermath of the 2011 Libyan Conflict', in Andrew J. Zwitter et al. (eds.), *Humanitarian Action: Global, Regional and Domestic Legal Responses* (Cambridge: Cambridge University Press, 2014), pp. 447–474, 447 ('Principles').

enables the defence of boundaries.[133] In Leader's words, they comprise the 'long spoon' that humanitarian actors use in order to avoid being corrupted by other actors.[134] We will see in Chapter 4, however, that the seeming compatibility of distinction and the traditional humanitarian principles strains in the training spaces and breaks down in the operational context. Such tensions are often concealed, I argue, because humanitarian actors cultivate ambiguity around the relationship between distinction and the humanitarian principles.[135]

The question of what to do in the event of a clash between distinction and the traditional humanitarian principles invites us to consider the legal status of the humanitarian principles. As noted in Chapter 1, the principle of distinction is at the centre of IHL. The precise legal status of the traditional humanitarian principles, in contrast, is subject to debate. The Harvard Program on Humanitarian Policy and Conflict Resolution (HPCR) takes the view that following the humanitarian principles is an IHL requirement,[136] and Kuijt maintains that adherence to these principles allows humanitarian actors to claim IHL protections.[137] These contentions can more easily be made out with respect to the principle of impartiality, because IHL explicitly requires humanitarian assistance to be impartial in character.[138] It is less clear, however, what IHL asks of humanitarian actors in terms of neutrality and independence. Further, the concept of humanity as a traditional humanitarian principle refers to a very specific commitment to helping those in need; it is not to be confused with the IHL concept of humanity that governs the conduct of hostilities.[139] Some scholars thus conclude that there is nothing legal at all about the traditional humanitarian principles. De Waal depicts the principles as having been developed in isolation from law,[140] and argues that following the principles

[133] Udan Fernando and Dorothea Hilhorst, 'Everyday Practices of Humanitarian Aid: Tsunami Response in Sri Lanka', *Development in Practice*, Vol. 16, No. 3/4, 2006, pp. 292–302, 300 ('Everyday Practices').

[134] Nicholas Leader, 'Proliferating Principles; or How to Sup with the Devil Without Getting Eaten', *Disasters*, Vol. 22, No. 4, 1998, pp. 288–308 ('Proliferating Principles'). For a primer on the wider relationship between humanitarianism and politics see Michael Barnett and Thomas Weiss (eds.), *Humanitarianism in Question: Politics, Power, and Ethics* (Ithaca, NY: Cornell University Press, 2008), Chapter 1 (*Humanitarianism in Question*).

[135] Leaving the principle of distinction aside, a recognized dilemma in humanitarian assistance is that between the principle of humanity on one hand, and a commitment to impartiality and neutrality on the other. Sometimes, providing assistance to populations in need (humanity) may require humanitarian actors to accept conditions imposed by the parties to the armed conflicts, thus violating neutrality and impartiality. Discussed in Barrat, supra, 344 (*Status of NGOs*).

[136] HPCR, 'Humanitarian Action under Scrutiny: Criminalizing Humanitarian Engagement', *Harvard Program on Humanitarian Policy and Conflict Research Working Paper*, February 2011, 4 ('Humanitarian Action').

[137] Emily E. Kuijt, 'A Humanitarian Crisis: Reframing the Legal Framework on Humanitarian Assistance', in Andrew J. Zwitter et al. (eds.), *Humanitarian Action: Global, Regional and Domestic Legal Responses* (Cambridge: Cambridge University Press, 2014), pp. 54–80, 66–67 ('Humanitarian Crisis').

[138] See Section 2.3.1.

[139] As explained in Chapter 2, the principle of humanity in IHL is balanced with military necessity in the conduct of hostilities.

[140] de Waal, supra, 153 (*Famine Crimes*).

constitutes a disengagement from IHL.[141] Koddenbrock surmises that the principles could be seen as 'bureaucratic operating procedures or even slogans'.[142] My own view is that the traditional humanitarian principles form part of a larger legal regime relating to humanitarian assistance,[143] but they are largely moral values that guide operational practice rather than strict legal requirements.[144]

It merits mention that when humanitarian actors deploy the traditional humanitarian principles, they do not always (or only) rely upon them for legal protection. Rather, humanitarian actors believe that these principles offer moral guidance, ensure services are provided appropriately, and afford them actual protection on the ground. The principles form part of a larger 'acceptance' strategy, which was mentioned above in connection with the NATO CIMIC training and CM-Coord guidance.[145] Humanitarian actors seek to demonstrate that their agenda is purely a humanitarian one, and that they are not implicated in the conflicts in which they operate.[146] The demonstration aspect is crucial here, for it implies an audience. A concern for perceptions is evident in claims that: neutrality is 'in the eye of the beholder';[147] impartiality and independence must be 'experienced and perceived by the outside world';[148] and impartiality is 'also a state of affairs which hinges on perception'.[149] The aim, then, is not just to follow the traditional humanitarian principles but also to be *seen* to be following them. This dovetails with the performative aspects of the humanitarian distinction project, and spotlights an important role for the signs and symbols of humanitarianism.

Humanitarian signs and symbols

Both physically and metaphorically, humanitarian actors use signs, symbols, and spatial referents in their everyday distinction practices. This discussion highlights differences in the legal protection of the symbols belonging to Red Cross, UN, and NGO actors and engages with two critiques of humanitarian symbols.

A first observation is that the symbols of various humanitarian actors receive different levels of protection under international law. It remains the case that there is no humanitarian symbol more powerful or widely recognized than the Red Cross emblem.[150] The special treatment of the Red Cross emblem in IHL both emerges

[141] Ibid., 134.
[142] Koddenbrock, supra, 63 (*Humanitarian Intervention*).
[143] As per Aneja-Bod, supra (*Contesting*).
[144] Accounts that treat the principles as 'quasi-legal' include Herman, supra, 31 ('Humanitarian Space'). See also Mačák, supra, 447 ('Principles').
[145] See Section 2.3.2 and 3.2.1.
[146] Mackintosh, supra, 129 ('Beyond the Red Cross').
[147] Hilhorst, supra, 358 ('Dead Letter').
[148] Daniel Thurer, 'Dunant's Pyramid: Thoughts on the "Humanitarian Space"', *International Review of the Red Cross*, Vol. 89, No. 865, 2007, pp. 47–61, 60 ('Dunant's Pyramid').
[149] Demeyere, supra, 20 ('Stranger').
[150] See Pilloud et al. (eds.), supra, 832 (*AP Commentary*). Note that the focus here is on the Red Cross emblem, specifically, rather than the sun, crescent, lion, or crystal.

from, and perpetuates, the Red Cross fantasy. According to the dominant narrative of the ICRC, IHL serves as the primary authority for the legal protection of humanitarian assistance; the Red Cross emblem serves as the visible manifestation of this legal protection.[151] On this account, the misuse of the emblem threatens to dilute the power of humanitarian symbols, by blurring the lines between persons and objects that fall within IHL's protective remit and those that do not.[152] The policing of the Red Cross emblem suggests that if the emblem were to be used by the wrong person or in the wrong way, there would be a threat of contamination. A crucial feature of the legal treatment of the Red Cross emblem is its exclusivity: humanitarian NGO actors, for example, cannot use this emblem and cannot expect the same treatment for their own symbols.[153]

Many humanitarian NGO actors express concern about this disparity.[154] Some even call for a new humanitarian symbol or legal emblem to visibly signify NGOs' adherence to the humanitarian principles.[155] While no such symbol has yet materialized, observers suggest that a number of processes and objects already serve as emblems for humanitarian NGOs. Examples range from organizational logo signs,[156] T-shirts, car stickers, and flags[157] to the standard operating procedures of humanitarian actors, including their manner of dress and the white Land Cruisers they drive.[158] Smirl's book-length account, *Spaces of Aid*, is particularly important here for its exploration of the architecture of aid and the spatial and symbolic aspects of humanitarian practice.[159] As a matter of international law, the emblems and logos of UN humanitarian actors are better protected than those of NGOs; the blue laurel wreath of the UN and its logo are explicitly protected under international law.[160] This does not put UN logos on equal footing with the Red Cross emblem, however.

[151] Rolle and Lafontaine, supra, 763 FN 10 ('Emblem').

[152] Ibid., 759–761. See Article 37 of AP I (perfidy); see also Articles 23 and 27 of the 1906 GC (misuse or abuse of the emblem). The UN has also condemned misuse of the emblem. See Article 9.7 in UN Secretary-General (UNSG), Secretary-General's Bulletin: Observance by United Nations Forces of International Humanitarian Law, UN Doc ST/SGB/1999/13, 6 August 1999. Available at: http://www.unhcr.org/refworld/docid/451bb5724.html. See also Rule 59 of Jean-Marie Henckaerts and Louise Doswald-Beck, *Customary International Humanitarian Law* (ICRC, 2005) ('ICRC Customary IHL Study').

[153] Koenrad Van Brabant, 'Operational Security Management in Violent Environments', *Humanitarian Policy Network Good Practice Review*, June 2000, 336 ('Security Management'); Demeyere, supra, 11 ('Stranger').

[154] Demeyere, supra, 11 ('Stranger'). See also Rolle and Lafontaine, supra ('Emblem'). Mackintosh, supra, 41 ('Beyond the Red Cross').

[155] Mackintosh, supra, 126 ('Beyond the Red Cross').

[156] Linda Polman, *War Games: The Story of Aid and War in Modern Times* (London: Viking, 2011), 20 (*War Games*).

[157] Nicholas Stockton, 'In Defence of Humanitarianism', *Disasters*, Vol. 22, No. 4, 1998, pp. 352–360, 358 ('Defence').

[158] Lisa Smirl, *Spaces of Aid: Post Disaster Relief and Reconstruction* (Chicago, IL: University of Chicago Press, 2015) (*Spaces of Aid*).

[159] Ibid. (focusing on the cases of the Aceh tsunami and Hurricane Katrina).

[160] See Chapter 2.

Setting to one side the differential treatment of various humanitarian symbols for now, two critiques of humanitarian symbols are relevant to the investigation of humanitarian distinction practices. The first critique pertains to whether the distinction humanitarian actors promulgate is an alibi for hidden interests. In an operational context such as South Sudan, the very same logos and emblems that humanitarian actors emblazon themselves with—as well as their equipment, facilities, and projects—to assert distinction are often used for marketing purposes and to achieve 'visibility' for donors.[161] It can be exceedingly difficult to discern where the effort to assert one's civilian status (or humanitarianness) ends and where economics-driven marketing begins. In some instances, the individuals who deploy these symbols may not be certain, themselves. Similar issues arise with respect to the demarcation and policing of 'humanitarian space'[162] by humanitarian actors. Although humanitarian actors claim that safeguarding this space is about serving the victims of war, sceptics counter that it is about organizational survival[163] or excluding outsiders from the humanitarian establishment.[164] These concerns surface in South Sudan, where humanitarian actors are accused of deploying distinction—in the IHL targeting sense—as a cover for turf spats and competition for donor resources.

The second critique that merits examination is that which claims that humanitarian actors treat the protection of humanitarian symbols as an end in itself, rather than a means to the end of helping populations in need. Hopgood picks up this thread, critiquing the ICRC's claim about the relationship between IHL and the Red Cross emblem (see above).[165] Hopgood proposes that it was not IHL, but the suffering of the victims of war, that originally empowered the Red Cross emblem.[166] This suffering, in turn, gave the law moral authority and served as a totem.[167] The true aim of policing the emblem, he alleges, is not to preserve the emblem's protective functioning, as the ICRC claims.[168] Rather, it is to uphold the sacred value of the symbol itself.[169] The mischief here is that protecting the

[161] On humanitarian branding and marketing, see: Anne Vestergaard, 'Humanitarian Branding and the Media: The Case of Amnesty International', *Copenhagen Business School*, Working paper, No. 81, 2006 ('Branding'); Leclerc-Gagné, supra, 59–60 ('Inviolate Actor'); Cooley and Ron, supra ('NGO Scramble'); Hugo Slim, 'Marketing Humanitarian Space: Argument and Method in Humanitarian Persuasion', *Centre for Humanitarian Dialogue*, May 2003 ('Marketing'); Krause, supra, 48 (*Good Project*); Koddenbrock, supra, 56, 63 (*Humanitarian Intervention*); Eric James, 'The Professional Humanitarian and the Downsides of Professionalization', *Disasters*, Vol. 40, No. 2, 2016, pp. 185–206, 192 ('Professional Humanitarian').

[162] See Chapter 1.

[163] Nicholas Leader, 'The Politics of Principle: The Principles of Humanitarian Action in Practice', *Humanitarian Policy Group*, Report No. 2, 2000 ('Politics of Principle'); Collinson and Elhawary, supra (*Humanitarian Space*); Hilhorst, supra, 357 ('Dead Letter').

[164] Collinson and Elhawary, supra, 3–4 (*Humanitarian Space*); Fast, supra, 6, 10 ('Aid in Danger').

[165] Stephen Hopgood, *The Endtimes of Human Rights* (Ithaca, NY: Cornell University Press, 2014), 38 (*Endtimes*).

[166] Ibid.

[167] Ibid.

[168] Ibid., pp. 38–40

[169] Ibid.

humanitarian symbol potentially takes on more importance than protecting the victims of war.[170]

All of this invites us to reflect upon what the signs and symbols of humanitarian actors actually represent. It may be that what is symbolized is actually a state of exception, inequality, or hypocrisy.[171] It is also well established that humanitarian actors are often targeted *because* of, not in spite of, the fact that they are humanitarian.[172] Humanitarian actors themselves are alert to this possibility, and there are some operational contexts in which they seek to make no impression at all. They remove branding and logos and drive in local vehicles, all in an attempt to maintain a low profile and achieve invisibility.[173]

The issues that arise with respect to humanitarian signs and symbols offer an entry point for thinking about the underlying motivations, and actual functions, of humanitarian distinction practices. In drawing attention to the Red Cross fantasy that circulates in IHL and in the practices of international actors, this discussion has highlighted a Red Cross exceptionalism. As the investigation proceeds, it grapples with humanitarian exceptionalism in the broader sense—encompassing Red Cross and non-Red Cross actors alike. The question of interest is whether distinction practices bolster such exceptionalism, serving mostly (or only) to protect and privilege the lives of humanitarian actors. This possibility surfaces routinely in the empirical discussion, and it is something that many humanitarian actors are alive to.

Conclusion

This chapter has explored who draws the line in everyday practice, demonstrating in the operational context and in training spaces that humanitarian actors routinely take the initiative to do so.

When humanitarian actors in the Kinetic realm urge other international actors to support their vision of distinction, they do not often call upon IHL's authority. Instead, humanitarian actors implore others to consider what the local audience sees; the 'phantom local' thus does most of the heavy lifting. While the Pedagogical realm is a step removed from the operational context, the need to appease onlookers is also emphasized at the civil–military training grounds. The difference at the training sessions, however, is that humanitarian actors routinely combine the invocation of perceptions with an appeal to law. Still, international military actors

[170] Ibid., 37. See also Krause, supra, 113 (*Good Project*).

[171] Smirl, supra, 95 (*Spaces of Aid*); Hammond, supra ('Holding Humanitarianism Hostage').

[172] Smirl, supra, 129 (*Spaces of Aid*); Roth, supra (*Edgework*).

[173] Antonio Donini, 'Afghanistan: Humanitarianism under Threat,' *Feinstein International Centre*, Briefing, 2009 ('Humanitarianism under Threat'). Available online at: http://fic.tufts.edu/publication-item/afghanistan-humanitarianism-under-threat/.

are quick to contest humanitarian attempts to dissociate from them. The former might even engage in humanitarian-like activities themselves, or activate their 'rush to the intimate'. One has the impression that these military actors are moving, dimming, and erasing the lines faster than humanitarian actors can draw them. These struggles find parallels in humanitarian–peacekeeper interactions in South Sudan, as we will soon see.

The final part of this chapter focused on IHL's treatment of different humanitarian actors and contemplated the qualities associated with humanitarianness. Advancing the claim that IHL projects a Red Cross fantasy, I have also proposed that non-Red Cross actors sustain the stereotype through their attempts to approximate the Red Cross actor. Flagging tensions between the principle of distinction and the traditional humanitarian principles, the discussion also explored critiques of humanitarian signs and symbols. The notion that distinction might be an alibi for hidden interests, or that humanitarian symbols might become an end in themselves, prompts an enquiry into the actual functions of humanitarian distinction practices. As we will see in Chapter 4, it is often humanitarian actors themselves who are asking these questions.

4
How is the line drawn?

Introduction

This chapter focuses on the *how* of everyday distinction practices, attending to signs, symbols, and modalities of distinction as implemented by humanitarian actors. Leaving behind the notion of a (bright) line, the chapter elucidates a dynamic vision of distinction characterized by floating signifiers of 'civilianness' and 'combatantness'. While civilianness is connected to innocence, harmlessness, and non-participation, combatantness is linked to danger, complicity, and participation in conflict. These qualities can be affixed to any individual in accordance with their appearance and behaviour, as well as the surrounding context. Crucially, qualities of combatantness might circulate not only around those who would be categorized as combatants in IHL, but also civilians. The 'phantom local' again plays a pivotal role, as an imagined local audience is deemed to pluck these qualities from the air and assign them to different actors. Once we entertain the possibility that civilianness exists on a continuum, the operating logic of everyday distinction practices becomes easier to grasp. If nothing is stable, and everything is a matter of degree, then individuals wanting to assert their civilian identity must struggle to claim the highest degree of civilianness available. Non-humanitarian actors emerge here as a potential source of contamination, threatening to taint humanitarian actors through proximity or affiliation.

Moving once again from the field, to pedagogy, to doctrine, the discussion begins in the Kinetic realm. First, in South Sudan, humanitarian actors implement distinction practices while living and working in close physical proximity to UNMISS actors. Humanitarian actors also grapple with decision-making regarding the use of military assets, which can facilitate their work yet undermine their civilian identity. As the 'phantom local' manifests in various forms, everyday practices in South Sudan highlight the visual life of distinction and showcase the importance of optics. Second, at the civil–military training grounds, international military and peacekeeping actors accuse humanitarians of enacting distinction in an unpredictable manner. There are deeper grievances in play here: these other actors want lines drawn in accordance with their own vision and priorities, and they are personally aggrieved by humanitarian distinction practices. Third, the discussion of the Intellectual realm delves further into the civilian concept. It canvasses historic approaches to protection in war, highlighting qualities that have traditionally been associated with those who do not fight. This section also

The Humanitarian Civilian. Rebecca Sutton, Oxford University Press (2021). © Rebecca Sutton.
DOI: 10.1093/oso/9780198863816.003.0004

considers the adjudication of the civilian category in crimes against humanity cases. In the *Martić* and *Milošević* trials at the ICTY, it is shown that civilianness is being pushed in two directions. The overarching point conveyed across the three realms is that when it comes to the practice of distinction, being civilian is more a matter of degree than categorical difference. The chapter closes by introducing three new civilian figures, all of which are unfamiliar to IHL.

4.1 The Kinetic realm

Two aspects of daily life in South Sudan impose serious operational pressures on the implementation of humanitarian distinction practices: humanitarian–UNMISS colocation in the PoC sites and the use of UNMISS assets by humanitarian actors. This two-part discussion contemplates these issues at some length, signalling the importance of the visual and spatial life of distinction in the Kinetic realm. As is shown, UNMISS actors accuse humanitarian actors of implementing distinction both too strictly, and inconsistently. It is evident that peacekeeping actors experience humanitarian distinction practices as a personal affront, a dynamic that has parallels in the civil–military training spaces.

4.1.1 Co-Location in South Sudan's PoC sites

Regardless of their entitlement to civilian protection under IHL, UN peacekeepers' combatant-like appearance and direct engagement with conflict dynamics leads humanitarian actors to desire separation. The decision to live in close physical proximity thus makes humanitarian actors anxious that their vision of distinction may be compromised before they even get out of bed in the morning. As a starting point for exploring the spatial dimension of distinction practices, consider the construction of a 'humanitarian hub' inside South Sudan's PoC sites. The delineation of a separate space for humanitarian actors represents a move to assert distinction within a discrete segment of a larger setting—the PoC site—in which distinction is already compromised. As humanitarian actors invest resources in asserting distinction in and around the sites on a daily basis, other international actors both resent their presence and interpret it as a tacit agreement to affiliate.

'Why do you eat in our cafeteria?'

As one UN civilian actor notes, the PoC sites in South Sudan are spaces where the UN mission 'comes closest' to humanitarian actors. Another UN civilian surmises: 'I've never seen another example where humanitarians and UNMISS work so closely.' This issue of physical proximity is also flagged by a humanitarian NGO actor living in one of the PoC sites. He is concerned that the mere fact of his

> presence on site undermines his organization's efforts to distinguish itself from UNMISS. An individual working for a different humanitarian NGO chimes in on this point. He explains that colocating with UN military forces leads 'fiercely independent' humanitarian NGOs to fear that they are compromising the humanitarian principles of neutrality, independence, and impartiality. It is adhering to these principles, he explains, that helps humanitarian actors demonstrate they are distinct. OCHA plays a pivotal role in mediating relationships between humanitarian actors and military actors in South Sudan, and one OCHA staff member contemplates how his own presence in the PoC site impinges on these efforts. In a setting dominated by machine guns and people in uniform, he often finds himself eating breakfast in the same room as the soldiers. He must subsequently impress upon these very people the importance of distinction. He wonders: 'How do you have that conversation?' His concerns appear to be well-founded. When I ask a UNMISS peacekeeper whether such casual proximity affects his thoughts about distinction, he directs his reply to an imagined humanitarian actor: 'If you are so concerned, why do you eat in our cafeteria, why do you drink our water, why sleep in our camp, why use our toilets?'

Since the conflict began in December 2013, many international humanitarian actors have been housed 'inside the wire' of South Sudan's PoC sites. Colocation with a UN peacekeeping mission in this manner is unusual for humanitarian actors; global guidance on civil–military interaction generally discourages humanitarian actors from colocating with military actors in armed conflict settings or complex emergencies.[1] In response to the outbreak of violence in 2013, however, the UN Humanitarian Country Team (HCT) for South Sudan approved the use of (military) force protection for humanitarian actors so they could be based in the sites.[2] This formed a blanket clearance for the use of military and civil defence assets (MCDA) by humanitarian actors within the sites, avoiding the need for case-by-case clearance, as is usually required.[3] Apart from this, general rules regarding the use of military assets as a 'last resort' are in place. In 2015, the HCT emphasized the need for individual humanitarian agencies to consider how their own decision-making on being based in the sites impacts on other humanitarians. Humanitarians must inform it of future decisions to colocate in the sites, the HCT

[1] South Sudan Civil–Military Advisory Group, *Guidelines for the Coordination between Humanitarian Actors and the United Nations Mission in South Sudan (UNMISS)*, endorsed 6 December 2013 ('Humanitarian–UNMISS Guidelines').

[2] UN OCHA, 'Frequently Asked Questions: UN Humanitarian Civil–Military Coordination, Military Civil Defense Assets and the Use of Military Escorts in South Sudan' ('Humanitarian Civil–Military Guidelines'). See also UN, *Agreement of Division of Roles and Responsibilities between UNMISS and the Humanitarian Country Team in UNMISS POC Sites*, February 2014.

[3] 'Humanitarian Civil–Military Guidelines', supra; UN OCHA, *Guidelines on the Use of Foreign Military and Civil Defence Assets in Disaster Relief*, November 2007 ('Oslo Guidelines'). Available at: https://www.unocha.org/sites/unocha/files/OSLO%20Guidelines%20Rev%201.1%20-%20Nov%2007.pdf.

stated, as the behaviour of one agency 'may have an impact on the perception of the broader humanitarian community'.[4]

Enforcing distinction in close quarters

Being based inside South Sudan's PoC sites helps to ensure the safety of humanitarian personnel and facilitates proximity to populations in need—or, at least, to a subset thereof.[5] As one humanitarian actor states: 'We don't like the PoC site set-up, being associated with military, but we know that we have no other choice. Do we want to reach the people we want to reach?' Colocation in the PoC sites gives rise to problems of association on two levels.[6] First, humanitarian actors could be influenced through a close relationship or affiliation with UNMISS. Living with UNMISS actors might affect the way in which humanitarian actors position themselves with respect to the conflict in South Sudan, make operational decisions on a day-to-day basis, and select who receives humanitarian services. All of this could undermine humanitarian actors' ability to operate in an independent and impartial manner. Second, there is the concern for appearances. Qualities of combatantness hover around the PoC sites because they are guarded by armed UN forces, and a perceived humanitarian–UNMISS association could undermine humanitarian distinction. The prospect of the 'phantom foreigner' arises again here, as humanitarian actors worry that local onlookers will lump all international actors together.

A UNMISS civilian actor recalls lengthy conversations in the early days of the Bentiu PoC site about whether humanitarian actors would come there. One humanitarian NGO actor submits that humanitarian actors made the decision knowing that it would blur the lines and adversely impact local perceptions. For this individual, the blurring is between the 'humanitarian sphere' and 'military approaches to protection'.[7] Another humanitarian actor describes the PoC sites as a 'mélange', with principled humanitarian actors wanting 'to be as far away from the mission as possible'. Despite efforts to construct a separate humanitarian hub lying physically apart from the UN base, one humanitarian actor remarks: 'You can only separate so much—they are still all together'. Offering an extreme example of these overlapping spheres, Arensen documents how, in 2015, UNMISS established a new base inside an abandoned NGO compound in Leer, Unity State.[8] In addition to 'blurring the distinction between a military actor and humanitarians', this impeded the return of the NGO to its compound.[9]

[4] 'Humanitarian–UNMISS Guidelines', supra.

[5] A report on the 2013–2016 period shows that only 14 per cent of South Sudan's IDPs resided inside PoC sites. See Michael Arensen, *If We Leave We Are Killed: Lessons Learned from South Sudan Protection of Civilians Sites* (International Organization for Migration, 2016), 40 (*If We Leave*).

[6] This two-level account of association will be revisited in Section 5.2.2, where a SWEDINT trainer tells two stories from the field about how humanitarians become tainted.

[7] On differing concepts of protection between humanitarian and UNMISS actors see Section 3.1.1.

[8] Arensen, supra, 30 (*If We Leave*).

[9] Ibid.

Delving now into the role of perceptions, it will be shown that the conception of the 'phantom local' as an omnipresent observer coexists with daily engagement with actual interlocutors. Focusing first on the invocation of the attacker-perceiver in South Sudan's PoC sites, this is the figure most clearly connected to issues of targeting in IHL. As the head of one international NGO in South Sudan contends, it is the safety of humanitarian actors that is paramount. 'My biggest concern is safety and security of my personnel; that trumps everything, irrespective of what needs are. If I am unable to ensure their safety, my team members, then it's pointless to try to get the work done.' Rather than entrusting their security to the armed UN forces guarding the PoC sites, humanitarian actors work to convey to the attacker-perceiver that they are separate from UN forces.

A humanitarian actor who resides in the Bentiu PoC site says that managing the perceptions of nearby SPLA soldiers requires daily effort. He recounts an incident in which an SPLA soldier behaved menacingly towards him near the entrance gate to the PoC site. At the time, this humanitarian actor was standing close to the armed UN peacekeepers who guarded the site. He suspects that simply standing there put 'me and the peacekeepers in his head, as the same kind of thing'. Another humanitarian NGO actor residing in the same PoC site shares that SPLA soldiers have called him both 'UN' and 'military'. In an effort to mitigate this confusion, he spends a lot of time chatting to SPLA soldiers near the entrance to the POC site. '[If] something happened, I wanted them to know me.' Despite these exertions, he reports that a recent incident alarmed him. Upon observing an altercation between humanitarian actors and SPLA soldiers at the entrance to the site, he intervened and asked an SPLA soldier he was well acquainted with to tell his fellow soldiers not to 'threaten humanitarians'. To this, the first soldier responded: 'But you're UN.' The humanitarian NGO actor was aghast, imploring: 'You know me, you are my friend. Am I UN?' The soldier replied: 'Well, you are military as well.' The humanitarian actor pushed on, brandishing his civilian credentials: 'Do you ever see me carrying a gun?' Lifting up his shirt, he asked: 'Do I have an imaginary gun, an invisible gun?' Finally, he reminded the soldier that his humanitarian NGO 'has always been your friend, we always come here'. While this particular incident was resolved peacefully, the humanitarian actor concludes: 'That was a point where I was feeling a little close [to UNMISS].'

In this encounter, qualities of combatantness hover around the humanitarian actor, who is seen to have an inappropriate affiliation with armed UN forces. It is implicit in the commentary above that the SPLA soldiers have a negative judgement of the UN peacekeeping actors. Cutting the other way, humanitarian actors accuse UN forces of being too friendly with the SPLA. This is especially concerning because the latter are known to commit violence against the local population.[10]

[10] On violence against the civilian population in South Sudan, see Nicki Kindersley and Øystein H. Rolandsen, 'Who are the Civilians in the Wars of South Sudan?', *Security Dialogue*, Vol. 50, No. 5, 2019, pp. 383–397 ('Who are the Civilians?').

A possible UNMISS–SPLA affiliation might send the message that UN forces would not use force robustly to protect the sites—for example if SPLA soldiers were to breach the perimeter.[11] These are legitimate concerns, especially when considered in the context of evidence that UNMISS is failing to properly implement its robust PoC mandate.[12] One humanitarian actor highlights the optics of UN forces being linked to the SPLA: 'This is a big problem. IDPs see it, that can't be good …. There has to be some sanctity to the PoC [site]. I know it's porous as hell, but at least the visual has to matter a bit.' Note the transition here from violent actors to beneficiaries as the specific audience of concern. Humanitarian actors are apprehensive that, if IDPs feel unprotected, this will cloud their view of the humanitarian actors who are on site to provide services.

The way in which the beneficiary-perceiver, as a particular iteration of the 'phantom local', circulates in connection with distinction practices in South Sudan's PoC sites merits further attention. International humanitarian actors refer to the beneficiaries of their projects as a key audience—and the term 'audience' is one they employ—for the performance of distinction in the PoC sites. They want to ensure that beneficiaries can differentiate them from other international actors and trust them to provide appropriate services. When it comes to enacting distinction, one humanitarian actor asserts that the perceptions of beneficiaries matter above all else. For this individual, the 'element of distinction is purely from their perspective'. The accounts that follow here are fascinating from an IHL perspective, as they collapse concerns about the perceptions of local populations together with anxieties about targeting. This offers a striking example of the distinction vernacular.

International humanitarian actors emphasize that beneficiary perceptions vary significantly across the different PoC sites in South Sudan. The PoC site in Bor hosts the smallest population of IDPs. One humanitarian actor thus suggests that IDPs residing on site have a very good idea of who is who amongst international actors. Another humanitarian actor agrees: 'Civilians in Bor can tell you who everyone is …. They are a closed audience in a small camp that does not move in and out, they deal with only so many internationals or outsiders.' By comparison, the PoC sites in Bentiu and Juba host fluctuating IDP populations. In these larger, more porous sites, the prospect of a 'phantom foreigner' looms. The same individual who describes the Bor site as a small camp says that, in these larger sites, he 'would expect that people there have no idea who is with what agency and what they are doing'. A number of humanitarian actors at the Bentiu and Juba PoC sites are indeed distressed at the prospect of IDPs confusing them with the UN forces that guard the site.

[11] One example is the perimeter breach that occurred at the Bor PoC site in 2014. See Radio Tamazuj, 'Armed Youth, Uniformed Gunmen Attack UN Camp in Bor Killing 60', *Radio Tamazuj*, 17 April 2014. Available at: https://radiotamazuj.org/en/news/article/armed-youth-uniformed-gunmen-attack-un-camp-in-bor-killing-60.

[12] See Section 3.1.1.

One humanitarian NGO actor recalls being called 'Mongbatt' by IDPs when he first arrived. He suspects they mistook him for the Mongolian battalion of UNMISS, because the latter were the first foreigners present when the site formed. This resonates with Autessere's finding in the DRC, regarding the conflation of intervening military and civilian groups:[13]

> MSF and other NGOs have spent more than ten years trying to distinguish themselves from the UN Mission in Congo (the local peacekeeping mission, long called by its French acronym MONUC), but local people still call out 'MONUC, MONUC' when they see cars with MSF logos crossing through their villages.

In the account of the NGO actor who was called 'Mongbatt', qualities of combatantness affix to the humanitarian actor simply because he is present in the same physical space as armed UN forces. Another humanitarian NGO actor recalls how IDPs voiced anger with his organization after UNMISS announced there would be no accompanied daily firewood patrols out of the PoC site. Despite the fact that his NGO had nothing to do with this UNMISS decision, IDPs accused him: 'You don't help us anyway'. Such comments exemplify how a focus on distinction might engender a flattening of war-affected populations. Instead of examining whether the IDPs are being helped, the humanitarian actor who is consumed by worries about distinction fixates on whether the IDPs think he works for UNMISS. This is not to say that it is a bad thing for humanitarian actors to imagine how local actors see them. The narrower claim here is that, when enacting distinction, humanitarian actors sometimes treat the recipients of their services as less than three-dimensional.

These concerns about IDP confusion are more palpable in conversations with humanitarian actors working for NGOs, as opposed to the UN. One UNICEF staff member, who also resides in the large Bentiu PoC site, is confident that the visual cues his organization transmits help beneficiaries to distinguish UNICEF from other international actors. He elaborates: 'People look at [the UN] as very big, but people here are very quick to distinguish. They can tell you who runs the clinic, who provides medicine, who dug a bore hole.' Hearing these comments by the UNICEF staff member, a humanitarian NGO actor working in the same site balks. He counters that UN humanitarian actors fail to sufficiently differentiate themselves from the UN mission presence in the PoC sites. He suspects that many IDPs perceive UNICEF to be affiliated with UNMISS.

At the Juba office of a humanitarian NGO, the Head of Mission links distinction practices to the cultivation of beneficiary trust. 'If I give them a Puritab[14] to put in

[13] Severine Autessere, *Peaceland: Conflict Resolution and the Everyday Politics of International Intervention* (Cambridge: Cambridge University Press, 2014), 271 (*Peaceland*).

[14] This is the brand name of tabs for water purification.

their jerry can, they need to know it's not an anti-pregnancy tab or won't convert you into a Muslim. Any sort of misconception needs to be sorted at the beneficiary level.' Given that his NGO cannot reach the entire population of South Sudan, his aim is that, for 'the people we do reach, we are seen as someone who is there to work with them, assist in a dignified way'. The hope is that this reputation will be transmitted to other communities through word of mouth. He intimates that the perceptions of the beneficiary-perceiver rank above those of the authority-perceiver. If the GoSS requests a list of beneficiary names, for example, his organization must refuse. 'Again, it's a question of trust.' He believes that, when IDPs arrived at the gates of (what became) the PoC sites in December 2013, they approached his NGO for help because 'they knew we weren't perpetrators or military assets'. The staff of his organization always ask to wear his NGO's T-shirt, he adds, because 'they do protect us, people know that these guys provide water, etc. They immediately associate us with a need, which is not just felt, but also expressed'.

Building on the Chapter 3 discussion of signs and symbols, the function of the NGO T-shirt in this account demands scrutiny. Initially, this humanitarian actor talks about securing beneficiary trust. When he mentions the T-shirt, however, the goal shifts to protecting humanitarian actors. It is instructive to recall Hopgood's claim that the suffering of the victims of war imbues both law and the Red Cross emblem with authority.[15] When the humanitarian actor in South Sudan says that his organization's T-shirt protects staff because the symbol is associated with needs, the suffering of vulnerable populations grounds the humanitarian actor's humanitarianness and civilianness. Another humanitarian actor in South Sudan intertwines the safety of humanitarian actors with the quality of humanitarian programming. This person looks at the situation 'from the eyes of beneficiaries, because ultimately they will determine whether my intervention is successful or otherwise, whether my team is safe'. It could be that the protection referred to here is from the attacker-perceiver, whose perceptions are simply folded together with those of the beneficiary-perceiver. A further sentiment lurking beneath the surface might be that beneficiaries themselves pose a potential threat to humanitarian actors. It was noted earlier in this monograph that some humanitarian actors are indeed fearful of the persons they seek to assist.[16]

A final issue to consider here is that only a small proportion of populations in need actually reside within South Sudan's PoC sites. Arensen notes that, with the exception of MSF and the ICRC, 'the vast number of humanitarian actors have demonstrated a preference for establishing bases at the UNMISS PoC sites, as opposed to establishing operational capacity in the deep field, where humanitarian

[15] Stephen Hopgood, *The Endtimes of Human Rights* (Ithaca, NY: Cornell University Press, 2014), 38–40 (*Endtimes*').

[16] See e.g. Mark Duffield, 'Risk-Management and the Fortified Aid Compound: Everyday Life in Post-Interventionary Society', *Journal of Intervention and Statebuilding*, Vol. 4, No. 4, 2010, pp. 453–474, 471 ('Compound').

needs are particularly acute'.[17] He invites humanitarians to 'rationalize' their presence in the sites, as they would in global refugee camps or IDP sites.[18] In interviews for the present study, some humanitarian actors actively question the concentration of staff and resources within the PoC sites, voicing doubts about whether it is truly necessary to reside inside. In Bor, a number of humanitarian actors live 'outside the wire' because security conditions are deemed more favourable than in Bentiu or Malakal. Pointing to the looser arrangements in Bor, a humanitarian NGO actor in the Bentiu PoC site contends that humanitarian actors would achieve more by living outside the site. He thinks it is unnecessary to resort to the help of UNMISS 'unless there was a bunch of bullets—say I had to get to the airport'. He deduces that his colleagues are too risk-adverse and bureaucratic to find ways of working outside the PoC sites. A UN humanitarian actor asserts that more support from UN forces is needed for humanitarians to venture safely outside: 'There are places we want to go ... but we can't. We want to ensure safety and dignity of people in the PoC [site] but the forces can only do perimeter protection, not the details. It's very limited.'

Moving on, the perspectives of UNMISS actors confirm that humanitarian actors are right to worry that they have compromised distinction by residing in the PoC sites. Here, turf battles entwine with everyday distinction practices in intricate ways.

Humanitarian–UNMISS tensions

As noted, some humanitarian actors question whether it is truly necessary for them to reside in South Sudan's PoC sites. It turns out that many UNMISS actors, both peacekeeping forces and civilian staff, wonder the same thing. One humanitarian actor attributes strains in the humanitarian–UNMISS relationship to the trajectory of PoC site development after December 2013:

> My sense is that the mission, as a body, was caught by surprise with the emergency. Before, the base was airtight; they went out on missions. Now, suddenly, you have 20,000 people living in there, 200 humanitarians, everyone is taking your food, your shower, your place, so you get angry .... [UNMISS] couldn't see that this wasn't people's fault. I'm here as a humanitarian because of these 20,000 people, and they are here because of the war.

A humanitarian NGO actor reports 'huge fights' in the early days of the PoC sites, including an alleged incident in which UNMISS actors locked humanitarian actors out of the bathrooms in Malakal. He shares the story of a UNMISS engineer who

[17] Arensen, supra, 40 (*If We Leave*) (For the 2013–2016 period, 30 per cent of the humanitarian budget was spent inside the sites).

[18] Ibid.

took scissors and cut off a plug that was powering the small cluster of humanitarian tents on site. The engineer apparently told humanitarian actors that they could not simply show up and expect to be provided with electricity. The individual recounting this altercation says that he urged the UNMISS actor to stop cutting, entreating: 'You are talking like I came to your cabin in the woods and we're guests. Do you know why we are here? ... Do you know what will happen to you if we just leave?' At the Bor PoC site, a humanitarian actor has a similar message for UNMISS: 'You would not be able to do this without us.' He wishes UN forces would appreciate that, in the absence of humanitarian services, the physical protection that UN forces provide is for naught. He suspects that UN forces dismiss humanitarian actors in South Sudan as being completely disorganized.

Picking up the theme of the cabin in the woods, another humanitarian actor contends that UNMISS actors treat the PoC sites as a personal home. When humanitarian actors request an extension to a PoC site to make space for more IDPs, 'UNMISS doesn't see it as a programmatic purpose; it's as though you requested a piece of land to lay down on yourselves'. Although he reports that intergroup relations in the Bentiu PoC site are less fraught than in the Malakal site, he maintains that 'If there is a water flow [problem], if they have to switch off valves, they'll switch off humanitarians'. He also recalls that, in the site's early days, 'They would give you bad looks as a humanitarian when you would take a shower'. Then, 'you'd go to a meeting, they'd say, "These humanitarians, they don't know what they do, it's us and them"'. Matters are not helped by the fact that UN peacekeeping mandates have, in recent years, been interpreted as life-saving.[19] This leads to more overlap between the respective tasks of the two sets of actors.

The larger story being told here is one of hostility and resentment in the humanitarian–UNMISS relationship. The remarks of the last speaker merge the issue of water-hogging in the PoC site seamlessly with a coordination meeting at which UNMISS actors not only profess an 'us and them' mentality, but also claim that humanitarians do not know what they are doing.[20] These accounts provide important context for the OCHA actor's concerns about living alongside UNMISS actors (see opening vignette, above). The OCHA actor routinely finds himself surrounded by armed UN peacekeepers on site, sharing meals with them at one moment and trying to impress upon them the need for separation in the next. These dynamics acquire a new hue when one considers that these UNMISS actors might also view the PoC site as their own home.

[19] As reflected in comments of UN Secretary General António Guterres at a UN Security Council Meeting marking the 20th Anniversary of the PoC Agenda. UN Security Council meeting, 'Civilian Experiences, Needs in Conflict Critical to Creating Protection, Accountability Frameworks, Speaker Tells Security Council', SC/13822, 23 May 2019 (UN PoC efforts have 'saved countless civilian lives').

[20] While electricity cutting incidents and the like have abated since the early days of the PoC sites, the mistrust and resentment behind these stories was still palpable at the time of the field research in 2015.

When a UN peacekeeper is asked about whether this is the case, he confirms the OCHA actor's fears. He cannot fathom how humanitarian actors could feel so comfortable living and working in 'his' environment, if distinction is so important to them. In his view, humanitarian actors who reside in the PoC sites are no different from those who actively rely on UNMISS forces for protection or logistics. Their claims to distinction are weak, he argues, because 'they still use us'. Notably, this peacekeeper is more sympathetic when the ICRC and MSF wish to keep interactions with the military 'behind the curtain'. He explains: 'They don't want to face retaliations and people on the ground need them. People in need come first.' Suggesting that these humanitarians share certain capabilities, mentalities, and efficiencies with the military, he calls these two organizations the 'military of the humanitarians .... [T]hey are self-sufficient, they have planes, they go in in any emergency.' This UN peacekeeper ties humanitarianness to what is, in his view, the right kind of combatantness. Humanitarian actors who 'still use us' are, in contrast, seen to exhibit the wrong kind of combatantness.

This adds a further dimension to the claim articulated earlier about military actors not being aware of how their 'rush to the intimate' undermines distinction.[21] In South Sudan, UNMISS peacekeepers judge harshly those humanitarian actors who rely upon them, even as they work to get close to these same humanitarian actors. The next section addresses humanitarian actors who 'use' UNMISS by relying on military assets.

4.1.2 Military asset use

One form of the militarization of humanitarian assistance, explored in Chapter 3, is the direct engagement of military actors in humanitarian-like activities. Another variant, which is the focus of the present discussion, is the use of military logistical, security, and other resources by humanitarian actors.[22] Along with the choice to reside within the PoC sites, reliance upon UNMISS assets constitutes another way in which humanitarian actors in South Sudan actively participate in blurring the lines. Continuing with the exploration of how the line is drawn, this section organizes the differing humanitarian approaches to UNMISS asset use into two ideal types.

[21] See Section 3.2.2.

[22] Peter Hoffman and Thomas Weiss, *Sword and Salve: Confronting New Wars and Humanitarian Crises* (Lanham, MD: Rowman & Littlefield, 2006), 20; Hugo Slim, 'The Stretcher and the Drum: Civil–Military Relations in Peace Support Operations', *International Peacekeeping*, Vol. 3, No. 2, 1996, pp. 123–140, 124–125 ('Stretcher').

'You become tainted'

One day in 2015, a group of international humanitarian actors[23] takes a flight with UN peacekeeping forces in a UNMISS helicopter in South Sudan. According to the rumours circulating in connection with the incident, the humanitarian actors have not obtained permission from OCHA to take this flight. When the helicopter lands at its destination, the humanitarian actors embark on some humanitarian activities in an area where UNMISS peacekeepers are conducting a force patrol; UN civilian human rights monitors are also present, gathering information from the local population. The trip goes smoothly and the humanitarian actors return to their point of origin unharmed. As word spreads, however, the conduct of these humanitarian actors attracts the ire of the wider humanitarian community. Many humanitarian actors are aghast at the optics of flying with UNMISS peacekeepers in transport marked with the black UN logo, and delivering services in such close physical proximity to a force patrol. They deem this unsanctioned helicopter flight an ill-judged move that undermines distinction, putting all humanitarian actors in South Sudan at risk. Reflecting on the incident, one humanitarian actor is sympathetic to the impulse to reach populations in need. Nevertheless, he wishes his colleagues would consider the reasoning behind appeals to distinction. 'Why is it important for me not to board a UNMISS helicopter, why should I use a non-military asset?' The answer, he imparts, is 'you become tainted'. Amongst humanitarian actors, there is a small but discernible current of opinion that goes a different way. The fastidious commitment to distinction, some humanitarian actors assert, interferes with the alleviation of suffering. One humanitarian actor charges that the commitment to Do No Harm is mistranslated as Do No Good.

Questions regarding the use of military assets by humanitarian actors came to the fore in the 1990s, when humanitarian actors in Somalia, Rwanda, and the Balkans resorted to the use of military protection by local and international forces.[24] In terms of concrete benefits, these assets can prevent humanitarian actors from being soft (unprotected, easy) targets for violence by armed actors, and they can also help them gain access to populations that are difficult to reach.[25] Whatever the potential gains in terms of safety and access, Pugh observes that military asset use can also generate problems of association for humanitarian actors and impede

[23] The identity of the organization was widely acknowledged in private conversations but is not included here for reasons of confidentiality.

[24] Michael Pugh, 'The Challenge of Civil–Military Relations in International Peace Operations', *Disasters*, Vol. 25, No. 4, 2001, pp. 345–357, 352 ('Civil–Military Relations').

[25] Koenrad Van Brabant, 'Operational Security Management in Violent Environments', *Humanitarian Policy Network Good Practice Review*, June 2000, 74–87('Security Management'). See also Kate Mackintosh, 'Beyond the Red Cross: The Protection of Independent Humanitarian Organizations and their Staff in International Humanitarian Law', *International Review of the Red Cross*, Vol. 89, No. 865, 2007, pp.113–130, 122 ('Beyond the Red Cross').

adherence to the traditional humanitarian principles.[26] The association problems here are, once again, about perceptions as well as actual influence. Military asset use might, for example, incentivize the delivery of assistance to some segments of the war-affected population, but not others. As for the optics, reliance on UNMISS assets leads qualities of combatantness to swirl around humanitarian actors.

As discussed in Chapter 3, treating the humanitarian principles as a 'long spoon' or a 'distancing discourse' gives the impression that upholding distinction and implementing the principles go hand in hand.[27] While leaving some wiggle room at the level of abstract principles may enable humanitarian actors to defend a range of practices on the ground, there comes a point when it is impossible to uphold all commitments at once.[28] Daily decision-making about military asset use in South Sudan brings these latent tensions to the fore. As the principle of humanity requires humanitarian actors to address human suffering wherever it is found, this might entail delivering services in hard-to-reach places. In some cases, getting to these places safely requires humanitarian actors to use military resources, a move that potentially undermines distinction.

To capture the way in which humanitarian actors grapple with this dilemma in the Kinetic realm, this study characterizes humanitarian actors according to two ideal types.[29] The first ideal type takes a strict approach to distinction, treating it as a lynchpin of humanitarianness. These humanitarian actors narrowly interpret 'last resort' policies on military asset use and take a long-term view of the implications of their everyday choices for their future operations. For the first ideal type, distinction serves as a trump; this aligns with the paramount status of distinction in the civil–military guidelines canvassed in Chapter 2. The second ideal type is typified by a more flexible approach to the performance of distinction, treating it as a norm that should be balanced with other objectives. These actors typically take a short-term view of the consequences of their choices, and they ground humanitarianness in the humanitarian imperative. They view the first ideal type as out of touch with the values that should motivate humanitarian actors, while the first type faults them for being short-sighted. The split between these two types is

[26] Pugh, supra, 352 ('Civil–Military Relations'); Michael Pugh, 'The Role of Armed Protection in Humanitarian Action', in *Humanitarian Action: Perception and Security*, European Commission Seminar proceedings (Lisbon: European Commission Humanitarian Office and International Committee of the Red Cross, 27–28 March 2007).

[27] See Section 3.3.3.

[28] Koddenbrock makes a similar observation with respect to the traditional humanitarian principles, more generally. Kai Koddenbrock, *The Practice of Humanitarian Intervention: Aid Workers, Agencies, and Institutions in the Democratic Republic of the Congo* (London and New York: Routledge, 2016), 66 (*Humanitarian Intervention*).

[29] Some aspects of military asset use are also addressed in Rebecca Sutton, 'Operationalizing Distinction in South Sudan: Humanitarian Decision Making about Military Asset Use', in Matt Killingsworth et al. (eds.), *Who do the Laws of War Protect? Civility, Barbarity and IHL* (Cambridge: Cambridge University Press, forthcoming 2021).

brought into stark relief in episodes of decision-making about the use of UNMISS assets.

Two ideal types of humanitarian actor

The first ideal type of humanitarian actor in South Sudan proposes that, when deciding whether to use the capacity and resources of other international actors, the foremost consideration should be distinction. When it comes to declining offers to use UNMISS assets, a humanitarian actor of this type states: 'We are constantly challenged, negotiating, trying to explain to people why we do this.' Some of the people this message must be conveyed to, another humanitarian actor emphasizes, are fellow members of the humanitarian community. They might not understand that they should not rely upon or get too close to armed actors. The humanitarian actor who alleges that humanitarian actors become tainted by using UNMISS assets (see opening vignette, above) flags the fact that UNMISS has previously allowed the SPLA to travel on its flights. He contends that any humanitarian actors who now travel with UNMISS—and maybe even those who elect not to—are therefore compromised. This point is important: individuals who are several degrees removed from the decision of a particular humanitarian actor may still be seen to acquire features of combatantness. He elaborates: 'People will perceive us as part of UNMISS, which for some is code for supporting the SPLA.' The ultimate concern with using military assets, one humanitarian NGO actor argues, is 'we need trust, and to be distinct'.

As for the 'last resort' rules around military asset use, humanitarian actors belonging to the first ideal type advocate a stringent approach. One humanitarian actor is dismissive of colleagues who bend the last resort rules. He notes that some humanitarian actors say 'Oh, we use these assets because there's not enough donor money'—even though this is not an acceptable last resort scenario according to the rules. Those who adopt a more lenient approach are also faulted for yielding to the temptation of short-term gains. When humanitarian actors view rigid principles and guidelines as disabling, a humanitarian actor argues, they fail to understand that 'As [humanitarian] space collapses we can leverage this to negotiate access, ensure safety and welfare of staff'. One humanitarian actor recognizes that others tie humanitarianness to the need to reach vulnerable populations, at any cost. 'Yes, the humanitarian imperative is front and centre, getting to that place to provide assistance is paramount.' The problem, however, is that 'What is immediate, might not be best'. Another humanitarian actor contends that those who flout the civilian–combatant divide in South Sudan in order to reach war-affected populations simply 'haven't calculated that distinction has been compromised'. In these last few statements, the long-term time horizon does important work. These humanitarian actors do not dispute that alleviating suffering is central to their role. What they propose, however, is that relying on military assistance to help some people in need now might adversely impact both distinction and the potential to help more people at a later time. There may be a sleight of hand here, suggesting that no one is proposing distinction as a trump but that upholding distinction is simply one way to fulfil the traditional principle of humanity.

As for the unauthorized helicopter flight incident described in the opening encounter, humanitarian actors of the first ideal type propose several possible reasons why the humanitarian actors may have boarded the UNMISS flight. Some float the possibility that it was done out of malicious intent or a competitive instinct, enabling the actors to get a 'leg up' over other humanitarian actors; however, this view tends to be rejected out of hand. One humanitarian actor suggests the motivation was mostly one of ignorance: 'They don't understand that by using these assets, it is detrimental.' Another humanitarian actor also blames a lack of knowledge: 'It seems some humanitarians here didn't know about the humanitarian principles—that they can't just jump into a vehicle with a UN logo on it.' This last commentator does not consider the possibility that the traditional humanitarian principle of humanity might well prompt a humanitarian actor to jump into UN transport to deliver services. As with the UN humanitarian actor quoted in Chapter 3 who trusts that arrangements will be worked out 'so long as humanity remains the guiding light', this fuzzy treatment implies that distinction and humanity are mutually reinforcing. A further issue to address is the assumption that ignorance may have driven the humanitarian actors to take the unauthorized helicopter flight. Cutting against this belief, rumour has it that one of the individuals who took the flight protested: 'These are not *our* principles.' The individual is said to have attributed the principles to OCHA, instead.[30]

When humanitarian actors belonging to the second ideal type navigate military asset use, their understanding of humanitarianness drives a wedge between upholding distinction and implementing the traditional humanitarian principle of humanity. Advocating for a more flexible approach, they position distinction as a good that must compete with other priorities. A humanitarian actor says of 'last resort' rules around military asset use: 'It's "last resort". It doesn't say "No"!' One humanitarian actor, who has repeatedly had his requests for humanitarian transport on a UN Humanitarian Air Services flight declined, laments that this has impeded his efforts to reach populations in need outside the PoC site. A faint hint of combatantness tinges his comments, as he proposes that these refusals 'took the weapons out of our hands, because we didn't have any other option. We watch UNMISS go for missions here and there, but we can't do it'. The insinuation that a UNMISS mission is akin to a humanitarian mission is also worth noting. This viewpoint clashes with that of humanitarian actors who emphasize the differing

[30] For a study of how MSF staff understand and interpret the humanitarian principles, see Dorothea Hilhorst and Nadja Schmiemann, 'Humanitarian Principles and Organizational Culture: Everyday Practice in Médecins Sans Frontières-Holland', *Development in Practice*, Vol. 12, Nos. 3 and 4, 2002, pp. 490–500 ('Organizational Culture').

definitions of protection, access, and so on between humanitarian actors and UNMISS.[31]

Whatever inequality exists between humanitarian actors and war-affected populations at the outset, it may be reinforced and exacerbated by humanitarian distinction practices. As humanitarian actors of the second ideal type in South Sudan point out, when humanitarian actors refuse to use military assets, they often do not elect to proceed without the assets—they simply do not travel at all. One humanitarian actor contends: 'It's really costly, the risk management is stopping people from getting out to where the need is.' Another individual says of the fixation on service delivery within the PoC sites, simply: 'It's a distortion.' From this vantage point, distinction inappropriately privileges the personal safety of humanitarian actors over the delivery of services to war-affected populations. In attempting to avoid being tainted by the combatantness that floats around military assets, actors of the first type are seen to relinquish their humanitarianness. The concluding chapter revisits these anxieties, conducting a micro-level examination of the two ideal types and exposing fluidity between them.

Next, we will see that the misgivings articulated by humanitarian actors of the second ideal type resonate with the views expressed by many UNMISS actors.

UNMISS perspectives on asset use

A UNMISS civilian actor working in the Bor PoC site praises humanitarian actors belonging to the first ideal type for their strict approach to distinction. However, the actor thinks that such humanitarian actors are few and far between, and that most have become 'too comfortable using UN assets and not all [are] following the humanitarian principles'. This sweeping reference to 'the humanitarian principles' obscures whether distinction and humanity are, respectively, in or out.

The view that humanitarian actors are too quick to use UNMISS assets is far from an isolated one. In October 2015, an NGO that was commencing activities in a PoC site reportedly demanded that UNMISS donate assets in support of its programmes.[32] UNMISS actors were apparently resentful of such incidents, and of humanitarian reliance on their assets more generally.[33] However, most UNMISS actors interviewed for the present study also contend that humanitarian actors are not comfortable enough with the idea of relying upon UNMISS. They see humanitarian actors who take a stringent approach to distinction as obsessed with the purity of their humanitarianness. Humanitarian actors of the second ideal type, in contrast, are admired because they 'bend the rules' to reach populations in need. One UNMISS peacekeeper alleges that humanitarian actors of the first ideal type treat proximity to UNMISS 'like cursing the prophet'. He believes that if a

[31] See Section 3.1.1.

[32] Arensen, supra, 39 (*If We Leave*).

[33] Ibid.

humanitarian actor wishes to travel with UNMISS to places in South Sudan where no one is providing services, they should be supported to do so. Another UNMISS peacekeeper decries those who take a 'fundamentalist' approach to enforcing the humanitarian principles, calling a particular humanitarian actor known for zealously enforcing distinction 'the Taliban guy'. This muddled treatment of the relationship between distinction and the traditional humanitarian principles shows that humanitarian actors are not the only ones cultivating ambiguity.

International actors in South Sudan express frustration with humanitarian actors who are inconsistent in their usage of military assets, and we will see in the Pedagogical realm that this closely tracks with views expressed in the training spaces. International military and peacekeeping actors cannot comprehend the logic that leads humanitarian actors to vociferously insist on keeping their distance at one moment, and to be ready on a whim to use military assets at another. One UNMISS peacekeeper recounts a story of an armed escort he helped to arrange in Boma State, South Sudan. Although humanitarian actors initially requested that he organize the escort, his efforts were undermined when the actors abruptly broke off from the convoy. He recalls: 'They just changed their minds and left the area, just screwed off. I thought, "What's the point of being here?" They are keen to go on their own, they moan about us, but then this happens.' What irks this individual is that, once humanitarian actors asked for the escort, he took this as an explicit agreement to associate. This presumption of an on/off switch for association chafes with the notion that humanitarian actors navigate subtle gradations and degrees of civilianness that can be acquired or lost. The mention of how humanitarian actors 'moan about us' also shows that some UNMISS actors experience distinction practices as a personal affront.

The same UNMISS actor who accuses humanitarian actors of taking a fundamentalist approach to distinction also reports that even 'the Taliban guy' will rely on UNMISS for evacuation in the event of danger. After sharing his personal misgivings about this, he is quick to add that, as a member of UNMISS, he recognizes that humanitarian actors may need to limit their reliance on military assets. He clarifies: 'We're fine with DPKO use being last resort.' This splitting of the individual perspective from the institutional outlook is detectable in the practices of UNMISS civilian staff as well (see Section 5.2.1). It is worth recalling here the humanitarian NGO actor residing in the Bentiu PoC site who says that he would rely on UNMISS assets if there were a 'bunch of bullets' and he had to get to the airport. This particular individual—whose diligent approach to implementing distinction in all other respects would likely attract a 'fundamentalist' label from the UNMISS peacekeeping actor—believes that distinction must give way in a life-or-death situation. While making an exception for cases of evacuation is perfectly reasonable from his perspective—and likely compliant with international law—the UNMISS peacekeeping actor seizes on this reliance as proof of prevarication.

In sum, from the perspective of other international actors in South Sudan, international humanitarian actors try to have it all: they police the boundaries between actors, then overstep these boundaries when they deem it necessary.

4.2 The Pedagogical realm

Deepening the examination of humanitarian actors' vision of distinction, we now explore how humanitarian actors draw the line in the Pedagogical realm. Foregrounding the perspectives of international military actors, it will be shown that the performance of distinction by humanitarian actors can mystify outsiders.

This section is shorter than the Kinetic discussion that preceded it, and this is due to the nature of the civil–military training spaces as a site of study. In comparison with everyday practice in South Sudan, there is relatively less fine-grained empirical material available on modalities of distinction in the Pedagogical realm. It is those aspects of trainings that overlap more with the Kinetic realm—such as simulation exercises and stories from the field—that best illuminate on-the-ground line-drawing practices. The flipside of this, of course, is that the (more normative) nature of the civil–military training spaces affords a lengthier discussion of distinction in the conduct of hostilities.

4.2.1 The performance of distinction

When international military actors fault humanitarian actors for how they enact distinction, the underlying message is that military actors want to be in charge of drawing the line. If they were in this position, then they would not be subject to the proclivities of humanitarian actors. Of course, humanitarian actors do not see themselves as simply drawing the line on a whim. What others adjudge as equivocation is, for humanitarian actors, often a nuanced recalibration based on the changing nature of a situation—and, in many instances, the imputed perceptions of a local audience. Part of the problem here is the continuum of civilianness that humanitarian actors are promulgating, which relies not upon differences of category but instead of degree. Humanitarian actors are not drawing a line, as such, so much as they are hoping that qualities of civilianness will affix to them.

'We have magical front lines'

In a training session at CAMPO, a military trainer shares a story from Haiti where he offered to arrange a military convoy for humanitarian NGOs. Initially, the NGOs turned him down: 'The humanitarians refused to associate.' Subsequently, however, it became clear that there was no other way for them to travel safely and they changed their minds. All of the logistical arrangements were worked

> out and the necessary preparations were made. When time to travel ultimately came, however, the humanitarian NGOs 'fought over how much distance to have between the cars, because they didn't want to be seen with [the military]'. This dismayed the CAMPO trainer. He had viewed the agreement to join the convoy as an explicit decision to associate; he was incredulous that humanitarian actors would insist on avoiding an association that they had already agreed to. Weighing in, another CAMPO military trainer proposes that whether a given humanitarian request for distinction is reasonable is contingent on the pressures of the operational context. In a major conflict area with clear front lines, he understands when humanitarian actors say 'I do not want to mingle because my only protection is to be seen as non-partisan'. In less fraught settings, however, he thinks such refusals to mingle are misguided. He elaborates: 'It's hard when you say, "We have magical front lines that aren't real on the ground"'.

The following section highlights two grievances on the part of military actors, which concern the issue of how the line is drawn. First, military actors accuse humanitarian actors of taking an overly strict approach to distinction; humanitarian actors will not share information and refuse to be seen with military actors. Second, military actors fault humanitarian actors for being inconsistent in their distinction practices; the latter avoid the former, until they need their help. Whichever critique is activated, it is apparent that military actors often digest humanitarian distinction practices at the individual level and experience the enactment of distinction as a personal affront. As a point of clarification, the performance descriptors of 'strict' and 'inconsistent' are not offered here as iterations of the first and second ideal types discussed in the previous section. The focus presently is on the operating logic of humanitarian distinction practices, as viewed by international military actors.

The strict performance of distinction

The topic of information sharing is a contested matter in the field of military–humanitarian interaction,[34] and it is a key avenue through which distinction is addressed at all three civil–military training grounds. When it comes to dialogue, other international actors accuse humanitarian actors of instituting the bottleneck. To be sure, humanitarian actors often make no attempt to hide their reluctance to share information with military forces. Humanitarian actors cite fears that any information they provide could be used for military purposes,[35] or could more generally interfere with their ability to operate. While humanitarian actors also

[34] Humanitarian Policy Group, 'The Concept of Protection: Towards a Mutual Understanding', Humanitarian Policy Group and ICRC Roundtable on Civil–Military Coordination, December 2011, 9 ('Roundtable').

[35] Han Dorussen and Marian de Vooght, 'Putting Civilians First: NGO Perceptions and Expectations of UN Peacebuilding', *Folke Bernadotte Academy*, Brief 01, 2018, 5 ('FBA Report').

fault military actors for not sharing with them—for example, with respect to the 'caveats' under which some peacekeeping forces operate—the former are generally positioned as the withholding party in the relationship. As is shown here, military actors understand this reticence to share information—and to associate, more generally—to be fuelled by anti-military sentiment.

At the NATO CIMIC training, a humanitarian trainer outlines his organization's approach to dialogue with the military. He acknowledges that understanding the local context may require some form of proximity to international military actors, perhaps in order to receive warnings about dangerous areas. This depiction holds that, whatever risk is incurred by getting closer to military actors, the danger that is *averted* through such contact is of bigger concern. A number of NATO trainees still voice dissatisfaction with this approach. They view it as limited because humanitarian actors do not offer to share anything in return. At the SWEDINT training, a military trainee argues that humanitarian actors communicate poorly with other international actors in conflict zones. He suggests that this is because humanitarian actors lack appropriate training, but he also notes that such training might be for naught, as 'some don't care'. The insinuation is that the caginess of humanitarian actors stems from a distaste for military actors.

Drawing on his experiences in Afghanistan, one trainee at SWEDINT focuses on the example of the ICRC:

> I can see why they want to stay away from uniforms. The only way they could work in harsh places was because they weren't doing police, military, or spy [activities] .... So imagine if the Taliban sees the uniforms, especially foreign military, having connection with ICRC. They will think they are all carrying information, reporting on insurgents, and ICRC could no longer work there.

This trainee deems the refusal to share information and to be seen near people in uniform an appropriate interpretation of the demands of distinction. In this account, ICRC actors simply seek to ensure that their humanitarianness is not compromised by contact with actors who attract qualities of combatantness. A military trainee at SWEDINT further suggests that asking a humanitarian actor for information about 'bad guys' is like 'asking a journalist to reveal their source for a story'. If humanitarian actors provide military forces with information about a target and this target is subsequently hit, 'The rebels will know where it came from, and this puts them at risk'. His colleague at SWEDINT concedes this point but argues that humanitarian actors could at least engage in 'trusted information sharing'. They could, for example, pass along their assessments of the needs of local populations.

Other trainees at SWEDINT insist that, if the primary concern is the safety of humanitarian actors, then this would surely be bolstered, rather than undermined, by talking to military actors. One military trainee proposes: 'The situation has changed, this era of terrorism. Hospitals and NGOs themselves can be targeted.

So they need to talk to us, meet with us.' Another military trainee contributes: 'We never know where the civilians are going; it could be a rebel area.' Over at NATO, a military trainee has the impression that humanitarians simply think that 'as military we are going to harass them, for information, and nothing else'. In these last few accounts, military actors insist that the physical protection they can provide for humanitarian actors outweighs the risks engendered through information sharing.

The issue of withholding information flows seamlessly into the broader refusal of humanitarian actors to associate with military actors. A SWEDINT trainee laments that there is simply no relationship between humanitarian actors and military actors, because the former decline to meet. During the delivery of a group presentation at CAMPO, a police trainee mimics a military actor, performing robotic and machine-like moves with his hands. This performance draws knowing titters from around the room, but the laughter belies a deep-seated resentment. In subsequent conversation, a number of military actors express distress that others view them as mindless perpetrators of violence. A CAMPO trainer suspects that the operating humanitarian mindset is as follows: 'I never talk to you because you're a killing machine.' A trainee offers that he has no problem with humanitarian actors seeking to avoid association in the field, so long as it is for reasons he can understand. If it is simply done out of ideological motivations, however, 'then I am angry'. Another CAMPO trainee adopts his trainer's choice of words (see opening vignette, above) to mimic a humanitarian actor saying 'We don't want to mingle with you, you're military'. He cannot shake the feeling that humanitarian actors believe 'You're the killer and I'm the peace angel'. One military trainer at NATO proposes that humanitarian actors are driven away not by loathing, but by fear. He says that they are 'often instinctually scared of military and rank and uniform'. A military trainee at NATO corroborates this: 'at tactical level, NGOs look afraid to talk to you'. This combination of fear and loathing resonates with a claim I will advance later in this chapter, namely that the distinction practices of humanitarian actors are driven by both heroism and vulnerability. Whatever the underlying reasons may be for the refusal to associate, a NATO trainee protests the result: 'It is a cold liaison!' Evoking the notion of the 'long spoon', a NATO trainer adds, 'What they will put in your face is the humanitarian principles'. This is a further instance of actors preserving ambiguity around distinction's relationship to the traditional humanitarian principles.

Evidently, military actors often experience humanitarian distinction practices as a move to push them away. However, as is demonstrated in the following section, military actors also fault humanitarian actors for pushing *and* pulling.

The inconsistent performance of distinction

The story told by a CAMPO trainer in the opening vignette, about the frustrated efforts he made to arrange a convoy for humanitarian actors in Haiti, has close parallels with dynamics in the Kinetic realm. As discussed earlier in this chapter,

UNMISS actors are perplexed when humanitarian actors try to delineate a 'humanitarian hub' in the PoC sites, or when they change their minds about participating in a convoy to Pibor. The CAMPO trainer's concept of 'magical front lines' offers a fascinating way of thinking about how humanitarian distinction practices appear to outsiders. The CAMPO trainer anticipated that, by joining the convoy, the humanitarian actors were agreeing to associate with military actors; but they surprised him by haggling over the distance between vehicles. In Haiti,[36] much like at the PoC sites, humanitarian actors likely knew their participation in the convoy already undermined distinction. Nonetheless, they sought as much separation as possible within the constraints of the circumstances. One might infer that the aim, from the humanitarian actors' perspective, was to preserve distinction to the greatest extent possible within a larger context in which it was polluted. Here again we see the dynamism of humanitarian actors' vision of distinction: everything is adjudged according to subtle gradations, and the aim is to claim the highest degree of civilianness available. From the vantage point of other international actors, however, the behaviour of humanitarian actors could appear erratic.

One SWEDINT trainee describes the relationship with humanitarian actors in conflict zones as 'non-symbiotic', and even 'parasitic'. This generates 'frustration and dislike from uniformed personnel'. His colleague elaborates, with more than a hint of exasperation, 'They want to stay far away from us when it suits them, but they use us when they want [something]'. Growing palpably irritated, he protests: 'How am I supposed to take you seriously when you reject me and don't want to talk to me, but ask for help a week later?' Sounding now like a spurned lover, he likens humanitarian NGOs to an ex-girlfriend who 'only calls when she wants to cuddle'. A military trainee at SWEDINT paints the following picture: humanitarian actors 'don't always run away from us, but they sometimes don't want to associate with us, but also sometimes they need us'. His colleague depicts the relationship with humanitarian actors as one of love and hate. 'When humanitarians have armed men around them, they love them because they need their help. But when they don't need them in this way, they hate them.' The reference to hate here is not so unusual or extreme. As Slim recounts, humanitarian NGOs who strove to distance themselves from US military forces in Somalia in the 1990s were 'just appalled' by the US forces.[37] At the CAMPO training, a military trainer addresses an imaginary humanitarian actor: 'First you don't like us, but then you want us when you need us later.' In his experience, the smaller the humanitarian organization is, the more challenging this dynamic. This alludes to issues of competence and professionalism, which are explored further in Chapter 5. Another CAMPO trainer

[36] While there is not scope to discuss it here, an important question for IHL lawyers would be whether distinction practices make sense in contexts that do not meet the definition of 'armed conflict' and thus IHL is not triggered.

[37] Slim, supra, 133 ('Stretcher').

chimes in, saying of international military forces: 'Shit hits the fan and, last minute, NGOs do want them.'

It is evident that, on some level, military actors take humanitarian distinction practices personally. From the perspective of these training participants, humanitarian actors do not legitimately draw on the protections afforded to civilians under international law. Nor do they simply try to appease the 'phantom local', avoiding contamination through contact with those who fail to embody the right kind of civilianness. Instead, they are like mercurial ex-lovers who love their armed partner when needed but are prepared to discard the partner until the inevitable point at which 'shit hits the fan' again. As in the Chapter 3 discussion of who draws the line, issues of power and control are activated. The possibility that humanitarian actors might deem themselves superior is especially enervating for military actors. Lest the impression be given that this is all one-sided, it will be shown later that military actors view humanitarian actors through the prism of their own grievances.

During their respective sessions at the NATO CIMIC training, two humanitarian trainers appear carefully attuned to such sensitivities. For her part, one trainer stresses that her organization is not anti-militaristic. She opines: 'Being a soldier is no less noble than being a humanitarian worker.' She goes on: 'We have nothing to say against war in itself.' Following the *jus in bello*, humanitarian assistance is solely concerned with 'who needs help because of the war'. When explaining why military and peacekeeping actors must leave their weapons outside humanitarian programme sites, she underscores 'Our problem is not with *you*'; it is rather with 'your uniforms, your colours, but activities too'. She adds: 'This is why it's so important to dialogue with you but make sure the distinction is clear.' The other humanitarian trainer also engages in a bit of relationship damage control. He says of the connection between the military and his organization: 'It's historic. From the very beginning we have had the same working environment. We've always been present during warfare.' He continues: 'So it's important to have a dialogue. You are operators but also potential victims: the wounded dead [this elicits snickers from the soldiers in the room] ... so you can benefit from a relationship with us.' This notion of the combatant 'operator' becoming subject to the care of humanitarian actors once wounded squares with the historical discussion of the humanitarian figure in Chapter 3. As noted there, Dunant's vision of humanitarian service at Solferino revolved around tending to wounded soldiers.

As elucidated above, other international actors sometimes experience the distinction practices of humanitarian actors as a personal insult. This might happen not only when humanitarian actors cleave to a strict implementation of distinction, but also when they enact distinction in what appears to be an erratic manner. When humanitarian actors strive to keep their distance, or change their minds about what distinction requires in a given scenario, other actors read into these moves and detect feelings of hostility as well as a sense of superiority.

4.3 The Intellectual realm

In this monograph, contemporary civilianness is associated with the following traits: harmlessness, innocence, non-participation, and, in a general sense, vulnerability. Iterations of these qualities circulate in the everyday distinction practices of humanitarian actors, implicitly or explicitly. At their full expression, these qualities comprise a civilian ideal so pure that it lies just beyond reach.

Building on the empirical investigation of modalities of distinction in the two main preceding sections of this chapter, this section considers how the line has been drawn historically and how it is drawn in contemporary crimes against humanity cases.[38] Leaving the humanitarian figure to one side momentarily, the focus is on the civilian–combatant distinction and the features that make up civilian identity. The aim here is contemplate qualities of civilianness, as they exist separately from their circulation in the everyday distinction practices of humanitarian actors. As is shown, the civilian is as degraded a concept as it is a celebrated one—a point conveyed here with respect to South Sudan. The frailty of the civilian ideal sheds light on why humanitarian actors might long for a special civilian status, an issue that will be addressed at the end of the chapter. The first part of the discussion examines traits that have historically been associated with civilianness, the second considers the treatment of civilianness in the adjudication of crimes against humanity at the ICTY, and the third introduces the 'civilian plus' and its corollaries.

4.3.1 The civilian in historical context

Delving into the historical treatment of those who do not fight,[39] this section conveys a sense of how the rationale for protection in war has changed over time. While there is not scope for an extensive historical discussion, a few observations will be made about the relevance of qualities such as innocence, harmlessness, (lack of) danger, (non-) participation, loyalty, and value to society.[40] Attention is drawn to the absence of a binary configuration for organizing protection historically, and to the shifting relevance of an armed/unarmed marker.

As Kinsella outlines in her genealogy of the principle of distinction, IHL's protections were originally designed for wounded, sick, or captured combatants.[41] The

[38] While this monograph does not focus on objects, another useful avenue of investigation would be the treatment of civilian objects in IHL and, more specifically, the protection of cultural property. See e.g. *Prosecutor v. Ahmad Al Faqi Al Mahdi*, ICC-01/12-01/15 (involving UNESCO heritage sites).

[39] The focus here is primarily on individuals who would be categorized as civilians in contemporary conflicts, rather than 'protected persons' under IHL.

[40] The concept of vulnerability is not addressed explicitly here, but it circulates implicitly in connection with many of these concepts. See Section 4.3.2 for a discussion of vulnerability in ICTY jurisprudence.

[41] Helen Kinsella, *The Image Before the Weapon: A Critical History of the Distinction between Combatant and Civilian* (Ithaca, NY and London: Cornell University Press, 2011), 122 (*Image*). See also Yves Sandoz,

justifications for contemporary civilian protection have essentially been 'grafted onto' these protections for combatants.[42] A more general point is that there has, historically, been a lack of attention to the civilian in IHL doctrine. It is the combatant, not the civilian, who has traditionally been at the centre of the development of the laws of war.[43] Some legal version of the combatant has existed since the twelfth century,[44] and the requirements for combatant status were laid out in early IHL treaties such as the Hague Regulations of 1907.[45] In contrast, the civilian was not introduced as a protected legal figure until much later. The general conceptualization of the civilian, as someone who should be spared from violence in war, emerged in the nineteenth century.[46] Prior to this, the term 'civilian' was employed quite differently to how it is used in the modern context.[47] For example, in the eighteenth century, 'civilian' referred to Europeans of the East India Company who were 'not in military employ'; thus, a civilian came to be understood as a 'non-military man or official'.[48]

Alexander also emphasizes that the civilian figure we are familiar with from AP I is a relatively recent invention. She frames the civilian as a twentieth-century project, with its immediate precursor being the private citizen—who was seen not only as passive but also as potentially dangerous.[49] During the First World War, ideology combined with technological advances to render the non-combatant population vulnerable, and yet also valuable as a target.[50] It was these twin features of vulnerability and value, Alexander proposes, that came to define the contemporary civilian figure.[51] This point will be revisited shortly in connection with a claim about the 'civilian plus'.

'Land Warfare', in Andrew Clapham and Paola Gaeta (eds.), *Oxford Handbook of International Law in Armed Conflict* (Oxford: Oxford University Press, 2014), pp. 91–117, 100–101 ('Land Warfare')

[42] Kinsella, supra, 122 (*Image*).

[43] Karma Nabulsi, 'Evolving Conceptions of Civilians and Belligerents: One Hundred Years after the Hague Peace Conferences', in Simon Chesterman (ed.), *Civilians in War* (London: Lynne Rienner Publishers, 2001), pp. 9–24 ('One Hundred Years').

[44] Kinsella, supra, 29 (*Image*).

[45] Article 1 and 2 ('Qualification of Belligerents') of Annex to Hague Convention (IV) Respecting the Laws and Customs of War on Land and its Annex: Regulations Concerning the Laws and Customs of War on Land, The Hague, 18 October 1907 ('1907 Hague Regulations').

[46] Kinsella, supra, 28 (*Image*). See also Michael Schmitt, 'Discriminate Warfare: The Military Necessity–Humanity Dialectic of International Humanitarian Law', in David Lovell and Igor Primoratz (eds.), *Protecting Civilians During Violent Conflict: Theoretical and Practical Issues for the 21st Century* (Oxford and New York: Ashgate, 2012), Chapter 6, 87–88 ('Discriminate Warfare'). Schmitt argues that the principle of distinction is introduced as a customary law norm in the St Petersburgh Declaration. Citing the Declaration Renouncing the Use, in Time of War, of Explosive Projectiles Under 400 Grammes Weight, Saint Petersburg, 29 November / 11 December 1868 ('St Petersburgh Declaration').

[47] Kinsella, supra, 28–29 (*Image*).

[48] Ibid., 29.

[49] Amanda Alexander, 'The Genesis of the Civilian', *Leiden Journal of International Law*, Vol. 20, 2007, pp. 359–376, 375 ('Genesis').

[50] Ibid., 365.

[51] Ibid.

Focusing now on the concept of innocence, the discussion considers how its meaning evolved and how protection in war increasingly came to be associated with an individual's harmlessness and non-participation in fighting. Historically, innocence was connected to internal sentiment. Going back to the fifth century, Saint Augustine of Hippo conceptualized innocence as an internal spiritual condition—one that would be difficult to ascertain from the exterior.[52] In *City of God*,[53] he elucidated a tentative guilt–innocence opposition upon which protection in war was to be based.[54] This did not map onto a soldier/not-soldier dichotomy. Instead, several types of actors were singled out for protection due to their imputed innocence: those not involved in fighting; those no longer involved in fighting; and women and children.[55] In practice, Augustine believed that very few individuals were, in fact, innocent. Members of those populations whose leaders had committed wrongs were seen to share the burden of (moral) guilt for their leaders' unjust acts.[56]

Over time, innocence came to be associated more strongly with non-participation in fighting and an individual's concomitant harmlessness. As articulated by Francisco de Vitoria in the sixteenth century, innocence could be determined through the presence or absence of objectively verifiable criteria such as conduct or the bearing of arms.[57] Those who were not involved in war fighting were deemed to pose no threat of harm and to lack responsibility for the war. Bearing arms triggered a presumption of guilt, as armed individuals posed an immediate threat;[58] being unarmed, on the other hand, attracted a presumption of innocence.[59] These were rebuttable presumptions, and the potential for guilt was always present.[60] Protection was conceptualized as a contingent concept—an approach that also found favour in the medieval texts of Honoré Bonet[61] and the writings of Hugo Grotius[62] and Emer de Vattel.[63]

Vitoria's interpretation of innocence continued to influence more recent iterations of just war theory. For example, Walzer described innocent people as those who had

52 Colm McKeogh, *Innocent Civilians: The Morality of Killing in War* (New York: Palgrave, 2002), 26 (*Innocent Civilians*).

53 Augustine, and F. R. M. Hitchcock, St. Augustine's treatise on the City of God (London: Society for Promoting Christian Knowledge, 1922).

54 Richard Shelley Hartigan, *The Forgotten Victim: A History of the Civilian* (Chicago, IL: Precedent Publishing, 1982), 36 (*Forgotten Victim*).

55 Ibid., 31, 36.

56 McKeogh, supra, 65 (*Innocent Civilians*).

57 Ibid., 85; Hartigan, supra, 90 (*Forgotten Victim*).

58 McKeogh, supra, 86 (*Innocent Civilians*).

59 Ibid., 87; Betcy Jose, 'Would the Protected Please Stand Up? Historical Ambiguity and the Distinction Principle', in Edward Lorenz, Dana Aspinall, and J. Michael Raley (eds.), *Montesinos' Legacy: Defining and Defending Human Rights for Five Hundred Years* (London: Lexington Books, 2014), Chapter 5, 58 ('Historical Ambiguity').

60 Kinsella, supra, 68 (*Image*).

61 G. W. Coopland, *The Tree of Battles of Honoré Bonet: An English Version with Introduction by G. W. Coopland* (Liverpool: Liverpool University Press, 1949) (*Tree of Battles*).

62 Hugo Grotius, *The Law of War and Peace (De jure belli ac pacis libri tres* (Amsterdam, 1625). Discussed in Kinsella, supra, 75–81 (*Image*). Hartigan, supra, 99 (*Forgotten Victim*).

63 Emer de Vattel, *The Law of Nations, or, Principles of the Law of Nature, Applied to the Conduct and Affairs of Nations and Sovereigns, with Three Early Essays on the Origin of Nature and Natural Law and*

done—and were doing—nothing too warlike so as to entail a loss of rights.[64] Despite this move to tie innocence to more objective criteria such as the bearing of arms, the concern with internal sentiment did not disappear entirely after Vitoria's time. An example of how it resurfaced later can be found in the 1863 Lieber Code,[65] which introduced a hierarchy of protection based on loyalty.[66] The Code delineated three sub-categories of unarmed citizens: loyal, disloyal (sympathizing with the rebellion), and manifestly disloyal (giving 'positive aid and comfort' to the rebellious enemy).[67] Those deemed loyal citizens were to be protected as much as possible from war, while war's burden was to be placed on those belonging to the latter two categories.[68] The logic was that the external sign of (not) bearing arms only mattered if it was not contradicted by internal sentiment.[69] What is noteworthy about the Lieber Code approach, for the purposes of the present discussion, is how it set up internal divisions within the category of unarmed actors. This connects to one of the central themes of this monograph, namely that international humanitarian actors also perceive and enact distinctions amongst unarmed actors.

While innocence increasingly overlapped with harmlessness and non-participation in conflict, the latter also developed as separate bases for protection in war. The notion of sparing those who are harmless featured prominently in canonical decrees and chivalric codes; in the latter codes—as well as various medieval texts—harmlessness was equated with weakness.[70] Under the canonical decrees of the tenth and eleventh centuries, certain classes of people, their property, and their actions were protected in war.[71] Without going into the details of these approaches to protection, what is striking is their lack of reliance on a civilian–combatant binary. In the seventeenth century, Grotius carried forward the idea from the canonical decrees and chivalric codes that certain classes of people should be spared in war. He counted among them women, children, the elderly, and those holding

on Luxury, Bela Kapossy and Richard Whitmore (eds.) (Indianapolis, IN: Liberty Fund, 2008) (*Law of Nations*). Available at: http:// oll.libertyfund.org/ titles/ vattel- the- law- of- nations-lf- ed. Discussed in Jose, supra, 59 ('Historical Ambiguity').

[64] Michael Walzer, *Just and Unjust Wars: A Moral Argument with Historical Illustrations* (New York: Basic Books, 2015), 146 (*Just and Unjust Wars*).

[65] Also known as General Orders, Number 100, *Instructions for the Government of Armies of the United States in the Field* (Washington, DC: War Department, 24 April 1863) ('Lieber Code'). Discussed in Kinsella, supra, 86 (*Image*); Alexander, supra, 363 ('Genesis'). For an argument that the Lieber Code is the prototype of contemporary IHL, see Geoffrey Best, *Humanity in Warfare: Modern History of the International Law of Armed Conflicts* (New York: Columbia University Press, 1980), 171 (*Humanity*); Stephanie McCurry, 'Enemy Women and the Laws of War in the American Civil War', *Law and History Review*, Vol. 35, No. 3, pp. 667–710, 2017 ('Enemy Women').

[66] Discussed in Kinsella, supra, 86, 172 (*Image*).

[67] Article 155 of the 'Lieber Code', supra; Emily Camins, 'The Past as Prologue: The Development of the "Direct Participation" Exception to Civilian Immunity', *International Review of the Red Cross*, Vol. 90, No. 872, 2008, pp. 853–881, 863 ('Past as Prologue').

[68] Article 156 of the 'Lieber Code', supra.

[69] Kinsella, supra, 86 (*Image*).

[70] Coopland, supra, 130 (*Tree of Battles*).

[71] Kinsella, supra, 26 (*Image*).

certain peacetime occupations such as merchants, clerics, and farmers.[72] The rationale for protection was grounded in these persons' (in)ability to fight, as well as their value to society.[73] A variation on this concept of value to society is introduced in Chapter 5, in connection with the special acts that humanitarian actors perform in armed conflicts. By the eighteenth century, the main criterion for claiming protection in war was non-participation in unjust acts. Vattel proposed that those offering no resistance and not participating in fighting—such as women, children, the aged, and the sick—should not be harmed in war.[74] Here, it was not individuals' sex, age, or occupation that formed the basis for immunity, but the assumptions these characteristics generated about their participation.[75]

Reflecting on this brief historical discussion, the lack of a binary configuration for organizing protection is evident. As Kinsella illuminates, there is nothing inevitable about the civilian and combatant entities; IHL defines these entities and thereby produces the subjects it claims to protect.[76] What is also noteworthy is how consistently a high burden to secure protection is imposed on those who are not engaged in fighting. It is only the most innocent, harmless, worthy, and removed individuals—typically women, children, and the elderly—who are deemed to merit protection.[77] Furthermore, the concept of contingent protection means that an individual's claim to protection can be forfeited if he or she behaves in a manner that is deemed (potentially) threatening. Without overstressing continuity between past and present approaches, many of these dynamics still play out in contemporary wars. Enduring debates about women[78] and children[79] who participate in armed conflict offer an example. While these individuals may initially be deemed innocent due to assumptions about gender or age, this calculus changes the moment they join the fight. Chapter 5 will revisit these traits of civilianness, elucidating the way in which they manifest in the figure of the humanitarian actor.

[72] Jose, supra, 56 ('Historical Ambiguity'); Hartigan, supra, 99 (*Forgotten Victim*).

[73] Jose, supra, 56 ('Historical Ambiguity').

[74] Vattel, supra, Book 3, Chapter 8, sections 72, 145, 147 (*Law of Nations*).

[75] Hartigan, supra, 108 (*Forgotten Victim*).

[76] Kinsella, supra, 190–195 (*Image*).

[77] For an argument that it is women who are the essential non-combatants or civilians, see: Ibid., 16; McCurry, supra, 669 ('Enemy Women').

[78] Judith Gardam, 'Women and the Law of Armed Conflict: Why the Silence?', *International and Comparative Law Quarterly*, Vol. 46, No. 1, 1997, pp. 55–80 ('Women'); Orly Maya Stern, *Gender, Conflict and International Humanitarian Law: A Critique of the Principle of Distinction* (Oxford and New York: Routledge, 2019) (*Gender*); Claire Garbett, *The Concept of the Civilian: Legal Recognition, Adjudication and the Trials of International Criminal Justice* (Oxford: Routledge, 2015), 92–93 (*The Concept of the Civilian*).

[79] Mark Drumbl, *Re-imagining Child Soldiers in International Law and Policy* (Oxford: Oxford University Press, 2012) (*Child Soldiers*); Alex Sinha, 'Child Soldiers as Super-Privileged Combatants', *International Journal of Human Rights*, Vol. 17, No. 4, 2013, pp. 584–603; René Provost, 'Targeting Child Soldiers', *European Journal of International Law Blog EJIL: Talk!*, 12 January 2016. Available at: http://www.ejiltalk.org/targeting-child-soldiers/.

Next, the treatment of the civilian–combatant distinction in international criminal law is examined.

4.3.2 Distinction at the ICTY: civilianness pushed in two directions

Shifting gears now to focus on international criminal law, the discussion moves to the courtrooms of the International Criminal Tribunal for the Former Yugoslavia (ICTY).[80] As is shown, a concept of civilianness circulates in the adjudication of crimes against humanity at the ICTY. In comparison with the civil–military training spaces and the operational context of South Sudan, the ICTY is a more traditional site of lawmaking in which lawyers, judges, and legal proceedings are positioned at the centre of things. While it is perhaps easier to see these actors, rather than their counterparts in the Pedagogical and Kinetic realms, as lawmakers, this study puts all of these actors on the same plane. The courtrooms of the Hague are thus treated as simply one more site at which the everyday life of distinction is produced. This is not to diminish the importance of criminal tribunals to the discussion. As a branch of international law, international criminal law (ICL) plays an important role in interpreting and enforcing IHL.[81] International criminal tribunals are significant forums where the figure of the civilian is constituted, articulated, produced, and disseminated.

As a preliminary point, the 'civilian' protected under ICL from offences such as crimes against humanity is not necessarily the AP I civilian accorded with target immunity in the conduct of hostilities.[82] This is examined in more detail in what follows, with the ICTY cases of *Martić*[83] and *Milošević*[84] used as entry points for a discussion of the way in which civilianness is pushed in different directions. While *Martić* introduces a potentially vulnerable combatant who might be protected like a civilian, *Milošević* places a high burden on civilians to demonstrate

[80] The Court was established under UN Security Council (UNSC), *Security Council Resolution* 827 (1993), [International Criminal Tribunal for the Former Yugoslavia (ICTY)], 25 May 1992, S/RES/827 ('UNSC Resolution 827').

[81] Claus Kress, 'Towards Further Developing the Law of Non-International Armed Conflict: A Proposal for a *Jus in Bello Interno* and a New *Jus Contra Bellum Internum*', *International Review of the Red Cross*, Vol. 96, No. 893, 2015, pp. 30–44, 33 ('Law of NIAC'); Sandesh Sivakumaran, 'Re-Envisaging the International Law of Internal Armed Conflict', *European Journal of International Law*, Vol. 22, No. 1, 2011, pp. 219–264, 232–233 ('Re-Envisaging').

[82] On different definitions of terms in IHL and ICL, see Sivakumaran, supra, 239 ('Re-Envisaging'). On why transposing the AP I definition of the civilian in ICL is potentially problematic, see Robert Cryer et al. (eds.), *An Introduction to International Criminal Law and Procedure*, 3rd edition (Cambridge: Cambridge University Press, 2014), 231 (*An Introduction*).

[83] *Prosecutor v. Milan Martić*, Case No. IT-95-II-A, Appeal Judgment, ICTY, 8 October 2008 ('*Martić* Appeal Judgment').

[84] *Prosecutor v. Dragomir Milošević*, Case No. IT-98-29/1-T, Trial Judgment, ICTY, 12 December 2007 ('*Milošević* Trial Judgment').

that they are worthy of protected status. These contests over civilianness impugn the idea of a bright-line distinction and a stable civilian category. As Garbett observes, the navigation of the concept of the civilian at the ICTY undermines the IHL premise 'that all persons are either civilian or combatant'.[85] Again, the fluidity that is revealed sheds light on why international actors might jostle with each other along fault lines that do not appear to exist in international law.

The case of *Martić*

First, in *Martić*, soldiers *hors de combat* were found to be victims of crimes against humanity. The implication was that qualities associated with contemporary civilianness—particularly harmlessness and vulnerability—could attach to individuals who would otherwise be categorized as combatants, entitling them to be protected like civilians. What is more, ICTY judges entertained the possibility that solders *hors de combat* could also be classified as 'civilians' for the purpose of crimes against humanity. While the ICTY Appeals Chamber ultimately rejected this latter proposition, it may yet see the light of day in other international tribunals.

The first issue to be considered here is the breadth of the civilian category in the context of crimes against humanity. While war crimes, as a category of offence, explicitly protect combatants, those rendered *hors de combat*, and civilians, crimes against humanity are primarily designed to protect civilians. In brief, crimes against humanity are systematic crimes that are committed as part of a general policy of attacking a civilian population.[86] In Article 5 of the ICTY Statute, this category of crime is constructed in such a way that certain underlying offences (i.e. murder) must be committed in the context of an attack directed against 'any civilian population'.[87] This latter requirement is referred to as the *chapeau* element, and it refers to an attack that is widespread or systematic in nature;[88] neither the nationality nor the ethnicity of the civilians against whom the attack is directed are relevant.[89]

This construction of the offence prompts questions about whether specific civilians must be the target of the underlying offence; whether and to what extent the civilian population must be composed entirely of civilians; and the meaning of the term 'civilian' in both contexts. These issues came to the fore in the trial and appeal of Milan Martić. Martić had held various governmental positions within the Serbian Autonomous Region of Krajina, and subsequently became Commander of the Republic of Serbian Krajina (RSK) forces. He was accused of—amongst other offences

[85] Garbett, supra, 149 (*The Concept of the Civilian*).

[86] Article 5 of the UN Security Council, 1993, Statute of the International Criminal Tribunal for the Former Yugoslavia (as amended on 17 May 2002), 25 May 2003 ('ICTY Statute').

[87] Ibid.

[88] *Prosecutor v. Dusko Tadić*, Opinion and Judgment, Case No. IT-94-I, Trial Judgment, ICTY, 7 May 1997, para. 727 ('*Tadić* Trial Judgment').

[89] William J. Fenrick, 'The Crime against Humanity of Persecution in the Jurisprudence of the ICTY', *Netherlands Yearbook of International Law*, Vol. 32, 2001, pp. 81–96, 86 ('Persecution').

perpetrated individually or as a member of a joint criminal enterprise—planning and ordering the shelling of civilian areas and the civilian population of Zagreb in May 1995. Some, but not all, of the victims of these attacks were soldiers *hors de combat*.

A key question that arose in the *Martić* appeal was how the term 'civilian' in Article 5 of the ICTY Statute should be defined. In the trial judgment, the ICTY Trial Chamber had found that defining the civilian too expansively would 'impermissibly blur' the distinction between combatant and non-combatant.[90] Following suit, the Appeals Chamber applied the narrow AP I definition of the civilian,[91] citing the 'fundamental character of the notion of the civilian' in both IHL and ICL.[92] The Chamber also noted that the AP I definition accords with the ordinary meaning of the term 'civilian', as a person who is not a member of the armed forces.[93] The ICTY had not always hewn to such a narrow definition of the civilian, however. In *Prosecutor v. Kordić and Čerkez*, the Appeals Chamber appeared open to a more expansive interpretation of 'civilian'—one that could include members of the armed forces placed *hors de combat*.[94] A number of ICTY trial judgments have also evinced a broader approach to defining the civilian.[95] In *Prosecutor v. Kupreškić*, the ICTY Trial Chamber held that the word 'civilians' in Article 5 should be interpreted broadly, 'the more so because the limitation in Article 5 constitutes a departure from customary international law'.[96]

The second key question in the *Martić* appeal was whether all individual victims of crimes against humanity must be civilians. Article 5 of the ICTY statute is silent on this point.[97] While retaining the *chapeau* requirement of 'any civilian

[90] *Prosecutor v. Milan Martić*, Case No. IT-95-11-T, Trial Judgment, ICTY, 12 June 2007, para. 56 ('*Martić* Trial Judgment'). A similar approach is followed in *Prosecutor v. Tihomir Blaškić*, IT-95-14-A, Appeal Judgment, ICTY, 29 July 2004, paras. 113–114 ('*Blaškić* Appeal Judgment'); *Prosecutor v. Stanilav Galić*, IT-98-29-A, Appeal Judgment, ICTY, 30 November 2006, footnote 437 (members of armed forces cannot claim civilian status) ('*Galić* Appeal Judgment'); *Prosecutor v. Mrkšić* et al., Case No. IT-95-I3/I-T, Trial Judgement, ICTY, 27 September 2007, para. 461 ('*Mrkšić* Trial Judgement').

[91] '*Martić* Appeal Judgment', supra, para. 299. Following *Prosecutor v. Dragoljub Kunarać* et al., Case No. IT-96-23/IT-96-23/I-A, Appeal Judgment, ICTY, 12 June 2002, para 91 ('*Kunarać* Appeal Judgement').

[92] '*Martić* Appeal Judgment', supra, para. 91.

[93] Ibid., para. 297.

[94] *Prosecutor v. Dario Kordić and Mario Čerkez*, Case No. IT-95-14/2-A, Appeal Judgment, ICTY, 17 December 2004, paras. 421–422 ('*Kordićc and Čerkez* Appeal Judgment'). The Appeals Chamber also held that the AP I definition of civilians and civilian populations was relevant to crimes against humanity (para. 97).

[95] See, e.g.: *Prosecutor v. Kupreškić* et al., Case No. IT-95-16-T, Trial Judgment, ICTY, 14 January 2000 ('*Kupreškić* et al. Trial Judgment'); *Prosecutor v. Momcilo Krajišnik*, Trial Judgment, Case No. IT-00-39-T, ICTY, 27 September 2006, para. 706 (*Krajišnik* Trial Judgment'); *Prosecutor v. Fatmir Limaj* et al., Case No. IT-03-66-T, Trial Judgment, ICTY, 30 November 2005, para. 186 ('*Limaj* Trial Judgment').

[96] '*Kupreškić* et al. Trial Judgment', supra, paras. 547–549. Citing *Prosecutor v. Klaus Barbie*, French Court of Cassation (Criminal Chamber), 20 December 1985, 78 ILR 125 ('*Klaus Barbie*'). For an argument that there was slippage in these earlier cases between the use of the term 'civilian' in the underlying offence and the *chapeau* requirement, see Joakim Dungel, 'Defining Victims of Crimes against Humanity: *Martic* and the International Criminal Court, *Leiden Journal of International Law*, Vol. 22, 2009, pp. 727–752, 743 ('Defining Victims').

[97] Discussed in Dungel, supra, 736 ('Defining Victims').

population', the Appeals Chamber found that, within the wider civilian population, each individual victim does not have to be a civilian in the IHL sense.[98] Accordingly, members of armed forces who have been rendered *hors de combat* may also be victims of crimes against humanity.[99] One question that *Martić* left unresolved is what would happen in a scenario where every single individual targeted in an attack failed to meet the AP I definition of a civilian. This was addressed in the *Mrkšić* appeal, wherein the Appeals Chamber found that a population composed (almost) entirely of those who were *hors de combat*—in that case, prisoners of war—did not meet the criteria of 'any civilian population'.[100] To date, most international tribunals have followed *Martić* in excluding soldiers *hors de combat* from the civilian population.[101] The Extraordinary Chambers in the Courts of Cambodia (ECCC) will revisit the issue, in two cases involving attacks by the Khmer Rouge against its own soldiers in the 1970s.[102]

In *Martić*, the ICTY Appeals Chamber established the category of a suddenly-vulnerable combatant who merits the same protection as a civilian. This was the case, even if the Appeals Chamber did not go so far as to move the bright line by including soldiers *hors de combat* in the civilian population. Considering the rationale for protection in contemporary armed conflict,[103] it is perhaps not so surprising that soldiers *hors de combat* have emerged as figures worthy of special protection. It was Rousseau who first articulated the idea that once a soldier becomes wounded, sick, or captured, he ceases to be an instrument of the state; instead, he becomes an individual with rights that merit protection.[104]

[98] '*Martić* Appeal Judgment', supra, para. 307. Citing, e.g., '*Blaškić* Appeal Judgment', supra, paras. 114–115.

[99] '*Martić* Appeal Judgment', supra, para. 307. The Appeals chamber found this to reflect customary international law (para. 309).

[100] *Prosecutor v. Mrkšić* et al., Case No. IT-95-13/1-A, Appeal Judgment, ICTY, 5 May 2009, paras. 27–44. The same attack was still prosecuted as a war crime.

[101] See *Prosecutor v. Germain Katanga*, Case No. ICC-01/04-01/07, Judgment pursuant to Article 74 of the Statute, ICC, 7 March 2014, para. 1102 ('*Katanga* Trial Judgment'); *Prosecutor v. Issa Hassan Sesay, Morris Kallon and Augustine Gbao*, Case No. SCSL-04-15-T, Trial Judgment, SCSL, 2 March 2009, para. 82 ('*Sesay* Trial Judgment'); Case 001(*Prosecutor v. Kaing Guek Eav*), Case No. 001/18-07-2007-ECCC/TC, Trial Judgment, ECCC, 26 July 2010, paras. 304–305 ('Case 001'); Case 002/01 (*Prosecutor v. Nuon Chea and Khieu Samphan*), Case No. 002/19-09-2007/ECCC/TC, Trial Judgment, ECCC, 7 August 2014 ('Case 002/01'). See also the more expansive approach of the International Criminal Tribunal for Rwanda: *Prosecutor v. Jean-Paul Akayesu*, Case No. ICTR-96-4-T, Trial Judgment, ICTR, 2 September 1998, para. 582 ('*Akeyesu* Trial Judgment').

[102] Case 003 (*Prosecutor v. Meas Muth*) Case No. 003/ 07-09-2009-ECCC-OCIJ, ECCC; Case 004/01 (*Prosecutor v. Yim Tith*) Case No. 004/07-09-2009-ECCC-OCIJ, ECCC. Compare the Amicus Curiae submissions of Rachel Killean, Eithne Dowds, and Amanda Kramer, 'Soldiers as Victims at the ECCC: Exploring the Concept of "Civilian" in Crimes Against Humanity', *Leiden Journal of International Law*, Vol. 30, 2017, pp. 685–705 (articulating a human rights-based definition of the civilian); with Catherine Drummond, Philippa Webb, and Dapo Akande, *Amicus Brief for Cases 003 and 004*, submitted to the Co-Investigating Judges of the ECCC, 19 May 2016 (finding a narrower approach more consistent with law).

[103] See Section 4.3.1.

[104] Discussed in Michael Barnett, *Empire of Humanity: A History of Humanitarianism* (Ithaca, NY: Cornell University Press, 2011), 79 (*Empire*).

Next, in the *Milošević* trial, we will see that establishing the civilian bona fides of a given individual requires more than presenting them as the combatant's opposite.

The case of *Milošević*

In the *Milošević* trial, the issue of attacks directed at a civilian population arose in the context of crimes against humanity and the war crime of terrorizing the civilian population.[105] I propose that the ICTY, in this case, imposed a heavy burden on civilians to demonstrate their worthiness of civilian status. They not only had to show that qualities of combatantness did not attach to them at the time of the attack, but they also had to make the case that qualities of civilianness did. The practices canvassed at this trial introduce further instability to the civilian–combatant distinction, setting high standards for appearance, comportment, and behaviour for those claiming civilianness. This is relevant for thinking about how international humanitarian actors imagine and assert their own civilian status, and why they might seize onto particular civilian signifiers in their everyday practice.

In *Milošević*, the Trial Chamber explained that the term 'civilian' is defined negatively to include any person who is not a member of the armed forces or an organized military group belonging to a party to the conflict.[106] The Trial Chamber also noted that, in some circumstances, it may be difficult to ascertain whether a given individual is a civilian.[107] The Chamber highlighted the general requirement that combatants distinguish themselves by wearing a uniform (or distinctive sign) and carrying weapons openly.[108] It went on to list other factors that may be helpful in identifying civilians, such as the activities they were engaging in at the relevant time, their age, and their sex.[109] When considering the legal status of one particular victim, the Trial Chamber cited an expert report stating that the victim's clothing 'would have enabled the shooter to identify her as civilian'.[110] The Chamber proceeded to comment on the victim's age (13 years) and height, concluding that these characteristics gave 'no reason to identify the victim as a combatant'.[111] When seeking to establish the civilian status of a particular witness, the prosecution in *Milošević* routinely emphasized victim characteristics such as age, occupation,

[105] '*Milošević* Trial Judgment', supra, paras. 875, 882, 921–924. The subsequent *Milošević* appeal is not covered in detail here, as the focus in this discussion is the handling of civilian status at the trial, rather than the overall outcome of the case. See *Prosecutor v. Dragomir Milošević*, Case No. IT-98-29/1-A, Appeal Judgment, ICTY, 12 November 2009 ('*Milošević* Appeal Judgment').

[106] '*Milošević* Trial Judgment', supra, para. 945. Citing *Prosecutor v. Stanilav Galić*, IT-98-29-T, Trial Judgment, ICTY, 5 December 2003, para. 47 ('*Galić* Trial Judgment'). This paragraph draws on Garbett's account and first-person observation of the trial. See Garbett, supra, 107–112 (*The Concept of the Civilian*).

[107] '*Milošević* Trial Judgment', supra, para. 945.

[108] Ibid., paras. 945–946.

[109] Ibid., citing the '*Galić* Trial Judgment', supra, para. 50. The Appeals Chamber in the *Milošević* appeal found no error with this approach. '*Milošević* Appeal Judgment', supra, para. 198.

[110] '*Milošević* Trial Judgment', supra, para. 353, citing P514, Expert report by Lt. Patrick van der Weijden, p. 43.

[111] Ibid. Discussed in Garbett, supra, 112 (*The Concept of the Civilian*).

clothing, and other aspects of appearance, as well as the individual's actions at the relevant time.[112] As Garbett observes, the defence rarely interrogated the civilian status of the witnesses who testified, except when they were young males—insinuating that their male gender and youthful age gave rise to the possibility that they could have been combatants.[113] Significantly, the civilians who testified as witnesses at the *Milošević* trial also claimed that they had not worn a military uniform or military insignia (as a combatant would have). Garbett identifies three further ways through which these civilians asserted their civilian status: they emphasized their choice to not engage in military conduct or operations;[114] they recounted their efforts to go about their everyday lives as normally as possible during the conflict;[115] and they spoke of a shared experience of the conflict, connecting themselves to others who were beset by the same threats of harm.[116]

At the *Milošević* trial, the establishment of civilianness required something more than presenting as the combatant's opposite. The emphasis on characteristics such as age, sex, and conduct summoned signifiers of harmlessness, non-participation, and vulnerability. When attention was drawn to the fact that a particular victim had been wearing a woman's dress, for example, femaleness was linked to notions of vulnerability, harmlessness, and a particular vision of civilianness.[117] Based on her observations of this trial, Garbett finds that international actors at the ICTY delineate a positive definition of the civilian to supplant IHL's negative one.[118] To do so, they introduce clear markers of civilian identity and draw on social characteristics of group membership.[119] Dinstein, for his part, views such efforts as an exercise in futility. He characterizes the attempt to identify unequivocal civilian markers as 'chimerical' and emphasizes the difficulty of ascertaining what constitutes normal life in times of armed conflict.[120] While Dinstein's point about the elusiveness of definitive markers is well taken, what is interesting for this study is the fact that international actors cast about for such markers.

While it should be kept in mind that the civilian figure in ICL is not always one and the same as that in IHL, the *Milošević* trial and *Martić* appeal show how qualities of civilianness and combatantness might affix to any given individual at any given moment. This is yet one more instance in which civilianness is detached from the civilian.

[112] Garbett, supra, 109 (*The Concept of the Civilian*).
[113] Ibid., 110–112.
[114] Ibid., 105–106.
[115] Ibid., 106.
[116] Ibid., 107.
[117] On gender and the principle of distinction, see Stern, supra (*Gender*); Kinsella, supra (*Image*).
[118] Garbett, supra, 98 (*The Concept of the Civilian*).
[119] Ibid.
[120] Yoram Dinstein, *The Conduct of Hostilities under the Law of International Armed Conflict* (Cambridge: Cambridge University Press, 2004), 143 (*CoH*).

4.3.3 Three new civilian figures

Having jettisoned the idea of a bright line in the present chapter, I now want to introduce multiple lines—or rather, a triptych—into this story. As the empirical material canvassed so far in this monograph shows, the everyday practices of humanitarian actors are underpinned by a vision of distinction in which everything is a matter of degree and subtle gradation. This invites us to think of civilianness as existing along a continuum, which I propose is populated by three figures: the 'civilian plus', 'the civilian minus', and the 'mere civilian'. While these strange civilian figures are presented here as discrete entities, the process through which an individual actor claims (or is assigned) one of these designations depends upon shifting factors of self-presentation, behaviour, and circumstance. My intention is thus to preserve the dynamism of floating signifiers so far as is possible, rather than to conjure imagery of inert statuses fixed in place.

At one end of the civilianness continuum lies a special 'civilian plus'[121] figure. This unfamiliar figure emerges when features of innocence, vulnerability, harmlessness, and non-participation attach to individuals who are already imbued with qualities of civilianness. While the civilian aspect of the 'civilian plus' figure attracts the same target immunity accorded to all civilians in armed conflict, the 'plus' provides an added layer of inviolability in a legal, as well as a practical, sense.[122] We might think here of the paradigmatic civilian figures, women and children—though a caveat is needed because even such individuals are routinely accused of participation. A better example, perhaps, is that of civilians under GC IV and AP I who are deemed especially vulnerable, such as pregnant mothers and young children. These civilians are accorded priority access to services and extra protections in IHL, beyond what they would have if their civilianness were to only assume ordinary form.[123] Recognizing that humanitarian actors face myriad risks while operating in armed conflicts, the 'plus' is intended to serve as a shield against those who would harm them.[124] At the same time, the 'plus' denotes humanitarian

[121] The term 'civilian plus' is not to be confused with Hilhorst's concept of the 'humanitarian plus'. The latter refers to humanitarian actors who engage in development activities that go beyond life-saving humanitarian services. In Hilhorst's conceptualization, the 'plus' indicates that the actor in question has overstepped the bounds of traditional humanitarian action. In the present study, the 'plus' sets the relevant individual up as a sort of super-civilian. See Dorothea Hilhorst, 'Dead Letter or Living Document? Ten Years of the Code of Conduct for Disaster Relief', *Disasters*, Vol. 29, No. 4, 2005, pp. 351–369, 359 ('Dead Letter').

[122] Practical and juridical aspects of inviolability are also discussed in Lisa Smirl, *Spaces of Aid: Post Disaster Relief and Reconstruction* (Chicago, IL: University of Chicago Press, 2015), 31, 40, 94–95 (*Spaces of Aid*).

[123] The treatment of different segments of the civilian population is discussed in Section 5.3.2.

[124] Iterations of the shield motif surface in the humanitarian studies literature. See Laura Hammond, 'The Power of Holding Humanitarianism Hostage and the Myth of the Protective Principles', in Michael Barnett and Thomas Weiss (eds.), *Humanitarianism in Question: Politics, Power, and Ethics* (Ithaca, NY: Cornell University Press, 2008), pp. 172–195, 172–174 ('Holding Humanitarianism Hostage') (humanitarian actors deploy the principles as a sort of armour); Larissa Fast, *Aid in Danger: The Perils*

virtue, which derives from the social value of their important professional role. It can thus be said that international humanitarian actors' bid for special civilian status is grounded in both vulnerability and heroism—qualities which are embedded in the figure of the humanitarian actor.

While humanitarian actors long for this especially pure civilian status, they frequently have to stave off charges that they are somehow complicit, dangerous, and participating in the conflict. In some instances, they may be seen to merit a tainted civilian status, that of 'civilian minus'. This combatant-like figure represents a civilian entity whose features of innocence, harmlessness, and non-participation are impugned. A straightforward example is the civilian who directly participates in hostilities, and thus poses a threat of harm to those engaged in fighting. In the moment of participation, qualities of combatantness attach to this individual, who can be targeted like a combatant. Humanitarian actors may attract a 'minus' designator when they overstep the boundaries of their role, as when they serve as 'force multipliers' or a second front in armed conflict.[125] Crucially, qualities of combatantness might also swirl around humanitarian actors when they engage in quintessentially humanitarian tasks, such as delivering services to those in need (who happen to belong to the 'other side'). Humanitarian actors who lack competence and credentials may also be seen as dangerous or complicit, even where they have done nothing explicit to compromise their civilian status.

Residing in the middle of the civilianness continuum, the 'mere civilian' is a default status assigned to those civilians who are not eligible for special treatment, yet who do not present any of the features of combatantness. The 'mere civilian' is not stripped of any core quality of civilianness, and, like all civilians, may not be intentionally attacked in accordance with IHL's principle of distinction. Nonetheless, this entity is relatively worse off than both the 'civilian plus' and the mythical civilian figure that would exist in a world in which all civilians are considered equal. International humanitarian actors desire more than 'mere civilian' status, believing that its expression of (ordinary, degraded) civilianness is inadequate to meet their needs. Recalling the discussion of humanitarian signs and symbols in Chapter 3, it is difficult to ascertain whether a given attempt to escape ordinary civilianness is animated by anxieties about targeting, or instead by other concerns—perhaps turf wars and intra-civilian competition. Indeed, the distinction vernacular that

and Promise of Humanitarianism (Philadelphia, PA: University of Pennsylvania Press, 2014), 111(*Aid in Danger*) (humanitarians expect that good intentions and good acts will function as 'magic shields').

[125] As when Colin Powell referenced the role of humanitarian NGOs in the global war on terror as 'A force multiplier for us. Such an important part of our combat team'. Cited in Martin Woollacott, 'Humanitarians Must Avoid Becoming Tools of Power', *The Guardian*, 2 April 2004 ('Tools of Power'). See also Sarah Kenyon Lischer, 'Military Intervention and the Humanitarian "Force Multiplier" ', *Global Governance*, Vol. 13, No. 1, 2007, pp. 98–118 ('Force Multiplier').

humanitarian actors produce rejects such either/or propositions; it instead folds together many disparate fears and ambitions. This highlights once again the power of the 'phantom local' idea. That is, by tracking which audience is invoked in a particular instance, we can sometimes discern the underlying motivations of a given enactment of distinction.

Reflecting on these three figures, it can be said that humanitarian actors deploy the 'civilian plus' in two modes. First, humanitarian actors appeal to the 'civilian plus' to draw down qualities of especially pure civilianness that will differentiate them from the 'mere civilian'. This move both relies upon, and seeks to transcend, the civilian's vulnerability. Second, humanitarian actors deploy the 'civilian plus' to wipe away threats of contamination or ward off charges of complicity. Here, the 'plus' performs a cleansing function, scrubbing away any qualities of combatantness that might affix to humanitarian actors. Whereas in the first mode the 'plus' is deployed in an attempt to escape from the vulnerability of the ordinary civilian, in the second mode the 'plus' functions to claw back the ordinary civilian's promise. These dynamics will be illuminated further in Chapter 5.

As a point of clarification, the plus/mere/minus designators are not terms that international humanitarian actors themselves employ. They are, rather, concepts that I am introducing for their analytical utility. The potential drawbacks of this type of exercise must be explicitly acknowledged. First, insofar as this triptych sets up discrete civilian types, it risks losing some of the dynamism and fluidity that the present chapter has grappled with. The more we think in terms of concrete statuses, the less we are able to imagine, say, the civilian ascendant or descendant, or to contemplate the civilian as a scenery that gradually changes.[126] Second, it is not as though IHL is in need of new labels and categories. The introduction of three new civilian figures replicates IHL's tendency to over-taxonomize, an issue that arguably generated the very problem under discussion in this book. Third, by introducing the 'plus' label and its corollaries, I—and it is me who is doing this—am actively participating in naming greater and lesser civilians. This is against the backdrop of a world in which the concept of general civilian protection is imperilled, and in the context of a conversation about, amongst other things, who might be attacked in armed conflict. Without downplaying these drawbacks, I propose they are offset by the analytical payoff of engaging with these unfamiliar civilian figures. The conceptual framework of the 'civilian plus' sheds light on the way in which everyday distinction practices reshape the civilian concept, and it renders messy on-the-ground practices legible to IHL—which, I have argued, is also messy and chaotic.

[126] I thank Mark Drumbl for this alternative imagery.

Conclusion

While this chapter has engaged with the question of how the line is drawn, its central claim is that no line, as such, exists in practice. Instead, international humanitarian actors promulgate a vision of distinction in which degrees of civilianness might be claimed or lost. When these actors engage in contests over distinction with others, it is not civilian status they are after per se, but rather the purest form of civilianness available. Such practices are not legible if one thinks in terms of a bright-line binary distinction with a stable civilian category. These micro-distinctions are readily observable, however, when civilianness is conceived of as a continuum or spectrum.

In a place like a PoC site in South Sudan, humanitarian actors attempt to assert distinction within a context in which distinction is already compromised in the grander scheme of things. The construction of a separate 'humanitarian hub', within the confines of a base guarded by armed UN peacekeeping forces, evinces the important spatial component of everyday distinction practices. As they live, eat, and go about their daily lives in close proximity to UNMISS actors, humanitarian actors question how they might impress upon these actors the importance of distinction. It is evident that some UNMISS actors interpret the humanitarian presence in the sites as a tacit agreement to affiliate; the former's starting point in conversations about how to relate to humanitarian actors presumes collaboration rather than avoidance. Decision-making on military asset use gives rise to further tensions, as humanitarian actors belonging to the first and second ideal types adopt different views on distinction's paramountcy. Further, the approach of the second ideal type drives a wedge between distinction and humanity. A final point regarding the Kinetic realm is the work that the 'phantom local' is doing. When this figure is called upon in its attacker-perceiver form, issues of targeting in the conduct of hostilities are often in play. When the beneficiary-perceiver is summoned instead, relevant concerns might go more to trust, branding, and quality of humanitarian programming.

In the Pedagogical realm, international military actors react to the teachings about distinction in the civil–military training spaces. Continuing a theme that first arose with respect to questions of who draws the line, military actors engage in power struggles with humanitarian actors and have trouble acceding to the latter's vision of distinction. It is not simply a matter of military actors faulting humanitarian actors for being overly strict, or precious, about safeguarding distinction. It is, rather, inconsistency and equivocation on the part of international humanitarian actors that international military actors find especially difficult to accommodate. The magical front lines that military actors accuse humanitarians of activating appear less mysterious when one contemplates a vision of distinction characterized by floating signifiers.

Finally, the exploration of the Intellectual realm established that the messiness of distinction is not something new that humanitarian actors are introducing through their practices. As evinced by historical approaches to protection and the treatment of the civilian category at the ICTY, the civilian concept is, and has always been, contested. The notion of an innocent, harmless, and non-participating figure cleanly separated from fighting is in many respects more myth than reality. This is true even at the most abstract level, before the idea of the civilian hits the ground. As other actors outside the humanitarian realm push civilianness in different directions, humanitarian distinction practices are cast in a different light.

The narrative about distinction that has unfolded across this chapter is one of fluidity and complexity. While attempting to hold on to some measure of this dynamism, I ended the discussion by introducing civilian figures unfamiliar to IHL. The next chapter pursues the 'civilian plus' and its corollaries across the three realms.

5
Where is the line drawn?

Introduction

This chapter investigates the circulation of three unfamiliar civilian figures, grappling with the puzzle of '*distinction from whom?*'. The 'civilian plus' and the 'civilian minus' capture, respectively, the status humanitarian actors long for and the status that haunts their daily practice. The 'mere civilian' represents a status that humanitarian actors would prefer not to have; they will, nevertheless, cleave to it in the event that qualities of combatantness hover around them.

The empirical parts of this chapter trace these three civilian figures across the Kinetic and Pedagogical realms. The Kinetic realm first explores the circulation of the 'civilian plus' in humanitarian–civilian interactions, drawing attention to the anxieties of those civilians left behind. Next, accusations that humanitarian actors merit instead a 'civilian minus' status are addressed, and attention is paid to the differential positioning of humanitarian NGOs and UN humanitarian actors. The exploration of the Pedagogical realm adopts the same structure. The discussion turns first to the circulation of the 'civilian plus' in civil–military training spaces, where military actors complain about humanitarian superiority. As for the 'civilian minus', it is shown that even as military actors fault humanitarians for being too close to the conflict, the former remain eager to encroach upon the latter. The discussion in the Intellectual realm builds on the claim that distinction is a disrupted idea prior to, and apart from, the everyday practices of international actors. The discussion first canvasses IHL targeting rules that trouble a bright-line distinction, and next demonstrates that IHL's civilian category was split apart before the civilian was defined in AP I. Bringing the humanitarian actor back into the conversation, the last section examines the way in which IHL positions humanitarian actors vis à vis the general civilian population. Once again, a Red Cross fantasy is found to be circulating.

This chapter generates pressing questions about whether a special civilian status for international humanitarian actors is desirable, tugging at a seam that runs along the larger investigation. Rather than split this open in the present discussion, I want to first focus on describing the relevant practices so we can understand what is actually going on. The normative question is addressed in Chapter 6.

The Humanitarian Civilian. Rebecca Sutton, Oxford University Press (2021). © Rebecca Sutton.
DOI: 10.1093/oso/9780198863816.003.0005

5.1 The Kinetic realm

Drawing on the everyday distinction practices of international actors, this two-part discussion unearths the existence of fault lines within the civilian category. The first part focuses on how international humanitarian actors delineate boundaries between themselves and international civilian actors, as a clear instance in which the 'civilian plus' circulates. The second part examines allegations that humanitarian actors should instead have a lesser civilian status, akin to 'civilian minus'. All of these practices are compatible with a dynamic vision of distinction, in which degrees of civilianness might be acquired or lost. To claim the highest degree of civilianness available, humanitarian actors showcase their vulnerability and exhibit stereotypical features associated with the civilian. They also emphasize the social value of their role in war, and the fact that it is this role that separates them from other civilians. In a world where the civilian category is broken up into pieces, (non-humanitarian) international civilian actors find themselves in a precarious position. These other civilians question whether certain humanitarian actors can make authoritative claims to humanitarianness, or even to civilianness.

5.1.1 The 'civilian plus': the Kinetic realm

Humanitarian actors might promulgate a 'civilian plus' status when interacting with any international actors, be they civilians or combatants. Nonetheless, it is at the humanitarian–civilian contact point that it is most apparent that humanitarian actors stake a claim to a different kind of civilianness to that which is available to other civilians. It will be shown here that humanitarian actors are deeply concerned about how UNMISS civilian staff express their own civilianness in South Sudan. Intriguingly, the behaviour of UNMISS peacekeeping forces does not give rise to the same critiques. I propose that this is because humanitarian actors regard UN peacekeeping forces as so combatant-like—with qualities of combatantness swirling around their personnel, equipment, facilities, and transport—that the latter do not impugn civilianness in the same way.

A preliminary point is that other international civilians, such as the civilian staff of UN peacekeeping missions, generally see themselves as outside the fight.[1] These civilians, too, fear being targeted with violence. They believe that all the features of civilianness attach to them, and they might even see themselves as having some claim to a 'civilian plus' status, given that they also perform an important social role

[1] The situation of armed peacekeeping forces is more complicated, and likely to be context specific. While, in South Sudan, UNMISS peacekeepers are generally though to merit civilian protection, I found many of them identifying as combatants in casual conversation. Further, their counterparts in the DRC have been categorized as parties to the conflict. To simplify matters, the present section focuses on more stereotypical civilians such as UNMISS civilian staff.

in armed conflicts.[2] The 'civilian minus' status is one that they are eager to avoid, and it looms large when they participate in comprehensive or integrated missions. The prospect of a special civilian status for humanitarian actors is, against this backdrop, threatening to other civilians.

'It's not out of purity, it's to get access'

A noticeable feature of humanitarian distinction practices in South Sudan is that distinction is enacted with respect to UNMISS civilian actors. In some cases, humanitarian actors profess the general need to assert distinction from UNMISS as a wider mission. Elsewhere, they highlight concerns that are specific to UN civilian actors, extending beyond the latter's membership in the mission. One humanitarian actor elaborates on why he cannot be seen with UNMISS civilian actors: '[W]e have access to places because of our neutrality. We try to distinguish ourselves, by toning down our connections.' Anticipating his critics, he stresses, 'it's not out of purity, it's to get access'—meaning access to affected populations. This forging of a line within the civilian category provokes vexed responses from some UNMISS civilian actors. They fear that humanitarian actors are nudging them closer to the combatant category, disregarding their own anxieties about being associated with UN forces. One UNMISS civilian actor recalls an incident in which she and her civilian colleagues were interviewing local war-affected populations in South Sudan. Unexpectedly, armed UN peacekeepers came up behind her with their weapons visible. While she acknowledges that 'We're not exactly humanitarians', she is adamant that being seen with military forces troubled her in the same way that humanitarian actors profess it bothers them. The deployment of distinction to draw lines within the humanitarian category also attracts condemnation from other international actors in South Sudan. Many attribute this to interagency competition and the fight for donor resources. One UN civilian actor wonders aloud if humanitarian actors might not, in fact, aim for ambiguity in some cases. They fly a flag in the name of distinction, but this flag conveys many other things.

In South Sudan, humanitarian actors routinely make sweeping statements about the need for separation from the wider UN mission. A classic example of this is shown when a humanitarian actor simply states: 'The UN mission, we're not part of that.' A humanitarian actor sums up the humanitarian–UNMISS relationship (such that any singular relationship might be said to exist) across South Sudan's various PoC sites as follows: 'I know we are not ideal, I know there are many mistakes done,

[2] The present study does not investigate whether non-humanitarian international civilian actors have a special status under IHL. For a brief examination of this issue, see Lisa Smirl, *Spaces of Aid: Post Disaster Relief and Reconstruction* (Chicago, IL: University of Chicago Press, 2015), 40, 94–95 (*Spaces of Aid*).

but we simply need to try to stay away.' In such accounts, maintaining separation from UN civilian staff is placed on the same plane as dissociating from armed UN forces. The former may be imbued with too low a degree of civilianness, or even with combatantness. This is quite consistent with the South Sudan civil–military guidelines, which, as noted in Chapter 2, provide for a humanitarian–UNMISS distinction. However, some distinction practices clearly depart from the guidelines, such as when humanitarian NGOs call for a separation from UN humanitarian actors. The latter practices invite us to question what values, interests, and priorities are being conflated in the distinction vernacular.

Enforcing distinction from UNMISS civilian actors

A central reason why humanitarian actors strive to avoid affiliation with UNMISS civilian actors is the latter's connection to UN forces. Qualities of combatantness may affix to UN civilian actors because of the structure of the mission: 'UNMISS is a mission with a military component, and we can't be seen to have anything to do with this.' Alternatively, more specific entanglements of UNMISS civilians with armed actors may be problematized. UN civilians work 'with the military people, they fly with their assets, they go on patrol'. Crucially, humanitarian actors also express misgivings about UNMISS civilians that are not tied to UN mission membership. One individual alleges, 'the real tension is actually with UN civilians, not the UN military'. It is hinted that UNMISS civilians pose a bigger concern than military actors because the former 'are willing to break the rules' and 'they don't follow orders; they say "We're not in the military"'. Evidently, shared interests and overlapping mandates do not automatically translate into positive humanitarian–civilian relationships. This squares with a point that Barnett makes: he cites a veteran humanitarian actor who would rather have a beer with a soldier than with a human rights activist.[3] These observations belie an assumption that otherwise pervades the civil–military relations literature, namely that humanitarian–civilian relationships will be warmer than humanitarian–military relationships.[4] As we will soon also see in the Pedagogical realm, the present study finds that humanitarian–civilian relationships may sometimes be the prickliest. Further, humanitarian actors are more likely to be confused with international civilian actors than uniformed soldiers or peacekeeping actors. This issue of confusion should perhaps not be overemphasized, however, given that humanitarian actors are routinely targeted on purpose.

[3] Michael Barnett, *Empire of Humanity: A History of Humanitarianism* (Ithaca, NY: Cornell University Press, 2011), 16–17 (*Empire*).

[4] See Han Dorussen and Marian de Vooght, 'Putting Civilians First: NGO Perceptions and Expectations of UN Peacebuilding', *Folke Bernadotte Academy*, Brief 01, 2018, 4 ('FBA Report'). In that study, an NGO respondent states: 'Our best ties are with the civilian section for sure because most of the time with civilian affairs and human rights and political affairs, but mostly civilian affairs actually, we have common interests.'

Also of note, humanitarian actors accuse UNMISS civilian actors of competing with them, though UNMISS actors lack the requisite technical expertise and skills to deliver humanitarian services. One humanitarian actor says that UNMISS civilians think 'they are all humanitarians'. Another adds: 'They don't know how to measure arms and say "famine"'. In such accounts, humanitarian actors treat UNMISS civilian actors as 'mere civilians' at best, often hinting that a 'civilian minus' status would be appropriate. As humanitarian actors deploy the 'civilian plus' to set themselves apart from UNMISS civilian actors, the criterion of expertise is folded into the distinction vernacular.

Widening out to the UN mission as a whole, UNMISS's posture with respect to the Government of South Sudan (GoSS) poses a number of concerns for humanitarian actors. It is acknowledged at mission level that UNMISS has a political character; this 'can mean that some positions or activities are not considered neutral by all parties in the country'.[5] Here, neutrality requires separation from armed actors who are potentially implicated in the conflict, and also from the prospect of politicization in various forms. Humanitarian actors frame the UNMISS–GoSS relationship as both too warm and too cold. Their first allegation is that UNMISS is too friendly with state actors in South Sudan.[6] A humanitarian actor ventures that UNMISS has been too quick to 'jump into normal relations' with the GoSS, simply because the UN mission is so desperate for the country to find peace. While the international community was heavily involved in the 2011 referendum for independence, after the resurgence of violence in 2013, donors were more reluctant to be seen supporting the GoSS.[7] Humanitarian actors believe that the failure of the wider UN mission to sufficiently distance itself from the state after December 2013 has generated wariness from the international donors they rely upon for funding. More generally, humanitarian actors believe that if they become entangled with UNMISS, they will themselves become too close to the GoSS. Many of the concerns communicated here resonate with the Chapter 2 discussion of the problems integrated missions raise for distinction.

However, humanitarian actors fear that, if the UNMISS–GoSS relationship becomes strained, state actors will block their own access to war-affected populations. The 'phantom local' circulates in connection with such apprehensions, taking form as the authority-perceiver. The specific charge humanitarian actors advance is that UNMISS aggravates state actors by speaking out on political and

[5] South Sudan Civil–Military Advisory Group, *Guidelines for the Coordination between Humanitarian Actors and the United Nations Mission in South Sudan (UNMISS)*, endorsed 6 December 2013, 2 ('Humanitarian–UNMISS Guidelines').

[6] The FBA report finds that NGOs tend to view the work of UNPol and UN Civil Affairs as supporting governmental and transitional authorities. See Dorussen and de Vooght, supra, 4 ('FBA Report').

[7] For a discussion of how donors and other international actors changed approaches after the December 2013 violence, see Jeremy Astill-Brown, 'South Sudan's Slide into Conflict: Revisiting the Past and Reassessing Relationships', *Chatham House Research Paper*, December 2014 ('Slide into Conflict').

human rights issues.[8] One humanitarian actor accuses UNMISS civilian human rights monitors of 'jumping up and down about human rights violations'. Another humanitarian actor vents: 'There are some complete idiots in the UN system, getting up on Human Rights Day and saying blah blah blah.' A humanitarian actor submits that his fellow humanitarian actors in South Sudan mostly fail to appreciate the need to carefully modulate their interactions with UN human rights monitors. A point that has not yet been addressed with respect to the unauthorized helicopter trip in Chapter 4 is that UNMISS human rights monitors were also present. Contemplating this fact, the same individual says that his colleagues 'kind of get why we can't have soldiers in the heli[copter] with us, but they don't understand why not human rights monitors'. The implication is that the civilianness of human rights actors is tarnished by the political nature of their actions.

This last speaker who addresses the helicopter trip fits with the first ideal type of humanitarian actor.[9] However, not all who belong to the first ideal type call for a similar civilian–civilian distinction. A particularly thorny issue is the engagement of some humanitarian actors, themselves, in human rights activities (see Section 5.1.2). As for actors belonging to the second ideal type, they generally find efforts to dissociate from other civilian actors dubious. One such humanitarian actor reports chilly relations in South Sudan between humanitarian NGOs and political bodies such as the Inter-Governmental Authority on Development (IGAD)[10] and the Panel of Experts on South Sudan.[11] He protests: 'Are we really going to exclude someone ... because they are with a panel of experts?' Akande and Gillard also question whether onlookers fully appreciate the differing approaches of various humanitarian actors to engaging with accountability mechanisms. They find that:[12]

> ... it is less clear whether those who are in a position to impede operations are actually aware of the different positions adopted by humanitarian actors, or simply consider them all 'foreigners working with the ICC'. In certain contexts perceptions of humanitarian actors' impartiality, neutrality and independence are already tainted to such a degree that it is questionable whether cooperating with accountability mechanisms can in fact undermine them further.

[8] One example of an official UN report about human rights violations in South Sudan is the following: *The State of Human Rights in the Protracted Conflict in South Sudan* (UNMISS and UNOHCHR, 2015). Available at: https://reliefweb.int/sites/reliefweb.int/files/resources/UNMISS_HRD4December2015.pdf.

[9] The two ideal types are introduced in Section 4.1.2.

[10] IGAD is the regional body responsible for mediating peace talks in South Sudan.

[11] The Panel of Experts on South Sudan, which focuses on the issue of targeted sanctions, was established pursuant to UNSC, *Security Council Resolution* 2206 (2015), 3 March 2015, S/RES/2206 ('UNSC Resolution 2206').

[12] Dapo Akande and Emanuela-Chiara Gillard, 'Humanitarian Actors' Engagement with Accountability Mechanisms in Situations of Armed Conflict: Workshop Report', *Anuario De Direito Internacional*, 2016, pp. 105–132, 113 ('Accountability').

In addition to the issue of futility, an overarching concern here is that humanitarian actors who drive other international civilians away will become isolated and poorly informed of what goes on around them in South Sudan.

The perspectives of UNMISS civilian actors

UNMISS civilian actors are well aware that humanitarian actors are reticent to be seen with them. While some take umbrage, others are more understanding. One UNMISS civilian actor concedes: 'UNMISS is never neutral, [it] tries to be impartial, but not really. Humanitarians are well aware of that perception.'[13] This individual feels that, though he has civilian status under IHL, only 'the humanitarians are civilian in nature, literally and figuratively'. He emphasizes the fact that humanitarian actors have 'no uniform'—an observation that is interesting to hold up alongside claims made by humanitarian actors that their T-shirts and logos are their uniform.[14] Although humanitarian actors often depict their 'uniform' as protecting them, this UN civilian actor thinks that the absence of a uniform is what sets humanitarian actors apart. He states that every uniform is associated with a party to the conflict in South Sudan, and he depicts UNMISS civilian actors as also wearing a uniform. He continues: 'I am very confident about what I am. I am not humanitarian. We are clearly told that at the induction. They say "We are not humanitarian, we are the black UN". My car is painted with black. So, that I know so well.' While this individual has no illusions about his (lack of) humanitarianness, he emphasizes that it is part of his mandate, as a UN civilian, to support humanitarian actors.

The above account constitutes a fascinating example of how non-humanitarian actors participate in carving out a special civilian status for international humanitarian actors. While few other UNMISS civilian actors go so far as to propound the 'civilian plus', some of this actor's UN civilian colleagues voice support for clear boundaries and a division of labour. Their views are based partly on eradicating the prospect of a 'phantom foreigner' and partly on ensuring strategic variation across the different international organizations operating in South Sudan. One individual notes that UN actors tend to be big, slow, and risk averse, while also noting that 'You've got your ICRCs and your MSFs, and we know they're going to be on the front line'. Once again, the Red Cross (and MSF) fantasy informs the way in which humanitarianness is conceptualized. No mention is made of the qualities that other humanitarian actors, such as small NGOs, are deemed to possess.[15]

When humanitarian actors disseminate a 'civilian plus' status, UNMISS civilian actors feel that the prospect of being downgraded to 'mere civilian' or 'civilian minus' status looms large. As indicated by the UNMISS civilian actor who

[13] This individual was interviewed at the SWEDINT training but had deployed in South Sudan.

[14] See Section 4.1.1.

[15] See Section 5.1.2.

recoils when UN forces come up behind her unexpectedly (see opening vignette, above), UNMISS civilian actors are keen to affirm their own civilianness. They are also concerned that high-level UNMISS leadership appears to be driving the mission closer to the military. One international civilian actor working for a UN-affiliated organization imparts: '[T]here's less distinction between the black and the blue UN. I think we get lumped together. I think the UN is not as appreciated, the logo, because in a conflict both sides like to use the message "Oh, you're helping the other side more"'. A UNMISS civilian actor says of vehicles driving around South Sudan with black and blue UN logos, 'who the hell knows the difference'. Putting a different spin on the 'phantom local' and 'phantom foreigner' concepts, one UNMISS civilian actor reports that the South Sudanese staff who work for UNMISS routinely ask her if she is military. She says, exasperatedly: 'I wonder why they think that. They aren't thinking creatively, aren't piecing it together.' Finally, one UNMISS civilian actor suggests that, as requests to various international actors for help merge over time, the rather banal fact is that 'People get lazy'.

One UNMISS civilian actor speaks of the hostility that humanitarian actors feel towards him—particularly those not belonging to the UN. Raising up his hands in an abrasive manner, he impersonates a humanitarian NGO actor, exclaiming: 'No no no no, that's wrong, don't do things that way.' Much like military actors in the Pedagogical realm, he and many of his civilian UNMISS colleagues experience humanitarian distinction practices as a rejection of themselves and what they stand for. One UNMISS civilian actor explains that when he travelled to meet with international humanitarian actors in South Sudan, 'The last thing they would do is sit down with us'. Another UN civilian actor adds: 'Their independence makes them think they are somehow above us. Yes, I get paid more than you, but you're just doing a stint, you won't be working here forever. They can rub you the wrong way.' We see here that the 'civilian plus' is not only threatening because it nudges UNMISS civilian staff closer to peacekeeping forces, but also because it situates UNMISS civilians beneath humanitarian actors in a hierarchy of virtue. The UNMISS civilian actor who professes that only 'the humanitarians are civilian in nature' thus stands out as something of an outlier.

Drawing lines within the humanitarian category

When certain humanitarian actors take steps to differentiate themselves from other humanitarian actors, they are often criticized as doing so to promote their organizational brand. The possibility that distinction is a cover for turf spats and competition for donor resources makes a 'civilian plus' status for humanitarian actors even more difficult for other civilian actors to swallow. As discussed elsewhere in this monograph, it is difficult to verify whether a particular flag is flown for distinction in the IHL targeting sense or, say, to promote a particular organization.[16]

[16] See the first critique of the humanitarian symbols, in Section 3.3.3.

Other international actors in South Sudan, however, are quick to argue that it is the latter. One UN civilian actor wonders aloud if humanitarian actors may not, in fact, aim at ambiguity in their use of signs and symbols (see opening vignette, above). Highlighting fundraising pressures, an international civilian actor who conducts long-term development work in South Sudan shares: 'Sometimes I think distinction is a lie, an excuse for visibility.'

Although most humanitarian actors in South Sudan earnestly protest such charges, some belonging to the second ideal type ask similar questions. If distinction is deployed in the service of other goals, such as branding or marketing humanitarian projects, then this might well impact where distinction is deemed to sit in the order of things. Certainly, it adds a question mark to the belief that humanitarianness is grounded in distinction as much as in the imperative to alleviate suffering. One humanitarian actor believes that humanitarian actors 'use' distinction when it suits them, whether this is to win the 'resource wars' with other organizations or to protect staff. This prompts him to wonder whether the distinction that humanitarian actors promulgate is valid or honest. In this account, the (physical) protection of humanitarian actors is accorded the same validity as branding initiatives; the implication is that managing the perceptions of the attacker-perceiver is no worthier a cause than influencing what we might term the donor-perceiver.[17] In either case, humanitarian actors instrumentalize distinction to some end—stated or otherwise. A senior UN humanitarian actor in Juba also thinks that humanitarian actors are too motivated by economic interests. He believes that humanity is the principle that humanitarian actors have forgotten and emphasizes that in Pictet's original formulation of the principles, humanity was positioned at the top of the hierarchy.[18]

These allegations that humanitarian actors use distinction for marketing purposes and that they fail to deliver services to populations in need impugn their virtue and suggest that they are not fulfilling their valued social role. This could fatally undermine the main rationales for protecting humanitarian actors in war. At the very least, it would seem to weaken the legitimacy of the claims they make of holding something more than 'mere civilian' status. The next section explores the possible existence of a 'civilian minus' status for humanitarian actors.

[17] On donors as another audience, see: Alexander Cooley and James Ron, 'The NGO Scramble: Organizational Insecurity and the Political Economy of Transnational Action.' *International Security*, Vol. 27, 2002, pp. 5–39 ('NGO Scramble'); Monika Krause, *The Good Project: Humanitarian Relief NGOs and the Fragmentation of Reason* (Chicago, IL and London: University of Chicago Press, 2014), 48 (*Good Project*); Kai Koddenbrock, *The Practice of Humanitarian Intervention: Aid Workers, Agencies, and Institutions in the Democratic Republic of the Congo* (London and New York: Routledge, 2016), 56–57 (*Humanitarian Intervention*).

[18] Jean Pictet, *The Fundamental Principles of the Red Cross: Commentary* (Geneva: Henry Dunant Institute, 1979) (*Principles*). See also Chapter 1.

5.1.2 The 'civilian minus': the Kinetic realm

Sometimes, qualities of combatantness swirl around humanitarian actors, such that they are allocated a position on the most polluted end of the civilianness continuum. This section delves into the notion of a 'civilian minus' status for humanitarian actors, examining how their claims of harmlessness and their humanitarian credentials might be called into question. The opening encounter highlights the differential positioning of humanitarian NGO and UN humanitarian actors.

> **'I go without force protection'**
> A number of humanitarian NGO actors report that they struggle over distinction with UN humanitarian actors in South Sudan's PoC sites. As one individual confides: 'We had to make compromises here. Not all NGOs want to be seen, even with the UN humanitarian agencies.' It has not escaped the notice of UN humanitarian actors that humanitarian NGOs might attempt to keep their distance. One UN humanitarian actor faults the 'close' relationship between UN humanitarian actors and the UN peacekeeping mission. UN humanitarian actors, for example, are quick to rely upon UNMISS for protection when they travel outside of the PoC sites. Another UN humanitarian actor has noticed humanitarian NGOs avoiding him in public, and he interprets this as a warning sign. It suggests to him that other, potentially violent, actors such as the SPLA might also question his humanitarian status. He attempts to mitigate any potential downgrading of status in practical ways, such as by traveling without UNMISS outside of the PoC sites, whenever possible. 'What I do, and this is just me, I go without force protection because I want government and SPLA to see me first as a humanitarian, and second as UN.' He makes these adjustments not to ingratiate himself with humanitarian NGOs so much as to influence local perceptions of his status. As for humanitarian NGOs, the authority of certain humanitarian actors to perform distinction is brought into question. Some humanitarian actors, it is argued, lack competence and professionalism; others step too far outside the bounds of what is properly their humanitarian role.

The discussion first considers two respects in which humanitarian actors are accused of being too close to the conflict in South Sudan: UN humanitarian actors' affiliation with UNMISS, and all humanitarian actors' performance of humanitarian tasks. Next, the discussion addresses allegations that some humanitarian actors lack the requisite competence and credentials.[19]

[19] The discussion does not address situations where humanitarian actors cause harm to people in the context of conflict, such as in cases of corruption or sexual exploitation and abuse. See e.g. IASC Task Force on Protection from Sexual Exploitation and Abuse, 'Sexual Exploitation and Abuse by UN, NGO and INGO Personnel: A Self-Assessment', *Humanitarian Exchange Magazine: Special Feature on Humanitarian Accountability*, No. 52, October 2011, pp. 34–36 ('SEA'); Ronald Francis and Anona

Too close to the conflict: entanglement with UNMISS and helping the enemy
A key insight from the Kinetic realm is that humanitarian actors, themselves, utter some of the harshest critiques of humanitarian distinction practices. This is also the case with respect to proximity to UNMISS: humanitarian NGO actors level numerous accusations at UN humanitarian actors on this front. A humanitarian NGO actor characterizes living with UN humanitarian actors in the PoC sites as a compromise, conveying that humanitarian NGOs do not implement distinction practices in tandem with their UN humanitarian counterparts. UN humanitarian actors might be deemed to lack the authority to claim a special 'civilian plus' status, or even to possess a degraded form of civilianness. When humanitarian actors police each other's conduct in this way, an evident concern is contamination through the poor choices of others. The humanitarian actor who tells the story of the unauthorized helicopter trip in Chapter 4 says of his colleagues who took the flight, 'you become tainted'.[20] But what he is also saying is: '*I* become tainted'. Here, the 'phantom local' downgrades the civilianness of those humanitarian actors who make poor choices, as well as individuals who were not even present at the scene.

Some UN humanitarian actors are concerned that affiliation with UNMISS will adversely impact their status.[21] In terms of what this exact status is, UN humanitarian actors appear attuned to the prospect of attracting a 'mere civilian' status, rather than a 'civilian minus' status. In the opening vignette, the UN humanitarian actor who interprets being pushed away by humanitarian NGOs as a 'warning sign' clings to his humanitarianness more than his civilianness. While he understands that other humanitarian actors might view him as compromised, he tends to think of himself as having a special 'civilian plus' status. Evidently, his attempts to forgo force protection are not (primarily) about assuaging the concerns of other humanitarian actors. His dissociation from UNMISS is galvanized, instead, by the imputed perceptions of the authority-perceiver and the attacker-perceiver—assuming tangible form as the GoSS and the SPLA, respectively.

The above accounts shed new light on the situation facing the OCHA actor who worries about sharing a cafeteria with UNMISS forces in the PoC site.[22] Not only does his fellow UN humanitarian actor describe the relationship with UNMISS as 'close', but the humanitarian NGOs he believes he represents do not see themselves as implementing distinction alongside him. On the contrary, humanitarian NGO actors take steps to distance themselves from him and his UN colleagues.[23]

Armstrong, 'Corruption and Whistleblowing in International Humanitarian Aid Agencies', *Journal of Financial Crime*, Vol. 18, No. 4, 2011, pp. 319–335 ('Corruption').

20 See Section 4.1.2.
21 As noted, UNMISS actors generally say that UN humanitarian actors are easier for them to work with than non-UN humanitarian actors.
22 See Section 4.1.1.
23 See Section 5.1.1.

All of these practices point to a dynamic and fractured conceptualization of humanitarianness. Similar to the continuum of civilianness, in this perspective, humanitarianness is assessed according to nuanced gradations and perceived hierarchies.

As noted, humanitarian actors worry that the 'phantom local' will confuse or mistake them for other international actors. An additional fear is palpable in South Sudan, namely that it is humanitarian actors' very humanitarianness that attracts qualities of combatantness and renders them enticing targets. As humanitarian actors perform routinized tasks, they may be viewed as participants in the conflict who are neither harmless nor innocent. This idea revisits the Chapter 3 discussion about the actual meanings and representations of humanitarian symbols. In South Sudan, one humanitarian NGO actor is curious about what the SPLA thinks of humanitarian NGOs. Alluding to the existence of the 'phantom foreigner', he wants to know if his organization's T-shirts 'mean anything to them'. He refines this: 'Not even that, I want to know what they think of me because of my white skin.' He reasons that, if the SPLA has qualms with white Western actors, or indeed any actor who seeks to provide humanitarian services, then wearing a T-shirt will do nothing to ensure protection. Another humanitarian actor contemplates the reliance on visual cues of humanitarianness in South Sudan, and expresses similar worries: 'The question is always, if you wear [our organization's] T-shirt or hat, is it going to protect you or expose you?'

A further issue is how armed actors in South Sudan view the populations that humanitarian actors assist. Doubts about the civilian status of IDPs[24] help to explain why armed actors might take issue with international actors providing services in the PoC sites. One humanitarian actor who works in the Bor PoC site speaks of how he was once confronted by a group of local armed actors who berated him for 'helping our enemy'. This particular individual is South Sudanese, working as a national staff member of an international NGO. This fact, and the mention of white skin (see above), highlights the differential threats that local humanitarian actors face in South Sudan—whether due to ethnicity, nationality, or involvement in local politics. While there is no room to address this issue within the confines of the present study, other scholars have turned their attention to the matter[25] and it merits serious investigation. On a final note, this accusation of 'helping our enemy' finds a parallel in the Pedagogical realm, where humanitarian actors are faulted for assisting the 'other side'.

[24] The civilian status of IDPs in South Sudan is addressed in Section 3.1.1.

[25] On security risks to local humanitarian actors, see Ruben Andersson and Florian Weigand, 'Intervention at Risk: The Vicious Cycle of Distance and Danger in Mali and Afghanistan', *Journal of Intervention and Statebuilding*, Vol. 9, 2015, pp. 519–541, 529–533 ('Intervention at Risk'); Silke Roth, *Passionate Professionals: The Paradoxes of Aid Work* (London and New York: Routledge, 2015), 34 (*Paradoxes of Aid*); Jan Egeland, Adele Harmer, and Abby Stoddard, *To Stay and Deliver: Good Practice for Humanitarians in Complex Security Environments* (Geneva and New York: OCHA, 2011) (*Stay and Deliver*).

Questioning humanitarian credentials

UNMISS civilian actors variously describe humanitarian actors working in South Sudan's PoC sites as 'young and green', 'third world groupies', 'eager beaver, energizer bunnies', and people who are 'padding the CV'. Yet it is also said that some humanitarians stay too long and become 'very worn after they've done time in the PoC sites'. A UNMISS peacekeeper considers the difference between UN and non-UN humanitarian actors. The former 'get paid better, it's a gravy train. They are slightly less altruistic, let's say'. NGO actors are deemed to be more virtuous, because they want to 'make the world a better place'.

The humanitarian actors who travelled with UNMISS on the unauthorized helicopter flight in South Sudan did not belong to an unknown or peripheral agency.[26] However, the general claim in South Sudan is that smaller, lesser known humanitarian organizations are the least predictable. Even amongst humanitarian actors, the Red Cross fantasy circulates, though room is also made for a few other named organizations. The head of an international humanitarian NGO says: 'Every year we watch ICRC stand by itself. Oxfam, Mercy Corps, MSF will not use military assets or escorts. They might be even more principled than CARE, Save [the Children], Concern, Goal.' Apart from these reputable organizations, he explains, there are concerns about the decision-making of the myriad smaller humanitarian organizations operating across South Sudan. These concerns extend beyond issues of targeting in the conduct of hostilities, folding issues of commitment, reputation, professionalism, and competence into the distinction vernacular. While ICRC's move to 'stand by itself' is lauded, one humanitarian NGO actor denigrates humanitarian actors who go 'cowboy'. The latter undermine joint planning amongst international actors in South Sudan, fail to coordinate with others in the UN humanitarian cluster system, and refuse to engage in collective needs assessments. Interestingly, MSF is cited as one of the 'cowboy' organizations but touted as doing an excellent job of asserting distinction.

Aside from going 'cowboy', humanitarian actors unwittingly send signals that compromise their claims to virtue.[27] Such behaviours call to mind Goffman's depiction of expressive incongruities an individual might exhibit in performing a given role; he offers the example of the surgeon who picks his nose prior to entering the operating room.[28] Looking at humanitarian actors from the vantage point of the beneficiary-perceiver, one humanitarian actor in Juba wonders: 'What do you see when you see these big NGOs? The vehicle? It's probably brand new. I'm on the street begging for money. I see big offices, new offices. People say they're sending

[26] The identity of the organization has been withheld to protect confidentiality.

[27] The unintentional sending of signals that might undermine protection is also a theme in Larissa Fast, *Aid in Danger: The Perils and Promise of Humanitarianism* (Philadelphia, PA: University of Pennsylvania Press, 2014) (*Aid in Danger*).

[28] Erving Goffman, *Encounters: Two Studies in the Sociology of Interaction* (Eastford, CT: Martino Fine Books, 2013/1961), 101 (*Encounters*).

money, where is it going?' He suggests that more agile humanitarian actors with smaller offices and older vehicles get 'further into the community because they're not saying "I'm going to tell you what to do". Instead, they say "I'm going to work with you, we've got these programmes"'. He also notes that expatriate humanitarian actors go to parties and become intoxicated in public. 'This person is here for fun, are they here to help?'

Finally, humanitarian actors who engage in human rights activities may be seen to exceed their remit and compromise their civilianness. One humanitarian actor explains that, when humanitarian actors spend time behind the frontlines of conflict, they develop feelings of solidarity for the victims of violence. He believes that the impulse to speak out against atrocity is triggered when 'you start to see through someone else's eyes'. This account offers a striking counterpoint to the way in which humanitarian actors typically ascribe perceptions or 'see through the eyes' of the phantom local.[29] Instead of holding up a mirror to grasp how local actors perceive *him*, the humanitarian actor looks out at the world through the local actor's eyes in order to feel what this person feels. While his empathic approach is laudable for the gesture of solidarity, there appears to be a consensus amongst international actors that humanitarian engagement in human rights-type work is seriously problematic. One humanitarian NGO actor proposes that such practices are more likely to undermine distinction than anything a UNMISS actor might do.[30] Accordingly, this individual contends that all human rights work should be left to international human rights organizations such as Amnesty International and Human Rights Watch. These concerns surface again in the Pedagogical realm, where a CAMPO trainer warns that humanitarian actors who stray outside their remit 'burn their fingers'.[31]

The next stage in the discussion follows the idea of distinction to the Pedagogical realm, where the three civilian figures are circulating in civil–military training spaces.

5.2 The Pedagogical realm

Following the same structure as the preceding discussion on South Sudan, this part opens with an examination of the 'civilian plus' status humanitarian actors promulgate in civil–military training spaces. Once again, the focus here is on humanitarian–civilian dynamics, as the 'civilian plus' is easiest to detect when humanitarians engage with other civilians. At a virtual reality exercise in Sweden, a

[29] Compare with Section 4.1.1, wherein a humanitarian actor sees through the eyes of the beneficiary to ensure that his own team is safe.

[30] As noted in the earlier discussion of UNMISS's navigation of human rights issues, humanitarians are concerned that the mission might aggravate the GoSS. See Section 5.1.1.

[31] See Section 5.2.2.

volunteer actor hired to play the role of the humanitarian can be found staking out a position at the purest end of the civilianness continuum. The enactment of such intra-civilian distinctions attracts the ire of the civilian staff of international missions. Similar to the Kinetic realm, these other civilians fear that they are being nudged closer to combatant-like figures, and they are irritated by the insinuation that humanitarians are more virtuous. In the second section, international military actors allege that humanitarian actors possess a tainted form of civilianness. Humanitarians are accused of helping the enemy and getting involved in the fight—even where they do not overstep the bounds of the traditional humanitarian remit. These accounts depict the humanitarian actor as complicit and potentially dangerous, or as simply incompetent.

5.2.1 The 'civilian plus': the Pedagogical realm

At the training places, international humanitarian actors ground their 'civilian plus' status explicitly in the social value of their role in war. They bolster this effort by invoking the 'phantom local' and stressing how hard they must work to influence local perceptions. They do not tend to overtly extol their own virtue or moral uprightness in explicit terms; they are, perhaps, aware of the alienation this might engender in a setting populated mostly by non-humanitarians. Nonetheless, other international civilian actors—focusing here on civilian staff of international military and peacekeeping missions—read feelings of superiority into such distinction practices. These other civilians also discern that humanitarian distinction practices impugn their own claims to civilianness.

> **'I know you are allergic to the uniforms beside me'**
> Having been allocated roles as part of a joint international assessment mission in a mythical conflict zone, SWEDINT trainees gather in a virtual reality exercise room. Each team encompasses a diverse set of international actors, including peacekeeping forces and civilian staff of a UN political mission. Their assigned task is to conduct an assessment of local needs, and their virtual journey begins with a drive in a UN vehicle to the headquarters of a local humanitarian NGO named HELP. As the lights dim, the action unfolds on a large screen at the front of the room. Before long, the virtual HELP representative appears before the vehicle and greets the joint assessment team; he is friendly, wearing a blue T-shirt, black trousers and a black hat. Once this virtual encounter is underway, the lights come on and the trainees relocate to another training room. There they are faced with a live actor, now in female form, who serves as the real (though simulated) HELP representative. The team members take their seats, and the UN civilian leading the team introduces himself. He states that he is from the UN mission, then hastily appends 'but we are civilian'. Gesturing to his military counterparts, he

> says: 'I know you are allergic to the uniforms beside me.' The NGO representative nods and confirms that her commitment to independence does indeed require that she keep her distance from the military. She takes this a step further, now alleging that the entire UN is 'a military of sorts'. Bristling at this, the UN civilian tries to salvage the encounter. He assures her that he will not bring his military and police team members to their next meeting. The prospect of being jettisoned does not sit well with the rest of his team. Teetering on the edge of her seat, a military team member admonishes: 'Don't apologize for the military, we are part of the team!' Her military colleague rallies to her side, lamenting: 'If we continue to put up the boundaries between us, we are never going to function together.'

The discussion begins with a brief examination of intra-civilian distinctions and then analyses how other international civilian actors react to the humanitarian actor as 'civilian plus'.

Drawing lines within the civilian category

During the role play exercise at SWEDINT in the opening vignette, the humanitarian NGO representative from HELP calls for separation not only from international military actors, but also from international civilian actors belonging to the UN. This is a clear example of the dissemination of the 'civilian plus' figure, and the humanitarian actor assigns 'civilian minus' status to UN civilian staff, painting them as 'military'. This encounter is tinged with artificiality, especially as a volunteer actor plays the role (in the theatrical sense) of the HELP representative. Still, this volunteer has been instructed to act in this way and her behaviour emulates the posture that international humanitarian actors in South Sudan adopt with respect to the UN integrated mission. The exchanges in this virtual reality session have interesting parallels with one particular encounter that takes places between a humanitarian actor and an SPLA soldier at a PoC site in South Sudan.[32] Here, at the SWEDINT training, the actor hired to play the role of NGO representative claims the entire UN is a military, of sorts; she insists on maintaining separation from all UN actors. This move makes sense when one considers what befalls her counterpart in South Sudan: when he lifts up his shirt and asks the soldier if he has an invisible gun, the soldier replies by lumping all UN actors together and even sweeping in the NGO to this UN group as well. Painting the entire UN with a broad brush allows the HELP actor to steer clear of any potential affiliation.

During the SWEDINT exercise, the UN civilian who is leading the joint assessment team is placed in an awkward position. In order to successfully move the meeting forward, he needs to ingratiate himself with the humanitarian actor. He believes he can achieve this by burnishing his civilian credentials, yet doing so

[32] See Section 4.1.1.

also requires him to distance himself from the military members of his assessment team. When he attempts this delicate move, his military colleagues lash out. The thrust of their outbursts encapsulates the comprehensive ethos, perfectly capturing the 'working together' mentality. 'We are part of the team', they claim, before pronouncing that erecting boundaries will impede them from getting things done. The heated nature of this simulated encounter—in which the stakes are, precisely, zero—exhibits how the emotions of individual actors shape these exchanges, and how some actors take the distinction practices of humanitarian actors personally.

International military actors detect considerable friction between different kinds of international civilian actors, flagging intra-civilian conflicts at all three training venues. At the NATO CIMIC training, several participants describe humanitarian actors as being in competition with other civilians, such as those working for UN missions or the US State Department. They argue that the 'bigger battle' amongst international actors is along this humanitarian–civilian divide. Alluding to the existence of a 'civilian plus' figure, a military trainee contends that, when humanitarian actors separate themselves from other civilian actors, 'This divides the civilian population into castes'. From this individual's perspective, 'UN, NGOs … everyone should be the same'. At CAMPO, a military trainer argues that if the concern is about meeting the needs of war-affected populations, then 'It's the relationship amongst the civilian actors that is decisive'. Another CAMPO trainer is wary of depicting any given relationship as more consequential than another. He calls instead for a more holistic conversation that captures the overall diversity of international actors.

When they allude to line-drawing practices within the civilian category, military actors tend to imply that such practices are something that civilian actors bring about. It has been shown elsewhere in this monograph, however, that military actors often splinter the civilian category.

The perspectives of other international civilian actors

As a civilian trainer at SWEDINT confides, when he has previously worn clothing with a UN logo or travelled in UN vehicles in conflict zones, he has felt at best 'identified, but not protected'. He does not feel immune from violence as a UN civilian, he says, 'because the UN is a target'. He is alarmed by the possibility that humanitarian actors might call his civilianness into question, nudging him closer to the military actors he tries to distance himself from. His commentary attests to a tacit assumption that civilians can be ordered along a continuum, with floating signifiers of combatantness swirling around those at the more polluted end. The following passage is also instructive. It shows how a UN civilian might link his fate to humanitarian actors, and it highlights the twin features of vulnerability and value that Alexander deems characteristic of the civilian figure.[33] A UN civilian trainee

[33] Amanda Alexander, 'The Genesis of the Civilian', *Leiden Journal of International Law*, Vol. 20, 2007, pp. 359–376, 375 ('Genesis').

at SWEDINT contends that attacks against humanitarian actors are rarely due to confusion. Instead, 'there are bandits who do not respect the law, and they will target people, kidnap humanitarians and demand ransom, for economic reasons'. It is a serious concern, this individual adds, 'because we can be killed'. This 'we' is striking. The individual who is speaking is not a humanitarian actor in the traditional sense, but a civilian actor who deploys with UN political and peacekeeping missions. Nonetheless, he aligns himself with humanitarian actors because he shares their fears about being seen as complicit or as participating in the conflict. Similar to the SWEDINT trainer (above) who senses that he is unprotected by the UN logo, this individual may feel even more at risk than humanitarian actors that qualities of combatantness will fasten to him.

Contemplating how events unfolded in the simulated encounter with the HELP representative, a UN civilian trainee at SWEDINT says the dynamics resonated with her experience of working as civilian staff with the UN mission in the DRC (MONUSCO). When she introduces herself to humanitarian actors in the operational context, she is always careful to emphasize her civilian status.[34] In fact, she takes the very same approach her fellow trainee did in the simulation exercise. 'We are from MONUSCO, but we are civilians.' A civilian trainer at SWEDINT describes an incident in which humanitarian actors rebuffed him when he was working for the UN mission: 'I was slapped on my fingers by UNHCR, and I was UN mission so I thought we were UN as much as them .... [T]he feeling of being told off that I had nothing to do here, that was the first time I had the feeling, "Yeah, right! We are not the same."' Sounding much like the military actors who accuse humanitarian actors of implementing distinction unevenly, a civilian trainee says that humanitarian actors 'don't like us until they need us. And they will always need us'. Another civilian trainee asserts that humanitarian actors can be 'so focused on what they do that they forget we are not there to babysit them'. These sentiments recall commentary from the PoC sites in South Sudan, where UNMISS actors voice resentment that humanitarian actors want to live in 'their' home.[35]

A UN civilian trainee suspects that humanitarian actors look down on those of his ilk. 'The humanitarians never liked us because we did not deliver the goods. We are too bureaucratic, people don't have time and energy to stomach our bureaucracy.' This comes back to the caution offered previously against assuming that there is greater affinity between humanitarian actors and other civilians. Even when humanitarian actors work with the same populations as UN civilians, for example, their approaches differ in important ways. Further, although one might expect greater alignment between UN civilians and humanitarian actors who also

[34] This might be especially important in the DRC, where the case can be made that MONUSCO is, or certain components of it are, party to the conflict. See Scott Sheeran and Stephanie Case, 'The Intervention Brigade: Legal Issues for the UN in the Democratic Republic of the Congo' (International Peace Institute, 2014) ('Intervention Brigade').

[35] See Section 4.1.1.

work for the UN—as opposed to NGOs, for example—the story of the SWEDINT trainee being rebuffed by UNHCR in the field attests that this is not always the case. One UN civilian trainee warns that if humanitarian actors constantly criticize or struggle with UN mission actors, then humanitarians might find that the UN mission does not help them when they need it. A colleague disputes this last claim, countering that the UN mission is more likely to try to foster the relationship, in case humanitarian actors eventually become useful.

The commentary of the last two speakers highlights the perils of dismissing what might appear to be bickering or idle gossip between different kinds of international actors. The first UN civilian actor hints that constant criticism by humanitarian actors could adversely impact the way in which UN actors interpret their obligations to assist the latter under international law. This shows how interpersonal squabbles can inform and potentially overshadow the observance of legal mandates, such as the requirement that UN mission actors facilitate humanitarian access. As a matter of day-to-day reality, these two speakers are respectively concerned with avoiding the criticism of, and extracting information from, humanitarian actors.

Focusing now on claims about humanitarian superiority, a number of civilian trainees at the CAMPO training believe that humanitarian actors look down on other civilians. A UN civilian trainee says she only recently discovered prejudice against the UN mission. At a training event she attended, a humanitarian actor professed the view: 'I think all UN people are assholes.' She adds: 'It feels personal, how can you talk like this?' A civilian trainee also has the feeling that humanitarian actors 'think they are superior to everybody else—military, police, but even amongst civilians.' This individual says that MSF and other 'hardcore' humanitarians see UN civilians as essentially useless, and rank military actors and peacekeepers 'down at the bottom.' One UN civilian trainee suspects that humanitarian actors write her off when she drives in a UN mission vehicle. Another civilian trainee adds that, in social settings, humanitarian actors 'will talk to you as friends, but when you come to work they will freeze you. They are just separate.' In these scenarios, it is difficult to discern whether the relevant dynamics should be categorized as a simple turf spat or whether these actors can be said to be jostling for a better kind of (legal) civilian status. One thing is certain: the construction of civilianness by international actors, according to differing degrees and gradations, is inflected with emotions as well as value judgements.

A UN civilian trainee at CAMPO speculates on the way in which humanitarian actors see her versus the way in which they view her fellow trainee, who is a UN police actor in the DRC. She draws attention to the issues of gender and visual signifiers. 'Humanitarians probably see your police uniform. You are MONUSCO and you have a weapon and you are a man.' She remarks, however, that 'You see masculinity in humanitarian aid too.' Recounting her experience as a UN civilian actor in the DRC, she describes the (male) humanitarian actors who would arrive in

Goma, where they had a 'nice apartment and pool, but one to two hours away from real conflict. These guys, these cowboys, they come and go'. To conjure an image of these humanitarian actors, she puffs herself up and pulls back her shoulders. 'They are the hero of Oxfam. Oh, we say, "Another hero is coming". He thinks he is the most interesting man in Goma .... Sometimes I see the cowboys, I just smile.' This gendered account offers an interesting counterpoint to the traditional association of the military with masculinity, and humanitarian assistance with femininity.[36] A more general observation is that international civilian actors bring their own biases and grudges to their encounters with humanitarian actors.

It was noted previously that international civilian actors who deploy with political or peacekeeping missions risk being associated with military actors working for the same mission. Similar to humanitarian actors, these other international civilian actors are curious about whether local populations can distinguish between the various international actors. They, too, hold up the mirror of local perceptions and try to imagine how observers see them. Alluding to the prospect of a 'phantom foreigner', a civilian trainer at SWEDINT suspects that local actors cannot tell who is who because so many international actors come from Western countries. Invoking an angry beneficiary-perceiver, one UN civilian trainee reports that when local populations become embittered with UN military actors in the DRC, UN civilian actors are also faced with protests and marches. A UN civilian trainee disagrees, arguing that local actors in the DRC know very well who is who. He claims that it is 'easy to identify MONUSCO, with their white and black vehicles. OCHA has the emblems, every organization has their emblem and logo, even the NGOs'.[37] In his experience, locals are also able to identify the different humanitarian actors: 'This one is Merlin, this one is IRC, this one is Save the Children, this one is ICRC, this one is MSF.' These distinctions are accompanied by value judgements. He goes on: 'Locals know MSF, who is in the bush, we know they do not fight, they come with medicine ... we know also that the Red Cross cannot be attacked.' This perspective offers yet another example of the circulating Red Cross fantasy, wherein MSF is once again accorded the same special status. Here, an international civilian actor propagates the fantasy, and he says nothing of whether the other named humanitarian actors—OCHA, IRC, Merlin, and Save the Children—cannot be attacked.

On a further note, a UN civilian trainee at CAMPO adjudges that UN civilian actors are unreasonably hard on humanitarian actors. When her colleagues say to

[36] On gender and civil–military relations see: Laura Sjoberg and Sandra Via, *Gender, War, and Militarism: Feminist Perspectives* (Westport, CT: Praeger Security International, 2010). On the relative lack of scholarly attention paid to gender in the (historical) study of humanitarian practice see Esther Moller, Johannes Paulmann, and Katharina Stornig, 'Call for Proposals for Conference on "Gender and Humanitarianism: (Dis) Empowering Women and Men in the Twentieth Century"', 2017. Available at: http://www.ieg-mainz.de/media/public/Call%20for%20Papers/CfP_Gender_and_Humanitarianism_2017.pdf.

[37] French to English translation carried out by the author.

her, 'Be careful with the humanitarians', she takes this with a grain of salt. As an individual, she has developed various techniques for warming relations with humanitarian actors: she engages them on a personal level, maintains an open attitude, and shares information generously. Another UN trainee at CAMPO takes care not to defend the UN when speaking to humanitarian actors:

> I have this feeling that I want to get sympathy from the humanitarians and get close to them, so I can do that by separating myself from [my] institution ... but you have to be careful, if you want to stay in your organization. So I'll criticize [the UN mission] while giving an option of collaboration.

When confronted by the distinction practices of humanitarian actors, these UN civilian actors find ways to engage with humanitarian actors and engender proximity. In some instances, they make headway by shrugging off their institutional affiliation and fostering interaction at the individual level. In so doing, they assure humanitarian actors that if they (the UN civilian actors) possess the wrong kind of civilianness, it will not be transmitted to the humanitarian actors. These techniques have interesting parallels with military actors' 'rush to the intimate', showing the importance of interactions at the individual level.

5.2.2 The 'civilian minus': the Pedagogical realm

The Red Cross fantasy is alive and well in the above discussion of the 'civilian plus', and one military trainee at SWEDINT offers a twist on this. He respects the ICRC's desire to maintain separation from others because ICRC actors are not 'total humanitarians ... I would even say they are translating military language into civilian language'. This is clearly intended as a compliment, and it resonates with the UNMISS peacekeeper's claim, also voiced in an approving manner, that MSF and the ICRC are the 'military of the humanitarians'.[38] The allegation that humanitarian actors might edge into the military sphere is more often articulated disparagingly, however. International military actors believe that some humanitarian actors attract qualities of combatantness because of their entanglement in the conflicts in which they operate. While the impugned activities very rarely comprise direct participation in hostilities under IHL, they often create a perception that humanitarian actors might be complicit. Humanitarian actors who are seen to lack humanitarian credentials are also viewed as dangerous—in the sense not that they would intentionally harm others, but that their actions create dangers for those around them. As is shown in what follows, international military actors do

[38] See Section 4.1.1.

not tend to think their own efforts to engender proximity with humanitarian actors are problematic.

> **'You are feeding the armed groups'**
> A white Land Rover emblazoned with a black UN on its side comes to a stop a few metres in front of a checkpoint manned by local armed actors. After a few terse exchanges, the vehicle drives slowly away and one of the men at the checkpoint can be heard muttering 'There is no need for the UN here, we provide security'. While this encounter takes place on-screen as part of a virtual reality simulation exercise, it galvanizes a heated discussion amongst SWEDINT trainees about humanitarian actors who pay at checkpoints. Noting how armed actors set up roadblocks and checkpoints as a tactic to garner resources, one trainee reproaches humanitarian actors who pay to reach populations on the other side. He charges: 'You are feeding the armed groups ... trying to be special and giving money to armed groups, you're fuelling the armed conflict.' Although the intentions of humanitarian actors may be noble, another trainee asserts, this does not give them a free pass in dealing with armed actors. When they pay at checkpoints, give food, treat the wounded, and provide other forms of aid, humanitarian actors 'bring care to the enemy' and 'prolong the rebellion'. Further, their sheer presence in the conflict zone renders them part of the conflict. Humanitarian actors inevitably become part of the wars in which they operate, one trainee says, 'even if they are in the middle'. One trainee recounts an incident in which, as a member of the international military forces in Afghanistan, he was called to assist a humanitarian NGO who was stuck at a roadside. When he and his colleagues arrived at the scene, the first question from the NGO was whether they had to bring their guns. 'I couldn't believe it. Do you grasp the severity of the events happening around [you]? They act like it's a fairy tale and we're fucking being shot at.' Another trainee bemoans: 'We are not the enemy.'

This three-part discussion considers humanitarian actors who: accept political funds and help the 'other side'; are deemed to lack competence and credentials; and become too close with international military actors. While the first two issues are explored from the perspective of military actors, I argue that military actors are oblivious to the third issue.

Too close to the conflict: political funding and helping the 'other side'

A first sticking point for trainees at the three training grounds is how humanitarian actors garner resources for their programming in conflict zones. Many trainees cannot fathom how humanitarian actors are able to accept money from—but not be beholden to—(political) donors. At the NATO CIMIC training, military trainees fixate on the fact that humanitarian actors accept funding from the very same organizations they claim to distance themselves from. After a training session on the traditional humanitarian principles, a trainee alights on the use of government funding by the humanitarian trainer's organization. He inquires of the trainer: 'Are *you* not too close with government?' The trainer responds that government donors are not permitted to dictate where assistance is delivered, or how. Unconvinced, a number of trainees shake their heads in disbelief. Equally, NATO trainees are bewildered by one humanitarian organization's extremely strict funding policies. When a humanitarian trainer explains that her organization does not accept money from Coca Cola, given its link with health problems, a trainee sputters 'You ... are too complicated!' Over lunch in the cafeteria, another military trainee voices incredulity: 'As if people in Afghanistan care about Coca Cola.' As summoned by the military actors, the 'phantom local' faults humanitarian actors for their reliance on political donors, but it is not bothered by the use of resources from corporate purveyors of unhealthy products.

Allegations of 'civilian minus' status become more glaring when participants discuss how humanitarian actors perpetuate armed conflicts. Critiques of this nature are not new, and in the 1990s they galvanized the development of the 'Do No Harm' agenda inside the humanitarian community. The central insight of Do No Harm is that 'when international assistance is given in the context of a violent conflict, it becomes a part of that context and thus also of the conflict'.[39] It is also recognized that, while humanitarian actors may adopt a neutral position with respect to the parties to an armed conflict, their actions and the aid they provide inevitably interact with the conflict context.[40] Contemporary humanitarianism is embedded with responses to such critiques, such as the move to professionalize the humanitarian sector.[41] Still, international military actors view humanitarian actors as working against them when they provide assistance to all. It is important to note that the conduct international military actors find fault with is not a violation of the traditional humanitarian principles, but rather the effort to *uphold* principles of neutrality and impartiality. Such activities are anathema for international military actors because they potentially help their adversaries win the war.

At the NATO CIMIC training, a military trainee outlines a hypothetical scenario in which a suicide bomber badly injures one of his fellow soldiers in battle. If a doctor working for MSF provides care that allows this bomber to return to the fight, international military forces will become hostile towards MSF, as well as other humanitarian actors. In such instances, the trainee believes that military discipline plays a crucial role, because 'It's harder to stay rational'. A NATO military

[39] Mary B. Anderson, *Do No Harm: How Aid Can Support Peace—Or War* (London: Lynne Reinner Publishers, 1999) (*Do No Harm*).

[40] Ibid., 1.

[41] See e.g. Peter Walker and Catherine Russ, 'Fit for Purpose: The Role of Modern Professionalism in Evolving the Humanitarian Endeavour', *International Review of the Red Cross*, Vol. 93, No. 884, 2011, pp. 1193–1210 ('Professionalism'). The broader efforts of the humanitarian sector to absorb critiques are considered in Krause, supra (*Good Project*).

trainer corroborates this, adding that when a soldier's unit comes under attack, the most difficult thing is to not blame international humanitarian actors who have helped 'the other side'. As the humanitarian actor participates in or becomes complicit in the conflict, his or her status is downgraded to 'civilian minus'. What is notable about such accounts is how characteristics of combatantness are seen to attach to humanitarians doing quintessentially humanitarian activities. Unlike the issue of political funding, which could potentially compromise the independence and impartiality of humanitarian actors, the provision of services based on need is at the heart of the humanitarian endeavour. Moreover, such activities are consistent with the role of civilian humanitarian actors under IHL.[42] This is one clear example of dissonance between what IHL provides and what international actors perceive.

A humanitarian trainer confronts this last issue directly at the NATO CIMIC training. She explains that, when a humanitarian organization treats a wounded combatant in an armed conflict, 'In that moment he's not a combatant, really. He's a human.' Reflecting on this, a civilian trainee at NATO notes that the trainer 'got everyone going' in her session. He surmises: 'It's good for these guys in uniform to see someone like her talk about what it would be like on the other side, how they understand the humanitarian principles.' The implication here seems to be that humanitarian actors may have one interpretation of the humanitarian principles, but other international actors are entitled to have another. At the CAMPO training, a military trainer refers to humanitarian NGOs as 'unguided missiles' during a session. A humanitarian actor who is present balks at this, protesting: 'Are you calling me a weapon system?' Most trainees take this to be an amusing joke, but the humanitarian actor does not laugh. While the imagery of a missile depicts the humanitarian actor as nudging closer to the combatant category, the use of the word 'unguided' dovetails with the next strand of critique that is examined here. This is the allegation that some humanitarian actors lack the competence and credentials to make authoritative appeals to distinction.

Questioning humanitarian credentials

As Weir observes, the humanitarian community as a whole remains something of a mystery to military actors—never mind individual humanitarian agencies.[43] Similar to South Sudan, international military and peacekeeping actors in the training spaces view smaller organizations and lower-profile humanitarian actors as the least predictable. More than this, military actors doubt that these peripheral humanitarian actors possess the requisite competence, professionalism, or

[42] Note that IHL explicitly empowers those who qualify as humanitarian actors, or relief workers, to assist all parties to the conflict.

[43] Erin Weir, 'Conflict and Compromise: UN Integrated Missions and the Humanitarian Imperative', *Kofi Annan International Peacekeeping Training Centre Monograph*, 2006, 41 ('Conflict and Compromise').

humanitarian credentials to implement distinction in a coherent way. These humanitarian actors are also alleged to pose a potential danger to those around them.

Returning to the virtual reality exercise at SWEDINT,[44] a UN civilian trainee recalls how the local NGO HELP faced resistance when trying to execute her vision of distinction. This trainee surmises that an ICRC actor would have had an easier time. 'If we compare someone who is famous and not famous, this is it. The Geneva Conventions is basically them. And HELP, what does this organization stand for, what do they do? ICRC has worked hard for their fame in comparison.' At the CAMPO training, a military trainer says that the ICRC is the only humanitarian actor 'I really respect. The rest, it's a political thing'. She describes the individuals who work for small, lesser known NGOs as 'funny figures' and 'strange characters'. By sending young people 'who have no idea' to work in dangerous conflict zones, she argues that 'NGOs can *cause* danger ... these guys are idealistic, emotional. They don't grasp the complexity, politically, of the place they're going to'. Another CAMPO trainer proposes that 'bigger organizations are more professional. You also have the exotic guys on the side, who can be a problem'. His colleague adds: 'Yes, it's an old stereotype but for sure still applies to the small ones. They barely have mission statements, and the necessity to get money leads them to this activity and that.' One military trainer at CAMPO says this kind of activity leads humanitarian actors to 'burn their fingers'. A police trainee confesses that she is generally wary of humanitarian actors. There is 'always a suspicion that maybe they are working for someone else'. Smirking at this, another trainee questions whether one can trust that humanitarian actors are who they appear to be. She speculates, with a raised eyebrow, 'Maybe they are not really humanitarian'. As is discussed earlier in this chapter, humanitarian actors who enter the human rights arena in South Sudan are also seen to be playing with fire.

One military trainer at the NATO CIMIC training says exasperatedly of humanitarian organizations that there are 'millions of them. We only know the hugest ones'. A trainee suggests that less organized NGOs endanger people and risk injury to their staff. Recalling accusations from South Sudan that expatriate humanitarian actors party too much in public,[45] a military trainee at the SWEDINT training proposes that some NGOs are simply in conflict zones on holiday. He is suspicious of humanitarian actors who 'want freedom, no responsibility, and not to be like military or diplomatic [actors]'. Another military trainee calls for humanitarian actors to prove that they can 'deliver the goods'. In a subsequent CAMPO training session, a trainer induces laughter when he introduces a new use for the acronym CIA: 'Confused International Agencies'. Later, over dinner, the same trainer softens his view. He confesses: 'I find I miss the messy humanitarians, who care about

[44] Examined in Section 5.2.1.
[45] See Section 5.1.2.

people.'[46] His colleague dismisses this as overly sentimental. 'You don't go somewhere as a professional and try to save [people]. You have to be cool-headed and rational. Otherwise you will cause trouble.' There is overlap here with the claims that some humanitarian actors are too idealistic or emotional to behave with adequate professionalism in conflict zones. This denigration of the effort to 'save lives', however, is not consistently espoused by CAMPO trainers. At other junctures in the training, trainees are reminded that humanitarian actors are not the only ones in conflict zones who save people. Indeed, there is a mixed message in this respect in all three of the civil–military training programmes. Even as they fault humanitarian actors for being naïve, military actors at the CAMPO and NATO training sessions also express an earnest desire to help.

Reminiscent of the previous discussion of international civilian actors, the way in which international military actors understand the distinction practices of humanitarian actors is shaped by a larger set of grievances. While international military actors express concern that humanitarian actors are anti-military, they also bring their own prejudgements and misgivings to their encounters with humanitarian actors. The crucial difference, of course, is that while humanitarian actors want to dissociate from international military actors, military actors seek to foster proximity. As Goodhand summarizes in the case of Afghanistan: 'Generally, NGOs have tended to argue for sharp boundaries and a clear delimitation of tasks, whilst the default position of the military is to blur or demolish these boundaries through integration.'[47] We now arrive at a significant blind spot of international military actors: they do not appear attuned to how their efforts to engage with humanitarian actors could undermine the latter's civilianness.

Too close to the conflict: proximity to international military actors

The final way in which humanitarian actors might attract a 'civilian minus' label is through contact with international military actors. As noted, international military actors accuse humanitarian actors of feeding and caring for the enemy. These same military actors grow frustrated when humanitarian NGO actors do not want to be seen with them and their guns on the roadside. What is more, through their 'rush to the intimate', military actors strive to encroach upon humanitarian actors. These active efforts to move, dim, or erase the lines that humanitarian actors draw sit uneasily with accusations that humanitarian actors are too close to the conflict.

A viable interpretation of these dynamics is that when international military actors protest against humanitarian actors' entanglement in armed conflict, they

[46] This outlook encapsulates a key strand of pushback against the move to professionalize humanitarian assistance. Discussed in Eric James, 'The Professional Humanitarian and the Downsides of Professionalization', *Disasters*, Vol. 40, No. 2, 2016, pp. 185–206 ('Professional Humanitarian').

[47] Jonathan Goodhand, 'Contested Boundaries: NGOs and Civil–Military Relations in Afghanistan', *Central Asian Survey*, Vol. 32, No. 3, 2013, pp. 287–305, 297 ('Contested Boundaries').

are narrowly concerned with conflict actors who fight for the other side. The exception to this is where international military actors take issue with humanitarian actors who receive funding from (political) donors on the 'good' side of the conflict. Perhaps this problem is easier for military actors to see because they do not feel personally implicated. Ultimately, these military actors are primarily fixated upon how they might achieve their own goals through contact with humanitarian actors. Notably, some of the measures these military actors adopt—such as 'speaking civilian'—downplay their own combatantness.

Although few military actors concede it is problematic to get close to humanitarians, others with less skin in the game readily acknowledge this. A SWEDINT trainer, who previously held the position of humanitarian–military coordinator, explains how this association can taint the civilian status of humanitarian actors:

> [T]he moment you get too close to the military, you are sort of lost .... I noticed when I was advising people in the field, people would say 'It's so great, I was invited to a military BBQ'. You have to be really cautious and tell them 'The military is likely to open their arms and invite you to everything, and these are the people you need distance from'.

While acceding to military advances in the social sphere might seem innocuous to humanitarian NGOs, the trainer argues that this familiarity and comfort spills over into operational decision-making. When humanitarian actors happily accept military support, he says, 'I feel like asking them, putting them in a chair and saying, "Are you out of your mind?!" There is no thinking about what the consequences would be.'[48] To flesh out the way in which humanitarian actors become contaminated, he recounts two experiences from the field. These stories, which respectively deal with optics and influence, perfectly capture the two dimensions of association.

The first example comes from Darfur, where some humanitarian NGOs acquired the habit of carelessly relying on UN assets. The SWEDINT trainer describes an incident in which an NGO in Darfur asked the UN/AU hybrid mission, UNAMID, to recover the NGO's broken vehicle. OCHA recommended that this NGO refrain from direct communication with UNAMID and advised that if the decision were made to accept help from UN forces, the NGO's logo should be removed from the car. The NGO, however, disregarded this advice. As a result, 'UNAMID was driving a convoy with a broken NGO car on top of it'. This generated concerns with respect to optics, as humanitarian NGOs in Darfur would be visibly associated with the UN mission. In this account, the 'phantom local' spots the convoy as it makes its way along the sandy road in

[48] Like the first ideal type of humanitarian actor, this individual adopts a long-term view and prioritizes distinction over other goals.

Darfur. It sees the UNAMID and NGO logos juxtaposed and assigns qualities of combatantness to the humanitarian actors.

The SWEDINT trainer's second story demonstrates that affiliation concerns will not always be about what is externally observed. Instead, proximity might lead one to become inappropriately influenced as a matter of actual fact. The context of this story is an intervention in the Middle East,[49] wherein members of an international military coalition developed a close relationship with the UN humanitarian–military coordinator. As the SWEDINT trainer explains, this coordinator became so friendly with the military that he started to advocate on their behalf with the wider humanitarian community. Having developed sympathy for the military perspective, this UN humanitarian coordinator over-identified and 'took that line'. He began telling UN humanitarian agencies to deliver services in places where the coalition forces wanted them to work for strategic reasons. As the conflict progressed, other humanitarian actors grew uncomfortable with the coordinator's positioning and showed increasing reluctance to approach the UN mission. In the end, there was considerable professional fallout for this individual as a result of his missteps. The message is that one's humanitarianness can become compromised as a matter of actual fact, even when there are no witnesses to it. The SWEDINT trainer's parting advice is simple: 'You need to know what game you're playing in.'

Moving on to consider where the line is drawn in the Intellectual realm, the next section proposes that 'civilian minus' and 'civilian plus' figures circulate in international law.

5.3 The Intellectual realm

This part of the discussion identifies openings for both 'civilian plus' and 'civilian minus' status in international law, and more generally highlights the existence of a continuum of civilianness. While the first two sections respectively focus on the conduct of hostilities and the provision of services to the general civilian population, the third engages with the figure of the humanitarian actor. The main findings are as follows. First, the way in which the principle of distinction interacts with other IHL rules relating to targeting in the conduct of hostilities undermines a binary civilian–combatant distinction. Second, when it comes to protection and access to services, some civilians are treated differently to others in IHL. Third, IHL constitutes some humanitarian actors—namely those who conform to the Red Cross fantasy—as 'civilian plus'.

[49] Location withheld to maintain confidentiality.

5.3.1 IHL targeting rules that muddle the distinction

A number of IHL targeting rules interact with the binary formulation of distinction and potentially trouble the notion of a stable civilian category. Four AP I rules are examined here, in turn: the prohibition on perfidy, the expansion of the combatant category, the concept of direct participation in hostilities (DPH), and the presumption in favour of civilian status. Collectively, these rules undermine a clear civilian–combatant distinction. The DPH concept, in particular, introduces fluidity between the civilian and combatant categories that makes a bright-line distinction impossible to sustain.

In contemporary armed conflict, the prohibition on perfidy requires those engaged in fighting to stay on their side of the line. Briefly, this prohibition forbids those engaged in war fighting from feigning civilian status in an attempt to deceive or to secure concomitant benefits.[50] Compliance with this rule is incentivized by the fact that a soldier who misleadingly wears civilian clothing may be legally targeted during this time.[51] Historically, this prohibition was grounded in concerns about the honour and dignity of the fighter.[52] Whatever the underlying motivation, perfidy is, in essence, about trust. It concerns the issue of whether one can have confidence that the person in front of them is who or what they appear to be.[53] The overall thrust of the prohibition on perfidy is to preserve and reinforce the notion of a binary civilian–combatant distinction. It also puts a premium on authentic civilianness. That is, IHL outlaws the feigning of civilian status, while it treats many other forms of deception as lawful ruses.[54] All of this would seem to suggest that the prohibition on perfidy stabilizes a binary distinction. That notion is undermined, however, by two things. First, the rule exists because individuals can and do, in practice, jump over the line. Second, the prohibition on perfidy reveals the capacity for authentic and fake civilians. This does not promote, but instead undercuts, a bright-line binary. The issue of perfidy is revisited later in this part of the discussion, with respect to the simulation of humanitarian actors.

While the IHL rule on perfidy bars combatants from feigning or simulating civilian status, Article 44(3) of AP I provides that, in specified circumstances,

[50] See Article 37 of AP I, based on Article 23(b) of the Hague Regulations of 1899; Article 37(1) in Claude Pilloud, Yves Sandoz, Christophe Swinarski, et al. (eds.), *ICRC Commentary on Additional Protocols of 8 June 1977 to the Geneva Conventions of 12 August 1949* (Geneva: ICRC, 1987), 435 (*AP Commentary*); Rule 65 of Jean-Marie Henckaerts and Louise Doswald-Beck, *Customary International Humanitarian Law* (Geneva: ICRC, 2005) (*ICRC Customary IHL Study*); Gabriella Blum, 'The Laws of War and the "Lesser Evil"', *Yale Journal of International Law*, Vol. 35, No. 1, 2010, pp. 1–69, 41 ('Lesser Evil').

[51] Gabriella Blum and Philip Heymann, 'Law and Policy of Targeted Killing', *Harvard National Security Journal*, Vol. 1, 2010, pp.145–170, 146 ('Targeted Killing').

[52] Blum, supra, 41 ('Lesser Evil').

[53] Ibid.

[54] On lawful ruses in customary IHL, see Rule 57 of Henckaerts and Doswald-Beck, supra (*ICRC Customary Law Study*).

combatants are relieved of the obligation to distinguish themselves from the general civilian population.[55] While combatants must still carry weapons openly while engaging directly in hostilities, they are permitted to blend in with the civilian population between combat phases.[56] The effect of this provision, which accommodates the tactics of irregular fighters, is to expand the combatant category.[57] Those who oppose this IHL rule argue that it leads parties to the conflict to regard civilians as potential combatants in disguise.[58] This points again to the trust issue, suggesting that one's appearance might not be an accurate indication of one's status. It should be stressed that, when within sight of the enemy, persons are prohibited from feigning protected status in order to carry out a hostile act.[59] Nonetheless, the Article 44(3) exception has a destabilizing impact on the civilian–combatant binary.

Whereas the two provisions discussed thus far address combatants who look like civilians, the DPH concept is concerned with civilians who join in the fighting. While AP I provides for the most robust form of civilian immunity that has so far been codified in positive law, it also contains the crucial caveat that civilians who participate in war may lose their immunity.[60] As stipulated in Article 51(3): 'Civilians shall enjoy the protection afforded by this part, unless and for such time as they take a direct part in hostilities.'[61] Introducing temporal fluidity, the DPH concept challenges the notion that the civilian and combatant categories are alternative and exhaustive. At any given moment, there may be actors located in the civilian category who have recently engaged in fighting or are about to do so. These individuals, who would otherwise have civilian status, forfeit immunity and may be lawfully targeted on the basis of their conduct.[62]

[55] Article 43(3) of AP I states that, where a combatant cannot distinguish himself due to the nature of hostilities,

> 'he shall retain his status as a combatant, provided that, in such situations, he carries his arms openly: (a) during each military engagement, and (b) during such time as he is visible to the adversary while he is engaged in a military deployment preceding the launching of an attack in which he is to participate'.

[56] Yves Sandoz, 'Land Warfare', in Andrew Clapham and Paola Gaeta (eds.), *Oxford Handbook of International Law in Armed Conflict* (Oxford: Oxford University Press, 2014), pp. 91–117, 96 ('Land Warfare').

[57] Emily Crawford, *Identifying the Enemy: Civilian Participation in Armed Conflict* (Oxford: Oxford University Press, 2015), 41–42 (*Identifying the Enemy*); Helen Kinsella, *The Image Before the Weapon: A Critical History of the Distinction between Combatant and Civilian* (Ithaca, NY and London: Cornell University Press, 2011), 6, (*Image*).

[58] United Kingdom Ministry of Defence, *The Joint Service Manual of the Law of Armed Conflict*, JSP 383 (2004), 4.5.1. Cited in Crawford, supra, 43 (*Identifying the Enemy*).

[59] Sandoz, supra, 95–96 ('Land Warfare').

[60] Article 51(3) of AP I; Crawford, supra, 233 (*Identifying the Enemy*).

[61] Article 51(3) of AP I. See also Article 13(3) of AP II. On special problems with DPH in NIACs and the notion of a 'continuous combat function', see Yoram Dinstein, *The Conduct of Hostilities under the Law of International Armed Conflict* (Cambridge: Cambridge University Press, 2004), 42 (*CoH*). See also Rule 6 of Henckaerts and Doswald-Beck, supra (*ICRC Customary Law Study*) ('Civilians are protected against attack, unless and for such a time as they take a direct part in hostilities').

[62] On the relationship between status and conduct, see Dinstein, supra, 42 (*CoH*).

Furthermore, unlike combatants, they are liable for prosecution due to their acts, as well as punishment by a Detaining Power.[63] Civilians who directly participate are thus treated differently from combatants, as well as from civilians who do not DPH.

In the mid 2000s, international lawyers expected the concept of DPH to re-invigorate IHL.[64] However, the intensive global discussions of DPH that ensued did not ultimately have the desired effect. On the contrary, delving into DPH drew attention to the fact that the principle of distinction was widely viewed as 'a disputed concept, one that was open to multiple reasonable interpretations'.[65] Contemplating the implications of DPH for a binary distinction, some commentators suggest that it allows actors to cross the civilian–combatant line.[66] This view maintains the binary formulation but jettisons the notion of a bright line. Others contend that DPH sets up a third category of actor.[67] While Hellestveit maintains that IHL's principle of distinction has, in fact, 'always been stretched' to cover a third category,[68] she goes on to characterize the distinction as 'otherwise orderly'.[69] This latter view is not at all unusual. Many international actors interviewed for this study—including lawyers—manage to hold a vision of a binary distinction in mind, at the same time as they acknowledge that rules like DPH undermine it. This suggests that the clarity afforded by a binary framework remains appealing, regardless of how troubled it might be. We might also recall here the case of *Martić* at the ICTY,[70] where the soldier *hors de combat*—who was a victim of crimes against humanity—was essentially

[63] A combatant is entitled to PoW status upon capture and can engage in certain types of violent conduct. Discussed in Crawford, supra, 48 (*Identifying the Enemy*).

[64] Naz Modirzadeh, 'Folk International Law: 9/11 Lawyering and the Transformation of the Law of Armed Conflict to Human Rights Policy and Human Rights Law to War Governance', *Harvard National Security Journal*, Vol. 5, No. 1, 2014, pp. 225–304, 301 ('Folk IL').

[65] Ibid., 302. It also exposed the lack of agreement regarding what actually constitutes DPH. For the relevant ICRC guidance and critiques, see: ICRC, 'Interpretive Guidance on the Notion of Direct Participation in Hostilities Under International Humanitarian Law', *International Review of the Red Cross*, Vol. 90, No. 872, December 2008, pp. 991–1047 ('ICRC Interpretive Guidance'); Ryan Goodman and Derek Jinks, 'The ICRC Interpretive Guidance on the Notion of Direct Participation in Hostilities Under International Humanitarian Law: An Introduction to the Forum', *NYU Journal of International Law and Politics*, Vol. 42, 2010, pp. 637–640 ('DPH').

[66] Colm McKeogh, *Innocent Civilians: The Morality of Killing in War* (New York: Palgrave, 2002), 138, 140 (*Innocent Civilians*) (arguing that AP I actually did away with a 'no man's land' or gap between the civilian and combatant categories that had previously been occupied by irregular fighters).

[67] Kinsella, supra, 144 (*Image*) (arguing that DPH sets up a new category of civilian); Dinstein, supra, 58, 175, 177 (*CoH*); Richard Baxter, 'So-Called "Unprivileged Belligerency": Spies, Guerrillas, and Saboteurs', *British Yearbook of International Law*, Vol. 28, 1951, pp. 323–345, 328 ('Unprivileged Belligerency') (on the concept of unprivileged belligerents).

[68] Cecilie Hellestveit, 'The Geneva Conventions and the Dichotomy between International and Non-International Armed Conflict: Curse or Blessing for the "Principle of Humanity"?', in Kjetil Mujezinovic Larsen, Camilla Guldahl Cooper, and Gro Nystuen (eds.), *Searching for a 'Principle of Humanity' in International Humanitarian Law* (Cambridge: Cambridge University Press, 2013), pp. 86–123, 102–103 ('Curse or Blessing?').

[69] Ibid., 103.

[70] See Section 4.3.2.

treated as part of the civilian population. This wounded, sick, or captured (former) fighter was deemed to merit the same protection as a civilian.[71] As the suddenly harmless and vulnerable soldier *hors de combat* looks out at a suddenly dangerous civilian, they might find themselves sharing a status—one that is unfamiliar to IHL: the 'civilian minus'.[72]

Further to the promise of clarity, Article 50(1) of AP I provides that, in cases of doubt, there is a presumption in favour of civilian status. Ostensibly, this supports the vision of a broad, unified civilian category populated by all those who are not combatants. Although it may be argued that all legal doctrine is imbued with some level of indeterminacy, doubt, or ambiguity,[73] what is interesting here is the explicit inclusion of dubious civilians in the civilian category. Reflecting on the function of doubt in Article 50(1), Kinsella proposes that it 'becomes an integral attribute of the category itself as well as the basis for the injunction to extend the category'.[74] Through this presumption, Kinsella argues, IHL admits that the distinction between combatant and civilian is imprecise.[75] Put differently, IHL asserts that only some individuals in the civilian category are 'definitely' civilians.[76]

It merits emphasis that all of this messiness occurs at the normative level of legal doctrine and concepts, before one accounts for the murkiness of on-the-ground implementation. The next section pivots away from the conduct of hostilities, to consider the provision of services and protection to civilian populations. The IHL rules examined here do not pertain so directly to targeting issues as those discussed above, but I will suggest that they nonetheless contribute to the existence of a continuum of civilianness in international law.

[71] Notably, commentators who argue that the ICTY's approach in *Martić* was too narrow emphasize the harmlessness and vulnerability of soldiers *hors de combat* at the moment of targeting. See Joakim Dungel, 'Defining Victims of Crimes against Humanity: Martic and the International Criminal Court', *Leiden Journal of International Law*, Vol. 22, 2009, pp. 727–752 ('Defining Victims'); William A. Schabas, *The UN International Criminal Tribunals: The Former Yugoslavia, Rwanda and Sierra Leone* (New York: Cambridge University Press, 2006), 191. Citing *Prosecutor v. Kupreškić* et al., Case No. IT-95-16-T, Trial Judgment, ICTY, 14 January 2000 ('*Kupreškić* et al. Trial Judgment'); Handsdeep Singh, 'Critique of the *Mrskic* Trial Judgment: A Re-Evaluation on Whether Soldiers *Hors De Combat* Are Entitled to Recognition as Victims of Crimes Against Humanity', *The Law and Practice of International Courts and Tribunals*, Vol. 8, 2009, pp. 247–296, 293, 296 ('Critique of *Mrskic*'); Kai Ambos and Steffen Wirth, 'The Current Law of Crimes Against Humanity: An Analysis of UNTAET Regulation 15/2000', *Criminal Law Forum*, Vol. 13, No.1, 2002, pp. 1–90 ('Crimes Against Humanity').

[72] This study is primarily interested in civilians and not those categorized as 'protected persons' under IHL.

[73] On the indeterminacy of international legal rules generally see Martti Koskenniemi, *From Apology to Utopia: The Structure of International Legal Argument* (Cambridge: Cambridge University Press, 2009). Indeterminacy is discussed in Section 1.2.

[74] Kinsella, supra, 143, 144, 185 (*Image*).

[75] Ibid., 5.

[76] For a broader discussion of civilian ambiguity, see Hugo Slim, *Killing Civilians: Method, Madness, and Morality in War* (Oxford: Oxford University Press, 2010), 182–184 (*Killing Civilians*).

5.3.2 Disaggregating civilians for the purpose of protection and services

In this monograph, the distinction vernacular includes, but also encompasses more than, issues of targeting in the conduct of hostilities. The 'plus' designator that I have introduced in connection with the civilian figure has implications for who might be harmed in armed conflicts, but that is not all: it is also loaded with features pertaining to broader concepts of survival, protection, and privilege. Opening out to consider issues beyond immunity from attack, this section canvasses IHL provisions that afford different segments of the civilian population special treatment. These legal rules rely upon intra-civilian distinctions, and thus shed light on the logic of humanitarian distinction practices. If civilianness is a matter of degree, then individuals seeking protected status will naturally wish to claim the most robust iteration with the highest level of entitlements.

As mentioned in Chapter 1, GC IV does not define the civilian entity that is supposed to be the object of legal protection. While it is often taken for granted that GC IV contains a unified civilian category, this legal instrument does something that significantly undermines the notion of a unified civilian category: it disaggregates the civilian population for the purposes of receiving protection and accessing humanitarian assistance.[77] This means that before the civilian was defined in IHL, and before the principle of distinction was codified in AP I, GC IV of 1949 splintered the civilian category. It did this by allocating some civilians who were deemed especially vulnerable additional entitlements to protection and assistance that other civilians could not claim. I propose that civilians who were singled out for special treatment acquired 'civilian plus' status, while those who were left behind were relegated to 'mere civilian' (and perhaps 'civilian minus') status.

In some instances, GC IV disaggregates civilians on the basis of social characteristics such as age and gender. In the context of occupation, for example, Article 50 states that the Occupying Power shall not impede any preferential measures in regard to food, medical care, and protection for children younger than 15 years, expectant mothers, and mothers of children under 7 years.[78] There are further provisions in GC IV that single out certain civilians for special treatment. Some of these relate to setting up hospitals and safety zones to protect designated groups,[79] granting the passage of essential supplies to pregnant women and children,[80] and providing members of listed groups with special access to evacuation.[81] Article

[77] I thank Dino Kritsiotis for this point, in response to the author's presentation on the 'Emotional Warfare' panel at the conference 'The Historicization of International Law', 2016, Uppsala, Sweden.

[78] Article 50 of GC IV.

[79] Article 14 of GC IV (providing for hospitals and safety zones that aim at protecting certain groups from the effects of war).

[80] Article 23 of GC IV (granting passage to essential supplies for pregnant women and children).

[81] Article 17 of GC IV (granting special access to evacuation for members of listed groups).

16(2) further stipulates that the wounded and sick, the infirm, and expectant mothers 'shall be the object of particular protection and respect'.[82] This last provision addresses not only those who would otherwise be categorized as civilians, but also fighters who have become vulnerable by virtue of being *hors de combat*. It is important to recall here that IHL's protections were first designed for wounded soldiers on the battlefield, and that the concept of 'wounded and sick' was subsequently expanded to all those who are particularly vulnerable and in need of care.[83]

From a relational perspective, the question that arises here is how IHL situates individuals who are accorded special treatment in relation to members of the general civilian population. The ICRC *Commentary to GC IV* stipulates that granting something extra to certain segments of the civilian population is not supposed to take anything away from others.[84] According special respect or protection to some individuals, it states, does not free belligerents from their obligation to respect and protect the wider civilian population.[85] The *Commentary* further asserts that special protections are 'not instead of, but in addition to the protection given generally'.[86] I want to contest these claims, and suggest that something *is* being taken away from those civilians who are not accorded special treatment. This argument is supported by this study's findings about on-the-ground practice. As we have seen in the Kinetic and Pedagogical realms, international (non-humanitarian) civilian actors express serious anxiety regarding the prospect of a spectrum—or hierarchy—of civilian actors.

Van Engeland, too, is alert to the possibility that special treatment of the kind under discussion here can destabilize the civilian category. She suggests that these GC IV provisions establish a subcategory of civilians and introduce individuals who potentially 'fall in between the categories' of civilians and combatants.[87] In the parlance of the present study, it may be said these extra entitlements set up a continuum of civilianness populated by different civilian figures.[88] Even if what is given is 'in addition to' general civilian protection, my concern is that the singling out of certain civilians fundamentally alters the concept of (general) civilian protection. Civilians who are not selected for special treatment take on 'mere civilian'

[82] Article 16(2) of GC IV.

[83] Discussed in Sandoz, supra, 101 ('Land Warfare'), citing the definition of 'wounded and sick' in Article 8(a) of AP I.

[84] Jean Pictet (ed.), *Commentary: IV Geneva Convention, Relative to the Protection of Civilian Persons in Time of War* (Geneva: ICRC, 1958) (*Commentary to GC IV*). Discussing Art 16(2) of GC IV.

[85] Ibid.

[86] Ibid.

[87] See Anicée Van Engeland, *Civilian or Combatant? A Challenge for the 21st Century* (Oxford: Oxford University Press, 2011), 75, 161 (*Civilian or Combatant?*).

[88] This is not to say that humanitarian assistance that accords preferential treatment to especially vulnerable populations cannot be impartial. See Dapo Akande and Emanuela-Chiara Gillard, *Oxford Guidance on the Law Relating to Humanitarian Relief Operations in Situations of Armed Conflict* (UN OCHA, 2016), 9 (*Oxford Guidance*).

status, and there are also hints that a 'civilian minus' status is in circulation—a possibility that becomes clearer when the DPH concept is considered.

A few remarks are merited here on how AP I delineates the populations that are entitled to receive assistance and protection in armed conflict. The relevant AP I rules deviate somewhat from the GC IV approach that has just been outlined.[89] Significantly, AP I expressly states that humanitarian assistance is for the entire civilian population, rather than only specified vulnerable groups.[90] Nonetheless, AP I stipulates that certain members of the civilian population, including children, expectant mothers, and nursing mothers, have priority access to assistance and protection.[91] Both women and children are again referred to in the relevant AP I provisions as 'the object of special respect'.[92] So, while AP I provides that humanitarian assistance should be given to the entire civilian population, it still engages in disaggregation of the sort envisioned in GC IV.

The next section proposes that IHL also treats some humanitarian actors as special civilians.

5.3.3 The humanitarian actor as special civilian

The discussion of the Red Cross fantasy in Chapter 3 considered how IHL situates different humanitarian actors in relation to one another, highlighting the existence of a Red Cross exceptionalism. The present discussion opens out to explore how IHL situates humanitarian actors, as a larger group, in relation to the civilian category. I advance the claim that IHL treats some humanitarian actors as special civilians, building towards an examination of the desirability of the 'civilian plus' in Chapter 6.

I will suggest here that by the time humanitarian actors were considered more directly in AP I, IHL had already set at least some humanitarian actors apart from the wider civilian population. Implicitly, humanitarianness is connected here to a higher form of civilianness.[93] While there is little room for this prospect if one envisions a unified civilian category, it makes sense in a world where civilianess exists along a continuum. As will be shown, the treatment of the humanitarian actor in the Rome Statute of the International Criminal Court (ICC)

89 The humanitarian actor under AP I is discussed separately in Chapter 3.

90 Articles 69 and 70 of AP I.

91 Article 70(1) of AP I. See also Article 76 of AP I (additional protection for women); Article 77 of AP I (additional protection for children); Article 76 of AP I (evacuation of children).

92 Articles 76 and 77 of AP I; see also Article 4(3d) of AP II (special protection for captured children who have engaged in DPH who are younger than 15).

93 See also Bruno Demeyere, 'Turning the Stranger into a Partner: The Role and Responsibilities of Civil Society in International Humanitarian Law Formulation and Application', *Harvard Program on Humanitarian Policy and Conflict Research Thematic Brief*, 2016, 13 ('Stranger') (asking the following question about NGO status: 'Can "ordinary" NGOs have any more special status under IHL than that accruing to "ordinary" civilians, in recognition of the special assistance they are ready to deliver?').

and the public pronouncements of the UN further give the impression that a special status is carved out for humanitarian actors from the civilian category. While the exact shape of this humanitarian actor is hazy, it refers to the Red Cross figure.

To examine how the humanitarian actor is constituted vis à vis the civilian category in AP I, it is helpful to bracket the differences between different kinds of humanitarian actors. Article 71(2) of AP I stipulates that, in IACs, those engaged in war fighting are required to 'respect and protect'[94] humanitarian actors.[95] The question of interest is how this situates humanitarian actors in relation to the general civilian population. The notion that AP I positions humanitarian actors alongside other civilians in a unified civilian category is supported in the respective accounts of Fast and Barrat.[96] Barrat points out that the APs extend the requirement of 'respect and protect' to all non-combatants.[97]

Alternatively, one can emphasize the fact that the APs explicitly attend to personnel engaged in the provision of relief, remedying a previous lack of protection under IHL. This view is promoted in Durham and Wynn-Pope's account, which contends that the AP I obligation to 'respect and protect' humanitarian actors provides these actors with 'more substantial footing and a specific status' under IHL than what they previously had under the GCs.[98] I am persuaded by the latter view of the *lex lata*, though I would emphasize that only Red Cross actors and actors resembling the Red Cross figure are legible to IHL in this way.[99] This claim will now be fleshed out further.

To begin, scholars often assert or imply that humanitarian actors have a special status without specifying the legal basis for it. While these discussions are not all centred on the conduct of hostilities, they go to the more general notion that humanitarians are a special kind of civilian. In an examination of crimes against humanity, for example, Fernandez and Estapa mention as an aside that humanitarian

[94] The term 'respect' here is interpreted to mean 'to spare, not to attack', while protect means 'to come to someone's defence, to lend help and support'. See Pictet (ed.), supra, 146 (*Commentary to GC IV*). Discussed in Helen Durham and Phoebe Wynn-Pope, 'Protecting the "Helpers": Humanitarians and Health Care Workers During Times of Armed Conflict', *Yearbook of International Humanitarian Law*, Vol. 14, December 2011, pp. 327–346, 337 ('Protecting the "Helpers"').

[95] Article 71(2) of AP I. There is no equivalent rule in AP II, though medical relief is clearly protected under Article 9 of AP II. Protections for humanitarian actors in NIACs can be derived from customary law. Kate Mackintosh, 'Beyond the Red Cross: The Protection of Independent Humanitarian Organizations and their Staff in International Humanitarian Law', *International Review of the Red Cross*, Vol. 89, No. 865, 2007, pp. 113–130, 118 ('Beyond the Red Cross').

[96] For an argument that IHL protects humanitarian actors as civilians, see Fast, supra, 197 (*Aid in Danger*); Claudie Barrat, *Status of NGOs in International Humanitarian Law* (Leiden: Brill Nijhoff, 2014), 323 (*Status of NGOs*).

[97] Barrat, supra, 323 (*Status of NGOs*).

[98] Durham and Wynn-Pope, supra, 337 ('Protecting the Helpers').

[99] On the lack of coverage for most 'relief personnel' see Mackintosh, supra, 113 ('Beyond the Red Cross'). Compare with Barrat, supra ('Status of NGOs') (arguing that humanitarian NGOs are comprehensively covered).

personnel have 'differentiated status' from other civilians.[100] In other instances, scholars flag a special status but only for Red Cross humanitarian actors. In a discussion of IHL rules on perfidy and the misuse of emblems, Bartels remarks that IHL accords special protection to Red Cross actors, while 'a "regular" civilian "only" enjoys regular/standard protection'.[101] Bartels reports these findings in a questioning manner, intimating a lack of clarity in IHL on this matter.

The special status of the Red Cross figure also receives attention in the ICRC *Commentary to the APs*. The authors of the *Commentary* find:[102]

> Apart from the personnel involved in actions under the responsibility of the ICRC, who consequently enjoy the protection of the red cross emblem, personnel participating in relief actions are only protected, outside the régime of the Protocol, by general rules applicable to civilians of States which are not Parties to the conflict. Such persons certainly enjoy the general protection of populations against certain consequences of war, and, as civilians, may not be attacked, but not all of them are covered by the Fourth Convention which excluded certain categories from its field of application ....

In this account, the entitlements of non-Red Cross humanitarian actors are not clear; but it does appear that ICRC personnel are granted something more than civilian status.[103]

The possibility that humanitarian actors are constituted as special civilians finds some support in international criminal law. Article 8(2)(e)(ii) of the Rome Statute prohibits intentional attacks against buildings, material, medical units, and transport systems, as well as personnel using the 'distinctive emblems of the Geneva Conventions in conformity with international law'.[104] Further, Article 8(2)(b)(iii) prohibits intentional attacks against 'personnel, installations, material, units or vehicles involved in a humanitarian assistance or peacekeeping mission' in accordance with the UN Charter, 'as long as they are entitled to the protection given to

[100] Rosa Fernandez and Jaume Estapa, 'Towards a Single and Comprehensive Notion of "Civilian Population" in Crimes Against Humanity', *International Criminal Law Review*, Vol. 17, 2017, pp. 47–77, 51 ('Civilian Population').

[101] Rogier Bartels, 'Killing with Military Objects Disguised as Civilian Objects is Perfidy', *Just Security* blog, March 2015. Available at: https://www.justsecurity.org/21285/disguising-military-weapons-civilian-equipment-perfidy-or-be/.

[102] Pilloud et al. (eds.), supra, 832 (*AP Commentary*). Referring to GC I–IV of 1949, AP I, and AP II.

[103] The only other humanitarian actors who have unambiguous claims to special protection are UN humanitarian actors (see Chapter 2) and medical personnel of the armed forces. See Julia Brooks, 'Protecting Humanitarian Action: Key Challenges and Lessons from the Field', *A Report for Harvard Humanitarian Initiative and ATHA*, October 2016, 10 ('Protecting Humanitarian Action').

[104] Article 8(2)(e)(ii) of the UN General Assembly, Rome Statute of the International Criminal Court (last amended 2010), 17 July 1998 ('Rome Statute'); Felix Schwendimann, 'The Legal Framework of Humanitarian Access in Armed Conflict', *International Review of the Red Cross*, Vol. 93, No. 884, 2011, pp. 993–1008, 1005 (noting that a nexus with an armed conflict is required) ('Legal Framework').

civilians or civilian objects' under IHL.[105] This latter provision merits careful scrutiny for its treatment of the humanitarian actor in relation to the civilian figure.[106] Of note, the Rome Statute also deems intentional attacks against the general civilian population war crimes.[107] If humanitarian actors were protected as members of the wider civilian population, one might expect that they would be amply covered by that provision. The separate provision thus appears to establish humanitarian actors as a category of actor that is set apart from the wider civilian population.[108] This special treatment in the Rome Statute is amplified in the Resolutions and public pronouncements of the UN Security Council, the UN General Assembly, and other UN leadership regarding attacks on humanitarian actors.[109] Collectively, such statements convey the sentiment that intentional violence against humanitarian actors is especially egregious.

While the general civilian population is protected from targeting under IHL, and attacks against civilians are also prohibited as war crimes, the instruments and discourse canvassed above accord humanitarian actors a higher form of civilianness. Only a narrow slice of the humanitarian community—that is, Red Cross actors and those who resemble them—are deemed to merit 'civilian plus' status in international law. The protections that IHL accords other humanitarian actors are, comparatively speaking, opaque. The Rome Statute language ('as long as they are entitled to the protection given to civilians') also highlights the fact that humanitarian actors can *lose* civilian protection. This might happen, for example, if an individual humanitarian actor were to engage in DPH.[110] Rogers argues that participation in peace-enforcement operations could generate the same

[105] Article 8(2)(b)(iii) of the 'Rome Statute', supra. See also Article 4 of the Statute of the Special Court for Sierra Leone, 2178 UNTS 138, 145; UN Doc. S/2002/246, 16 January 2002, Appendix II ('Statute of the SCSL').

[106] See Durham and Wynn-Pope, supra, 339 ('Protecting the Helpers') ('relief workers who maintain their civilian status according to the Geneva Conventions are better protected than ever before').

[107] Article 8(2)(b)(i) of the 'Rome Statute', supra (prohibiting 'Intentionally directing attacks against the civilian population as such or against individual civilians not taking direct part in hostilities').

[108] Leclerc-Gagné also highlights that the prohibition on attacks against the wider civilian population appears only two clauses prior to Article 8(2)(b)(iii). Elise Leclerc-Gagné, *The Construction of the Humanitarian Worker as Inviolate Actor* (unpublished PhD thesis, 2014), 137–139 (*Inviolate Actor*).

[109] See e.g. United Nations Security Council, 'Increased Attacks on Aid Workers Due to Lack of Respect for International Humanitarian Law, Deputy Secretary-General Tells Security Council', *United Nations Meetings Coverage*, 19 August 2014, SC/11524. Resolutions calling for those engaged in warfighting to respect and protect humanitarian actors include: UNSC, *Security Council Resolution* 2139 (2014), 22 February 2014, S/RES/2139 ('UN Security Council Resolution 2139'); UNSC, *Security Council Resolution* 1894 (2009), 11 November 2009, S/RES/1894 ('UN Security Council Resolution 1894'); UNSC, *Security Council Resolution* 1502 (2003), 26 August 2003, S/RES/1502 ('UN Security Council Resolution 1502'). See also: UNGA, *General Assembly Resolution* 52/167 (1997), A/RES/52/167 ('UN General Assembly Resolution 52/167') (condemning any act or failure to act 'which obstructs or prevents humanitarian personnel from discharging their humanitarian functions'); UNGA, *General Assembly Resolution* 53/164 (1998), A/RES/53/164; UNGA, *General Assembly Resolution* 54/192 (1999), A/RES/54/192 ('UN General Assembly Resolution 53/164').

[110] DPH is addressed in Chapter 2 and Section 5.3.1.

result.[111] Thus, it may be that a 'civilian minus' status—if not a recategorization as a combatant—can be assigned to some humanitarian actors.[112]

A final issue to consider is how the visual cues of humanitarianness relate to those associated with civilianness. As noted, IHL provides little indication of the visual signification of civilianness.[113] Starting from the assumption that civilians generally do not wear military uniforms or bear arms, it can be said that humanitarian actors present differently. As Barker observes: 'For one thing, aid workers look like aid workers and not like civilians.' [114] The most crucial discrepancy is that humanitarian actors have recourse to an arsenal of signifiers that the wider civilian population cannot use, such as the aforementioned T-shirts with logos, car stickers, and flags. Of course, humanitarian actors do not tend to simply emblazon the generic term 'humanitarian' on their clothing, equipment, and facilities. More often, they signify the particular organization they belong to, such as UNICEF, Mercy Corps, or World Vision. This links to the first critique of humanitarian symbols, which concerns whether the distinction humanitarian actors promulgate is an alibi for hidden interests.

Conclusion

Problematizing the common assumption that civilians get along better with each other than with military actors, this chapter identified marked intra-civilian tensions in the Kinetic and Pedagogical realms. The Kinetic realm showcases international humanitarian actors trying to maintain distance from other international civilian actors; the former insist that this is not about purity but rather about saving lives. Other civilians question the motives underlying such practices, not wanting to find themselves with tarnished civilianness nor at the bottom of a hierarchy of virtue. Meanwhile, the 'civilian minus' circulates around humanitarian actors whose claims to harmlessness are impugned, whose humanitarian credentials are brought into question, and who are seen as too close to the fight. The 'civilian minus' materializes here as the shadow side of the special status humanitarian actors promulgate.

[111] Humanitarian actors and personnel involved in peacekeeping missions are protected, as opposed to those involved in peace enforcement. A. P. V. Rogers, *Law on the Battlefield*, 3rd edition (Manchester: Manchester University Press, 2012), 319 (*Law on the Battlefield*).

[112] Note that humanitarians who operate without (state) consent do not lose civilian status under IHL. When consent is withheld, no duty arises to facilitate the rapid and unimpeded passage of relief supplies, equipment, and personnel. Akande and Gillard, supra, 51 (*Oxford Guidance*).

[113] See Claire Garbett, *The Concept of the Civilian: Legal Recognition, Adjudication and the Trials of International Criminal Justice* (Oxford: Routledge, 2015), 100 (*The Concept of the Civilian*); See Chapter 1.

[114] Camilla Barker, 'Aid Workers Could Secure Better Protection Under the Protection of Civilians Mandate', *International Law Grrls*, 15 August 2014. Available at: https://ilg2.org/2014/08/15/aid-workers-could-secure-better-protection-under-the-protection-of-civilians-mandate/.

Similar dynamics unfold in the Pedagogical realm. The circulation of the 'civilian plus' leads other international civilian actors to fear that they are being nudged closer to combatants, whom they too wish to avoid. Evidently, the way in which humanitarian actors deploy the 'plus' also rubs other actors the wrong way. Even where humanitarian actors do not extol their virtue explicitly, others read into their distinction practices a sense of superiority. Once again, humanitarian actors stand accused of meriting not a special status but instead a 'civilian minus' status. Humanitarian actors accept political funding, they pay at checkpoints, they feed the enemy, and sometimes they are dangerous because of plain incompetence. Although international military actors fault humanitarians for being too close to the conflict, they are not alive to the way in which their own efforts to encroach upon the humanitarian sphere compound this problem.

Finally, in the Intellectual realm, various targeting rules were found to destabilize distinction. The concept of DPH, in particular, makes a bright-line binary framework difficult to sustain. It is also shown that in GC IV, different segments of the civilian population were deemed to merit priority access to services and special protections due to their ascribed vulnerability. While again this is not strictly about targeting in the conduct of hostilities, it suggests not only that IHL makes intra-civilian distinctions, but also that the civilian category was split before the civilian was first defined in AP I. Finally, I argued that IHL accords some humanitarian actors a special civilian status, and here again the Red Cross fantasy circulates. All of these observations from the Intellectual realm support the claim that, through their everyday practices, humanitarian actors are engaging with an IHL rule that is already deeply disrupted.

6
Conclusion

Introduction

This multi-sited study has interrogated the idea of distinction across three domains: the Kinetic, the Pedagogical, and the Intellectual. As the idea of distinction was followed across each of these realms, it was not only the civilian–combatant distinction that was broken up. Other, unfamiliar, distinctions were also introduced and subsequently troubled—such as that between the 'civilian plus' and the 'mere civilian'. By devoting attention to unconventional actors and choosing unconventional sites of study, this monograph has revealed that many distinctions are constituted and reconstituted by international actors in many places, on a daily basis. The dynamics that have been scrutinized here are mostly hidden, both to IHL and to legal scholars. This opacity can largely be attributed to the tendency to see everything through the prism of a civilian–combatant divide. While this study has foregrounded actual practice, it has also taken care to show that messiness is not confined to the operational context. At every level, including legal text and doctrine, the disorder of distinction is palpable.

This concluding discussion commences with one last bottom-up engagement with the empirical material from South Sudan, in a final effort to tease out the work that the idea of distinction does in humanitarian practice. This encounter highlights an important role for the temporal element and attests that tensions about distinction play out at the level of the individual humanitarian actor. Having deferred normative questions throughout the investigation, the second section confronts them head on. I consider whether a 'civilian plus' status is desirable for how it 'helps the helpers', or, instead, whether it gives legal imprimatur to humanitarian exceptionalism. I ultimately come down on the latter side, offering some thoughts on why the 'civilian plus' might be a dangerous idea. The third section contemplates what this sideways look at distinction has told us about humanitarianness and the idea of the civilian. Finally, the discussion opens out and gestures towards potential avenues of future inquiry.

6.1 Everyday distinction practices: the temporal element

This section embarks on a granular description at the micro level of the way in which the idea of distinction circulates amongst humanitarian actors in South

The Humanitarian Civilian. Rebecca Sutton, Oxford University Press (2021). © Rebecca Sutton.
DOI: 10.1093/oso/9780198863816.003.0006

Sudan. Here we return to the two ideal types of humanitarian actor, and thus to the tension between upholding distinction and implementing the principle of humanity. As the following encounter demonstrates, these seemingly clashing approaches are not so far apart as they initially appear. Indeed, the two ideal types might even meet on the other side when the temporal element is adjusted.

> **'In a true emergency, I think distinction isn't something that matters'**
> There has recently been active fighting in Upper Nile, South Sudan, and most humanitarian actors have had to leave the area for security reasons. There is no steady provision of humanitarian services. Civilian populations residing in Upper Nile have mostly been required to fend for themselves, while also being targets of violence. Pointing to this situation, a humanitarian NGO actor inquires: 'If you're wounded, do you care if our [international NGO] or a UN surgeon operates? Do you care who your food comes from, in a true emergency?' He goes on to say: 'Where there is an acute need, in an emergency, I think distinction isn't something that matters. I think it matters more on a policy level: What will the rest of the world, the government here, the press think?' Subsequently, he acknowledges that the above attitude is open to accusations of short-term thinking. He ventures: 'I think it's an ethical dilemma. You don't care about distinction at that point in time, but then you think: Do you want someone who is a non-mutual party doing that work?' Another humanitarian NGO actor in South Sudan also vacillates on this issue. He initially espouses a strong commitment to distinction, attesting to the way in which it infuses all of his decision-making on a daily basis. However, he believes that, at a certain point, its observance is diametrically opposed to helping populations in need. Discussing the plight of war-affected populations in South Sudan's Southern Unity state, he explains: 'For obvious reasons, I support distinction as much as possible. But I think it hits a threshold where the need to just get in and provide services and do something outweighs the distinction risks. That comes way, way, down the line, [when] you've tried everything else.' In a context in which war-related violence leads to many civilian deaths daily, he probes: 'So we're not going to bring food in because it would involve a military helicopter? Really?'

It will be recalled that the first ideal type of humanitarian actor prioritizes distinction and takes a long-term view. In contrast, the second type balances distinction against other goals on a case-by-case basis, tending to prioritize the immediate need to help. The two speakers in the opening vignette begin from diametrically opposed positions, but they work their way towards each other. This suggests that humanitarian actors cannot simply be statically characterized as belonging to the first or second ideal types. To some extent, each individual may be capable of both ways of thinking and assume a particular outlook as a default. Juxtaposing these two accounts illuminates the crucial work that the temporal aspect performs in the production of distinction and the conceptualization of humanitarianness.

6.1.1 The second ideal type, reconsidered

In the above encounter, the first speaker initially exhibits all of the proclivities of the second ideal type. Leaning on the importance of implementing the principle of humanity, he draws attention to injured and hungry people in need of service. In a 'true emergency', he argues, distinction does not matter. Or, he adjusts, it matters—but only to those who are removed from the pressing needs of the victims of war. Here he cites the world, the press, and the GoSS as the relevant audiences, couching these diverse stakeholders as the 'policy level'. Having said this with firm conviction, he senses he is open to critique, particularly by humanitarian actors who might think of the longer-term implications. In his words: 'You don't care about distinction at that point in time, but . . . .' The reference to a non-mutual party also casts the UN surgeon in a different light to before. Previously, the surgeon was treated as almost a pair of disembodied hands that could heal. In this second take, the UN surgeon forms part of an international mission with political and military aspects. The surgeon is now potentially implicated in, or at least not doing enough to stop, the conflict in South Sudan—the same conflict that led to the injury of the wounded person on the operating table.

The temporal aspect of the distinction calculus is pivotal: the very same scenario looks completely different when the humanitarian NGO actor widens his perspective beyond immediate needs. It is also important to note how the 'phantom local' is mobilized in this account. Initially, the imagined audience takes the form of the (wounded) beneficiary-perceiver, who simply wishes to have needs met and is ostensibly unconcerned with which international actor will provide the service. Next, when the goal of meeting the needs of war-affected populations is held up against the importance of safeguarding distinction, distinction matters to three stakeholders: local government, the press, and the world. While the GoSS is not at the kind of remove that the press and the world are, it is insinuated that the perceptions of the authority-perceiver can be dealt with once the humanitarian imperative is met.

6.1.2 The first ideal type, reconsidered

Turning now to the second speaker from the opening encounter (see above), this humanitarian actor begins by encapsulating the tendencies of the first ideal type. He positions distinction as a priority and states that it inflects all of his daily decisions. Taking this as a point of departure, he too finds himself in situations where enforcing distinction seems impossible without compromising humanity. While he asserts that this only comes 'way, way, down the line', when all other options have been exhausted, his commitment to distinction comes with a caveat. He supports distinction, but only 'as much as possible'. Here, he begins to sound more like the second ideal type, emphasizing that there are other values and priorities to consider. He is alert to the risks of compromising distinction, but he believes that, at a certain point, 'the need to just get in and provide services and do something' prevails. Again, the temporal aspect does crucial work here, as he shifts to focus on immediate need. His crossover to the second ideal type is complete when he says: 'So we're not going to bring food in because it would involve a military helicopter? Really?'

In a similar vein, one humanitarian actor[1] confides that he has discreetly joined UNMISS forces on a few unauthorized trips outside of the PoC site where he resides. He says that had he not gone on these journeys he would not have been able to see anything. He elaborates: 'I would think twice if bending the rules involved a bunch of agencies, but if I, just myself, if I could see myself, touch the ground, then I can come back.' At one point he asserts that he does not feel personally bound by the rule of distinction. Subsequently, he modifies this to say that he believes that distinction is subsumed by other pressing priorities. While it appears that other members of the humanitarian community are not aware of this particular individual's discreet trips with UNMISS, the much-discussed unauthorized helicopter trip in Chapter 4 suggests how opinions might divide.

In a similar vein, a UN humanitarian actor contends that distinction should not stand in the way of responding to vulnerable populations who have nowhere else to turn for help. 'When you are between a rock and a hard place, you have to choose. There are pluses and minuses. Maybe I will lose on distinction, but I will win on something ... I would gain more than I would lose.' Another humanitarian actor is adamant that distinction stands in the way of real humanitarian work. He alleges that distinction prevents humanitarian actors 'from even thinking about what could be possible—it's hampering *thinking* even before *doing*'. He offers the hypothetical situation of an armed attack on UN food distribution to local civilian populations in South Sudan, and proposes:

> If we remove all distinction issues, the best scenario is to plunk in a bunch of peacekeepers, set a perimeter, do patrols, lay the smack-down. 'No shit's going down while we're here.' That's what we could do if we removed everything we know about distinction.

[1] Organizational affiliation and location are omitted to preserve confidentiality.

This individual's attention is not on the identity of the international actor providing the service, but on the service itself, and the fact that it is provided. From this perspective, competent military engagement in humanitarian assistance is preferable to a humanitarian organization doing it poorly for the sake of ensuring it is purely humanitarian. This perspective can be contrasted with that of the discussion in Chapter 3 regarding the direct engagement of military actors in humanitarian-type activities.[2] It was noted there that, while humanitarian actors recognize the (technical) capability of military actors to deliver humanitarian assistance, they question whether it can be done in an appropriate and principled manner. This speaker in South Sudan pushes such doubts to the side, centring the fact of service provision. Far from disseminating the 'civilian plus' figure, or even 'mere civilian' status, this humanitarian actor in South Sudan links humanitarianness to a sort of virtuous 'civilian minus'. In the image conjured here, the humanitarian actor is more agile and does not let fears of proximity to armed actors stand in the way of getting things done. The abdication of distinction is explicit in this account: the individual openly admits that his plan requires neglecting 'everything we know about distinction'.

In this encounter from the Kinetic realm, projections about the implications for populations in need render decision-making about distinction a fraught enterprise and lend it a sense of urgency. It is not my intention to resolve these tensions here, but rather to bring them to light and expose the work they are doing in everyday practice. The next section brings war-affected populations further into the foreground, grappling with whether a special civilian status is something humanitarian actors should have. As the focus shifts from considering distinction's paramountcy to assessing the desirability of a special civilian status, it is worth noting that these are two discrete, albeit related, problems. The issue of whether distinction should serve as a trump goes to distinction's place in the order of things; distinction is held up here against other priorities, particularly the humanitarian commitment to addressing human need wherever it is found. The conundrum of the 'civilian plus', for its part, concerns the move to split open the civilian category and establish intra-civilian distinctions. These two issues might well dovetail: in some instances, the fault line along which distinction is enacted will influence views about whether distinction should prevail over some other valued good.

6.2 The desirability of the 'civilian plus'

The empirical portions of this monograph establish that international humanitarian actors are longing for a special status and that they are making claims to

[2] See Section 3.2.2.

this status in the course of routine practice. It has further been shown that IHL in fact grants some humanitarian actors legal protection over and above that which is accorded to ordinary civilians. Turning now to normative questions about the 'civilian plus', I will make the stakes explicit by introducing a debate between two composite outlooks. These are, respectively, the 'help the helpers' and the 'against humanitarian exceptionalism' perspectives. For clarity, I should mention that a sustained debate on this matter is not yet underway in international legal circles—though I believe it should be, given the practices outlined in this monograph.

6.2.1 The 'civilian plus': two ways of seeing

First, the 'help the helpers'[3] view is grounded in the belief that humanitarian actors should have an extra layer of inviolability that protects them and enables them to execute their tasks.[4] In short, a special status allows humanitarian actors to save lives and to assist war-affected populations without becoming targets themselves.[5] Special protections are typically presented here as a means to an end—that of ensuring that war-affected populations receive humanitarian assistance and protection. [6] Observing how the GCs of 1949 accord humanitarian actors the same protection as other civilians, Durham and Wynn-Pope submit that 'it is questionable whether such general protection would be adequate'.[7] Additional protection is merited, they suggest, because humanitarian actors often face greater risk to their personnel, supplies, and facilities than the general civilian population.[8] This perspective embeds global efforts to develop extra protections for humanitarian actors over the past four decades, such as through the pronouncements of various UN bodies, and provisions in the Rome Statute of the International Criminal Court.[9]

Considered on its own, a special status for humanitarian actors might appear quite appealing: it denotes recognition of their particular needs and could incentivize their important work in armed conflicts. As a general proposition, few would contest the validity of enhancing the safety of humanitarian actors and improving their access to beneficiaries. A significant drawback of the 'help the helpers' position, however, is that it overlooks the way in which a carve-out for humanitarian

[3] Loosely based on Helen Durham and Phoebe Wynn-Pope, 'Protecting the "Helpers": Humanitarians and Health Care Workers During Times of Armed Conflict', *Yearbook of International Humanitarian Law*, Vol. 14, December 2011, pp. 327–346, 327 ('Protecting the Helpers').

[4] This tracks along with Durham and Wynn-Pope's arguments in Ibid.

[5] Fiona Terry, 'The International Committee of the Red Cross in Afghanistan: Reasserting the Neutrality of Humanitarian Action', *International Review of the Red Cross*, Vol. 93, No. 881, 2011, 173–188 ('ICRC in Afghanistan').

[6] Durham and Wynn-Pope, supra, 340 ('Protecting the Helpers').

[7] Ibid., 334.

[8] Ibid., 334, 329, 339. They also argue that humanitarian actors do in fact have a special status under the APs, as noted in Chapter 5.

[9] See Section 5.3.3.

actors impacts on the concept of general civilian protection. The more relational approach of the 'against humanitarian exceptionalism' perspective gets at this missing piece, though only implicitly because much of the latter literature neglects the legal dimension.[10] My aim here is thus to identify some fruitful contact points between the legal concept of the civilian and these critiques of humanitarian exceptionalism.

Those espousing the 'against humanitarian exceptionalism' perspective[11] greet the idea of a special status for humanitarian actors with trepidation. In scholarship addressing the figure of the humanitarian-as-outsider,[12] the humanitarian actor appears distant and perhaps even estranged from other actors around her—as well as from the wider context in which she works.[13] Through their attempts to set themselves apart, humanitarian actors may drift further away from the very people who legitimize their presence in conflict zones.[14] An important argument advanced in this literature is that the altruistic humanitarian act of 'saving lives' relies upon an imbalance. While the life of the humanitarian actor is freely risked, Fassin points out, the life of the vulnerable individual is treated as a bare life facing dangers not of their own choosing.[15] Beerli explores how these lives are weighed against each other through a routine calculus, as humanitarian actors decide whether a given course of action falls within the limits of acceptable sacrifice.[16] For her part, Fast queries the general expectation that humanitarian actors would be exempted from the violence that befalls war-affected populations.[17] She problematizes the treatment of humanitarian actors as a 'special category of civilians deserving attention and protection',[18] and asks whether this might undermine legal protection for the broader civilian population.[19] These are the very dynamics that the present study

[10] Fast is something of an exception here, see later in this section.

[11] While this is a composite perspective, this phrase 'humanitarian exceptionalism' is widely used in critical literature on humanitarianism. See, for example, Larissa Fast, *Aid in Danger: The Perils and Promise of Humanitarianism* (Philadelphia, PA: University of Pennsylvania Press, 2014), 112 (*Aid in Danger*).

[12] A term used in Didier Fassin, 'Inequality of Lives, Hierarchies of Humanity: Moral Commitments and Ethical Dilemmas of Humanitarianism', in Illana Feldman and Miriam Ticktin (eds.), *In the Name of Humanity: The Government of Threat and Care* (Durham, NC: Duke University Press, 2010), pp. 238–255, 239 ('Inequality of Lives').

[13] Fast, supra, 5 (*Aid in Danger*).

[14] Building on a point made by Fassin, supra ('Inequality of Lives').

[15] Didier Fassin, 'Humanitarianism as a Politics of Life', *Public Culture*, Vol. 19, No. 3, 2007, pp. 499–520, 500 ('Politics of Life'). Citing Giorgio Agamben, *Homo Sacer: Sovereign Power and Bare Life*, Daniel Heller-Roazen (trans.) (Stanford, CA: Stanford University Press, 1998). See also Fassin, supra ('Inequality of Lives').

[16] Monique J. Beerli, 'Saving the Saviors: Security Practices and Professional Struggles in the Humanitarian Space', *International Political Sociology*, Vol. 12, No. 1, 2018, pp. 70–87, 70 ('Saving the Saviors').

[17] Fast, supra, 112, 205 (*Aid in Danger*). See also Alex de Waal, *Famine Crimes: Politics and the Disaster Relief Industry in Africa* (Oxford: James Currey, 1997), 6 (*Famine Crimes*) (asking if humanitarian actors are given impunity that privileges them above other civilians).

[18] Fast, supra, 22, 197 (*Aid in Danger*).

[19] Ibid., 205.

aims to expose through its introduction of the 'civilian plus', 'mere civilian', and 'civilian minus' figures. Sometimes, what is privileged might not be the life of the humanitarian actor, but rather the symbols of humanitarianism—of which the Red Cross emblem is the paradigmatic example. As discussed in connection with critiques of humanitarian symbols, the risk is that preserving the purity of these symbols may become an end in itself.[20]

When considered in a vacuum, granting a special status to humanitarian actors might seem merited and morally sound. However, when one considers the possibility that humanitarian virtue may be founded upon the devaluation of the lives of populations in need, the 'civilian plus' acquires a different hue. In the logic of the 'against humanitarian exceptionalism' perspective, giving something extra to humanitarian actors marshals IHL to further entrench pre-existing inequalities between humanitarian actors and the civilian populations they serve. It is this prospect, in particular, that gives me pause. On a more practical note, there is a further aspect of the 'help the helpers' viewpoint that is potentially problematic: the assumption that a special status would actually prevent humanitarian actors from becoming targets. As noted in Chapter 4, Alexander characterizes the twin features of the civilian as vulnerability and value; value, in this account, refers to the civilian's appeal as a target.[21] Contemplating a special status for humanitarian actors, one might wonder whether a special status could have the perverse effect of making them *even more valuable* as targets. To the extent that violence against humanitarian actors is intentional as well as performative,[22] this prospect merits serious consideration.

6.2.2 The 'civilian plus': cui bono?

A further question that lingers on the edges of this investigation is the following: who benefits from granting a special status to humanitarian actors? This invites us to consider which interests are furthered by the 'civilian plus', and which interests are stifled or suppressed. As a general matter, designating the recipients of assistance as 'beneficiaries' might impede an examination of who the actual beneficiaries of humanitarianism are. Krause emphasizes that only a subset of

[20] Monika Krause, *The Good Project: Humanitarian Relief NGOs and the Fragmentation of Reason* (Chicago, IL and London: University of Chicago Press, 2014), 113, 144 (*Good Project*); Stephen Hopgood, *The Endtimes of Human Rights* (Ithaca, NY: Cornell University Press, 2014), 37–38 (*Endtimes*).

[21] See Chapter 1; Amanda Alexander, 'The Genesis of the Civilian', *Leiden Journal of International Law*, Vol. 20, 2007, pp. 359–376, 365 ('Genesis').

[22] As argued in Laura Hammond, 'The Power of Holding Humanitarianism Hostage and the Myth of the Protective Principles', in Michael Barnett and Thomas Weiss (eds.), *Humanitarianism in Question: Politics, Power, and Ethics* (Ithaca, NY: Cornell University Press, 2008), pp. 172–195 ('Holding Humanitarianism Hostage'). Discussed also in Silke Roth, *Passionate Professionals: The Paradoxes of Aid Work* (Abingdon and New York: Routledge, 2015), 32 (*Paradoxes of Aid*). See Section 3.2.1.

populations in need receive services, in practice, or benefit from an intervention.[23] Roth further considers that 'almost everyone involved in the aid sector could be considered a beneficiary'.[24] Those in favour of a special status for humanitarian actors extol the benefits for the receiving populations, first and foremost. The 'help the helpers' position, as outlined, posits that secure access for humanitarian actors translates into the delivery of assistance to populations in need. According to this logic, the beneficiaries of humanitarian assistance are the beneficiaries of a special status for humanitarian actors. Concepts of humanitarian virtue and sacrifice implicitly inform this outlook, which treats humanitarian actors as vehicles or instruments for assistance.

Consider now the 'against humanitarian exceptionalism' perspective, which draws attention to the way in which human lives are valued. As a baseline, this perspective frames the relationship between humanitarian actors and war-affected populations as one that is unequal. If humanitarian actors are able to claim a special status in international law, this may mobilize law to imbue their lives with (extra) value. Humanitarian actors are already set apart from the populations they serve, and a special status would give legal imprimatur to this imbalance. Proponents of a special status might counter here that the 'plus' merely recognizes humanitarian actors' particular needs. Moreover, in the grand scheme of the injuries inflicted on ordinary civilians in wartime, a special status for humanitarian actors is hardly the worst eventuality. A likely rejoinder from the 'against humanitarian exceptionalism' side—and I think this merits serious consideration—is that there is potentially a violence done to ordinary civilians in the bestowing of special protections and privileges upon those who are supposed to offer them succour.

The figure of the 'mere civilian' conveys the implications. These ordinary civilians are positioned equidistant from the 'plus' and 'minus' poles on the civilianness continuum, but this puts them that much closer to the 'minus' figure than their 'plus' counterparts are. Here again we must consider why a special status for humanitarian actors would be so appealing. It is in part because the civilian concept is beleaguered, undermined, and questioned at every turn that there is an impetus for humanitarian actors to escape the civilian's vulnerability (however illusory such an escape might be). Relegating civilian populations to 'mere civilian' status only serves to further compound the fragility of the civilian ideal, at the same time as it entrenches pre-existing inequalities between humanitarian actors and other civilians. The latter would be better off in a world where all civilians are considered equal, and where the ideal of general civilian protection is sufficiently robust as to render a special status unnecessary.

23 Krause, supra, 40 (*Good Project*) (Krause also argues that beneficiaries form part of a commodity that is sold to donors in a quasi-market).

24 Roth, supra, 9 (*Paradoxes of Aid*).

Having articulated some reasons to be wary of the 'civilian plus', the discussion finally moves on to reflect on the wider implications of this study's findings.

6.3 Implications and future directions

This section considers this study's contributions to our understanding of the civilian concept, as well as the practice of humanitarianism and the figure of the humanitarian actor. It also comments upon recent calls for more *lex specialis* for other groups of civilian actors and suggests that the 'civilian plus' is circulating in these appeals. Finally, the discussion identifies some potentially fruitful avenues for further research, both acknowledging the limitations of the present study and offering entry points for scholars interested in building on its findings.

6.3.1 The civilian concept

This study contributes to the burgeoning literature on the civilian by showing how the civilian is produced in the practices and interactions of international actors operating in armed conflicts. In this monograph, the international humanitarian actor has not been treated as an isolated entity. Instead, the humanitarian actor has been situated alongside other international civilian and military actors, as well as the general civilian populations that comprise IHL's civilian category. Many of the other international actors examined, such as NATO soldiers and UN peacekeepers, do not share the goals or world view of humanitarian actors. By attending to the perspectives of the former actors, this study has showcased how distinction is produced on the ground, through struggle and contestation. This grounded empirical investigation complements other emerging scholarship on the civilian, much of which adopts a normative or more critical genealogical approach to distinction. Effort has also been made in this study to engage with relevant historical approaches, in order to appropriately contextualize and situate contemporary practice. It has been demonstrated that the idea of a stable distinction—and the related notion of a unified civilian category populated by (equally) protected civilians—is more myth than historical reality. This understanding should inform our thinking about contemporary practices that impugn the idea of a bright-line binary and a mythically pure civilian.

The study has also highlighted the efforts that international humanitarian actors make to distinguish themselves from others, introducing the concept of everyday distinction practices. This marks an important contribution to the IHL literature, as little attention has been paid to the need for *civilian* actors to enact distinction. While the civilian self-protection literature generated by political science and international relations scholars illuminates the way in which civilians protect themselves in war,[25] scholars engaged in the study of the civilian as a legal entity have not yet grappled with these dynamics. This monograph has offered a way of doing so. By empirically describing and analysing the existence of a series of distinctions amongst international actors, this study has demonstrated that the civilian–combatant divide is not the only—or even the most significant—distinction at play. Overall, practices in South Sudan and at the civil–military training grounds map onto a fragmented vision of distinction, characterized by dynamism and a splintered civilian category. To be sure, individual actors self-conceptualize as civilians or combatants in a general sense, and they routinely reach for a bright-line distinction and its promise of clarity. Yet their everyday organization of relationships belies the notion of discrete entities. Instead, they behave as though individuals might be imbued with qualities of both civilianness and combatantness, which are swirling around in the air. The 'rush to the intimate' that military actors engage in marks something of an exception here, as it ignores how military actors' own characteristics of combatantness might contaminate humanitarian actors.

A final contribution this study makes to our understanding of the civilian is its elucidation of the important role that perceptions play in the practices of international actors. This remedies a notable gap in the legal literature, which has so far paid insufficient attention to the ways in which the perceptions of individual actors shape the implementation of international legal rules. As has been shown, international humanitarian actors generally seek to tie humanitarianness to the highest degree of civilianness available. Much as they endeavour to 'distinguish themselves', there is a shared understanding amongst international actors that the 'phantom local' has the final say. At the same time, international actors are the ones who project ascribed perceptions onto the 'phantom local' in its various manifestations. In the everyday encounters of international actors, it often seems as though the main function of the 'phantom local' is to provide an avenue through which international actors might speak to each other about distinction.

6.3.2 Humanitarianism and the humanitarian actor

A concerted effort has been made in this study to implement a genuinely interdisciplinary approach, bringing the theory and practice of humanitarianism together with international law. Noting that doctrinal and normative approaches have had an outsized influence in the scholarship on law and humanitarianism, this study has charted an alternative path. Espousing concern for the everyday aspects of both subjects, the study has elucidated a new way of putting the humanitarian

[25] See Chapter 1.

imaginary[26] in contact with the international legal imagination.[27] In applying a critical, sociolegal lens to IHL and drawing on an ethnographic sensibility that foregrounds day-to-day practice, this study shines a light on aspects of distinction's production that would otherwise remain concealed.

As a consequence of this engagement, the study makes a number of contributions to the literature on humanitarianism and to our understanding of the humanitarian actor. First, it contributes to scholarship on everyday humanitarianism. The study does so by positioning civil–military training grounds and armed conflicts as sites in which everyday humanitarian practices unfold, and by illuminating the ways in which law and the daily practices of humanitarian actors are co-constitutive. Second, it adds to the literature that adopts a relational understanding of humanitarian practice. By bringing the practices of international humanitarian actors into contact with the practices, perceptions, and preferences of other kinds of international actors, this study has revealed how so much of daily humanitarian practice revolves around interactions—and struggles—with others. Third, the monograph sheds light on the figure of the humanitarian actor, in all its attendant complexity. By delineating IHL's Red Cross fantasy, this study has exposed the limitations of IHL's understanding of the humanitarian actor. It has also shown that humanitarians are protected according to their ability to approximate a very particular vision of humanitarianess. Finally, the study has grouped critiques of humanitarian (distinction) practices into the 'against humanitarian exceptionalism' outlook, articulating the form such critiques might take if they were to engage more explicitly with law. The insights thereby derived are potentially devastating for what I have termed the 'help the helpers' position.

Recognizing that populations in need ostensibly serve as the *raison d'être* for humanitarian actors and justify their presence in armed conflicts, it is also important to scrutinize how summoning the 'phantom local' affects these populations. This study depicts the 'phantom local' as a composite figure that collapses together the beneficiary-perceiver, the attacker-perceiver, and the authority-perceiver.[28] When this amorphous entity is invoked, the actual lives, desires, and perspectives of war-affected populations are flattened. The recipients of humanitarian assistance might take on the specific form of the beneficiary-perceiver, or perhaps be folded together with the attackers and the authorities. In either scenario, the main role assigned to beneficiary populations is to serve as an audience for the performance of distinction. While this practice might be wholly unintentional, it engenders a subtle shift. A preoccupation with what the victims of war see, think, and feel *about*

[26] The humanitarian imaginary is discussed in Chapter 2 of Lilie Chouliaraki, *The Ironic Spectator: Solidarity in the Age of Post-Humanitarianism* (Cambridge: Polity Press, 2012) (*Ironic Spectator*).

[27] Mark Drumbl, *Re-imagining Child Soldiers* (Oxford: Oxford University Press, 2012), 9 (*Child Soldiers*).

[28] See Section 3.1.2.

humanitarian actors displaces concerns about how the former might be helped—never mind what they want and desire for their own lives, more broadly. In accordance with the 'against humanitarian exceptionalism' perspective, such treatment of war-affected populations exacerbates inequalities that are already embedded in the humanitarian-beneficiary encounter. When this point is considered alongside the possibility that distinction might serve as an alibi for other interests, or that protecting humanitarian purity might be prioritized over serving populations in need, the implications of humanitarian distinction practices for recipients of aid appear rather bleak. This is a significant finding, and it calls into question humanitarian actors' claims that their distinction practices enable them to alleviate the suffering of war-affected populations.

6.3.3 The yearning to be #NotATarget

It is not the case—at least not yet—that international lawyers are rushing out to create new legal treaties bestowing a special civilian status upon international humanitarian actors. Humanitarian actors, themselves, are also ambivalent about making overt claims to something more than civilian status. The findings of Mackintosh's 2007 study remain relevant:[29]

> [M]any in the humanitarian community are wary of appearing to ask for 'more' protection than the civilian population affected. In the words of one aid worker, 'Why should we get more protection than other civilians just because we decide to go to dangerous areas while they have no choice?'

And yet, humanitarian actors, international lawyers, advocates, and policymakers engage in myriad activities on a daily basis that keep the 'civilian plus' in circulation. The numerous UN resolutions condemning attacks against humanitarian actors as especially abhorrent are a case in point. The circulation of the #NotATarget hashtag on social media in connection with humanitarian actors is arguably another.[30] It is, accordingly, possible to imagine a scenario in which the formalization of special protections is explicitly put on the table in Geneva, New York, or elsewhere in the global halls of power. In offering a way of thinking about the circulation of the idea

[29] Kate Mackintosh, 'Beyond the Red Cross: The Protection of Independent Humanitarian Organizations and their Staff in International Humanitarian Law', *International Review of the Red Cross*, Vol. 89, No. 865, 2007, pp. 113–130, 123.

[30] See e.g. Voluntary Organizations in Cooperation in Emergencies (VOICE), 'World Humanitarian Day 2018: Join the #NotATarget Campaign', 9 August 2018. Available at: https://voiceeu.org/news/world-humanitarian-day-2018-join-the-notatarget-campaign; MSF, '#NotATarget: No More Attacks Against Civilians and Health Care Workers in Conflict Zones'. Available at: https://www.doctorswithoutborders.ca/issues/notatarget-no-more-attacks-against-civilians-and-healthcare-workers-conflict-zones.

of distinction in everyday life and illuminating the winners and losers of a special status, this study suggests that any such proposals should be greeted with caution.

Opening out beyond the field of humanitarianism, the 'civlian plus' may also be detected in calls for the special treatment of other types of civilians in armed conflict. This desire for ever more *lex specialis* merits scrutiny in light of this study's findings.[31] Appeals have recently been made for a special status for children,[32] for example, and for media professionals.[33] In each case, there is a sense that the particular circumstances of the actor in question need to be taken into account—whether due to their vulnerability, identity, professional role, or particular function in war. In keeping with the 'help the helpers' mentality, the impetus for such requests may indeed be the simple desire to have differential needs and circumstances recognized. Yet, if we contemplate the (cumulative) impact on civilians as a larger group, this ought to give us pause. The question, I propose, is whether meeting these demands for *lex specialis* establishes so many carve-outs from IHL's civilian category that the concept of general civilian protection is eroded to the point of meaninglessness. Whether or not it is anyone's intention that those with 'plus' status would be elevated above other civilians, the move to set some civilians apart compels us to consider the implications for those not singled out for special protection—both as a matter of law and of perception.

6.3.4 Avenues for further research

One limitation of this single-author study, as mentioned, is that it was not possible to conduct an extensive empirical investigation of actual local perceptions of distinction. While articulating definitive findings on this matter is challenging for the reasons identified in Chapter 3, much work can and should be done to expand on the efforts of those who have chipped away at this question over the past decade or so. A related point is that, for analytical purposes, this study has employed a simplified categorization of 'local' and 'international' actors. It will be important for future projects to probe these categories further. Such inquiries should recognize, for example, the fact that many 'local' actors might well be foreigners, and that many individuals working for international humanitarian organizations are in fact 'local' actors—not to mention regional and subregional dynamics, and so on. A study of distinction practices that more explicitly attends to the nuances within organizations and between different types of humanitarian actor would form a

[31] I thank Sarah Nouwen for this point.

[32] Shaheed Fatima, *Protecting Children in Armed Conflict* (Oxford: Hart, 2018) (*Children*).

[33] This argument was raised at the public event 'Media Professionals and Armed Conflict: Protection and Responsibilities under International Humanitarian Law' hosted by the British Red Cross and the British Institute for International and Comparative Law at London's Frontline Club on 28 November 2018.

useful contribution to the literature on humanitarianism. Further in this vein, a more explicitly decolonial and intersectional approach to humanitarian practice in general, and to concepts of risk in particular, would be welcome. There are pressing questions about gender, race, ethnicity, class, age, and ability that merit much more attention than I have given them here. Although such accounts are becoming more prevalent in the humanitarian literature, international legal rules and doctrine could usefully receive more attention in these conversations.

Another aspect of the study's empirical findings that merits further attention pertains to the feelings and emotions of international actors. While conducting field research for the study, it was striking how frequently international actors—without prompting—chose to speak about their feelings towards other international actors in their midst. Feelings of hostility and resentment, as well as affinity and respect, seemed to shape not only their interactions with each other but also their interpretations of their obligations under international law. While there was not scope to fully elucidate the affective dimension in the present study, I am pursuing the emotional life of IHL in a separate research project. I hope that other scholars will increasingly take an interest in IHL's human component, perhaps drawing on some of the empirical findings presented here.

Finally, an important avenue for future research—admittedly a niche one—is the work of untangling the various uses of distinction. While this study has made an earnest foray in this respect, there is certainly more to be done to tease apart the functions of distinction as practiced by international actors. One of the most demanding aspects of this untangling work is determining the underlying motivations of humanitarian actors' distinction practices. The reader will note an omission in the chapter titles, which included 'What is the Distinction?', 'Who Draws the Line?', 'How is the Line Drawn?', and 'Where is the Line?'. A missing piece is '*Why* is the line drawn?'.[34] An intellectually honest but admittedly unsatisfactory summary of what this study has discovered with respect to this question is: it depends on who you ask. In order to understand the 'why' of these distinction practices, it will be necessary to further probe the disconnect between what international actors say they are up to and what they are actually up to. Some of the practices canvassed in this study suggest that these actors might not be altogether sure, themselves.

The perspectives of other (non-humanitarian) international actors have helped to reveal much of what lies beneath humanitarian distinction practices, but it would be misguided to think that these external perceptions reveal the truth about distinction. As noted, these other actors also view humanitarian actors through the prism of their own biases and grievances. Both civilian and military actors working for international missions have their reasons for not wanting to support the vision of distinction that humanitarian actors propound. In the present study,

[34] The question of when the line is drawn, that is in what circumstances, is implicitly covered elsewhere—particularly in the discussion of how the line is drawn.

the technique of participant observation was absolutely crucial in grappling with some of these dynamics. A NATO soldier might bemoan the special distinction demanded by humanitarian actors in a simulation exercise in a civil–military training programme, but in a subsequent interview profess respect for humanitarian actors and the concerns they articulate regarding personal safety. This adds further nuance to the point made above—that the 'why' of distinction depends not only on who is asked, but also when and where they are asked and what circumstances prevail. Further engagement with these questions by scholars in other disciplines would be welcome, particularly from (legal) anthropologists with the training and resources to carry out fine-grained qualitative studies. Having suggested this, it should be recognized that generalizing such micro-level findings and linking them back to categories of international law is no easy feat. This highlights a key benefit of this multi-sited investigation's approach to its object of study. The micro and the macro were consistently put into conversation with each other, so as to facilitate understanding of how the practices in question implicate the relevant legal rule.

Conclusion

What does it mean if distinction is a perpetually disrupted idea? Nouwen's articulation of the two souls dwelling in each sociolegal scholar strikes a chord:[35] one soul seeks to clarify and explain, while the other is overwhelmed by the complexity of what has been found.[36] There is a temptation to simplify what is messy, but, given the multiplicity this monograph has contended with, it seems problematic to offer neat assertions about what should be done.

As a point of clarification, it is not necessarily desirable to have legal rules that reflect empirical reality. Alexander locates the value of IHL's civilian entity in its very artificiality: it aims not to reflect but to supplant the realities of war-affected populations.[37] Whatever distance there is between a real-life civilian and the IHL version, from this vantage point, is understood as an achievement.[38] Taking a cue from this, I will not end this discussion by issuing a call for legal reforms that make the principle of distinction more reflective of actual practice. My aim here has instead been to uncover and engage with the ambiguity and indeterminacy of IHL rules, and to highlight the large swath of actors who enact distinction on a daily basis. As this study has pursued the idea of distinction across a number of global

[35] Sarah Nouwen, 'As You Set Out for Ithaka: Practical, Epistemological, Ethical and Existential Questions about Socio-legal Empirical Research in Conflict', *Leiden Journal of International Law*, Vol. 27, No. 1, 2014, pp. 227–260, 233 ('Ithaka').

[36] Ibid.

[37] Amanda Alexander, *The Idea of the Civilian in International Law* (unpublished PhD thesis, 2013), 36.

[38] Ibid., 35–36.

sites, it has consistently found ambiguity at its side. Ambiguity is the shadow that follows distinction around, allowing different actors to speak to each other about distinction without realizing—or, perhaps, knowing full well—that they are not even having the same conversation. This fact has both confounded this investigation and yielded one of its most important discoveries. The revelation that distinction means many things to many people may seem obvious at first glance, but it could have enormous implications for our understanding of the daily enactment of IHL.

As this monograph has shown, some of the distinction practices of international actors reshape distinction beyond recognition as a bright-line rule in IHL. I have identified a number of new fault lines, and, while these may be unfamiliar, they are not inexplicable. The study has sought to capture and analyse the relevant dynamics by introducing the 'civilian plus', 'mere civilian', and 'civilian minus' figures. I have argued that these strange entities have as much relevance to the everyday interactions of international actors as the civilian–combatant divide—if not more. The claim here is not that all of the distinction dynamics described in this study directly (or even in any way) implicate concerns of targeting in the conduct of hostilities. The point, rather, is that the idea of distinction is circulating in different ways, amongst different people, in different kinds of spaces. As it travels, the IHL targeting rule is routinely collapsed together with other values, aspirations, and priorities. This distinction vernacular, as I have called it, represents distinction as it is found in actually existing practice.

Reflecting on the normative question of whether a special status for international humanitarian actors is desirable, this study has built on critiques of humanitarian exceptionalism to identify the potential pitfalls of the 'civilian plus'. I have proposed that the main cost is a downgraded status for some other civilian, somewhere else. With respect to the implications for other international actors, the findings from South Sudan capture the stakes poignantly. In particular, this study has highlighted the anxiety of UN civilian actors that their own civilian status might be adversely affected by the distinction practices of humanitarian actors. On an everyday basis in South Sudan, humanitarian actors jostle with these other civilians in hopes of claiming the highest degree of civilianness available. Indeed, the whole point of the 'civilian plus' is to set humanitarian actors apart from these other actors; the latter are viewed as having the wrong kind of civilianness, and qualities of combatantness might even circulate around them. As for the general civilian population, I have drawn attention to two ways in which they could be adversely affected by humanitarian distinction practices. First, local civilian populations, who are not eligible for special treatment, might find themselves relegated to 'mere civilian' or even 'civilian minus' status. Second, when the 'phantom local' is invoked, populations caught up in war's upheaval are repackaged as the beneficiary-perceiver. Often, they are also lumped together with other audiences for distinction, namely the attacker-perceiver and the authority-perceiver. The collapsing together of different kinds of local actors becomes more ominous when one considers that a special status for humanitarian actors might downgrade the civilianness of local populations in a relative sense. Ultimately, the 'civilian plus' presents a paradox. It is the beleaguered nature of the civilian ideal that leads humanitarian actors to long for a special status, and this special status has the effect of undermining the civilian ideal. The more strained the civilian ideal becomes, the more intoxicating the prospect of an escape from ordinary civilianness appears.

If it achieves nothing else, this monograph extends an invitation to spend time in a world where distinction's perpetually disrupted nature no longer remains hidden. This study has sought to make distinction strange and unfamiliar, reconceptualizing it in new forms. It is only when we recognize these three new civilian figures that we can begin to fathom why international actors struggle with each other for recognition of different degrees of civilianness. As this study has demonstrated, the distinction between the civilian and the combatant is more a matter of degree than category. Nonetheless, the notion of a bright-line civilian–combatant distinction remains alluring for its promise of clarity. Many of the international actors examined in this study, from NATO soldiers to UN peacekeepers and international humanitarian actors, continue to reach for this bright-line binary vision, even as it slips through their fingers.

Bibliography

Abu-Sada, C. (ed.), *Dilemmas, Challenges, and Ethics of Humanitarian Action: Reflections on Médecins Sans Frontières Perception Project* (Montreal and Kingston: McGill-Queens University Press, 2012).

Abu-Sada, C. (ed.), *In the Eyes of Others: How People in Crises Perceive Humanitarian Aid* (MSF and NYU Centre on International Cooperation, 2012).

Abu-Sada, C., 'Part I: Studying How MSF is Perceived', in Abu-Sada, C (ed.), *In the Eyes of Others: How People in Crises Perceive Humanitarian Aid* (MSF and NYU Centre on International Cooperation, 2012), pp. 10–96.

Adler, E. and Pouliot, V. (eds.), *International Practices* (Cambridge: Cambridge University Press, 2011).

African Affairs, 'Making Sense of South Sudan, Virtual Issue', 2016. Available at: https://academic.oup.com/afraf/pages/south_sudan_virtual_issue.

African Press Organization, 'South Sudan: Aid Workers Freed, Humanitarian Deaths Reach 100 since 2013', Press Release, Distributed by APO Group on Behalf of OCHA, 1 May 2018. Available at: https://search-proquest-com.ezproxy.is.ed.ac.uk/docview/2032567038/fulltext/E6B01DDAED4C4F28PQ/1?accountid=10673.

Agamben, G., *Homo Sacer: Sovereign Power and Bare Life*, Heller-Roazen, D. (trans.) (Stanford, CA: Stanford University Press, 1998).

Agreement on Outstanding Issues on Governance and Security Arrangements, 5 August 2018. Available at: https://www.peaceagreements.org/masterdocument/2111.

Agreement on the Resolution of the Conflict in the Republic of South Sudan, 17August2015. Available at: https://unmiss.unmissions.org/sites/default/files/final_proposed_compromise_ agreement_for_south_sudan_ conflict.pdf.

Akande, D. and Gillard, E. C., 'Arbitrary Withholding of Consent to Humanitarian Relief Operations in Armed Conflict', *International Law Studies*, Vol. 92, 2016, pp. 483–511.

Akande, D. and Gillard, E. C., 'Humanitarian Actors' Engagement with Accountability Mechanisms in Situations of Armed Conflict: Workshop Report', *Anuario De Direito Internacional*, 2016, pp. 105–132.

Akande, D. and Gillard, E. C., *Oxford Guidance on the Law Relating to Humanitarian Relief Operations in Situations of Armed Conflict* (UN OCHA, 2016).

Alexander, A., 'The Genesis of the Civilian', *Leiden Journal of International Law*, Vol. 20, 2007, pp. 359–376.

Alexander, A., *The Idea of the Civilian in International Law* (unpublished PhD thesis, 2013).

Alexander, A., 'A Short History of International Humanitarian Law', *European Journal of International Law*, Vol. 26, No. 1, 2015, pp. 109–138.

Alexander, A., 'International Humanitarian Law: Postcolonialism and the 1977 Geneva Protocol I', *Melbourne Journal of International Law*, Vol. 17, No. 1, 2016, pp. 1–36.

Alexandra, A., 'Private Military and Security Companies and the "Civilianization" of War', in Lovell, D. and Primoratz, I. (eds.), *Protecting Civilians During Violent Conflict: Theoretical and Practical Issues for the 21st Century* (Ashgate, 2012), pp. 183–189.

Allen, M. E., Sibahi, Z., and Sohm, E. D., *Evaluation of the Office of the United Nations Disaster Relief Coordinator*, JIU/REP/80/11, 1980. Available at: https://www.unjiu.org/

sites/www.unjiu.org/files/jiu_document_files/products/en/reports-notes/JIU%20 Products/JIU_REP_1980_11_English.pdf.

Ambos, K. and Wirth, S., 'The Current Law of Crimes Against Humanity: An Analysis of UNTAET Regulation 15/2000', *Criminal Law Forum*, Vol. 13, No. 1, 2002, pp. 1–90.

Anderson, M. B., *Do No Harm: How Aid Can Support Peace—Or War* (London: Lynne Reinner Publishers, 1999).

Andersson, R. and Weigand, F., 'Intervention at Risk: The Vicious Cycle of Distance and Danger in Mali and Afghanistan', *Journal of Intervention and Statebuilding*, Vol. 9, 2015, pp. 519–541.

Aneja-Bod, U., *Contesting the Humanitarian Regime in Political Emergencies: International NGO Policies and Practices in Sri Lanka & Afghanistan, 1990–2010* (unpublished DPhil thesis, 2013).

Annex to Hague Convention (IV) Respecting the Laws and Customs of War on Land and its Annex: Regulations Concerning the Laws and Customs of War on Land, The Hague, 18 October 1907.

Arensen, M., *If We Leave We Are Killed: Lessons Learned from South Sudan Protection of Civilians Sites* (Geneva: International Organization for Migration, 2016).

Aresseguier, A., 'The Moral Sense of Humanitarian Actors: An Empirical Exploration', *Disasters*, Vol. 42, No. 1, 2018, pp. 62–80.

Ashworth, J., 'The Relationship between Capitalism and Humanitarianism', *The American Historical Review*, Vol. 92, No. 4, 1987, pp. 813–828.

Astill-Brown, J., 'South Sudan's Slide into Conflict: Revisiting the Past and Reassessing Relationships', *Chatham House Research Paper*, December 2014.

Augustine, and F. R. M. Hitchcock, St. Augustine's treatise on the City of God (London: Society for Promoting Christian Knowledge, 1922)

Autessere, S., *Peaceland: Conflict Resolution and the Everyday Politics of International Intervention* (Cambridge: Cambridge University Press, 2014).

Baines, E. and Paddon, E., '"This is How We Survived": Civilian Agency and Humanitarian Protection', *Security Dialogue*, Vol. 43, No. 3, 2012, pp. 231–247.

Barakat, S., Deely, S., and Zyck, S., '"A Tradition of Forgetting": Stabilization and Humanitarian Action in Historical Perspective', *Disasters*, Vol. 34, No. S2, 2010, pp. 297–319.

Barker, C., 'Aid Workers Could Secure Better Protection Under the Protection of Civilians Mandate', *International Law Grrls*, 15 August 2014. Available at: https://ilg2.org/2014/08/15/aid-workers-could-secure-better-protection-under-the-protection-of-civilians-mandate/.

Barnett, M., *Empire of Humanity: A History of Humanitarianism* (Ithaca, NY: Cornell University Press, 2011).

Barnett, M. and Weiss, T. (eds.), *Humanitarianism in Question: Politics, Power, and Ethics* (Ithaca, NY: Cornell University Press, 2008).

Barrat, C., *Status of NGOs in International Humanitarian Law* (Leiden: Brill Nijhoff, 2014).

Barros, A. and Thomas, M. (eds.), *The Civilianization of War: The Changing Civil-Military Divide 1914–2014* (Cambridge: Cambridge University Press, 2018).

Barros, A. and Thomas, M., 'Introduction', in Barros, A. and Thomas, M. (eds.), *The Civilianization of War: The Changing Civil-Military Divide 1914–2014* (Cambridge: Cambridge University Press, 2018), pp. 1–21.

Bartels, R., 'Killing with Military Objects Disguised as Civilian Objects is Perfidy', *Just Security* Blog, March 2015. Available at: https://www.justsecurity.org/21285/disguising-military-weapons-civilian-equipment-perfidy-or-be/.

Baughan, E., et al., 'Empire and Humanitarianism: Special Edition', *Journal of Imperial and Commonwealth History*, Vol. 40, No. 5, 2012, pp. 727–896.

Baxter, R., 'So-Called "Unprivileged Belligerency": Spies, Guerrillas, and Saboteurs', *British Yearbook of International Law*, Vol. 28, 1951, pp. 323–345.

Baylis, E., 'The Transformative Potential of Rigorous Empirical Research', *American Society of International Law Annual Meeting*, Vol. 104, March 2010.

Beauchamp, S., 'Humanitarian Space in Search of a New Home', in Perrin, B (ed.), *Modern Warfare: Armed Groups, Private Militaries, Humanitarian Organizations, and the Law* (Vancouver: UBC Press, 2012), pp. 199–234.

Beerli, M. J., 'Saving the Saviors: Security Practices and Professional Struggles in the Humanitarian Space', *International Political Sociology*, Vol. 12, No. 1, 2018, pp. 70–87.

Berman, N., 'Privileging Combat? Contemporary Conflict and the Legal Construction of War', *Columbia Journal of Transnational Law*, Vol. 43, No. 1, 2004, pp. 1–71.

Best, G., *Humanity in Warfare: Modern History of the International Law of Armed Conflicts* (New York, NY: Columbia University Press, 1980).

Blanchard, L. P., *Conflict in South Sudan and the Challenges Ahead* (Washington, DC: Congressional Research Service, 2016).

Blank, L. R., 'The Limits of Inviolability: The Parameters for Protection of United Nations Facilities During Armed Conflict', *International Law Studies*, Vol. 93, 2017, pp. 45–101.

Blum, G., 'The Laws of War and the "Lesser Evil"', *Yale Journal of International Law*, Vol. 35, No. 1, 2010, pp. 1–69.

Boehland, N., *The People's Perspectives: Civilian Involvement in Armed Conflict* (Oxford: Oxford University Press, 2010).

Boer, L. M., 'The Greater Part of Juriconsults: On Consensus Claims and their Footnotes in Legal Scholarship', *Leiden Journal of International Law*, Vol. 29, 2016, pp. 1021–1042.

Bothe, M. et al. (eds.), *New Rules for Victims of Armed Conflicts: Commentary on the Two 1977 Protocols Additional to the Geneva Conventions of 1949*, 2nd edition (Hague, the Netherlands: Brill, 2013/1982).

Bourdieu, P., *Outline of a Theory of Practice* (Cambridge: Cambridge University Press, 1977).

Bourdieu, P., *The Field of Cultural Production* (Cambridge: Cambridge University Press, 1993).

Bourloyannis-Vrailas, C., 'The Convention on the Safety of United Nations and Associated Personnel', *International and Comparative Law Quarterly*, Vol. 44, 1995, pp. 560–590.

Bradbury, M., 'Normalising the Crisis in Africa', *Disasters*, Vol. 22, No. 4, 2002, pp. 328–338.

Briggs, C., *Protection of Civilians Sites: Lessons from South Sudan for Future Operations* (Norwegian Refugee Council, 2017).

Brooks, J., 'Protecting Humanitarian Action: Key Challenges and Lessons from the Field', *A Report for Harvard Humanitarian Initiative and ATHA*, October 2016.

Brunée, J. and Toope, S., *Legitimacy and Legality in International Law* (Cambridge: Cambridge University Press, 2010).

Bryman, A., 'The Debate about Quantitative and Qualitative Research: A Question of Method or Epistemology', *The British Journal of Sociology*, Vol. 35, No. 1, 1984, pp. 75–92.

Bugnion, F., *The International Committee of the Red Cross and the Protection of War Victims* (Geneva: Macmillan, 2003).

Camins, E., 'The Past as Prologue: The Development of the "Direct Participation" Exception to Civilian Immunity', *International Review of the Red Cross*, Vol. 90, No. 872, 2008, pp. 853–881.

CARE International, *Policy Framework for CARE International's Relations with Military Forces*, 2009. Available at: https://www.careemergencytoolkit.org/wp-content/uploads/2017/03/39_1.pdf.

Carle, A. and Chkam, H., 'Humanitarian Action in the New Security Environment: Policy and Operational Implications in Iraq', *Humanitarian Policy Group Background Paper*, September 2006.

The Carter Center, 'Observing the 2011 Referendum on the Self-Determination of Southern Sudan: Final Report', 2012.

Case 001 (*Prosecutor v. Kaing Guek Eav*), Case No. 00I/18-07-2007-ECCC/TC, Trial Judgment, ECCC, 26 July 2010.

Case 002/01 (*Prosecutor v. Nuon Chea and Khieu Samphan*), Case No. 002/19-09-2007/ECCC/TC, Trial Judgment, ECCC, 7 August 2014.

Case 003 (*Prosecutor v. Meas Muth*), Case No. 003/ 07-09-2009-ECCC-OCIJ, ECCC.

Case 004/01 (*Prosecutor v. Yim Tith*) Case No. 004/07-09-2009-ECCC-OCIJ, ECCC.

Cassese, A., 'Current Challenges to International Humanitarian Law', in Clapham, A. and Gaeta, P. (eds.), *Oxford Handbook of International Law in Armed Conflict* (Oxford: Oxford University Press, 2014), pp. 3–19.

Charmaz, K., *Constructing Grounded Theory: A Practical Guide Through Qualitative Analysis* (London: SAGE, 2006).

Chayes, A. and Chayes, A., 'On Compliance', *International Organization*, Vol. 47, No. 2, 1993, pp. 175–205.

Checchi, F. et al., *Estimates of Crisis-Attributable Mortality in South Sudan: December 2013–April 2018* (London: London School of Hygiene and Tropical Medicine, 2018).

Chouliaraki, L., *The Ironic Spectator: Solidarity in the Age of Post-Humanitarianism* (Cambridge: Polity Press, 2012).

Collinson, S. and Elhawary, S., *Humanitarian Space: A Review of Trends and Issues* (London: Overseas Development Institute, 2012).

Cooley, A. and Ron, J., 'The NGO Scramble: Organizational Insecurity and the Political Economy of Transnational Action', *International Security*, Vol. 27, 2002, pp. 5–39.

Cooley, C. H., *Human Nature and the Social Order* (New York: Scribner, 1902).

Coopland, G. W., *The Tree of Battles of Honoré Bonet: An English Version with Introduction by G. W. Coopland* (Liverpool: Liverpool University Press, 1949).

Cooren, F. and Matte, F., 'At the Limits of Perception: Humanitarian Principles in Action', in Abu-Sada, C. (ed.), *Dilemmas, Challenges, and Ethics of Humanitarian Action: Reflections on Médecins Sans Frontières Perception Project* (Montreal and Kingston: McGill-Queens University Press, 2012), pp. 29–47.

Cowan, D., Mulcahy, M., and Wheeler, S., 'Introduction', in Cowan, D., Mulcahy, M., and Wheeler, S. (eds.), *Major Works in Socio-Legal Studies* (London: Routledge, 2013).

Cowan, D. and Wincott, D., 'Exploring the "Legal"', in Cowan, D. and Wincott, D. (eds.), *Exploring the 'Legal' in Socio-Legal Studies* (London: Palgrave, 2016), pp. 1–32.

Crawford, E., *Identifying the Enemy: Civilian Participation in Armed Conflict* (Oxford: Oxford University Press, 2015).

Cryer, R. et al. (eds.), *An Introduction to International Criminal Law and Procedure*, 3rd edition, (Cambridge: Cambridge University Press, 2014).

d'Aspremont, J., 'International Law-Making by Non-State Actors: Changing the Model or Putting the Phenomenon into Perspective?', in Noortmann, M. and Ryngaert, C. (eds.), *Non-State Actor Dynamics in International Law: From Law-Takers to Law Makers* (London: Routledge, 2010).

Davey, E., 'Famine, Aid and Ideology: The Political Activism of Médecins Sans Frontières in the 1980s', *French Historical Studies*, Vol. 34, No. 3, 2011, pp. 529–558.

Davey, E., with Borton, J. and Foley, M., 'A History of the Humanitarian System: Western Origins and Foundations', *Humanitarian Policy Group Working Paper*, June 2013.

Davies, K., *Continuity, Change and Contest: Meanings of 'Humanitarian' from the 'Religion of Humanity' to the Kosovo War* (London: Humanitarian Policy Group, 2012).

de Coning, C., 'Is Stabilization the New Normal? Implications of Stabilization Mandates for the Use of Force in UN Peace Operations', in Nadin, P. (ed.), *The Use of Force in UN Peacekeeping* (Oxford and New York: Routledge, 2018), pp. 85–99.

de Montclos, M. A. P., 'The (de)Militarization of Humanitarian Aid: A Historical Perspective', *Humanities*, Vol. 3, 2014, pp. 232–243.

de Waal, A., *Famine Crimes: Politics and the Disaster Relief Industry in Africa* (Melton, Suffolk: James Currey, 1997).

Debuf, E., 'Tools to Do the Job: The ICRC's Legal Status, Privileges and Immunities', *International Review of the Red Cross*, Vol. 97, No. 897/8, 2016, pp. 319–344.

Declaration Renouncing the Use, in Time of War, of Explosive Projectiles Under 400 Grammes Weight, Saint Petersburg, 29 November/11 December 1868.

Demeyere, B., 'Turning the Stranger into a Partner: The Role and Responsibilities of Civil Society in International Humanitarian Law Formulation and Application', *Harvard Program on Humanitarian Policy and Conflict Research Thematic Brief*, 2016.

Deng, F. and Deng, D., *Bound by Conflict: Dilemmas of the Two Sudans* (New York: Fordham University Press, 2015).

Deng, F. M., *War of Visions: Conflict of Identities in the Sudan* (Washington, DC: The Brookings Institution, 1995).

Desmond, M., 'Relational Ethnography', *Theory and Society*, Vol. 43, No. 5, 2014, pp. 547–579.

Development Initiatives, *Global Humanitarian Assistance Report 2018*. Available at: http://devinit.org/wp-content/uploads/2018/06/GHA-Report-2018.pdf.

Dinstein, Y., *The Conduct of Hostilities under the Law of International Armed Conflict* (Cambridge: Cambridge University Press, 2004)

Donini, A., 'Afghanistan: Humanitarianism under Threat,' *Feinstein International Centre*, Briefing, 2009. Available online at: http://fic.tufts.edu/publication-item/afghanistan-humanitarianism-under-threat/.

Donini, A., 'Between a Rock and a Hard Place: Integration or Independence of Humanitarian Action', *International Review of the Red Cross*, Vol. 92, No. 880, 2010, pp. 141–157.

Donini, A. (ed.), *The Golden Fleece: Manipulation and Independence in Humanitarian Action* (Virginia: Kumarian Press, 2012).

Donini, A. et al., 'Mapping the Security Environment: Understanding the Perceptions of Local Communities, Peace Support Operations, and Assistance Agencies', *Feinstein International Famine Centre Report*, June 2005.

Donini, A. et al., *Humanitarian Agenda 2015: Final Report: The State of the Humanitarian Enterprise* (Boston: Feinstein International Famine Centre, 2008).

Dormann, K. and Maresca, L., 'The ICRC and its Contribution to the Development of IHL in Specialized Instruments', *Chicago Journal of International Law*, Vol. 5, No. 1, 2004–5, pp. 217–232.

Dorussen, H. and de Vooght, M., 'Putting Civilians First: NGO Perceptions and Expectations of UN Peacebuilding', *Folke Bernadotte Academy*, Brief 01, 2018.

Drumbl, M., *Re-imagining Child Soldiers in International Law and Policy* (Oxford: Oxford University Press, 2012).

Drummond, C., Webb, P., and Akande, D., *Amicus Brief for Cases 003 and 004*, submitted to the Co-Investigating Judges of the ECCC, 19 May 2016.

Duffield, M., 'Risk-Management and the Fortified Aid Compound: Everyday Life in Post-Interventionary Society', *Journal of Intervention and Statebuilding*, Vol. 4, No. 4, 2010, pp. 453–474.

Dunant, H., *A Memory of Solferino* (Geneva: International Committee of the Red Cross, 1986).

Dungel, J., 'Defining Victims of Crimes against Humanity: *Martic* and the International Criminal Court', *Leiden Journal of International Law*, Vol. 22, 2009, pp. 727–752.

Durham, H. and Wynn-Pope, P., 'Protecting the "Helpers": Humanitarians and Health Care Workers During Times of Armed Conflict', *Yearbook of International Humanitarian Law*, Vol. 14, December 2011, pp. 327–346.

Egeland, J., Harmer, A., and Stoddard, A., *To Stay and Deliver: Good Practice for Humanitarians in Complex Security Environments* (Geneva and New York: OCHA, 2011).

Elhawary, S. and Pantuliano, S., 'UN Integration and Humanitarian Space', Panel at University of Ottawa Centre for International Policy Studies, 31 January 2012. Available at: https://www.youtube.com/watch?v=3SfTYAVvHyU.

Epstein, L. and King, G., 'The Rules of Inference', *University of Chicago Law Review*, Vol. 69, No. 1, 2002.

Escorihuela, A. L., 'Humanitarian Law and Human Rights Law: The Politics of Distinction', *Michigan State Journal of International Law*, Vol. 19, No. 2, 2013, pp. 300–407.

Eslava, L., *Local Space, Global Life: The Everyday Operation of International Law and Development* (Cambridge: Cambridge University Press, 2015).

Falzon, M., 'Introduction: Multi-Sited Ethnography: Theory, Praxis and Locality in Contemporary Research', in Falzon, M. (ed.), *Multi-Sited Ethnography: Theory, Praxis and Locality in Contemporary Research* (Burlington, VT: Ashgate, 2009), pp. 1–24.

Fassin, D., 'Humanitarianism as a Politics of Life', *Public Culture*, Vol. 19, No. 3, 2007, pp. 499–520.

Fassin, D., 'Inequality of Lives, Hierarchies of Humanity: Moral Commitments and Ethical Dilemmas of Humanitarianism', in Feldman, I. and Ticktin, M. (eds.), *In the Name of Humanity: The Government of Threat and Care* (Duke University Press, 2010), pp. 238–255.

Fassin, D., *Humanitarian Reason: A Moral History of the Present* (University of California Press, 2011).

Fassin, D. and Pandolfini, M. (eds.), *Contemporary States of Emergency: The Politics of Military and Humanitarian Interventions* (New York: Zone Books, 2010).

Fast, L., *Aid in Danger: The Perils and Promise of Humanitarianism* (Philadelphia, PA: University of Pennsylvania Press, 2014).

Fenrick, W. J., 'The Crime against Humanity of Persecution in the Jurisprudence of the ICTY', *Netherlands Yearbook of International Law*, Vol. 32, 2001, pp. 81–96.

Ferme, M., *The Underneath of Things: Violence, History and the Everyday in Sierra Leone* (Berkeley, CA: University of California Press, 2001).

Fernandez, R. and Estapa, J., 'Towards a Single and Comprehensive Notion of "Civilian Population" in Crimes Against Humanity', *International Criminal Law Review*, Vol. 17, 2017, pp. 47–77.

Fernando, U. and Hilhorst, D., 'Everyday Practices of Humanitarian Aid: Tsunami Response in Sri Lanka', *Development in Practice*, Vol. 16, No. 3/4, 2006, pp. 292–302.

Ferraro, T., 'The Applicability of International Humanitarian Law to Multinational Forces', *International Review of the Red Cross*, Vol. 95, No. 891/2, 2013, pp. 561–612.

Ferreiro, M., 'Blurring of Lines in Complex Emergencies: Consequences for the Humanitarian Community', *Journal of Humanitarian Assistance*, December 2012.

Ferrell, W., 'No Shirt, No Shoes, No Status: Uniforms, Distinction, and Special Operations in International Armed Conflict', *Military Law Review*, Vol. 78, 2003, pp. 94–140.

Ferris, E., 'Faith and Humanitarianism: It's Complicated', *Journal of Refugee Studies*, Vol. 24, No. 3, 2011, pp. 606–623.

Final Act of the International Peace Conference, The Hague, 1899, Laws of Armed Conflicts.

Final Act of the Second International Peace Conference, The Hague, 1907, Laws of Armed Conflicts.

Finnemore, M., *National Interests in International Society* (Ithaca, NY: Cornell University Press, 1996).

Fishtein, P. and Wilder, A., 'Winning Hearts and Minds? Examining the Relationship between Aid and Security in Afghanistan', *Feinstein International Centre Report*, January 2012.

Flick, U., *An Introduction to Qualitative Research* (London: SAGE, 2009).

Forte, M., 'The Human Terrain System and Anthropology: A Review of Ongoing Public Debates', *American Anthropologist*, Vol. 113, No. 1, 2011, pp. 149–153.

Francis, R. and Armstrong, A., 'Corruption and Whistleblowing in International Humanitarian Aid Agencies', *Journal of Financial Crime*, Vol. 18, No. 4, 2011, pp. 319–335.

Frerks, G., 'Who Are They? Encountering International and Local Civilians in Civil–Military Interaction', in Lucius, G. and Rietjens, S. (eds.), *Effective Civil–Military Interaction in Peace Operations: Theory and Practice* (New York: Springer, 2016), pp. 29–44.

Garbett, C., *The Concept of the Civilian: Legal Recognition, Adjudication and the Trials of International Criminal Justice* (Oxford: Routledge, 2015).

Gardam, J., *Non-Combatant Immunity as a Norm of International Humanitarian Law* (Dordrecht: Martinus Nijhoff, 1993).

Gardam, J., 'Women and the Law of Armed Conflict: Why the Silence?', *International and Comparative Law Quarterly*, Vol. 46, No. 1, 1997, pp. 55–80.

General Orders, Number 100, *Instructions for the Government of Armies of the United States in the Field* (War Department, Washington, DC, 24 April 1863).

Geneva Academy, *Rule of Law in Armed Conflicts (RULAC)* project, 'Non-International Armed Conflict in South Sudan'. Available at: http://www.rulac.org/browse/conflicts/non-international-armed-conflict-in-south-sudan#collapse4accord.

Geneva Convention for the Amelioration of the Condition of the Wounded and Sick in Armed Forces in the Field, 12 August 1949, 75 UNTS 31, Can TS 1965 No. 20.

Geneva Convention for the Amelioration of the Condition of Wounded, Sick and Shipwrecked Members of Armed Forces at Sea, 12 August 1949, 75 UNTS 85, Can TS 1965 No. 20.

Geneva Convention Relative to the Treatment of Prisoners of War, 12 August 1949, 75 UNTS 135, Can TS 1965 No. 20.

Geneva Convention Relative to the Protection of Civilian Persons in Time of War, 12 August 1949, 75 UNTS 287, Can TS 1965 No. 20.

Gerring, J., 'Mere Description', *British Journal of Political Science*, Vol. 42, No. 4, 2012, pp. 721–746.

Gilder, A., 'The Effect of "Stabilization" in the Mandates and Practice of UN Peace Operations', *Netherlands International Law Review*, Vol. 66, No. 1, 2019, pp. 47–73.

Glad, M., *A Partnership at Risk? The UN–NGO Relationship in Light of Integration* (Norwegian Refugee Council, 2011).

Goffman, E., *Encounters: Two Studies in the Sociology of Interaction* (Eastford, CT: Martino Fine Books, 2013/1961).

Goodhand, J., 'Contested Boundaries: NGOs and Civil–Military Relations in Afghanistan', *Central Asian Survey*, Vol. 32, No. 3, 2013, pp. 287–305.

Goodman, R. and Jinks, D., 'The ICRC Interpretive Guidance on the Notion of Direct Participation in Hostilities Under International Humanitarian Law: An Introduction to the Forum', *NYU Journal of International Law and Politics*, Vol. 42, 2010, pp. 637–640.

Green, L., *The Contemporary Law of Armed Conflict*, 3rd edition (Manchester: Manchester University Press, 2008).

Greenwood, C., 'Historical Development and Legal Basis', in Fleck, D. (ed.), *Handbook on International Humanitarian Law*, 2nd edition (Oxford: Oxford University Press, 2008), pp. 1–43.

Gregory, D., 'The Rush to the Intimate: Counterinsurgency and the Cultural Turn', *Radical Philosophy*, Vol. 150, 2008, pp. 8–23.

Grenfell, K., 'Perspective on the Applicability and Application of International Humanitarian Law: the UN Context', *International Review of the Red Cross*, Vol. 95, No. 891/2, 2013, pp. 645–652.

Grotius, H., *The Law of War and Peace (De jure belli ac pacis libri tres* (Amsterdam, 1625)

Gupta, A. and Ferguson, J. (eds.), *Anthropological Locations: Boundaries and Grounds of a Field Science* (Oakland, CA: University of California Press, 1997).

Hammond, L., 'The Power of Holding Humanitarianism Hostage and the Myth of the Protective Principles', in Barnett, M. and Weiss, T. (eds.), *Humanitarianism in Question: Politics, Power, and Ethics* (Ithaca, NY: Cornell University Press, 2008), pp. 172–195.

Haque, A., 'Indeterminacy in the Law of Armed Conflict', *International Law Studies*, Vo. 95, No. 118, 2019, pp. 118–160.

Harmer, A., 'Aid Worker Deaths: The Numbers Tell the Story', *OCHA News*, 16 August 2018. Available at: https://www.unocha.org/story/aid-worker-deaths-numbers-tell-story.

Hartigan, R. S., *The Forgotten Victim: A History of the Civilian* (Chicago, IL: Precedent Publishing, 1982).

Haysom, S. and Jackson, A., '"You Don't Need to Love Us": Civil–Military Relations in Afghanistan, 2002–2013', *Stability*, Vol. 2, No. 2, 2013, pp. 1–16.

Hellestveit, C., 'The Geneva Conventions and the Dichotomy between International and Non-International Armed Conflict: Curse or Blessing for the "Principle of Humanity"', in Larsen, K. M., Cooper, C. G., and Nystuen, G. (eds.), *Searching for a 'Principle of Humanity' in International Humanitarian Law* (Cambridge: Cambridge University Press, 2013), pp. 86–123.

Henckaerts, J. M. and Doswald-Beck, L., *Customary International Humanitarian Law* (Geneva: ICRC, 2005).

Herman, J., 'International Law and the Humanitarian Space in the Twenty-First Century: Challenged Relationships', in Zwitter, A. J. et al. (eds.), *Humanitarian Action: Global, Regional and Domestic Legal Responses* (Cambridge: Cambridge University Press, 2014), pp. 11–32.

Hilhorst, D., 'Dead Letter or Living Document? Ten Years of the Code of Conduct for Disaster Relief', *Disasters*, Vol. 29, No. 4, 2005, pp. 351–369.

Hilhorst, D. and Schmiemann, N., 'Humanitarian Principles and Organizational Culture: Everyday Practice in Médecins Sans Frontières-Holland', *Development in Practice*, Vol. 12, Nos. 3 and 4, 2002, pp. 490–500.

Hoffman, P. and Weiss, T., *Sword and Salve: Confronting New Wars and Humanitarian Crises* (Lanham, MD: Rowman and Littlefield, 2006).

Hopgood, S., *The Endtimes of Human Rights* (Ithaca, NY: Cornell University Press, 2014).

HPCR, 'Humanitarian Action under Scrutiny: Criminalizing Humanitarian Engagement', *Harvard Program on Humanitarian Policy and Conflict Research Working Paper*, February 2011.

Hull, C., *Integrated Missions: A Liberia Case Study* (Division of Defence Analysis, Swedish Defence Research Agency, 2008.

Humanitarian Outcomes, *Aid Worker Security Report: 2018*, August 2018. Available at: https://reliefweb.int/report/world/aid-worker-security-report-figures-glance-2018.

Humanitarian Outcomes, *Aid Worker Security Report: 2019*, August 2019. Available at: https://www.humanitarianoutcomes.org/sites/default/files/publications/awsr_figures2019.pdf.

Humanitarian Policy Group, 'The Concept of Protection: Towards a Mutual Understanding', Humanitarian Policy Group and ICRC Roundtable on Civil–Military Coordination, December 2011.

Hyndman, J., 'Preventive, Palliative, or Punitive? Safe spaces in Bosnia-Herzegovina, Somalia, and Sri Lanka', *Journal of Refugee Studies*, Vol. 16, No. 2, 2003, pp. 167–185.

IASC Task Force on Protection from Sexual Exploitation and Abuse, 'Sexual Exploitation and Abuse by UN, NGO and INGO Personnel: A Self-Assessment', *Humanitarian Exchange Magazine: Special Feature on Humanitarian Accountability*, No. 52, October 2011.

IASC, *Civil–Military Relationship in Complex Emergency: A Reference Paper*, 2004. Available at: http://www.refworld.org/pdfid/4289ea8c4.pdf.

IASC, *Non-Binding Guidelines on the Use of Armed Escorts for Humanitarian Convoys*, February 2013. Available at: http://www.refworld.org/pdfid/523189ab4.pdf.

IASC, *Review of the Impact of UN Integration on Humanitarian Action*, 2015, 36–37. Available at: https://interagencystandingcommittee.org/system/files/150908_un_integration_review_-_iasc_pha_tt_2015.pdf.

Ibreck, R., *South Sudan's Injustice System: Law and Activism on the Front Line* (London: Zed Books, 2019).

ICRC, *Red Cross Code of Conduct for the International Red Cross and Red Crescent Movement and Non-Governmental Organizations (NGOs) in Disaster Relief* (ICRC, 1996), Preamble.

ICRC, 'Respect for and Protection of the Personnel of Humanitarian Organizations', *ICRC Report*, September 1998.

ICRC, 'Interpretive Guidance on the Notion of Direct Participation in Hostilities Under International Humanitarian Law', *International Review of the Red Cross*, Vol. 90, No. 872, December 2008, pp. 991–1047.

IFRC, 'The Emblem Debate'. Available at: http://www.ifrc.org/en/who-we-are/the-movement/emblems/the-emblem-debate/.

IFRC, 'The Seven Fundamental Principles: Impartiality'. Available at: http://www.ifrc.org/en/who-we-are/vision-and-mission/the-seven-fundamental-principles/impartiality/.

IFRC, 'The Seven Fundamental Principles: Neutrality'. Available at: http://www.ifrc.org/en/who-we-are/vision-and-mission/the-seven-fundamental-principles/neutrality/.

International Crisis Group, 'South Sudan: A Civil War by Any Other Name', *Africa Report*, No. 217, 2014, pp. 18–26. Available at: https://www.crisisgroup.org/africa/horn-africa/south-sudan/south-sudan-civil-war-any-other-name.

International Group of Experts, *Leuven Manual on the International Law Applicable to Peace Operations* (Cambridge: Cambridge University Press, 2017).

International Peace Institute, 'Prioritization and Sequencing of Security Council Mandates: The case of UNMISS' (International Peace Institute, The Stimson Center and Security Council Report, 2019).

International Peace Institute, 'UN Special Representative to the Secretary General Hilde Johnson: South Sudan Crisis Changed UNMISS Mindset', July 2014. Available at: https://www.ipinst.org/2014/07/srsg-johnson-south-sudan-crisis-changed-unmiss-mindset.

James, E., 'The Professional Humanitarian and the Downsides of Professionalization', *Disasters*, Vol. 40, No. 2, 2016, pp. 185–206.

Janowitz, M. (ed.), *W.I. Thomas on Social Organization and Social Personality* (Chicago, IL: University of Chicago Press, 1966/1931).

Jochnick, C. and Normand, R., 'The Legitimation of Violence: A Critical History of the Laws of War', *Harvard International Law Journal*, Vol. 35, No. 1, Winter 1994, pp. 49–95.

Jose, B., 'Would the Protected Please Stand Up? Historical Ambiguity and the Distinction Principle', in Lorenz, E., Aspinall, D., and Raley, J. M. (eds.), *Montesinos' Legacy: Defining and Defending Human Rights for Five Hundred Years* (London: Lexington Books, 2014), Chapter 5.

Jose, B. and Medie, P. A., 'Understanding Why and How Civilians Resort to Self-Protection in Armed Conflict', *International Studies Review*, Vol. 17, No. 4, 2015, pp. 515–535.

Kebedde, G., 'Sudan: The North–South Conflict in Historical Perspective', *Contributions in Black Studies*, Vol. 15, 1997, pp. 15–45.

Keen, D., *The Benefits of Famine: A Political Economy of Famine and Relief in Southwestern Sudan, 1983–1989* (Princeton, NJ: Princeton University Press, 1994).

Kellenberger, J., 'The Role of the International Committee of the Red Cross', in Clapham, A. and Gaeta, P. (eds.), *Oxford Handbook of International Law in Armed Conflict* (Oxford University Press, 2014), pp. 20–36.

Kennedy, D., *The Dark Sides of Virtue: Reassessing International Humanitarianism* (Princeton, NJ: Princeton University Press, 2005).

Kennedy, D., *Of War and Law* (Princeton, NJ: Princeton University Press, 2006).

Khartoum Declaration of Agreement Between Parties of the Conflict in South Sudan, 27 June 2018. Available at: https://igad.int/attachments/article/1874/Khartoum%20Declaration.pdf.

Killean, R., Dowds, E., and Kramer, A., 'Soldiers as Victims at the ECCC: Exploring the Concept of "Civilian" in Crimes Against Humanity', *Leiden Journal of International Law*, Vol. 30, 2017, pp. 685–705.

Kindersley, N. and Rolandsen, Ø. H., 'Civil War on a Shoestring: Rebellion in South Sudan's Equatoria Region', *Civil Wars*, Vol. 19, No. 3, 2017, pp. 308–324.

Kindersley, N., and Rolandsen, Ø. H., 'Who are the Civilians in the Wars of South Sudan?', *Security Dialogue*, Vol. 50, No. 5, 2019, pp. 383–397.

Kinsella, H., *The Image Before the Weapon: A Critical History of the Distinction between Combatant and Civilian* (Ithaca, NY and London: Cornell University Press, 2011).

Koddenbrock, K., *The Practice of Humanitarian Intervention: Aid Workers, Agencies, and Institutions in the Democratic Republic of the Congo* (London and New York: Routledge, 2016).

Koskenniemi, M., *The Gentle Civilizer of Nations: The Rise and Fall of International Law 1870–1960* (Cambridge: Cambridge University Press, 2001).

Koskenniemi, M., *From Apology to Utopia: The Structure of International Legal Argument* (Cambridge: Cambridge University Press, 2009).

Krause, J., 'Stabilization and Local Conflicts: Communal and Civil War in South Sudan', *Ethnopolitics*, Vol. 18, No. 5, 2019, pp. 478–493.

Krause, M., *The Good Project: Humanitarian Relief NGOs and the Fragmentation of Reason* (Chicago, IL and London: University of Chicago Press, 2014).

Kress, C., 'Towards Further Developing the Law of Non-International Armed Conflict: A Proposal for a *Jus in Bello Interno* and a New *Jus Contra Bellum Internum*', *International Review of the Red Cross*, Vol. 96, No. 893, 2015, pp. 30–44.

Kritsiotis, D., 'Humanitarian Warfare: Towards an African Appreciation', in Levitt, J. I. (ed.), *Africa: Mapping New Boundaries in International Law* (Oxford: Hart, 2008), pp. 149–180.

Kuijt, E. E., 'A Humanitarian Crisis: Reframing the Legal Framework on Humanitarian Assistance', in Zwitter, A. J. et al. (eds.), *Humanitarian Action: Global, Regional and Domestic Legal Responses* (Cambridge: Cambridge University Press, 2014), pp. 54–80.

Leader, N., 'Proliferating Principles; or How to Sup with the Devil Without Getting Eaten', *Disasters*, Vol. 22, No. 4, 1998, pp. 288–308.

Leader, N., 'The Politics of Principle: The Principles of Humanitarian Action in Practice', *Humanitarian Policy Group*, Report No. 2, 2000.

Leclerc-Gagné, E., *The Construction of the Humanitarian Worker as Inviolate Actor* (unpublished PhD thesis, 2014).

Levitt, P., and Merry, S., 'Vernacularization on the Ground: Local Uses of Global Women's Rights in Peru, China, India and the United States', *Global Networks*, Vol. 9, No.4, 2009, pp. 441–461.

Lilly, D., 'Protection of Civilians Sites: A New Type of Displacement Settlement?', *Humanitarian Exchange Magazine*, No. 62, September 2014. Available at: http://odihpn.org/magazine/protection-of-civilians-sites-a-new-type-of-displacement-settlement/.

Lippman, W., *The Phantom Public* (Piscataway, New Jersey: Transaction Publishers, 2006/1926).

Lischer, S. K., *Dangerous Sanctuaries: Refugee Camps, Civil War, and the Dilemmas of Humanitarian Aid* (Ithaca, NY and London: Cornell University Press, 2005).

Lischer, S. K., 'Military Intervention and the Humanitarian "Force Multiplier"', *Global Governance*, Vol. 13, No. 1, 2007, pp. 98–118.

Lohne, K. and Sandvik, K. B., 'Bringing Law into the Political Sociology of Humanitarianism', *Oslo Law Review*, Vol. 4, No. 1, 2017, pp. 4–27.

Long, A., 'Counter Insurgency', in Gheciu, A. and Wohlforth, W. (eds.), *The Oxford Handbook of International Security* (Oxford: Oxford University Press, 2018).

Luedke, A. and Logan, H., 'That Thing of Human Rights: Discourse, Emergency Assistance, and Sexual Violence in South Sudan's Current Civil War', *Disasters*, Vo. 42, No. S1, 2017, pp. S99–S118.

Macak, K., 'Principles of Neutrality and Impartiality of Humanitarian Action in the Aftermath of the 2011 Libyan Conflict', in Zwitter, A. J. et al. (eds.), *Humanitarian Action: Global, Regional and Domestic Legal Responses* (Cambridge: Cambridge University Press, 2014), pp. 447–474.

McCurry, S., 'Enemy Women and the Laws of War in the American Civil War', *Law and History Review*, Vol. 35, No. 3, pp. 667–710.

McDonald, A., 'The Challenges to International Humanitarian Law and the Principles of Distinction and Protection from the Increased Participation of Civilians in Hostilities', *Spotlight on Issues of Contemporary Concern in International Humanitarian Law and International Criminal Law*, Working Paper, University of Tehran Round Table, April 2004.

MacDonald, A., 'Local Understandings and Experiences of Transitional Justice: A Review of the Evidence', *London School of Economics Justice and Security Research Program*, Paper No. 6, July 2013.

McFate, M. and Laurence, J., *Social Science Goes to War: The Human Terrain System in Iraq and Afghanistan* (Oxford: Oxford University Press, 2015).

MacGinty, R., 'Against Stabilization', *Stability*, Vol. 1, No. 1, pp. 20–30.

Macionis, J. and Gerber, L., *Sociology*, 7th edition (Toronto: Pearson, 2011).

McKeogh, C., *Innocent Civilians: The Morality of Killing in War* (New York: Palgrave, 2002).

Mackintosh, K., 'Beyond the Red Cross: The Protection of Independent Humanitarian Organizations and their Staff in International Humanitarian Law', *International Review of the Red Cross*, Vol. 89, No. 865, 2007, pp. 113–130.

Macrae, J. and Leader, N., 'Shifting Sands: The Search for "Coherence" Between Political and Humanitarian Responses to Complex Emergencies', *Humanitarian Policy Group Report*, No. 8, August 2000.

Malinowski, B., *Argonauts of the Western Pacific: An Account of Native Enterprise and Adventure in the Archipelagoes of Melanesian New Guinea* (London: Routledge, 1922/1984).

Malkki, L. H., *The Need to Help: The Domestic Arts of International Humanitarianism* (Durham, NC: Duke University Press, 2015).

Mann, I., *Humanity at Sea: Maritime Migration and the Foundations of International Law* (Cambridge: Cambridge University Press, 2016).

Marcus, G., 'Ethnography In/Of the World System: The Emergence of Multi-Sited Ethnography', *Annual Review of Anthropology*, Vol. 24, 1995, pp. 95–117.

Marcus, G., *Ethnography through Thick and Thin* (Princeton, NJ: Princeton University Press, 1998).

Marriage, Z., *Not Breaking the Rules, Not Playing the Game: International Assistance to Countries at War* (London: Hurst, 2006).

Matar, L., 'UN Human Rights Body Should Renew South Sudan Investigation', *Human Rights Watch*, 20 February 2019. Available at: https://www.hrw.org/news/2019/02/20/un-human-rights-body-should-renew-south-sudan-investigation.

Matthews, H., 'The Other Side of COIN: The Civilian–Combatant Distinction, Terrorism, and the Laws of War', SSRN, 2013. Available at: https://ssrn.com/abstract=2316758.

Mégret, F., 'From "Savages" to "Unlawful Combatants": A Postcolonial Look at International Humanitarian Law's "Other"', in Orford, A. (ed.), *International Law and its Others* (Cambridge: Cambridge University Press, 2006), pp. 265–317.

Mégret, F., 'Beyond the "Salvation" Paradigm: Responsibility to Protect (Others) vs. the Power of Protecting Oneself', *Security Dialogue*, Vol. 40, No. 6, 2009, pp. 575–579.

Mégret, F., 'Thinking about what International Humanitarian Lawyers "Do": An Examination of the Laws of War as a Field of Professional Practice', in Werner, W., de Hoon, M., and Galán, A. (eds.), *The Law of International Lawyers: Reading Martti Koskenniemi* (Cambridge: Cambridge University Press, 2017).

Meron, T., *War Crimes Law Comes of Age* (Cambridge: Oxford University Press, 1998).

Meron, T., 'The Humanization of Humanitarian Law', *American Journal of International Law*, Vol. 94, No. 2, 2000, pp. 239–278.

Merry, S. E., 'International Law and Sociolegal Scholarship: Towards a Spatial Global Legal Pluralism', in Sarat, A. (ed.), *Special Issue: Law and Society Reconsidered (Studies in Law, Politics and Society)*, Vol. 21, 2007, pp. 149–168.

Merry, S. E., 'Ethnography of the Global', Workshop at the Berkeley Centre for the Study of Law and Society, February 2013.

Metcalfe, V. and Berg, M., 'Country-Specific Civil–Military Coordination Guidelines', *Humanitarian Policy Group Working Paper*, August 2012.

Metcalfe, V. et al., 'UN Integration and Humanitarian Space: An Independent Study Commissioned by the UN Integration Steering Group', *Stimson Center and Overseas Development Institute*, 2011.

Minear, L. (ed.), *Humanitarianism Under Siege: A Critical Review of Operation Lifeline Sudan* (New Jersey: Red Sea Press, 1991).

Minear, L., 'Humanitarian Action and Peacekeeping Operations', *Background paper for UNITAR/IPS/NIRA Singapore Conference*, 1997. Available at: https://sites.tufts.edu/jha/archives/110.

Minear, L. and Donini, A., 'International Troops, Aid Workers, and Local Communities: Mapping the Perceptions Gap', *Humanitarian Exchange Magazine*, No. 32, December 2005, pp. 26–29.

Modirzadeh, N., 'Folk International Law: 9/11 Lawyering and the Transformation of the Law of Armed Conflict to Human Rights Policy and Human Rights Law to War Governance', *Harvard National Security Journal*, Vol. 5, No. 1, 2014, pp. 225–304.

Mold, F., 'Bitter Foes Reunite to Sign Revitalized Peace Agreement to End Civil War in South Sudan,' *UNMISS*, 13 September 2018. Available at: https://unmiss.unmissions.org/bitter-foes-reunite-sign-revitalized-peace-agreement-end-civil-war-south-sudan.

Moller, E., Paulmann, J., and Stornig, K., 'Call for Proposals for Conference on "Gender and Humanitarianism: (Dis-) Empowering Women and Men in the Twentieth Century"', 2017. Available at: http://www.ieg-mainz.de/media/public/Call%20for%20Papers/CfP_Gender_and_Humanitarianism_2017.pdf.

Mosse, D. (ed.), *Adventures in Aidland: The Anthropology of Professionals in International Development* (New York: Berghahn, 2013).

MSF, '#NotATarget: No More Attacks Against Civilians and Health Care Workers in Conflict Zones'. Available at: https://www.doctorswithoutborders.ca/issues/notatarget-no-more-attacks-against-civilians-and-healthcare-workers-conflict-zones.

Nabulsi, K., *Traditions of War: Occupation, Resistance, and the Law* (Oxford: Oxford University Press, 1999).

Nabulsi, K., 'Evolving Conceptions of Civilians and Belligerents: One Hundred Years after the Hague Peace Conferences', in Chesterman, S. (ed.), *Civilians in War* (London: Lynne Rienner Publishers, 2001), pp. 9–24.

NATO Multi-National CIMIC Group, *Functional Specialist Course*. Available at: https://www.cimicgroup.org/c_id/119.

Nouwen, S., *Complementarity in the Line of Fire: The Catalysing Effect of the International Criminal Court in Uganda and Sudan* (Cambridge: Cambridge University Press, 2013).

Nouwen, S., 'As You Set Out for Ithaka: Practical, Epistemological, Ethical and Existential Questions about Socio-legal Empirical Research in Conflict', *Leiden Journal of International Law*, Vol. 27, No. 1, 2014, pp. 227–260.

O'Sullivan, K., 'Humanitarian Encounters: Biafra, NGOs and Imaginings of the Third World in Britain and Ireland, 1967–70', *Journal of Genocide Research*, Vol. 16, No. 2–3, 2014, pp. 299–355.

Okiror, S., 'Briefing: All You Need to Know about South Sudan's New Power Sharing Accord', *The New Humanitarian*, 14 August 2018.

Oosterom, M. A., 'It May Approach as Quickly as Bushfire: Gendered Violence and Insecurity in South Sudan', *IDS Research Report*, 2014.

Oppenheim, L., *International Law: A Treatise* (London: Longmans, Green, 1905).

Optional Protocol, adopted on 8 December 2005, to the UN Convention on the Safety of United Nations and Associated Personnel, 9 December 1994, 2051 UNTS 363.

Orchard, P., 'Revisiting Humanitarian Safe Areas for Civilian Protection', *Global Governance*, Vol. 20, No. 1, 2014, pp. 55–75.

Orford, A., 'In Praise of Description', *Leiden Journal of International Law*, Vol. 25, No.3, 2012, pp. 609–625.

Parlett, K., *The Individual in the International Legal System: Continuity and Change in International Law* (Cambridge: Cambridge University Press, 2011).

Philpot, H., 'Operation Lifeline Sudan: Challenges During Conflict and Lessons Learned', *University of Denver Case-Specific Briefing Paper*, 2011. Available at: https://www.du.edu/korbel/crric/media/documents/hollyphilpot.pdf.

Philpott, D. and Powers, G. (eds.), *Strategies of Peace: Transforming Conflict in a Violent World* (Oxford: Oxford University Press, 2010).

Pictet, J. (ed.), *Commentary: IV Geneva Convention, Relative to the Protection of Civilian Persons in Time of War* (Geneva: ICRC, 1958).

Pictet, J., *The Fundamental Principles of the Red Cross: Commentary* (Geneva: Henry Dunant Institute, 1979).

Pilloud, C., Sandoz, Y., and Swinarski, C. (eds.), *ICRC Commentary on Additional Protocols of 8 June 1977 to the Geneva Conventions of 12 August 1949* (Geneva: ICRC, 1987).

Plattner, D., 'ICRC Neutrality and Neutrality in Humanitarian Assistance', *International Review of the Red Cross*, No. 311, 1996.

Polman, L., *War Games: The Story of Aid and War in Modern Times* (London: Viking, 2011).

Pouligny, B., *Peace Operations Seen from Below: UN Missions and Local People* (London: C. Hurst and Company, 2006).

Protocol Additional to the Geneva Conventions of 12 August 1949, and Relating to the Protection of Victims of International Armed Conflicts, 8 June 1977, 1125 UNTS 3, Can TS 1991 No 1.

Protocol Additional to the Geneva Conventions of 12 August 1949, and Relating to the Protection of Victims of Non-International Armed Conflicts, 8 June 1977, 1125 UNTS 609, Can TS 1991 No 2.

Protocol Additional to the Geneva Conventions of 12 August 1949, and Relating to the Adoption of an Additional Distinctive Emblem, 8 December 2005.

Provost, R., 'Targeting Child Soldiers', *European Journal of International Law Blog EJIL: Talk!*, 12 January 2016. Available at: http://www.ejiltalk.org/targeting-child-soldiers/.

Pugh, M., 'The Challenge of Civil–Military Relations in International Peace Operations', *Disasters*, Vol. 25, No. 4, 2001, pp. 345–357.

Pugh, M., 'The Role of Armed Protection in Humanitarian Action', in *Humanitarian Action: Perception and Security*, European Commission Seminar proceedings (Lisbon: European Commission Humanitarian Office and International Committee of the Red Cross, 27–28 March 2007).

Pugh, M., 'Civil–Military Relations in Peace Support Operations: Hegemony or Emancipation?', *Overseas Development Institute Seminar on Aid and Politics*, February 2001. Available at: https://www.odi.org/sites/odi.org.uk/files/odi-assets/events-documents/3774.pdf.

Radio Tamazuj, 'Armed Youth, Uniformed Gunmen Attack UN Camp in Bor Killing 60', *Radio Tamazuj*, 17 April 2014. Available at: https://radiotamazuj.org/en/news/article/armed-youth-uniformed-gunmen-attack-un-camp-in-bor-killing-60.

Rana, R., 'Contemporary Challenges in the Civil–Military Relationship: Complementarity or Incompatibility?', *International Review of the Red Cross*, Vol. 86, No. 855, 2004, pp. 565–591.

Ratner, S., 'Law Promotion Beyond Law Talk: The Red Cross, Persuasion, and the Laws of War', *European Journal of International Law*, Vol. 22, No. 2, 2011, pp. 459–506.

Report of the Commission on Human Rights in South Sudan, A/HRC/40/69, 12 March 2019.

Rhoads, E. P., *Taking Sides in Peacekeeping: Impartiality and the Future of the United Nations* (Oxford: Oxford University Press, 2016).

Richey, L. A., 'Conceptualizing "Everyday Humanitarianism": Ethics, Affects, and Practices of Contemporary Global Helping', *New Political Science*, Vol. 40, No.4, 2018, pp. 625–639.

Riles, A., 'Anthropology, Human Rights and Legal Knowledge: Culture in the Iron Cage', *American Anthropologist*, Vol. 108, 2008, pp. 52–65.

Riles, A., 'Afterword: A Method More than a Subject', in Cowan, D. and Wincott, D. (eds.), *Exploring the 'Legal' in Socio-Legal Studies* (London: Palgrave, 2016), pp. 257–264.

Rogers, A. P. V., *Law on the Battlefield* (Manchester: Manchester University Press, 2012).

Rolandsen, Ø. H., 'A Quick Fix? A Retrospective Analysis of the Sudan Comprehensive Peace Agreement', *African Political Economy*, Vo. 38, No. 130, 2011, pp. 551–564.

Rolandsen Ø. H. et al., 'A Year of South Sudan's Third Civil War', *International Area Studies Review*, Vol. 18, No. 1, 2015, pp. 87–104.

Rolle, B. and Lafontaine, E., 'The Emblem that Cried Wolf: ICRC Study on the Use of Emblems', *International Review of the Red Cross*, Vol. 91, No. 876, 2009, pp. 759–778.

Rossner, M. et al., *The Process and Dynamics of Restorative Justice: Research on Forum Sentencing* (Sydney: University of Western Sydney, 2013).

Roth, S., 'Aid Work as Edgework: Voluntary Risk-Taking and Security in Humanitarian Assistance, Development and Human Rights Work', *Journal of Risk Research*, Vol. 18, No. 2, 2015, pp. 139–155.

Roth, S., *Passionate Professionals: The Paradoxes of Aid Work* (London and New York: Routledge, 2015).

Sandoz, Y., 'Land Warfare', in Clapham, A. and Gaeta, P. (eds.), *Oxford Handbook of International Law in Armed Conflict* (Oxford: Oxford University Press, 2014), pp. 91–117.

Sarat, A. and Kearns, T. R., 'Beyond the Great Divide: Forms of Legal Scholarship and Everyday Life', in Sarat, A. and Kearns, T. R. (eds.), *Law in Everyday Life* (University of Michigan Press, 1993), pp. 21–62.

Sassoli, M., Bouvier, A., and Quintin, A. (eds.), *How Does Law Protect in War?* (Geneva: ICRC, 2011).

Schabas, W. A., *The UN International Criminal Tribunals: The Former Yugoslavia, Rwanda and Sierra Leone* (New York: Cambridge University Press, 2006).

Scharf, M. P., 'International Law in Crisis: A Qualitative Empirical Contribution to the Compliance Debate', *Cardozo Law Review*, Vol. 31, 2009, pp. 45–97.

Schirch, L., 'Research Gaps on Civil–Military Policy Trends', *Humanitarian Practice Network*, May 2014. Available at: https://odihpn.org/magazine/research-gaps-on-civil-military-policy-trends/.

Schmitt, M., 'Military Necessity and Humanity in International Humanitarian Law: Preserving the Delicate Balance', *Virginia Journal of International Law*, Vol. 50, No. 4, 2010, pp. 796–839.

Schmitt, M., 'Discriminate Warfare: The Military Necessity–Humanity Dialectic of International Humanitarian Law', in Lovell, D. and Primoratz, I. (eds.), *Protecting Civilians During Violent Conflict: Theoretical and Practical Issues for the 21st Century* (Oxford and New York: Ashgate, 2012), Chapter 6.

Schmitt, M. and Watts, S., 'State *Opinio Juris* and International Humanitarian Law Pluralism', *International Law Studies*, Vol. 91, 2015, pp. 171–215.

Schwendimann, F., 'The Legal Framework of Humanitarian Access in Armed Conflict', *International Review of the Red Cross*, Vol. 93, No. 884, 2011, pp. 993–1008.

The Sentry, 'War Crimes Shouldn't Pay: Stopping the Looting and Destruction in South Sudan', September 2016. Available at: https://thesentry.org/reports/warcrimesshouldntpay/.

Shafer, G. and Ginsburg, T., 'The Empirical Turn in International Legal Scholarship', *American Journal of International Law*, Vol. 106, No. 1, 2012, pp. 1–48.

Shaheed F., *Protecting Children in Armed Conflict* (Oxford: Hart, 2018).

Sheeran, S. and Case, S., *The Intervention Brigade: Legal Issues for the UN in the Democratic Republic of the Congo* (New York: International Peace Institute, 2014).

Silbey, S. and Cavicchi, A., 'The Common Place of Law: Transforming Matters of Concern into the Objects of Everyday Life', in Latour, B. and Weibel, P. (eds.), *Making Things Public: Atmospheres of Democracy* (Cambridge, MA: MIT Press, 2005), pp. 556–565.

Silbey, S. and Sarat, A., 'Critical Traditions in Law and Research', *Law and Society Review*, Vol. 21, 1987, pp. 165–174.

Silverman, D. (ed.), *Doing Qualitative Research: A Practical Handbook*, 3rd edition (London: SAGE, 2010).

Singh, H., 'Critique of the *Mrskic* Trial Judgment: A Re-Evaluation on Whether Soldiers *Hors De Combat* Are Entitled to Recognition as Victims of Crimes Against Humanity', *The Law and Practice of International Courts and Tribunals*, Vol. 8, 2009, pp. 247–296.

Sinha, A., 'Child Soldiers as Super-Privileged Combatants', *International Journal of Human Rights*, Vol. 17, No. 4, 2013, pp. 584–603.

Sivakumaran, S., 'Re-Envisaging the International Law of Internal Armed Conflict', *European Journal of International Law*, Vol. 22, No. 1, 2011, pp. 219–264.

Sivakumaran, S., 'Making and Shaping the Law of Armed Conflict', *Current Legal Problems*, Vol. 71, No. 1, 2018, pp. 119–160.

Sjoberg, L. and Via, S., *Gender, War, and Militarism: Feminist Perspectives* (Westport, CT: Praeger Security International, 2010).

Slim, H., 'The Stretcher and the Drum: Civil–Military Relations in Peace Support Operations', *International Peacekeeping*, Vol. 3, No. 2, 1996, pp. 123–140.

Slim, H., 'Marketing Humanitarian Space: Argument and Method in Humanitarian Persuasion', *Centre for Humanitarian Dialogue*, May 2003.

Slim, H., 'How We Look: Perceptions of Humanitarian Action', *Centre for Humanitarian Dialogue*, Presentation, April 2004. Available at: https://reliefweb.int/sites/reliefweb.int/files/resources/CFBFB047170078CFC1257222004D3AFD-HDC-Apr2004.pdf.

Slim, H., *Killing Civilians: Method, Madness, and Morality in War* (Oxford: Oxford University Press, 2010).

Slim, H., *Humanitarian Ethics: A Guide to the Morality of Aid in War and Disaster* (Oxford: Oxford University Press, 2015).

Smirl, L., *Spaces of Aid: Post-Disaster Relief and Reconstruction* (Chicago, IL: University of Chicago Press, 2015).

Smith, M. J., *Social Science in Question* (London: Open University Press/SAGE, 1998).

South Sudan Civil–Military Advisory Group, *Guidelines for the Coordination between Humanitarian Actors and the United Nations Mission in South Sudan (UNMISS)*, endorsed 6 December 2013.

Southern Sudan Referendum Act, 2009.

Sphere, *The Sphere Project: Humanitarian Charter and Minimum Standards in Humanitarian Response*, 2011 edition (Rugby, UK: Practical Action Publishing, 2011).

Status of Forces Agreement between the United Nations and the Government of the Republic of South Sudan Concerning the United Nations Mission in South Sudan, 2011.

Steering Committee for Humanitarian Response, 'Some NGO Views on the Humanitarian Implications of Implementing the Brahimi Report', 2000.

Stern, O. M., *Gender, Conflict and International Humanitarian Law: A Critique of the Principle of Distinction* (Oxford and New York: Routledge, 2019).

Stockton, N., 'In Defence of Humanitarianism', *Disasters*, Vol. 22, No. 4, 1998, pp. 352–360.

Stockton, N., 'The Accountable Humanitarian', *Humanitarian Accountability Partnership*, 2005. Available at: http://hapinternational.org/pool/files/the-accountable-humanitarian-2-12-05.pdf.

Stoddard, A., 'Humanitarian NGOs: Challenges and Trends', *Humanitarian Policy Group*, Briefing paper, No. 1, July 2003.

Stoffels, R., 'Legal Regulation of Humanitarian Assistance in Armed Conflict: Achievements and Gaps', *International Review of the Red Cross*, Vol. 86, No. 855, September 2004, pp. 515–546.

Stoler, A. L. and Bond, D., 'Refractions Off Empire: Untimely Comparisons in Harsh Times', *Radical History Review*, Vol. 95, 2006, pp. 93–107.

Sutton, R., *The Humanitarian Actor as 'Civilian Plus': The Circulation of the Idea of Distinction in International Law* (unpublished PhD thesis, 2018).

Sutton, R., 'The "Phantom Local" and the Everyday Distinction Practices of Humanitarian Actors in War: A Socio-Legal Perspective', *New Political Science*, Vol. 40, No. 4, 2018, pp. 640–657.

Sutton, R., 'Enacting the "Civilian Plus": Humanitarian Actors and the Conceptualization of Distinction', *Leiden Journal of International Law*, Vol. 33, No. 2, 2020, pp. 429–449.

Sutton, R., 'Operationalizing Distinction in South Sudan: Humanitarian Decision Making about Military Asset Use', in Killingsworth, M. et al (eds.), *Who do the Laws of War Protect? Civility, Barbarity and IHL* (Cambridge: Cambridge University Press, forthcoming 2021).

Tanner, L. and Moro, L., 'Missed Out: The Role of Local Actors in the Humanitarian Response in the South Sudan Conflict', *Consortium Report for CAFOD UK, Christian Aid, Oxfam and Tearfund*, 2016. Available at: https://www.alnap.org/help-library/missed-out-the-role-of-local-actors-in-the-humanitarian-response-in-the-south-sudan.

Terry, F., 'The International Committee of the Red Cross in Afghanistan: Reasserting the Neutrality of Humanitarian Action', *International Review of the Red Cross*, Vol. 93, No. 881, 2011, 173–188.

The Comprehensive Peace Agreement: Between the Government of the Republic of the Sudan and the Sudan People's Liberation Movement/Sudan People's Liberation Army, signed at Naivasha, Kenya, 26 May, 2005. Available at: https://peacemaker.un.org/sites/peacemaker.un.org/files/SD_060000_The%20Comprehensive%20Peace%20Agreement.pdf.

The Revitalized Agreement on the Resolution of the Conflict in South Sudan (R-ARCISS), 12 September 2018. Available at: https://www.peaceagreements.org/wview/2112/Revitalised%20Agreement%20on%20the%20Resolution%20of%20the%20Conflict%20in%20the%20Republic%20of%20South%20Sudan%20.

The State of Human Rights in the Protracted Conflict in South Sudan (UNMISS and UNOHCHR, 2015). Available at: https://reliefweb.int/sites/reliefweb.int/files/resources/UNMISS_HRD4December2015.pdf.

Thurer, D., 'Dunant's Pyramid: Thoughts on the "Humanitarian Space"', *International Review of the Red Cross*, Vol. 89, No. 865, 2007, pp. 47–61.

Trubeck, D. M. and Esser, J., 'Critical Empiricism in American Legal Studies: Paradox, Program, or Pandora's Box?', *Law and Social Inquiry*, Vol. 14, 1989, pp. 1–52.

UN, *Agreement of Division of Roles and Responsibilities between UNMISS and the Humanitarian Country Team in UNMISS POC Sites*, February 2014.

UN Convention on the Privileges and Immunities of the United Nations, 13 February 1946, 21 UST 1418, TIAS No. 6900, 1 UNTS 15.

UN Convention on the Safety of United Nations and Associated Personnel, 9 December 1994, 2051 UNTS 363.

UN Department of Peacekeeping Operations, *Civil–Military Coordination Policy*, September 2002. Available at: http://www.refworld.org/pdfid/451ba7624.pdf.

UN General Assembly, Rome Statute of the International Criminal Court (last amended 2010), 17 July 1998.

UN OCHA, 'Clusters'. Available at: https://www.humanitarianresponse.info/en/coordination/clusters.

UN OCHA, 'Frequently Asked Questions: UN Humanitarian Civil–Military Coordination, Military Civil Defense Assets and the Use of Military Escorts in South Sudan'.

UN OCHA, 'Humanitarian Civil–Military Coordination (UN-CMCoord)'. Available at: https://www.unocha.org/themes/humanitarian-civil-military-coordination.

UN OCHA, 'Policy Instruction: OCHA's Structural Relationships within an Integrated UN Presence', 1 May 2009. Available at: https://www.humanitarianresponse.info/sites/www.humanitarianresponse.info/files/documents/files/OCHA%E2%80%99s%20Structural%20Relationships%20Within%20An%20Integrated%20UN%20Presence.pdf.

UN OCHA, 'Republic of South Sudan 2018 (Humanitarian Response Plan),' *Financial Tracking Service*, 2018. Available at: https://fts.unocha.org/appeals/646/summary.

UN OCHA, 'South Sudan: Operational Presence (3W: Who, What, Where),' June 2018. Available at: https://reliefweb.int/report/south-sudan/south-sudan-county-level-operational-presence-3w-who-what-where-june-2018.

UN OCHA, *Civil–Military Coordination Handbook* (OCHA, 2015).

UN OCHA, *Guidelines on the Use of Foreign Military and Civil Defence Assets in Disaster Relief*, November 2007. Available at: https://www.unocha.org/sites/unocha/files/OSLO%20Guidelines%20Rev%201.1%20-%20Nov%2007.pdf.

UN OCHA, *Guidelines on the use of Military and Civil Defence Assets to Support United Nations Humanitarian Activities in Complex Emergencies*, March 2003. Available at: https://www.unocha.org/publication/guidelines-use-military-and-civil-defence-assets-support-united-nations-humanitarian.

UN Secretary-General, Secretary-General's Bulletin: Observance by United Nations Forces of International Humanitarian Law, UN Doc ST/SGB/1999/13, 6 August 1999. Available at: http://www.unhcr.org/refworld/docid/451bb5724.html.

UNGA, *General Assembly Resolution* 45/6 (1990), A/RES/45/6.

UNGA, *General Assembly Resolution* 52/167 (1997), A/RES/52/167.

UNGA, *General Assembly Resolution* 53/164 (1998), A/RES/53/164.

United Kingdom Ministry of Defence, *The Joint Service Manual of the Law of Armed Conflict*, JSP 383 (2004).

United Nations Security Council, 'Increased Attacks on Aid Workers Due to Lack of Respect for International Humanitarian Law, Deputy Secretary-General Tells Security Council', *United Nations Meetings Coverage*, 19 August 2014, SC/11524.

United Nations, *Delivering as One: UN Report of the Secretary General's High-Level Panel* (New York: United Nations, 2006). Available at: https://www.undp.org/content/undp/en/home/librarypage/capacity-building/delivering-as-one-report-of-the-secretary-generals-high-level-panel.html.

United Nations, *Evaluation of the Implementation and Results of Protection of Civilians Mandates in United Nations Peacekeeping Operations: Report of the Office of Internal Oversight Services*, A/68/787, 7 March 2014.

United Nations, *UN High-Level Panel on Threats, Challenges, and Change. A More Secure World: Our Shared Responsibility*, UN Report A/59/565, 2 December 2004.

United Nations, *UN Report of the Panel on United Nations Peace Operations*, UN Report A/55/305—S/2000/809, 21 August 2000.

UNSC meeting, 'Civilian Experiences, Needs in Conflict Critical to Creating Protection, Accountability Frameworks, Speaker Tells Security Council', SC/13822, 23 May 2019.

UNSC, 1993, Statute of the International Criminal Tribunal for the Former Yugoslavia (as amended on 17 May 2002), 25 May 2003.

UNSC, *Security Council Resolution* 827 (1993) [International Criminal Tribunal for the Former Yugoslavia], 25 May 1992, S/RES/827.

UNSC, *Security Council Resolution* 1502 (2003), 26 August 2003, S/RES/1502.

UNSC, *Security Council Resolution* 1590 (2005), 24 March 2005, S/RES/1590.

UNSC, *Security Council Resolution* 1894 (2009), 11 November 2009, S/RES/1894.

UNSC, *Security Council Resolution* 1996 (2011), 8 July 2011, S/RES/1996.

UNSC, *Security Council Resolution* 2098 (2013), 28 March 2013, S/RES/2098.

UNSC, *Security Council Resolution* 2139 (2014), 22 February 2014, S/RES/2139.

UNSC, *Security Council Resolution* 2155 (2014), 27 May 2014, S/RES/2155.

UNSC, *Security Council Resolution* 2206 (2015), 3 March 2015, S/RES/2206.

Valentino, B. A., 'Why We Kill: The Political Science of Political Violence Against Civilians', *Annual Review of Political Science*, Vol. 17, No. 1, 2014, pp. 89–103.

Van Brabant, K., 'Operational Security Management in Violent Environments', *Humanitarian Policy Network Good Practice Review*, June 2000.

Van Engeland, A., *Civilian or Combatant? A Challenge for the 21st Century* (Oxford: Oxford University Press, 2011).

Vattel, E., *The Law of Nations, or, Principles of the Law of Nature, Applied to the Conduct and Affairs of Nations and Sovereigns, with Three Early Essays on the Origin of Nature and Natural Law and on Luxury*, Kapossy, B. and Whitmore, R. (eds.) (Indianapolis, IN: Liberty Fund, 2008). Available at: http://oll.libertyfund.org/titles/vattel-the-law-of-nations-lf-ed.

Venturini, G., 'International Disaster Response Law in Relation to Other Branches of International Law', in de Guttry, A., Gestri, M., and Venturini, G. (eds.), *International Disaster Response Law* (The Hague, Netherlands: Asser Press, 2012), pp. 45–64.

Vestergaard, A., 'Humanitarian Branding and the Media: The Case of Amnesty International', *Copenhagen Business School*, Working paper, No. 81, 2006.

Vestergaard, M., 'Biafra, 1967–1970: Ethical Dilemmas of Humanitarian Relief', *Online Atlas on the History of Humanitarianism and Human Rights*. Available at: http://hhr-atlas.ieg-mainz.de/articles/vestergaard-biafra.

Voluntary Organizations in Cooperation in Emergencies (VOICE), 'VOICE Position on Civil–Military Relations in Humanitarian Action: Recommendations to the European Union', 2009.

Voluntary Organizations in Cooperation in Emergencies (VOICE), 'World Humanitarian Day 2018: Join the #NotATarget Campaign', 9 August 2018. Available at: https://voiceeu.org/news/world-humanitarian-day-2018-join-the-notatarget-campaign.

Wagner, J. G., 'An IHL/ICRC Perspective on "Humanitarian Space"', *Humanitarian Exchange Magazine*, No. 32, 2005.

Walker, P., 'Cracking the Code: The Genesis, Use and Future of the Code of Conduct', *Disasters*, Vol. 29, No. 4, 2005, pp. 323–336.

Walker, P. and Maxwell, D., *Shaping the Humanitarian World* (London: Routledge, 2009).

Walker, P. and Pepper, K., *Follow the Money: A Review and Analysis of the State of Humanitarian Funding* (Boston, MA: Feinstein International Center, 2007).

Walker, P. and Russ, C., 'Fit for Purpose: The Role of Modern Professionalism in Evolving the Humanitarian Endeavour', *International Review of the Red Cross*, Vol. 93, No. 884, 2011, pp. 1193–1210.

Walzer, M., *Just and Unjust Wars: A Moral Argument with Historical Illustrations* (New York: Basic Books, 2015).

Weir, E., 'Conflict and Compromise: UN Integrated Missions and the Humanitarian Imperative', *Kofi Annan International Peacekeeping Training Centre Monograph*, 2006.

Western European Union (1999), *WEU Draft Concept on Civil–Military Cooperation (CIMIC)*, WEU Brussels, WEU-DMS 99246, 17 February 1999.

Wheeler, V. and Harmer, A. (eds.), 'Resetting the Rules of Engagement: Trends and Issues in Military–Humanitarian Relations', *Humanitarian Policy Group Report*, March 2006.

Woollacott, M., 'Humanitarians Must Avoid Becoming Tools of Power', *The Guardian*, 2 April 2004.

Yayboke, E., 'Accessing South Sudan: Humanitarian Aid in a Time of Crisis', *Centre for Strategic and International Studies Brief*, May 2018. Available at: https://www.csis.org/analysis/accessing-south-sudan-humanitarian-aid-time-crisis.

Yngvesson, B., 'Inventing Law in Local Settings: Rethinking Popular Legal Culture', *Yale Law Journal*, Vol. 98, No. 8, 1989, pp. 1689–1709.

Young, K., 'UNHCR and ICRC in the Former Yugoslavia: Bosnia-Herzegovina', *International Review of the Red Cross*, Vol. 83, No. 843, 2001, pp. 781–805.

Zentrum fur Internationale Friedenseinsatz (Zif), 'Comprehensive Approaches to Multi-Dimensional Peacekeeping Operations'. Available at: http://www.zif-berlin.org/en/training/zif-training-courses/specialization-courses/campo.html.

'South Sudan Army Claims UN peacekeepers Harbouring Rebels in Juba', *Sudan Tribune*, 19 September 2016. Available at: http://www.sudantribune.com/spip.php?article60283.

'South Sudan: The Humanitarian Toll of a Decade of War', *The New Humanitarian*, 21 March 2019. Available at: https://www.thenewhumanitarian.org/in-depth/south-sudan-humanitarian-toll-half-decade-war.

'Sudan Accuses U.N. Peacekeepers of Killing Seven Civilians in Darfur', *Reuters*, 27 April 2015. Available at: https://uk.reuters.com/article/us-sudan-darfur-unamid/sudan-accuses-u-n-peacekeepers-of-killing-seven-civilians-in-darfur-idUSKBN0NI1SC20150427.

Index

For the benefit of digital users, indexed terms that span two pages (e.g., 52–53) may, on occasion, appear on only one of those pages.

The manufacturer's authorised representative in the EU for product safety is Oxford University Press España S.A. of el Parque Empresarial San Fernando de Henares, Avenida de Castilla, 2 – 28830 Madrid (www.oup.es/en or product.safety@oup.com). OUP España S.A. also acts as importer into Spain of products made by the manufacturer.

www.ingramcontent.com/pod-product-compliance
Lightning Source LLC
LaVergne TN
LVHW011755200926
848484LV00003B/711
9780198863816